INVENTING A SOCIALIST NATION

Twenty years after the collapse of the German Democratic Republic, historians still struggle to explain how an apparently stable state imploded with such vehemence. This is the first book to show how 'national' identity was invented in the GDR and how citizens engaged with it. Jan Palmowski argues that it was hard for individuals to identify with the GDR amid the threat of Stasi informants and with the accelerating urban and environmental decay of the 1970s and 1980s. Since socialism contradicted its own ideals of community, identity and environmental care, citizens developed rival meanings of nationhood and identity. They learned to mask their growing distance from socialism beneath regular public assertions of socialist belonging. This stabilized the party's rule until 1989. However, when the revolution came, the alternative identifications citizens had developed for decades allowed them to abandon their 'nation', the GDR, with remarkable ease.

JAN PALMOWSKI is Professor of Modern and Contemporary History and Head of the School of Arts and Humanities at King's College London. His previous publications include *Urban Liberalism in Imperial Germany: Frankfurt am Main, 1866–1914* (1999) and *Citizenship and National Identity in Twentieth-Century Germany* (as co-editor, with Geoff Eley, 2008).

NEW STUDIES IN EUROPEAN HISTORY

Edited by

PETER BALDWIN, University of California, Los Angeles
CHRISTOPHER CLARK, University of Cambridge
JAMES B. COLLINS, Georgetown University
MIA RODRÍGUEZ-SALGADO, London School of Economics
and Political Science
LYNDAL ROPER, University of Oxford
TIMOTHY SNYDER, Yale University

The aim of this series in early modern and modern European history is to publish outstanding works of research, addressed to important themes across a wide geographical range, from southern and central Europe to Scandinavia and Russia, from the time of the Renaissance to the Second World War. As it develops the series will comprise focused works of wide contextual range and intellectual ambition.

For a full list of titles published in the series, please see the end of the book.

INVENTING
A SOCIALIST NATION

HEIMAT AND THE POLITICS OF EVERYDAY LIFE IN THE GDR, 1945–1990

JAN PALMOWSKI

King's College London

CAMBRIDGE
UNIVERSITY PRESS

CAMBRIDGE UNIVERSITY PRESS
Cambridge, New York, Melbourne, Madrid, Cape Town,
Singapore, São Paulo, Delhi, Mexico City

Cambridge University Press
The Edinburgh Building, Cambridge CB2 8RU, UK

Published in the United States of America by Cambridge University Press, New York

www.cambridge.org
Information on this title: www.cambridge.org/9781107690424

First published 2009
First paperback edition 2013

A catalogue record for this publication is available from the British Library

Library of Congress Cataloguing in Publication Data
Palmowski, Jan.
Inventing a socialist nation : Heimat and the politics of everyday life in the
GRD, 1945–90 / Jan Palmowski.
p.   cm. – (New studies in European history)
ISBN 978-0-521-11177-5 (hardback)
1. Germany (East) – Politics and government.   2. Nationalism – Germany (East)
3. Nationalism and socialism – Germany (East)   4. Sozialistische Einheitspartei Deutschlands.
5. Political culture – Germany (East)   6. National characteristics, East German.   7. Germany
(East) – Social conditions.   I. Title.   II. Series.
DD283.P35   2009
943'.1087–dc22
2009035487

ISBN 978-0-521-11177-5 Hardback
ISBN 978-1-107-69042-4 Paperback

To Alf Lüdtke, Sue Matthew and Heather Williams

Contents

Illustrations

Maps

Acknowledgements

It is ten years since I began thinking about this book, and in the process I have incurred many debts. I am grateful to the Arts and Humanities Research Council for the award of a major research grant in 2001–4, to the Berlin Senate for the award of a Research Fellowship in 2002–3, and the Alexander von Humboldt Foundation for the award of a Fellowship in 2004–5. I also wish to record my thanks to my own institution, King's College London: it has been a stimulating, demanding and fulfilling place to work in, and I am immensely grateful to my colleagues for allowing me the time to finish this book.

I will never forget the generosity with which colleagues have supported me over the years. At a very early stage in this project, Dieter Langewiesche provided invaluable advice which included introducing me to the work of Alf Lüdtke. Richard Bessel was similarly crucial to laying the foundations for this study, not least by tirelessly providing references and offering advice at a time when I was a completely unknown quantity amongst GDR scholars. Whatever he may think of this book, the help he gave me at that stage is emblematic of his encouragement to other scholars more generally. I am also grateful to Alon Confino, Celia Applegate, Nick Stargardt, Chris Clark, Geoff Eley and Thomas Lindenberger. This book attests to how deeply I admire their scholarship (even where I disagree with it), and for this reason their words of encouragement at critical junctures were more significant than they can know.

A number of conferences and seminars have provided critical feedback for important arguments presented here. I would like to thank participants and commentators of the University of London German History Seminar, the German Historical Institute, the German Studies Association in Houston and Pittsburgh, and the University of Oxford German History Seminar for their valuable comments. I am particularly grateful for the opportunity to speak at Paul Nolte's seminar at the Free University in Berlin – this was not the strongest paper I ever gave, but for that very reason

the experience was invaluable. Of all the seminars and workshops I participated in, the importance of Alf Lüdtke's colloquium, which I had the
privilege to attend regularly between 2002 and 2007, stands out. The
personal support and academic comments enriched my work immeasurably. Even though it is against the spirit of the seminar to mention
individuals, I would like to record my debt to Christina Hartig, whose
comment on my final presentation to the seminar caused me to rewrite
important parts of the book.

Over the past ten years I have been sustained by the support of many
friends, colleagues and relatives. My life, and my work for this book, have
been enriched immeasurably by my extended family even if they still do
not understand what I actually 'do' for a living; my sense of my sister's joy
in motherhood; and my parents' extraordinary courage, determination and
love as they battle against my father's Parkinson's disease. Among my
friends, I would like to thank Barbara and Chris O'Reilly, Tore and
Norunn Rem, Franz Mayer and Hanne Neuhauser for their support
despite my constant lack of time, and I am forever indebted to Michael
Suarez SJ and Robin Griffith-Jones not only for their friendship, but also
for their spiritual support. Finally, Katherine and Leo Martin have been
extraordinarily generous in offering me their time, their counsel, and their
home when I needed it. This book could not have been written without
them.

Amongst my friends and colleagues, I am particularly indebted to
S. Jonathan Wiesen, who heroically battled through an earlier version of
the manuscript, and to Helmut Walser Smith for almost making it through
the manuscript. Their advice was critical for its quality and its timing, and I
truly appreciate the huge amount of time and energy they devoted to me. I
am equally grateful to David Crew, who read through two chapters even
though he had met me only a few times. Like Helmut and Jonathan, he had
his own deadlines to keep, and his unflinching willingness to help has been
truly humbling. I would like also to thank Deborah Neill, for reading parts
of the book and providing me with characteristically sound and expert
advice, and also for her wonderful friendship and counsel, especially during
a very difficult year in Berlin. I have benefited immeasurably from the help
of Anne Reissig, who transcribed most of my interviews, proved to be a
valuable sounding board for ideas, and introduced me to the Vogtei region.
Last but not least, I am grateful to Anna Patton, who did a wonderful job at
turning my Germanic sentences into something slightly more intelligible;
and I thank David Monger for his insightful work in helping me to prepare
the final manuscript for publication.

Throughout this project on everyday history, I have become ever more aware of the historian's dependence on her or his environment. The choice of topics I studied, the files I chose to read, the persons I decided to interview and ultimately the arguments I came up with were not simply the result of rational thought, but also of emotions, personal circumstances and the kindness of others. Three individuals influenced this book in particular ways. Sue Matthew provided a home for me whenever I needed it, and being able to stay in Oxford particularly over one summer provided me with a wonderful opportunity to develop this book conceptually. Since meeting him for the first time in 2002, I have benefited enormously from the example of Alf Lüdtke, who had weathered extraordinary personal and academic attacks to realize his vision of rigorous scholarship and astonishing support for others. This book would have been completely different without his questions, comments and inspiration. Finally, the life of this book coincides almost perfectly with my relationship with Heather Williams, who has been with me in good times and in bad. While our lives changed with and in part through the work undertaken for this book, our time together also deeply affected what I explored, and how I explored it. It is to these three individuals that I dedicate this book.

Abbreviations

AIM	archivierter IM-Vorgang (archived file of an unofficial informant)
AOP	archivierter operativer Vorgang
AOPK	archivierte operative Personenkontrolle (an investigation into the life of an individual)
ARD	Arbeitsgemeinschaft der öffentlich-rechtlichen Rundfunkanstalten der Bundesrepublik Deutschland (Community of the Public Broadcasting Services in West Germany - First TV Channel of the FRG)
BArch-SAPMO	Bundesarchiv – Stiftung Archiv der Parteien und Massenorganisationen der DDR
BDV	Bund Deutscher Volksbühnen (League of German Folk Theatres)
BStU	Die Bundesbeauftragte für die Unterlagen des Staatssicherheitsdienstes der ehemaligen DDR (Federal Commission for the Records of the state security services of the former German Democratic Republic)
BV	Bezirksverwaltung (district administration)
DEFA	Deutsche Film Aktiengesellschaft (German Film Corporation)
DFF	Deutscher Fernsehfunk (German Television Broadcasting House, renamed GDR TV in 1972)
DM	Deutsche Mark (West German currency unit, 1948–2001)
DRA	Deutsches Rundfunkarchiv Babelsberg
FP	*Freie Presse*
FRG	Federal Republic of Germany (West Germany)
GDR	German Democratic Republic
GDR TV	Fernsehen der DDR (cf. DFF)

GHI	geheimer Hauptinformator (secret/unofficial informer)
GHZ	*Gothaer Heimatzeitung*
GNU	Gesellschaft für Natur- und Heimatfreunde (Society for the Friends of Nature and the Environment)
HA	Hauptabteilung
HStD	Heimatstube Dabel
IG	Interessengemeinschaft
IM	Inoffizieller Mitarbeiter (Unofficial or covert informer for the state security services, the Stasi)
JbVkKg	*Jahrbuch für Volkskunde und Kulturgeschichte*
'Join in!'	'Mach mit! – schöner unsere Städte und Gemeinden' (Join in! – more beautiful our towns and communities)
KA	Kreisarchiv (County Archive)
KD	Kreisdienststelle (County Office)
LHA	Landeshauptarchiv (State Central Archives)
M	Mark (East German currency unit from 1968)
MDN	(Deutsche) Mark der Deutschen Notenbank (East German currency unit, 1948–67)
Mark	Mark Brandenburg: the historical centre of Brandenburg, derived from the Margravate of Brandenburg. In the GDR, its territory extended from east of Magdeburg to the Polish border, including the northern half of Potsdam and Frankfurt districts
NAW	Nationales Aufbauwerk (National Reconstruction Effort)
NBI	*Neue Berliner Illustrierte*
NDR	Norddeutscher Rundfunk (North German Broadcasting Station)
NF	Nationale Front (National Front, the umbrella organization for all mass organizations)
NL	Nachlaß (private papers)
RdG	Rat der Gemeinde (Village Council)
RdK	Rat des Kreises (County Council)
StA	Stadtarchiv
Stasi	Staatssicherheit (State Security Services)
SVZ	*Schweriner Volkszeitung*
ThHStAWe	Thüringisches Hauptstaatsarchiv Weimar
ThStA	Thüringisches Staatsarchiv Altenburg
ZDF	Zweites Deutsches Fernsehen (Second German Television Station)

CHAPTER I

Introduction

This study explores the significance and the meanings of nation, homeland and patriotism under the conditions of socialism in the German Democratic Republic (GDR). The GDR hardly constitutes a 'typical' socialist state. A central pillar of the Soviet domination of Eastern Europe and a frontline state in the Cold War, the GDR remained under tight Soviet control until 1989. What made the GDR unique within the socialist bloc was the absence of a distinctive nationhood, which was constantly challenged by the larger and more prosperous part of Germany, the Federal Republic of Germany (FRG). For this reason, those scholars who have considered the issue have argued that in the GDR, nationalism played next to no role 'as movement, as political idea, and as popular sentiment' before 1989.[1] The idea of the nation, such as it existed, was closely tied to the promise of consumerism in the FRG – 'DM Nationalismus', as Jürgen Habermas called it. National identity appeared to be of little consequence in assessing the history of the GDR and its collapse. Even German reunification 'was not so much a nationalist idea as a route for East Germans to an imagined world of prosperity and freedom'.[2]

This book shows that the ruling Socialist Unity Party (SED) was extremely concerned to construct a GDR-specific sense of nationhood precisely because the Federal Republic provided a constant threat to the viability of the GDR, with socialism having only a tenuous hold over the majority of the population. From the 1950s, the SED tried to construct an

---

[1] Mary Fulbrook, 'Nationalism in the second German unification', in John Breuilly and Ron Speirs (eds.), *Germany's Two Unifications: Anticipations, Experiences, Responses* (Basingstoke: Palgrave, 2005), pp. 241–60; here p. 243.

[2] The arguments advanced by Mary Fulbrook and John Breuilly are very similar indeed. John Breuilly, 'Conclusion: nationalism and German Reunification', in John Breuilly (ed.), *The State of Germany: The National Idea in the Making, Unmaking and Remaking of a Modern Nation-State* (Harlow: Longman, 1992), pp. 224–38; here p. 231. Fulbrook, 'Nationalism', pp. 241–60. Mary Fulbrook, 'Nation, state and political culture in divided Germany, 1945–90', in Breuilly (ed.), *The State of Germany*, pp. 177–200.

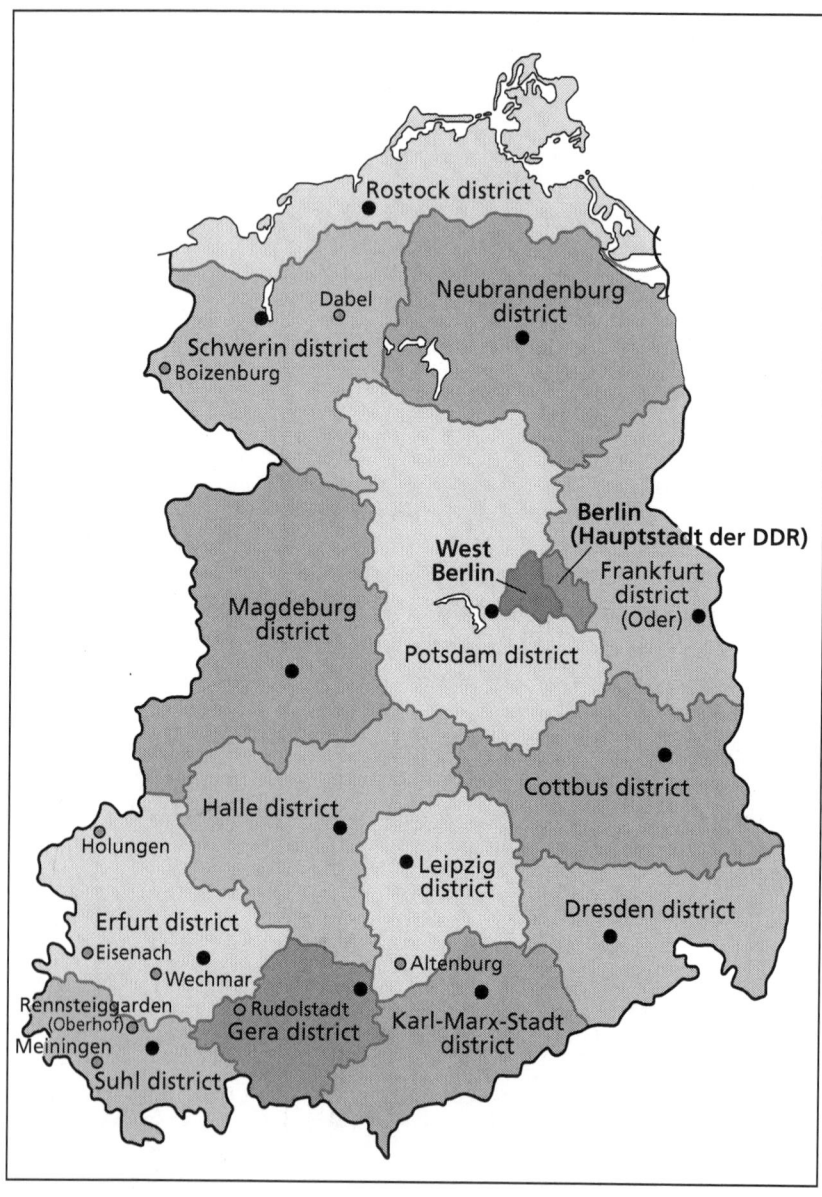

1. The GDR and its districts, 1952–90

emotional attachment to the GDR that would be reflected in individual identifications and popular practices. This study explores how the party invented the GDR as a distinctive 'nation', and how citizens and communities responded to this. In examining the SED's ability to realize its ideal of national identity in popular practice, this book provides a new understanding of the power of socialism in everyday life.

This examination of how nationhood was constructed in socialist Germany helps to overcome a tendency to perceive the GDR as a special case in history, in relation both to Eastern Europe and to Germany. In other states under Soviet domination, socialist parties came to rely on an ethnic construction of nationhood to sustain their legitimacy.[3] Soviet scholars have argued that during the Stalinist era 'nation' came to replace 'class' as the primary category for social ordering, with the 1936 constitution formalizing the transition from 'class' to 'people' (*narod*).[4] Similarly, historians of Eastern Europe have shown that as communist regimes matured in the 1960s, they sought to engender popular support primarily in relation to claims of national, rather than social, belonging.[5] In contrast to other states in Eastern and Central Europe, the GDR could not lay claim to an ethnic sense of nationhood. However, the party could, and did, develop a socialist ideal of nationhood that defined itself through class, local affinities, and the local and regional traditions that were specific to the GDR. As in other socialist states, the party tried to appropriate popular notions of locality and place to define traditions that expressed the socialist nation.

More striking even than the parallels to other socialist states are the ways in which the party, despite its claims to break with the German 'capitalist'

[3] Yuri Slezkine, 'The USSR as a communal apartment, or how a socialist state promoted ethnic particularism', in Sheila Fitzpatrick (ed.), *Stalinism: New Directions* (London: Routledge, 2000), pp. 313–47.

[4] Terry Martin, *The Affirmative Action Empire: Nations and Nationalism in the Soviet Union, 1923–1939* (Ithaca, NY/London: Cornell University Press, 2001); here pp. 449–50. Greg Castillo, 'Peoples at an exhibition: Soviet architecture and the national question', in Thomas Lahusen and Evgeny Dobrenko (eds.), *Socialist Realism without Shores* (Durham, NC/London: Duke University Press, 1997), pp. 91–119. Ronald Grigor Suny, *The Making of the Georgian Nation*, 2nd edn (Bloomington: Indiana University Press, 1994), ch. 13. Francine Hirsch, 'The Soviet Union as work-in-progress: Ethnographers and the category of nationality in the 1926, 1937 and 1939 census', *Slavic Review* 56 (1997), 251–78.

[5] Katherine Verdery, *National Ideology under Socialism: Identity and Cultural Politics in Ceauşescu's Romania*, 2nd edn (Berkeley: University of California Press, 1995). Gail Kligman, *The Wedding of the Dead: Ritual, Poetics and Popular Culture in Transylvania* (Berkeley: University of California Press, 1988). Gail Kligman, *Căluş: Symbolic Transformation in Romanian Ritual*, 2nd edn (Bucharest: The Romanian Cultural Foundation Publishing House, 1999). Kenneth C. Farmer, *Ukrainian Nationalism in the Post-Stalin Era: Myth, Symbols and Ideology in Soviet Nationalities Policy* (The Hague: Martin Nijhoff Publishers, 1980), pp. 40–3.

past, attached its ideals of nationhood to a German tradition of heimat. Literally translated as 'homeland', during the nineteenth and twentieth centuries heimat acquired rich connotations of protectedness, familiarity and order. In German history, heimat expressed notions of community and belonging through a physical, geographical sense of place. It also allowed the articulation of that which was lost: one's childhood, the community of times past, and, especially after 1945, one's birthplace.[6] Heimat acquired its significance over time through its malleability. It could accommodate the transformations of modernity and the political changes of the twentieth century. It allowed individuals to experience these challenges through the traditions of the locality, the familiar and communal relations that defined it, and the physical environment expressed in landscape, monuments and buildings. Heimat, in other words, allowed Germans to maintain a sense of community in the face of constant territorial, political, economic and social ruptures. It was located at the centre of an emotional and political discourse about place, belonging and identity throughout the nineteenth and twentieth centuries in Germany,[7] and the GDR era was no exception.

This work contributes to a flourishing academic debate about the relationship between locality and nationhood in Germany. In her pioneering work, Celia Applegate argued that heimat mediated the emergence of the nation state, reconciling the 'local world with the larger, more impersonal national one'.[8] Further studies have demonstrated just how close nationhood was to local notions of belonging in the German-speaking lands from the middle of the nineteenth century.[9] Debates about the nature of the locality, and its relation to the German nation, existed not just in more remote small towns and regions, but also in fast-changing towns like Hamburg or Frankfurt.[10]

---

[6] Johannes von Moltke, *No Place like Home: Locations of* Heimat *in German Cinema* (Berkeley: University of California Press, 2005), pp. 6–18.

[7] Celia Applegate, *A Nation of Provincials: The German Idea of* Heimat (Berkeley: University of California Press, 1990), ch. 1 ('Heimat and German Identity'). See also Elizabeth Boa and Rachel Palfreyman, Heimat: *A German Dream. Regional Loyalties and National Identity in German Culture, 1890–1990* (Oxford University Press, 2000), pp. 23–9.

[8] Applegate, *Nation*, p. 115.

[9] David Blackbourn and Jim Retallack (eds.), *Localism, Landscape, and the Ambiguities of Place: German-Speaking Central Europe, 1860–1930* (Toronto University Press, 2007).

[10] Jennifer Jenkins, *Provincial Modernity: Local Culture and Liberal Politics in Fin-de-Siècle Hamburg* (Ithaca, NY/London: Cornell University Press, 2003); here pp. 218–19. Jan Palmowski, *Urban Liberalism in Imperial Germany: Frankfurt am Main, 1866–1914* (Oxford University Press, 1999), esp. ch. 4. Till van Rahden, *Juden und andere Breslauer: Die Beziehungen zwischen Juden, Protestanten und Katholiken in einer deutschen Großstadt von 1860 bis 1925* (Göttingen: Vandenhoeck & Ruprecht, 2000).

While the significance of heimat for the construction of German nation-hood has become widely accepted, Alon Confino has challenged precisely how the locality related to the nation. Confino argues that the imagination of the German nation through heimat became so ubiquitous that heimat turned into an interchangeable representation of the local, the regional and the nation. The nation, in this reading, was not imagined through a specific local context; rather the heimat became a universally applicable metaphor for state and nation.[11] The value of Confino's work lies not only in generating a debate about how the locality related to the imagination of the nation; he also highlighted the significance of Germany's component territorial states in the construction of German national identity. The ways in which such states and their rulers shaped a memory culture of their own further complicated and affected individual and communal notions of locality and nationhood.[12]

The disagreement about the nature of heimat and national identity reflects the quintessential ambiguity of heimat, which allowed Germans to project on to it shifting notions of place and identity over time.[13] In the GDR, by contrast, the socialist party developed very clear ideas about how heimat, socialism and nationhood should relate to one another. What happened when the idea of heimat was appropriated so comprehensively by the state, and how did this impact upon popular culture? In the admin-istrative reform of 1952, the SED replaced the federal states with fourteen districts, in order to improve central control over the regions. The bounda-ries of these districts were drawn according to economic and political criteria, in an attempt to overcome regional traditions tied to historical dynastic and ecclesiastical boundaries. How successful could the party be in reshaping popular traditions that signified the joy of socialism, given the obduracy of heimat culture? These questions raise a wider issue which scholars of nationalism have discussed: what, if any, are the limits on the ability of political elites to 'construct' nationhood, particularly as regards the extent to which successful concepts of nationhood rely on pre-existing

---

[11] Alon Confino, *The Nation as a Local Metaphor: Württemberg, Imperial Germany, and National Memory, 1871–1918* (Chapel Hill: University of North Carolina Press, 1997); here p. 184.

[12] Andreas Fahrmeir, 'National colours and national identity in early nineteenth-century Germany', in David Laven and Lucy Riall (eds.), *Napoleon's Legacy: Problems of Government in Restoration Europe* (Oxford: Berg, 2000), pp. 199–216. Jim Retallack, '"Why can't a Saxon be more like a Prussian?" Regional identities and the birth of modern political culture in Germany, 1866–67', *Canadian Journal of History* 32 (1997), 26–55. Abigail Green, *Fatherlands: State-Building and Nationhood in Nineteenth-Century Germany* (Cambridge University Press, 2001). Siegfried Weichlein, *Nation und Region: Integrationsprozesse im Kaiserreich* (Düsseldorf: Droste, 2004).

[13] Von Moltke, *Place*, p. 8.

'cultural resources'?[14] For the GDR, this book explores the limitations of the state and party's ability to invent 'national' traditions.

Inasmuch as the GDR has featured in discussions about heimat, scholars have largely limited their focus to the 1950s. In looking at the production of popular heimat culture, and the organization of heimat practices, historians have found a surprising accommodation between socialism and heimat.[15] However, we still have little sense of how the idea of heimat developed beyond the 1950s, while even for that decade the compatibility of heimat and socialism is unclear. Ultimately, Alon Confino argued, 'poetics of nationhood and the ideology of class' could not be reconciled.[16] If this was so, what was it about class that was so much more incompatible with German concepts of nationhood than capitalism? Moreover, if socialist ideology had such a detrimental effect on conceptions of heimat in the GDR, how did successive ideological reformulations of socialism affect the construction of heimat? This study explores in more depth how heimat related to socialist ideology, and how this relationship evolved from the 1940s to the 1980s. In doing so, the book shows that both in socialist ideology and in popular custom, ideals and practices of heimat proved remarkably responsive to ongoing changes in socialist ideology.

Heimat was not the only ideal through which the party attempted to construct legitimacy. Scholars have shown how the party used anti-fascism to define a country that in overcoming the past was distinct from West Germany and morally superior to it.[17] Moreover, as this book confirms, the party's claims to be constructing a socialist society that could provide a

---

[14] Anthony D. Smith, *Chosen Peoples: Sacred Sources of National Identity* (Oxford University Press, 2003); here pp. 42–3.

[15] Willi Oberkrome, *„Deutsche Heimat": Nationale Konzeption und regionale Praxis von Naturschutz, Landschaftsgestaltung und Kulturpolitik in Westfalen-Lippe und Thüringen (1900–1960)* (Paderborn: Schöningh, 2004). Thomas Schaarschmidt, *Regionalkultur und Diktatur: Sächsische Heimatbewegung und Heimat-Propaganda im Dritten Reich und in der SBZ/DDR* (Weimar/Cologne/Vienna: Böhlau, 2004). Jan Palmowski, 'Building an East German nation: the construction of a socialist heimat, 1945–61', *Central European History* 37 (2004), 365–99. Von Moltke, *Place*, ch. 7. Thomas Lindenberger, 'Home, sweet home: desperately seeking heimat in early DEFA films', *Film History* 18 (2006), 46–58.

[16] Alon Confino, *Germany as a Culture of Remembrance: Promises and Limits of Writing History* (Chapel Hill: University of North Carolina Press, 2006), pp. 93, 111.

[17] Josie McLellan, *Antifascism and Memory in East Germany: Remembering the International Brigades, 1945–1989* (Oxford: Clarendon Press, 2004). On the problems and internal contradictions in the GDR's anti-fascism ideal, see Annette Leo and Peter Reif-Spirek (eds.), *Vielstimmiges Schweigen: Neue Studien zum DDR-Antifaschismus* (Berlin: Metropol, 2001). Benita Blessing, *The Antifascist Classroom: Denazification in Soviet-Occupied Germany, 1945–9* (New York: Palgrave Macmillan, 2006). Insa Eschenbach, 'Zur Umcodierung der eigenen Vergangenheit: Antifaschismuskonstruktionen in Rehabilitationsgesuchen ehemaliger Mitglieder der NSDAP, Berlin 1945/46', in Alf Lüdtke and Peter Becker (eds.), *Akten, Eingaben, Schaufenster: Die DDR und ihre Texte* (Berlin: Akademie-Verlag, 1997), pp. 79–90.

preferable alternative to capitalism also became constitutive of the GDR.[18] What distinguished heimat from these ideals was that it did not just help reinforce the legitimacy of the second German *state*: it allowed the party to go further and lay claim to a distinctive *nationhood* for the GDR.

For the party, the invention of the GDR as a socialist nation was as difficult as it was important because of the deep-seated, and continuing, unpopularity of Germany's division. Moreover, at the Yalta Conference in 1945 the Allied powers had defined the GDR's borders according to geopolitical rather than cultural and historical considerations. When the GDR was created in 1949, there were no specific sites of memory that were shared by its composite regions but not by West Germany. If the party wanted to ensure the viability of the GDR as a 'nation' it was crucial that it create such sites of memory, by redefining places of all-German importance in exclusive relation to the GDR.

The party could succeed in forging a distinctive nationhood only if it managed to capture the popular imagination. Since anti-fascism and socialism never acquired sufficient popularity on their own, these sources of legitimacy were also increasingly formulated through images and practices of heimat. This allowed the party to relate its ideals to local traditions shaped by amateur choirs, hobby groups and beautification activists. Heimat affinities were also the subject of countless songs, publications and television shows. This was a culture which resonated amongst a majority of the population, in north and south, in towns and in the countryside. Of course, cultural practices relating to heimat can easily be dismissed as a sphere of cultural banality in which politics had no place.[19] However, the state's attempt to construct a 'national' identity through heimat became so pervasive that even the most acerbic teenager could not have remained unaware of the party's 'socialist heimat' ideal. The political significance of heimat lay precisely in its apparent banality and its omnipresence. It could potentially enable the party to reach the majority of the population on whom socialism alone had little impact.

By investigating how nationhood and the imagination of the GDR were constructed and popularized, this book addresses a question that is central not just to the study of heimat, but also to GDR historiography more generally, namely how the party's actions affected its citizens, and how the citizens responded. How did individuals and communities respond to the

[18] Peter C. Caldwell, *Dictatorship, State Planning and Social Theory in the German Democratic Republic* (Cambridge University Press, 2003). Jonathan R. Zatlin, *The Currency of Socialism: Money and Political Culture in East Germany* (Cambridge University Press, 2007).
[19] Sandrine Kott, 'Zur Geschichte des kulturellen Lebens in DDR-Betrieben: Konzepte und Praxis der betrieblichen Kulturarbeit', *Archiv für Sozialgeschichte* 39 (1999), 167–95.

appropriation of their heimat identifications as acts of socialist citizenship? To what extent did heimat offer a viable framework in which actors could appropriate socialism in their own way, and what strategies were left to individuals to keep the party's influence at bay through strategies of sub-version or foot-dragging? Because of the singular importance which heimat acquired both in socialism and in popular practices, it provides a unique perspective through which we can examine the relationship between power, ideology, cultural practices and individual meanings.

In its subject and its methodology, this book makes a distinctive contri-bution to the historiography of the GDR. Since the 1990s, scholars have focused on the formal mechanisms through which the SED and its fellow mass organizations exercised power. Their work suggests that the SED was the lynchpin of power, leaving individuals and communities with little autonomy.[20] Such overviews have been accompanied by research into the country's economic, political, military and legal structures.[21] Combined with vigorous research on the workings of the state security services (the Stasi),[22] these works have yielded much valuable insight into how the party exerted control over institutions and structures, and how it co-opted elites.[23] Closely related to some of these concerns was the renaissance of 'totalitarian' approaches as a conceptual framework. Emphasizing the 'totalitarian' aspects of power allowed historians to study the GDR in a comparative framework, not least in relation to the preceding German dictatorship, the Third Reich.[24] Power and repression, from this point of view, were imposed by the party, so

[20] Sigrid Meuschel, *Legitimation und Parteiherrschaft: Zum Paradox von Stabilität und Revolution in der DDR 1945–89* (Frankfurt: Suhrkamp, 1992). Klaus Schroeder, *Der SED-Staat: Partei, Staat und Gesellschaft, 1949–1990* (Munich: Hanser, 1999).

[21] Hermann Wentker, *Justiz in der SBZ/DDR 1945–53: Transformation und Rolle ihrer zentralen Institutionen* (Munich: Oldenbourg, 2001). Dierk Hoffmann, *Aufbau und Krise der Planwirtschaft: Die Arbeitskräftelenkung in der SBZ/DDR 1945–63* (Munich: Oldenbourg, 2002). Hans Ehlert and Mathias Rogg (eds.), *Militär, Staat und Gesellschaft in der DDR* (Berlin: Links, 2004) as well as other volumes in the series of the Military Research Institute (Militärgeschichtliches Forschungsamt) in Potsdam. Curiously, there are more monographs now on the client parties of the SED than on the SED itself. Theresia Bauer, *Blockpartei und Agrarrevolution von oben: Die Demokratische Bauernpartei Deutschlands, 1948–1963* (Munich: Oldenbourg, 2003). Ulf Sommer, *Die Liberal-Demokratische Partei Deutschlands: Eine Blockpartei unter der Führung der SED* (Münster: Agenda, 1996).

[22] The best overviews are Jens Gieseke, *Die hauptamtlichen Mitarbeiter der Staatssicherheit: Personalstruktur und Lebenswelt 1950–1989/90* (Berlin: Links, 2000), and Jens Gieseke, *Der Mielke-Konzern: Die Geschichte der Stasi 1945–90*, 2nd edn (Munich: Deutsche Verlags-Anstalt, 2006). The research department of the BStU has produced a wealth of information on the workings of the Stasi: www.bstu.bund.de.

[23] John Connelly, *Captive University: The Sovietization of East German, Czech and Polish Higher Education* (Chapel Hill: University of North Carolina Press, 2000).

[24] For an excellent overview of this approach and its results, see Günther Heydemann and Detlef Schmiechen-Ackermann (eds.), *Diktaturen in Deutschland – Vergleichsaspekte* (Bonn: Bundeszentrale für Politische Bildung, 2003).

that the collapse of the GDR in 1989 could be understood only as a break-down of political (and economic) power.

Against this perspective, a host of scholars have pointed to ever more limitations on the reach of state and party. Not only did the party fail in its economic goals,[25] but its ideal of the classless society was belied by the persistence of inter- and intra-class divisions.[26] The party also found it difficult to reach the population ideologically. In relation to youth culture, for instance, the party had difficulty in inculcating the young with many of its own values,[27] and found it even harder to dissuade them from habits which it considered to be subversive.[28] Even in relation to the party itself, citizens were not quite as powerless as more structural accounts suggest. The tone, number and subjects of petitions sent in to the state show that the population was far from docile. Citizens had apparently learned to 'play the rules' of the political system, forcing the party in turn to respond and sometimes even concede the petitioners' demands.[29]

Paradoxically, then, GDR research has established the sometimes extra-ordinary reach of the party and its security apparatus, while also noting the wide spheres of autonomy that individuals maintained and even acquired vis-à-vis the party. Pointing to the 'limits of dictatorship', Richard Bessel and Ralph Jessen suggested that state and party were so concerned to invade every facet of private and public life, enlisting almost every citizen into at least one of their mass organizations, that this attempt at 'total' control could not fail to create individual spheres of autonomy in the process.[30]

---

[25] Jeffrey Kopstein, *The Politics of Economic Decline in East Germany, 1945–1989* (Chapel Hill: University of North Carolina Press, 1997). André Steiner, *Von Plan zu Plan* (Munich: Deutsche Verlags-Anstalt, 2004). Mark Landsman, *Dictatorship and Demand: The Politics of Consumerism in East Germany* (Cambridge, MA/London: Harvard University Press, 2005).

[26] Hartmut Kaelble, Jürgen Kocka, Hartmut Zwahr (eds.), *Sozialgeschichte der DDR* (Stuttgart: Klett-Cotta, 1994).

[27] Alan McDougall, *Youth Politics in East Germany: The Free German Youth Movement, 1946–1968* (Oxford: Clarendon Press, 2004).

[28] Mark Fenemore, *Sex, Thugs and Rock'n'Roll. Teenage Rebels in Cold-War East Germany* (New York / Oxford: Berghahn, 2008). Mark Fenemore, 'The limits of repression and reform: youth policy in the early 1960s', in Patrick Major and Jonathan Osmond (eds.), *The Workers' and Peasants' State: Communism and Society in East Germany under Ulbricht, 1945–71* (Manchester University Press, 2002), pp. 171–89. Alan L. Nothnagle, *Building the East German Myth: Historical Mythology and Youth Propaganda in the German Democratic Republic, 1945–89* (Ann Arbor: Michigan University Press, 1999). Uta G. Poiger, *Jazz, Rock and Rebels: Cold War Politics and American Culture in a Divided Germany* (Berkeley: University of California Press, 2000).

[29] Ina Merkel, *Wir sind doch nicht die Meckerecke der Nation! Briefe an das Fernsehen der DDR* (Berlin: Schwarzkopf, 1997).

[30] Richard Bessel and Ralph Jessen, 'Einleitung: Die Grenzen der Diktatur', in Richard Bessel and Ralph Jessen (eds.), *Die Grenzen der Diktatur: Staat und Gesellschaft in der DDR* (Göttingen: Vandenhoek und Ruprecht, 1996), pp. 7–24; here pp. 14–16.

Others have noted that in many areas, such as in welfare policies, the party did achieve genuine support, so that for many citizens the dictatorial aspects of the regime receded into the background.[31] Mary Fulbrook has even suggested that the GDR is best understood as a 'participatory dictatorship'. Taking full account of the repressive mechanisms at the regime's disposal, she argues that, from the mid-1960s to the mid-1980s, it was nevertheless possible for most citizens to lead 'normal' lives. Given that there were millions who assisted state and party through voluntary offices (which included that of unofficial informer for the state security services), it appears that most individuals had accepted the 'normality' of their existence, without necessarily losing their critical distance.[32]

The notion of the 'participatory dictatorship', like so many others, rephrases rather than solves the central issue of how everyday practices related to the dictatorial regime of the party. What did it signify for their commitment to the state when individuals became unofficial informants for the Stasi, when they joined the Cultural League, or when they volunteered for participatory campaigns organized by the National Front? We still have insufficient knowledge about how activity within the institutions of state and party affected the ways in which individuals identified with their circumstances. Nor is it sufficiently clear how the citizens' participation in the GDR's mass organizations and its other institutions helped to sustain existing power relations; after all, millions of citizens continued to be active in this manner until 1989, when the socialist order imploded nonetheless.

This book addresses these issues by looking more closely at how the power of state and party was appropriated, subverted, and even resisted in everyday life. By exploring contestations of heimat and 'national' identity in day-to-day situations, it seeks to examine some of the social and cultural practices through which people learned to 'make do' with their circumstances.[33] This perspective is essential for avoiding an understanding of history that is partial at best. By taking seriously the meanings of the 'many', those who normally remain 'nameless' in historical accounts,[34]

---

[31] Konrad Jarausch (ed.), *Dictatorship as Experience: Towards a Socio-Cultural History of the GDR*, trans. Eve Duffy (New York/Oxford: Berghahn, 1999).

[32] Mary Fulbrook, *The People's State: East German Society from Hitler to Honecker* (New Haven: Yale University Press, 2005). Her idea of normalization is rigorously defended by Jeanette Madarász, *Working in East Germany: Normality in a Socialist Dictatorship, 1961–79* (Basingstoke: Palgrave Macmillan, 2006).

[33] Alf Lüdtke, 'Alltagsgeschichte – ein Bericht von Unterwegs', *Historische Anthropologie* 11 (2003), 278–95.

[34] Alf Lüdtke, 'Introduction: what is the history of everyday life and who are its practitioners?', in Alf Lüdtke (ed.), *The History of Everyday Life: Reconstructing Historical Experiences and Ways of Life* (Princeton University Press, 1995), pp. 3–40; here esp. pp. 3–4.

the book shows how the state affected everyday cultural practices, and how functionaries in turn had to respond to, and take account of, popular desires. For power is not simply imposed from the top down: it depends for its efficacy on the actions of the dominated.[35] By investigating social and cultural practices and the meanings which individuals attribute to them, we gain sight of the complex movements of individuals which affect, constrain and qualify the power exerted at the top.[36]

This is by no means the first attempt to apply this 'everyday' approach to an examination of power in the GDR. A number of scholars have shown how, on a range of issues from gender equality to consumer desires, the party was forced to respond to the expectations of the 'many' time and again.[37] Other historians have examined more carefully the 'transmission spaces' of power, that tiny space between 'the tree and its bark' (Hürtgen) in which power was transmitted between the 'commando heights' (Lüdtke) and the 'many' nameless individuals of the everyday.[38] They have pointed to the significance of local functionaries in transmitting power to the 'many', and in stabilizing the regime.[39] These studies have also begun to overcome the 'state–society dichotomy' (Fulbrook) which has characterized so many works on the GDR by demonstrating, from different perspectives, just how closely individual actors and the state were interlinked. The state and its functionaries reached deep into the community and the workplace, and affected even the most mundane aspects of everyday life.

Heimat practices constituted just one such 'mundane' arena of people's lives. Thuringians or Mecklenburgers had sung folk songs, pursued hobbies such as ornithology, and celebrated their heimat in festivals for centuries; how and why would such apparently innocuous practices change under socialism? And yet socialism did shape the ways in which heimat was articulated and consumed at the grass roots. Not only did millions engage

---

[35] Thomas Lindenberger, 'Diktatur der Grenzen: Zur Einleitung', in Thomas Lindenberger (ed.), *Herrschaft und Eigen-Sinn in der Diktatur: Studien zur Gesellschaftsgeschichte der DDR* (Cologne: Böhlau, 1999), pp. 22–3.

[36] Michel de Certeau, *The Practice of Everyday Life* (Berkeley: University of California Press, 1984), esp. pp. xx, 29–42.

[37] See, for instance, the pioneering work by Kathy Pence in: Katherine Pence, 'Schaufenster des sozialistischen Konsums: Texte der ostdeutschen "consumer culture"', in Alf Lüdtke and Peter Becker, *Akten, Eingaben, Schaufenster: Die DDR und ihre Texte* (Berlin: Akademie-Verlag, 1997), pp. 91–118. For an excellent overview, see David Crew (ed.), *Consuming Germany in the Cold War* (Oxford: Berg, 2003).

[38] Lüdtke, 'Alltagsgeschichte', pp. 281–2.

[39] Thomas Lindenberger, *Volkspolizei: Herrschaftspraxis und öffentliche Ordnung im SED-Staat 1952–68* (Cologne: Böhlau, 2003). Andrew I. Port, *Conflict and Stability in the German Democratic Republic* (Cambridge University Press, 2007); here pp. 275–7. Renate Hürtgen, *Zwischen Disziplinierung und Partizipation: Vertrauensleute des FDGB im DDR-Betrieb* (Cologne: Böhlau, 2005).

in state-sponsored campaigns to 'beautify' the heimat, they also celebrated socialist heimat festivals and regularly watched heimat shows on television. Even when intense frustration about the environmental degradation of the heimat developed, the party proved remarkably successful in keeping these frustrations mostly within the official language of heimat and environmentalism. Individuals engaged in heimat practices through the 'public transcript' whereby they testified to being citizens who cared for their socialist heimat, the GDR. By publicly acknowledging what the state wanted to hear, individuals created spaces in which they could pursue their own, private meanings.

This study of how nationhood was constructed and contested is fundamentally about how socialist elites impose their power on the subordinate masses, and what strategies the masses develop to resist these impositions. To address this issue, this book builds on James C. Scott's work, which has influenced scholarship on other socialist states,[40] but which has barely featured in studies of everyday life in the GDR. Dietrich Staritz, in a characteristically insightful essay, has argued that GDR society was characterized by a contract whereby the party accepted the formal assertions of loyalty of its citizens 'as if' they were based on reality.[41] Noting the 'as if' society points in the right direction, but does not go far enough, because it fails to provide an explanation as to why the party accepted this behaviour, especially since it never abandoned its goal of transforming the population into true socialist citizens.

Reflecting on societies characterized by great imbalances of power, Scott noted that the most effective strategy open to subordinates consists of a double technique. This involves open compliance with the 'public transcript' of the powerful, alongside strategies of avoidance, foot-dragging and other 'offstage' behaviour that remains hidden from, and thus beyond the reach of, the state.[42] The dominant classes are rarely unaware that 'hidden transcripts' exist, but since these transcripts are, by definition, hidden from their view, it is extraordinarily difficult for the dominant to prevent such

---

[40] See, for instance, Sheila Fitzpatrick, *Stalin's Peasants: Resistance and Survival in the Russian Village after Collectivization* (New York/Oxford: Oxford University Press, 1994).

[41] Dietrich Staritz, 'Die SED und die Opposition', in Dietrich Staritz, *Was War: Historische Studien zu Geschichte und Politik der DDR* (Berlin: Metropol, 1994), pp. 137–68; here pp. 156–8. On the description of the Soviet Union as a society composed of citizens acting 'as if' they supported the public rituals and language of the regime, see Alexei Yurchak, *Everything was Forever, Until It Was No More* (Princeton University Press, 2006), here pp. 16–18.

[42] James C. Scott, *Weapons of the Weak: Everyday Forms of Peasant Resistance* (New Haven: Yale University Press, 1985), esp. pp. 32–6. James C. Scott, *Domination and the Arts of Resistance: Hidden Transcripts* (New Haven: Yale University Press, 1990), pp. 18–19.

transgressions from happening. Thus the dominant and the dominated have an interest in maintaining compliance with the public transcript. For the dominated, subscribing to the public transcript acts as a form of concealment, allowing them to 'minimize compliance at the actual level of behavior'.[43] For the dominant, by contrast, the public transcript affirms their hegemony through the appearance of affirmation and unanimity. 'By controlling the public stage', Scott writes, 'the dominant can create an appearance that approximates what, ideally, they would want to see'.[44]

What stops the dominant from being openly challenged is the appearance that their power is unavoidable. Enlisting the dominated to the public transcript becomes central to the act of domination, because in formally complying, they signal that they expect existing power structures to be there to stay. Conversely, open defiance of the public transcript becomes particularly dangerous to the dominant, because it contains a challenge to existing hegemony *tout court*. In systems where power relations are particularly unequal, the public transcript is central to the art of domination, for it serves to euphemize the physical power of the dominant.[45]

This book argues that heimat became central to the public transcript of socialism. By expanding the public transcript beyond official holidays, party gatherings and the workplace into the arena of popular culture, the party forced citizens to acknowledge the designs of socialism in their everyday practices in the community and in their spare time. Through the multiplication of arenas in which individuals had to subscribe to the public transcript of socialism and national 'identity', the party reinforced a sense that it was there to stay. As part of the public transcript, heimat became integral to the party's domination.

The notion of the public transcript helps us to shed new light on a major problem in GDR history, namely the relationship between the physical power of the state and everyday life. After all, in the humdrum of day-to-day activity, most individuals were seldom if ever interrogated by the state security services (Stasi). As they went about their daily business, most may even have stopped thinking about the Berlin Wall. I shall argue that this was only possible because of the public transcript. For as long as individuals affirmed the public transcript of socialism in their everyday practices, they did not have to fear the state's physical power. Conversely, knowledge of the latency of the state's physical power convinced most citizens to get on with their daily lives by subscribing to the public transcript of socialism. In expressing their identification with the heimat through the

[43] Scott, *Weapons*, p. 26. [44] Scott, *Domination*, p. 50. [45] Ibid., pp. 193–205.

language of socialism and GDR patriotism, citizens learned to keep the physical power of the state at bay and 'work the system ... to their minimum disadvantage'.[46]

By submitting to the public transcript, citizens were able to claim considerable space in which they could develop alternative, private meanings. For most citizens, the ubiquity of socialism in public life meant that it was wisest not to express views that directly contrasted with the public transcript of socialism. It is unhelpful to characterize such assertions of individual autonomy against the party's domination as 'opposition' (Staritz) or 'resistance' (Scott). Instead, this book restricts the notion of 'resistance' to the few who chose to openly reject the public transcript of socialism. The greatest attention of the Stasi was reserved for such acts. Refusal to subscribe to the public transcript was not against the law, but it nevertheless constituted a most fundamental threat to the party's power, and the party considered it as such. I shall show how the party tried to keep individual and communal frustrations within the public transcript, and how it responded to those who threatened to transgress it.

Scott's model of the public transcript is applied here only partially. This book echoes criticism that the 'hidden' and 'public' transcripts were hardly ever separate,[47] and argues that citizens developed private transcripts that were visible and open, but whose meanings were nonetheless specific to the local community. A further issue that arises out of Scott's work is that individual meanings were affected as much by emotions as by rational choices. This emotional dimension is easily lost in Scott's model, whereby individuals act in order to maximize their own interests. Yet the everyday practices of individuals often appear to be 'tacking' or 'meandering' from one direction to another, often in ways that defy rationale. Just as a river meanders apparently aimlessly, so individuals take different positions depending on their emotional states, their predispositions and the context.[48] The term 'meandering' is not ideal: often individuals tack between positions with purpose and intent. Still, 'meandering' does capture the often unpredictable and emotional side of human behaviour. This is often expressed through *Eigen-Sinn*, which translates literally as 'individual meanings', applied to actions that denote a 'mixture of self-affirmation and prankish obstinacy'. *Eigen-Sinn* accounts for acts that subvert and 'enrich' – without openly challenging – the meanings of the powerful, as individuals 'appropriate' current power relations in their own ways, and in relation to

[46] Eric Hobsbawm, cited in Scott, *Weapons*, p. xv.   [47] Yurchak, *Everything*, pp. 16–29.
[48] This definition is taken from Lüdtke, 'Alltagsgeschichte', p. 283.

their environment.[49] By looking at how the construction of the socialist heimat affected individual meanings, this study aims to locate individual experiences and practices in relation to wider dynamics of power (*Kräftefeld*).[50] To this end, this book examines the development of individual and communal meanings from two perspectives: by looking at the direct responses of individuals and communities to the transcript of the socialist heimat (Part 2), and by exploring how meanings of heimat related to social relations and individual desires (Part 3).

This focus on how power was asserted, appropriated, and subverted has of course influenced the subjects and sources selected for analysis in the present book. Most analyses of heimat in other periods of German history have tended to focus on local history groups and tourist associations as the groups most consciously shaping representations of heimat to locals and outsiders alike.[51] I shall consider such groups, particularly in Chapters 2, 3 and 4. That said, my object is not to provide conclusive definitions of how Thuringians or Mecklenburgers felt, and how these identifications changed over time. Instead, because of its primary focus on how claims to identity were constructed and contested, this book has a more expansive definition of what constituted heimat groups. For any investigation, the elasticity of the term 'heimat' makes the definition of what activities expressed it somewhat arbitrary. I shall include those who contributed to the cultural life of the local community, with particular attention devoted to the activities of enthusiasts such as ornithologists, aquarists, local historians and even stamp collectors. These were enrolled in the 'Friends of Nature and Heimat', whose more than 50,000 members formed the largest sub-unit of the Cultural League, the GDR's official cultural mass organization originally founded to articulate the cultural desires of the intelligentsia. I shall also examine activists who were not primarily involved in the Cultural League (even if they may have been members of that organization), notably environmental officers, preservationists and those engaged in participatory movements. This collection of activities is as random as any other. Tin-statue collectors or

49 Alf Lüdtke, 'What happened to the "fiery red glow"? Workers' experiences and German fascism', in Lüdtke (ed.), *The History of Everyday Life*, pp. 198–251; here pp. 226–8, 234–7. The quotation is on p. 226.
50 Alf Lüdtke, 'Herrschaft als soziale Praxis', in Alf Lüdtke, *Herrschaft als soziale Praxis: Historische und sozialanthropologische Studien* (Göttingen: Vandenhoek und Ruprecht, 1991), pp. 9–63; here esp. pp. 12–19. Hans Medick, 'Quo Vadis, historische Anthropologie? Geschichtsforschung zwischen historischer Kulturwissenschaft und Mikro-Historie', *Historische Anthropologie* 9, no. 1 (2001), 78–92; here esp. 87–92.
51 In addition to the work previously cited, see also, for instance, Caitlin Murdock, 'Constructing a modern German landscape: tourism, nature and industry in Saxony', in Blackbourn and Retallack (eds.), *Localism*, pp. 195–213.

philatelists often contributed to local exhibitions, but otherwise pursued hobbies whose relation to the construction of local identity could be extremely tenuous. Yet drawing a line between local historians on the one hand and ornithologists, or even philatelists, on the other would have created a boundary that contemporary activists themselves would not have understood. As the case studies in Chapters 7 and 8 show, the baker directing the amateur dramatic society, the engineer leading the local fight against the expansion of a local slag heap, and the teacher overseeing the young philatelists were all integral to heimat culture. Such actors are included because their involvement was vital in formulating local identities.

However expansive this list of activities may be, it still excludes some hobbies that acted as conduits for local identity, notably sport. Footballers, handball players and others have been left out mainly for practical reasons; an investigation of how local identity was expressed through amateur and professional sport would (and does) require another book entirely. In addition, although this study highlights the importance of the city in the socialist construction of heimat, for pragmatic and methodological reasons the micro-studies featured here are drawn from smaller settlements, ranging from villages to medium-sized towns. A further important area that would have significantly enriched this study is a closer examination of expellee communities, notably how these were integrated into, and how they identified with, the heimat offered to them after 1945. Although scholars have considered this issue lately, the integration of expellees in the GDR still requires further attention as a subject in its own right, especially at the micro-level.[52] This book does provide evidence (especially in Chapters 2 and 8) that the integration of expellees into the heimat was protracted and incomplete, but it does not claim to provide a comprehensive examination of the issue. While including a greater variety of activities than other investigations, the book cannot and does not profess to explore the entire range of cultural practices and identifications that relate to the heimat.

My analytical focus on heimat as a site of power under the conditions of socialism precludes comparison with the FRG. In fact, heimat is one of the few themes that have been examined predominantly in a comparative perspective.[53] This has been conducive to exploring questions about how

---

[52] Two recent publications are symptomatic of the difficulty of dealing with the integration of expellees in the GDR: despite their comparative ambitions, both are far stronger on the FRG than on the GDR. Christian Lotz, *Die Deutung des Verlusts: Erinnerungspolitische Kontroversen im geteilten Deutschland um Flucht, Vertreibung und die Ostgebiete* (Cologne: Böhlau, 2007); Ian Connor, *Refugees and Expellees in Post-War Germany* (Manchester University Press, 2007).

[53] Oberkrome, *„Deutsche* Heimat". Schaarschmidt, *Regionalkultur*. Von Moltke, *Place*.

notions of heimat and a sense of place developed both east and west of the Iron Curtain. The salience of heimat in both parts of Germany continues to render this subject eminently suitable for further comparative investigation. However, a comparison with the FRG is less helpful if one seeks to explore how ideas of heimat and nation were contested between individuals, communities and authorities in the GDR. I shall examine what contestations of heimat and nationhood can tell us about power relations in a socialist state, in the specific context of the GDR.

This book is based on a wide range of sources at the macro-, mezzo- and micro-levels. For the GDR as a whole, findings are based on material from the central archives of the Cultural League, the SED and relevant government ministries, as well as books, popular journals and the national press, and files (plus recordings) from the German Radio and Television Archives. At the regional level, I shall concentrate on the states of Mecklenburg and Thuringia, with particular emphasis on the districts of Erfurt, Suhl, Schwerin and Neubrandenburg.[54] The selection of these two states was based on the desire to include the north and the south while avoiding Saxony, a state whose territorial integrity was particularly pronounced by East German standards. At the regional and local levels, I consulted sources from the Cultural League, the National Front, local and county authorities, newspapers and private papers.

Documents from the National Front, the umbrella for all mass organizations (including the political parties and the trade union), perfectly illustrate the difficulty of obtaining nuanced information beyond official rhetoric.[55] This is, however, the exception, for all other sources are surprisingly rich in expressions of frustration or criticism, presumably because they discuss matters that were considered to be at the margins of political discourse. Of course, the historian should still approach such written sources with due scepticism, but without dismissing them out of hand simply because they were written in the communist era.

The written and visual evidence is complemented by forty-five semi-structured interviews, conducted twelve to seventeen years after the collapse of the GDR (2002–7). I began interviewing from the centre, with leading

---

[54] It should be noted that the evidence presented from these areas is not homogeneous. For instance, Thuringian local archives are clearly much better endowed than their Mecklenburg counterparts, so that it was much easier to access local archives in Thuringia. For this reason, in Part 2 the local cases explored in greater depth are drawn mostly from Thuringia. By contrast, at the state level the Mecklenburg archives contain far more documents relating to culture and the National Front than the Thuringian state archives.

[55] Matthias Judt, '"Nur für den Dienstgebrauch" – Arbeiten mit Texten einer deutschen Diktatur', in Lüdtke and Becker (eds.), *Akten*, pp. 29–38.

functionaries of the Cultural League in Berlin, who in turn recommended activists at the regional and local levels. I complemented this with my own choice of activists based on contemporary newspaper and archival reports, and many activists also gave me critical introductions to others. My interviewees, in short, were mostly actors who were heavily involved in heimat practices. They were in no way representative of the population. Yet, if the party wanted to succeed in appropriating the heimat for its own ends, it had to convince such actors first and foremost of its own meanings of socialism.

Evidently, the memories which these actors communicated have been affected by the length of time that has passed, by personal experiences since unification, and by the questions asked. Though my West German origins were obvious, the fact that I could point (truthfully) to my Anglo-German background, evident not least in my affiliation to a British university, may well have caused interviewees to speak to me differently than they would have done if I had had a more conventional (West) German academic background. Nevertheless, individuals could (and did) withhold information (e.g. about party allegiance), while also at times exaggerating the significance of their actions. That said, the number of interviews I conducted helped greatly in identifying what sentiments and practices were more common than others.

Finally, these sources are complemented by the files of the state security services, the Stasi. It would have been impossible to consider such files for every one of the towns explored in greater detail here; hence the use of Stasi files is limited to Eisenach (Chapter 6), Holungen (Chapter 7) and Dabel (Chapter 8).[56] Clearly, these are extremely problematic sources, not least because the reports are indicative at least as much of the concerns of the writers and of the local Stasi officers as they are of the subjects they report on. Nevertheless, the files are a unique historical source and they do add an important dimension to our understanding of local life – of which the Stasi was, as this book will demonstrate, an integral part.

The book is structured in three parts. The first investigates how and why, in the first half of the GDR's lifetime, the party attempted to construct a 'national' identity through heimat. It was not at all to be expected, after all, that a party committed to creating a new, socialist human being would fall back on pre-existing popular traditions for the construction of national identity. The appropriation of Heimat by a centralist state was neither self-evident nor without contradictions. Still, by claiming that it was only in

---

[56] My search for individual activists, events and groups related to heimat in Holungen, Dabel and Eisenach alone necessitated a search through 546 files containing some 73,000 pages.

socialism that an unadulterated enjoyment of heimat was possible, the party embraced the notion during the 1950s as a vehicle through which the distinctiveness of the GDR could be articulated without openly advocating the division of Germany. Moreover, by the late 1960s party leaders recognized that by linking socialism and the GDR to heimat, the utopia of socialism could be endowed with cultural and historical roots. Heimat had become central to defining GDR nationhood.

During the Honecker era (1971–89), a love of the socialist heimat continued to define GDR nationhood and citizenship, with the party encouraging an ever-growing diversity of cultural practices as evidence of a love of heimat and the joy of GDR citizenship. The second part of the book examines why individuals involved themselves in heimat activities, even if it meant subscribing to the public transcript. Heimat festivals and other activities not only provided relaxation and enjoyment, they also strengthened social and cultural bonds in the community. Heimat also provided a framework for individual initiative, for as long as individuals subscribed to the public transcript. This part of the book explores how individuals developed meanings that were quite different from those desired by the socialist party, while the SED, in turn, was remarkably successful at keeping these meanings restricted to the private sphere. Despite the frustrations individuals felt about the dilapidation of the environment and the party's inability to provide for the heimat, most citizens did not openly challenge the public transcript of the socialist heimat until October 1989.

The final part examines two communities more closely, in order to provide a more comprehensive understanding of how individuals developed the meanings of community and heimat in relation to state and party. Through micro-studies of two very different villages, one in Thuringia and one in Mecklenburg, this part aims to show how local dynamics of power were affected by state structures, socialist ideology and the state security services, as well as local relations and individual predispositions. The two cases show how individuals and communities learned to 'play the system' to their maximum advantage through multiple strategies, by publicly subscribing to the language of the socialist heimat while pursuing their own individual agendas within, and in relation to, the local community. The two villages were chosen because they related to socialism in different, and in many respects opposite, ways. Unwittingly I chose villages which were both objects of intense interest to the Stasi. This also allows us to see just how invasive the party could be in everyday village life, and reveals the strategies villagers developed to maintain and reaffirm local community nevertheless. Contrary to the intentions of state and party, local inhabitants learned to keep their roles as villagers and neighbours as distinct as possible from their roles as citizens of the GDR.

'A nation', Ernest Renan wrote, 'is a daily plebiscite.' The unpopularity of the German division precluded this option: most East Germans never appropriated the GDR as 'their' nation. In this context, persuading the population to affirm the public transcript of the socialist nation on a daily basis was the next best thing. The party's ideal of socialist nationhood was acknowledged whenever citizens watched heimat shows on GDR television, celebrated local festivals, or engaged in hobby activities relating to heimat. By subscribing to the socialist idea of the nation, East Germans affirmed the party's hold on power in everyday life.

The price the party paid for this near-universal public acknowledgement of the socialist heimat ideal was a failure to generate the identity between the state and its citizens which the SED so desired. The party attempted to straitjacket heimat culture into its own socialist meanings. At the national and even district levels, the imagery and the associations relating to heimat were clearly defined and presented, with little room for alternative articulations by the citizens, for whom the socialist heimat had been constructed. Yet communal identifications developed through cultural practices like carnival and village festivals, and through social tension within a given locality.[57] At the local level, and only there, it was possible to articulate and develop meanings that were unscripted and spontaneous. Such creative moments gave local communities their vibrancy, and this allowed their identities to evolve without needing to refer back to socialism or to the GDR. Beneath the veneer of the socialist heimat, meanings thus developed that reinforced local and regional identifications that were distinct from socialism and the GDR. By openly subscribing to the socialist ideal of heimat and patriotism nevertheless, individuals acknowledged the inescapability of the state and its discourse without ever identifying with it. When the GDR collapsed, the ideal of the socialist heimat vanished without trace, with local and regional identities surviving the most centralized regime in German history with remarkable vitality.

---

[57] On the methodological problems of considering Stasi documents for the history of everyday life, see Jan Palmowski, 'Staatssicherheit und soziale Praxis', in Jens Giesecke (ed.), *Staatssicherheit und Gesellschaft: Studien zum Herrschaftsalltag in der DDR* (Göttingen: Vandenhoek und Ruprecht, 2007), pp. 253–72.

Socialism, heimat and the construction of identity

Part I discusses how and why a party committed to the creation of a new society and culture not only accepted the continuation of heimat practices, but ended up appropriating the ideal of heimat for its own purposes. The GDR was founded upon the utopian ideals of the social, cultural and moral transformation of its population. Yet socialism was never sufficient to define the GDR, precisely because in a divided Germany the national question could not be left unaddressed. From the GDR's founding period, the socialist party had to contend with the difficulty of establishing cultural practices that pointed to socialism.

The SED soon discovered the continued popularity of cultural practices relating to the homeland, or heimat, including local festivals, folklore and hobby groups. Faced with the question of how this culture could relate to the socialist order, the party argued that heimat could be expressive of authentic German popular culture, and allowed a sense of individual fulfilment. Moreover, heimat enabled the socialist state to define itself culturally through the traditions of its regions, and to reinvent these as germane to the GDR. During the Ulbricht years, the 'socialist heimat' came to express the socialist nation, the GDR.

Chapter 2 explores how, in the first decade of Germany's division, heimat, a term with emotive associations for all Germans, became imbued with connotations specific to the GDR, notably hostility to Americanization and exploitative capitalism. At a time when a separate national identity could not yet be formulated, state and party used their commitment to heimat to affirm the party's theoretical commitment to unification while entrenching notions of separateness and distinctiveness for the socialist part of Germany.

From the late 1950s, the SED began in earnest to construct the new socialist human being, irrespective of developments in the FRG. Chapter 3 demonstrates that this new departure, encapsulated in the 'Bitterfeld Path' of 1959, led to the creation of a new cultural infrastructure which promoted new cultural practices at the expense of heimat traditions. Yet, in its subsequent failure to establish a socialist popular culture, the party became more, rather than less, reliant on heimat practices for bringing local culture to life. In fact, during the 1960s the 'socialist heimat' became central to the representation of the GDR and the achievements of socialism. There were two fundamental reasons for this. Given that the project of socialist transformation constituted a rational utopia, the socialist heimat was necessary in order to evoke emotional feelings of patriotism and belonging. The 'poetics of heimat' became essential to realize the 'ideology of class' (Confino). Moreover, socialist experiments in the 1960s came and went: the socialist heimat ideal could easily be adjusted to each of them, all the while expressing its unaltered essence – a socialist community that loved the GDR. When the GDR celebrated its twentieth 'birthday' in 1969, it did so principally in terms of the socialist heimat.

CHAPTER 2

Cultural renewal and national division, 1945–c. 1958

INTRODUCTION

Following the collapse of Nazi Germany, the new authorities in East Berlin endeavoured to 'democratize' their zone according to the Soviet model. This entailed not just the formation of political parties and mass organizations, but also the reformation of the administration, the judiciary and education.[1] In conjunction, the authorities aimed at the economic restructuring of the Soviet Zone through central planning and the transformation of land ownership initiated with the land reform of November 1945.[2] Closely linked to these transformations was a third goal, the cultural renewal of Germany. To this end, Johannes R. Becher and others founded the 'Cultural League for the Democratic Renewal of Germany' (Cultural League) on 8 July 1945. Only through the 'renewal of all progressive humanist, truly national traditions of the German people', they argued, could Nazism be overcome in the hearts and minds of all Germans.[3]

The ideal of casting out the devil of Nazism through a reappraisal of the German classics was not confined to the Soviet-occupied zone of Germany. In the Western zones, prominent intellectuals also urged that the aberrations of the Nazi period be overcome by returning to the values and ideals that had distinguished the German bourgeoisie in the nineteenth century.[4] Distinctive to the Soviet-occupied zone, however, was the significance which anti-fascism acquired for the legitimacy of the state. The Socialist Unity Party (SED)

---

[1] Wentker, *Justiz*. Connelly, *Captive University*.   [2] Kopstein, *Politics*. Steiner, *Plan*.

[3] Magdalena Haider, *Politik – Kultur – Kulturbund: Zur Gründungs- und Frühgeschichte des Kulturbunds zur demokratischen Erneuerung Deutschlands 1945–54 in der SBZ/DDR* (Cologne: Verlag Wissenschaft und Politik, 1993), pp. 30–1, 36–7. David Pike, *The Politics of Culture in Soviet-Occupied Germany, 1945–1949* (Stanford University Press, 1992), esp. pp. 80–8.

[4] Friedrich Meinecke, *Die deutsche Katastrophe: Betrachtungen und Erinnerungen* (Wiesbaden: Eberhard Brockhaus, 1946). In general, see Ulrich Herbert, 'Liberalisierung als Lernprozeß: Die Bundesrepublik in der deutschen Geschichte', in Ulrich Herbert (ed.), *Wandlungsprozesse in Westdeutschland: Belastung, Integration, Liberalisierung 1945–1980* (Göttingen: Wallstein-Verlag, 2002), pp. 1–52.

justified the GDR's existence as the 'better' Germany whose citizens had acquired a new, anti-fascist morality, an ideal which the party constructed through film, literature, memorials and public commemorations.[5]

The GDR was inherently anti-fascist because here, in contrast to the Weimar era, the workers had been liberated, so that they had the power to resist fascism, as it was opposed to their objective class interests. This was the second pillar on which the party constructed the state's legitimacy: socialism and the rule of workers and peasants. In the first workers' and peasants' state on German soil, not only did workers own the means of production, they could also ensure, through the party, that they were finally able to participate fully in education and high culture.[6] In the newly created socialist journal *Einheit*, Franz Lepinski wrote in 1946 that

> We [the workers' movement] are the inheritors of the great German culture ... We know that in taking on this culture we are stewards of the most precious things that humans have thought and aspired to ... We take on this treasure! But not to lock it up in museums and libraries – accessible perhaps only on workdays from 9 a.m. to 1 p.m. We want to take these cultural goods to the masses. They must lift up and expand the life of every last working person.[7]

Under socialism, German workers and peasants could avail themselves of all that the German classics had to offer.

The self-representation of state and party in the late 1940s and 1950s contained a central problem: how to deal with those who were neither anti-fascist nor inspired by humanism and the classics. In principle, the party was prepared for this difficulty. As the chief editor of the journal *Aufbau* and future Minister of Culture Klaus Gysi explained in 1948, cultural progress was closely linked to a new popular morality, and to artistic and scientific progress. These developments were indispensable to the success of the central plan for the economy, which in turn would lead to a higher morality.[8] Workers might not yet have fully appreciated the significance of anti-fascism, nor fully enjoyed the classical arts. However, as they discovered the fruits of socialism, they would develop new tastes and acquire new, socialist values.

---

[5] Jon Berndt Olsen, 'Tailoring the truth: memory culture and state legitimacy in East Germany, 1945–1989', PhD Dissertation, University of North Carolina (2004).

[6] Wolfram Schlenker, *Das kulturelle Erbe in der DDR: Gesellschaftliche Entwicklung und Kulturpolitik 1945–1965* (Stuttgart: Metzler, 1977).

[7] Horst Haase *et al.* (eds.), *Die SED und das kulturelle Erbe: Orientierungen, Errungenschaften, Probleme*, Akademie für Gesellschaftswissenschaften (Berlin: Dietz, 1986); here p. 55, footnote 53. See also pp. 60–2.

[8] Christoph Kleßmann, *Die doppelte Staatsgründung: Deutsche Geschichte 1945–55* (Bonn: Bundeszentrale für Politische Bildung, 1991), p. 170.

For the time being, however, the party had to contend with very different realities on the ground. Far from longing for the classics, audiences yearned for light entertainment, folk music and amateur drama, while many also engaged in their own hobbies, from archaeology to ornithology. Cultural practices relating to the heimat re-emerged which had existed before, and were far removed from the theory and practice of socialism. While putting its faith in the moral and cultural renewal of socialist Germany, the party had to grapple with the revival of a culture of localism on the ground.

That heimat was popular among Germans is neither new nor surprising, but the idea did not originally feature among socialist aspirations. Heimat traditions did not relate to class. Instead, they often referred implicitly or explicitly to the history of dynastic and ecclesiastical boundaries which had demarcated the regions and helped invent their traditions.[9] The party's hostility to such continuities constituted one of the reasons why it introduced the administrative reform of 1952. By creating fourteen districts (plus Berlin), the SED sought to maximize central control based on economic and security considerations, and to overcome historically and dynastically defined regional boundaries.[10] How, then, did a party dedicated to central planning and socialist renewal respond to the proliferation of locally based heimat groups after the war?

This chapter begins by examining the growth of popular culture related to the heimat in the Soviet-occupied zone. The party accepted practices relating to heimat by 1949, with functionaries desperate for cultural activity on the ground. Functionaries even encouraged expressions of local culture. Still, the party continued to be sceptical towards heimat practices, wary that such manifestations of local culture appeared far removed from its ideal of socialist realism. If the party continued to accept the idea of heimat in socialist Germany, it was for two reasons. First, it added an important dimension to the central tenets of the GDR's legitimacy, notably anti-fascism and socialist transformation. In the familiar and protected sphere of Heimat, the economic and moral transformations achieved by socialism could be felt and verified. Second, in the early 1950s the GDR acquired a further, distinctive, sphere of legitimacy: that of the genuine heimat unsoiled by Americanization and firmly rooted in German traditions. The party thus enhanced a term that had emotive meanings for all Germans with

---

[9] Thomas Kühne, 'Imagined regions: The construction of traditional, democratic and other identities', in James Retallack (ed.), *Saxony in German History: Culture, Society and Politics, 1830–1933* (Ann Arbor: University of Michigan Press, 2000), pp. 51–62.

[10] Siegfried Wietstruk, 'Von den Ländern zu den Bezirken: Die DDR 1949 bis 1952', *Staat und Recht* 38, no. 9 (1989), 753–60.

connotations specific to the GDR. By constructing an emotional link between individuals and a heimat distinguished by socialism, the party attempted to establish a distinctive popular identification with the GDR. Even though the idea of heimat had not yet become closely linked to socialism, by the late 1950s it had become central to the construction of nationhood in East Germany.

THE RENAISSANCE OF HEIMAT PRACTICES

If socialist re-education was to succeed, it had to do so, above all, in the countryside. In 1946, only 19 per cent of the population lived in cities of more than 100,000 inhabitants, while almost a third of the population lived in communities of 2,000 residents or fewer.[11] Especially outside the large cities, the socialist authorities soon discovered how difficult it would be to fulfil popular demands for cultural entertainment in ways that corresponded to the ideals of socialism. One year after the war had ended, for example, the culture officials of Hagenow county (western Mecklenburg) were forced to admit that they had thus far largely failed in their efforts at promoting high-quality culture. Classical concerts still only attracted small audiences, and as many as 80 per cent of the seats remained empty. Truly popular entertainment consisted of operettas, heimat evenings with talks on the history and the landscape of the locality, and light amateur plays. An evening devoted to the 'undying melodies' of Johann Strauss drew a sell-out crowd of 700 people, with Eduard Künneke's light operetta 'The Cousin from Thingammabob' (*Der Vetter aus Dingsda*) not far behind.[12]

Light cultural fare was popular throughout Mecklenburg. In January 1948, the Cultural League of Crivitz, with a membership of 179, organized a literary evening that was attended by twenty-two people. By contrast, an audience of 345 turned up to see the Fritz Reuter stage company perform, in Low German, the comedy *Up Düwels Schuvkor* ('On the Devil's Wheelbarrow'). In nearby Gadebusch, where the Cultural League comprised 343 members, attendance figures for events like political and cultural talks ranged between ten and sixty-five. Attendance leapt, by contrast, at a music evening entitled 'Songs Yesterday and Today', which drew an audience of 510.

---

[11] *Statistisches Jahrbuch der Deutschen Demokratischen Republik 1956*, Staatliche Zentralverwaltung für Statistik (Berlin: Staatsverlag der DDR, 1957), p. 18, table 9.
[12] Landeshauptarchiv Schwerin (LHA Schwerin), Ministerium für Volksbildung 2712: 'Kultur- und Volksbildungsamt an den Präsidenten des Landes Mecklenburg-Vorpommern' (23 April 1946; 22 May 1946; 27 June 1946).

The Mecklenburg Cultural League did manage to put on cultural fare that was more demanding and more popular at the same time, but only in the state's traditional cultural centres, Schwerin and Greifswald.[13] In Schwerin, the popular highlight of the January 1948 programme consisted of a talk on the landscapes of Mecklenburg, which attracted 270 people. Musical evenings (both classical and popular), film evenings and presentations linked to the local heimat were regularly well attended, drawing audiences above 150. Talks on 'politics and morals', or events such as a Lenin memorial evening, tended to attract audiences of well below 100.[14]

The difficulty that socialist officials experienced in promoting classical humanist culture was not unique to the state of Mecklenburg. In Saxony, the communist founding member of the Chemnitz Cultural League despaired that he had to deal with popular tastes which for twelve years had been 'drenched in the syrup of light entertainment and operetta'.[15] The Cultural League's programme for Zittau county in early 1947 also mirrors the popularity of local heimat culture. Even in the county's smallest villages, talks on 'heimat, our joy' or the 'mysteriousness of the Alps' as well as heimat concerts regularly attracted more than 200 listeners, far outdoing other cultural genres in terms of popularity.[16]

To overcome the dearth of good-quality cultural entertainment in the countryside, the state theatres embarked on an extensive touring programme. In Mecklenburg in 1948, state theatres gave 160 performances in the countryside, with an additional 100 performances given by the state-sponsored Low German Fritz Reuter company on tour. The folkloristic plays staged by the Fritz Reuter company were not part of the classical canon. But even the state theatres did not use their tours to bring high culture to the countryside. In 1948, the only classical play in their repertoire was the popular comedy *Der zerbrochene Krug*, performed alongside plays entitled 'The Trousers', 'Little Snow White' (*Schneeweischen*) and 'The Goosemaiden' (*Gänseliesel*).[17]

---

[13] LHA Schwerin, Ministerium für Volksbildung 3176: 'Durchgeführte Veranstaltungen in den Ortsgruppen des Kulturbundes zur demokratischen Erneuerung Deutschlands im Lande Mecklenburg-Vorpommern in den Monaten Dezember 1945, Januar u. Februar 1946' (unpag.).

[14] LHA Schwerin, Ministerium für Volksbildung 3173: 'Aufstellung der im Januar 1948 durchgeführten Veranstaltungen der Wirkungsgruppen des Kulturbundes zur demokratischen Erneuerung Deutschlands Landesleitung Mecklenburg'.

[15] '... süßlicher Operetten- und Unterhaltungszauber'. BArch-SAPMO, DY27 (Kulturbund der DDR) 481: 'Wirkungsgruppe Dresden, Erwin Völzke' (no date [*c*. early 1948], unpag.).

[16] BArch-SAPMO, DY27 226: 'Veranstaltungen der Ortsgruppen des Kreises Zittau in den Monaten Januar, Februar, März 1947' (unpag.).

[17] LHA Schwerin, Ministerium für Volksbildung 2667: 'Jahresbericht 1949 der Abteilung Volkskultur', ff. 22–40; here f. 29.

In another attempt to respond to the scarcity of uplifting cultural entertainment, the Mecklenburg authorities organized touring cinema screenings as a priority. Here, too, the insignificant demand for the culture promoted by the socialist authorities is revealed in the audience figures. In Grevesmühlen, the new East German cinema (DEFA) production 'No Place for Love' (1947) and the German musical comedy 'A Waltz with You' (1943) attracted around 800 spectators per day. By contrast, the Soviet film 'Primaballerina', featuring the music of Tchaikovsky, attracted around 400 visitors per day, while the Soviet war film 'Wait for Me' (1945) and the political biography of the 'Baltic Deputy' (1936) had to make do with fewer than 300 viewers.[18]

In their desire to promote classical culture, functionaries were constrained not only by popular demand, but also by their own aesthetic concerns. State officials in Mecklenburg actually encouraged the performance of folklore by local amateur groups at the expense of the classics, preferring well-performed heimat fare to poorly presented classical pieces.[19] This meant that classical plays or classical concerts were only to be performed by professional or highly trained amateur groups; but these were expensive to hire. In smaller towns and villages, cash-strapped local authorities simply could not afford to subsidize loss-making events, and therefore discouraged expensive cultural performances whose success was unpredictable.[20] The local branches of the Cultural League also had to budget carefully and were often hard-pressed to balance their books.[21] By encouraging existing regional traditions and pastimes, local functionaries promoted cultural occupations that were cheap, truly popular and in plentiful supply. Choirs and folklore groups could give concerts in their local communities, at the workplace and in neighbouring towns and villages. Hobby groups of ornithologists, aquarists and philatelists emerged, and these provided recreation and regular activities for members, while activists enriched local culture further through exhibitions.

[18] The original titles are, respectively, *Kein Platz für Liebe, Ein Walzer mit dir, Ballettsolistin, Warte auf mich* and *Stürmischer Lebensabend.* LHA Schwerin, Ministerium für Volksbildung 2996: 'Gespielte Filme im Monat November 1947' (unpag.).

[19] LHA Schwerin, Ministerium für Volkskultur 2980: 'Arbeitstagung des Landesausschusses für Freizeit und Erholung am Sonntag, dem 8. August 1948 Im [*sic*] Maxim Gorki-Haus', p. 9.

[20] LHA Schwerin, Ministerium für Volksbildung 2712: 'Kultur- und Volksbildungsamt an den Präsidenten des Landes Mecklenburg-Vorpommern' (23 July 1946).

[21] BArch-SAPMO, DY27 226: 'Bericht des Kulturbundes Wirkungsgruppe Chemnitz Monat August 1948'.

From the statistics available at national, state and local levels, one can gain some impression of the proliferation of heimat culture at the time of the GDR's foundation. Across most of the GDR, the most popular cultural pastime was choral singing. Of the thirty-five folklore groups registered with the League of German Folk Theatres (BDV, Bund Deutscher Volksbühnen) in the Thuringian town of Altenburg around 1950, twenty-eight were choirs.[22] In early 1950 the Cultural League in Saxony-Anhalt comprised 177 choirs and amateur orchestras, though some of the 264 groups which the Cultural League registered as 'folklore/folk culture' groups ('Volkskunstgruppen') would also have been choirs or orchestras.[23] Throughout the state of Saxony, too, choral singing constituted the most popular folklore activity.[24] The only exception to the predominance of choral singing was Mecklenburg, where the significance of local dialect as an expression of locally rooted identities meant that amateur theatre was particularly popular, with 23,430 registered participants organized in 710 groups in 1949. The state's 391 choirs registered 12,903 members; there were 196 dance groups (6,468 members), as well as 148 bands, orchestras and other musical groups (4,884 members).[25] For the GDR at the beginning of its existence, one estimate puts the total number of amateur theatre groups, choirs and folklore groups in the widest sense at around 10,500, with a total of 239,000 members.[26]

The figures given for each state and locality are highly unreliable, because the authorities and the mass organizations had difficulty in keeping track of amateur societies. Such groups were frequently founded spontaneously, and many turned out to be short-lived. Often, officials only learned of a group's existence when they received demands for meeting space, exhibition venues or financial support.[27] As hobby and folklore groups proliferated across the Soviet-occupied zone in the immediate post-war era,[28] cultural officials noted with concern that some local hobby associations had begun to consider forming organizations regionally and – to the alarm of officials – across

---

[22] In Altenburg, folklore groups appear to have been allocated, in 1949, to the League of German Folk Theatres rather than the Cultural League. ThStA Altenburg, Deutsche Volksbühne Kreisleitung Altenburg 19, 33.

[23] BArch-SAPMO, DY27 1973: 'Mitgliederbewegung [1 January – 30 June 1950]. Zahl der Sektionen' (unpag.).

[24] Schaarschmidt, *Regionalkultur*, pp. 375–7.

[25] LHA Schwerin, Deutsche Volksbühne: 'Statistische Übersicht der Laienkunstgruppen in Mecklenburg [1950]' (unpag.).

[26] *Die Aussprache* 4, 'Von den Aufgaben des Laienspiels' (1949), no. 2/3, 9–10.

[27] See, for instance, the development of the Schwerin chess club in LHA Schwerin, Ministerium für Volksbildung 2993. 'An den Rat der Stadt Dresden'. Letter from Willi Trampenau (16 January 1947).

[28] Schaarschmidt, *Regionalkultur*, pp. 289–90.

other parts of eastern and even western Germany.[29] In Mecklenburg, more-over, functionaries in the Ministry of Public Education warned that its bureaucracy at the state and the local levels was simply too small and underfunded to deal with the sheer number of associations. An inability to cope with amateur groups was bound to result in a loss of authority for the state.[30]

On 12 January 1949, the Soviet Zone's department of home affairs responded to these concerns by issuing an ordinance that integrated all independent hobby and folklore groups into the existing mass organiza-tions.[31] Pastimes such as chess or choral singing were incorporated in the Free German Youth and the Free German Trade Union. Amateur theatre companies that were not linked to the workplace were now included in the short-lived BDV. By contrast, heimat enthusiasts, whose passions included collecting (anything from stamps to tin statuettes), involvement with nature, and an interest for local history or archaeology were organized as the 'Friends of Nature and heimat' and became part of the Cultural League. Overnight, heimat enthusiasts became the largest branch of an organization originally founded to promote the revival of the German classics.

The ordinance created a legal basis for the organization of hobby enthu-siasts across the five eastern German states. It was not without flaws. The allocation of hobby groups to the different mass organizations was quite random as choirs and other folklore groups, for instance, could be attached to any one of the mass organizations. Still, the ordinance signalled that the party formally accepted the existence of hobby and folklore groups. This allowed many enthusiasts and groups to continue the interests which they had developed in the Weimar and Nazi eras. The ordinance also permitted activities that related closely to cultural practices in West Germany, where the German Heimat League continued to promote heimat activities that reinforced anti-modernist socio-cultural identifications with privacy, domesticity, and the nuclear, patriarchal family.[32]

The party had obviously not been able to ignore the cultural renaissance that marked everyday life in the GDR, and which expressed the desires of

---

[29] By early 1948, for instance, a number of eastern chess groups had heeded western German calls for an all-German chess association so as to prevent a possible division between workers' and bourgeois associations. LHA Schwerin, Ministerium für Volksbildung 2993: 'Sitzung der führenden Schachinteressenten des Landes Mecklenburg in Rostock' (29 February 1948) (unpag.).

[30] LHA Schwerin, Ministerium für Volksbildung 2994: 'Vorschlag für die Organisation einer Bewegung für Volkskunst, Freizeit und Erholung' (5 January 1948) (unpag.).

[31] Deutsche Verwaltung des Innern, *Verordnung zur Überführung von Volkskunstgruppen und volksbil-denden Vereinen in die bestehenden demokratischen Massenorganisationen* (12 January 1949).

[32] Oberkrome, „*Deutsche* Heimat", pp. 438–47.

the majority of the population, especially outside the large cities. However, even if the party acknowledged the existence of cultural practices relating to heimat by trying to assert political control over them, this does not mean that the SED accepted their ideological or cultural value. SED functionaries in Berlin continued to view heimat groups with considerable ambiguity. It remained to be seen how the persistence of activities related to the Heimat could express the new conditions of socialism.

SOCIALISM AND HEIMAT

The party based the legitimacy of socialist Germany on the ideals of anti-fascism, social unity and the superiority of socialism and the plan. Heimat was used to represent and enhance each of these visions. As the party came to realize, however, expressing socialism through heimat was not without ambivalence in this period.

Of particular concern to communist officials in the state cultural ministries were the *völkisch* and even racist undertones which the ideal of heimat, and heimat organizations, had acquired before 1945. During the Third Reich, heimat propagandists in Saxony, for instance, held that a conscious rootedness in local culture would lead to 'strength of character, and to a proud and superior disposition' for every Saxon.[33] The Saxon 'people' had become associated with hard work and a will of steel, honed by regular interactions with non-German peoples across its southern borders. The blood and soil of heimat, in this perspective, strengthened German character in the 'struggle' against non-German cultural influences, and in the rejection of Jews.[34]

Heimat was significant in the Third Reich far beyond propaganda, as it had influenced wartime plans for conquered eastern lands which were to be adapted for the use of their new occupiers.[35] In fact, heimat related closely to the imagination of place, ideas of lands tamed and cultured by man, of 'laughing meadows and flourishing fields'. Such ideas had nourished German colonial fantasies of lands rid of all elements that sullied them in German eyes: ideas acted out most tragically in the Second World War.[36]

---

[33] Schaarschmidt, *Regionalkultur*, pp. 173–4.

[34] Thomas Schaarschmidt, 'Regionalbewusstsein und Regionalkultur in Demokratie und Diktatur 1918–61: Sächsische Heimatbewegung und Heimat-Propaganda in der Weimarer Republik, im Dritten Reich und in der SBZ/DDR', *Westfälische Forschungen* 52 (2002), 203–28; here 222. Schaarschmidt, *Regionalkultur*, pp. 190–1.

[35] Oberkrome, „*Deutsche* Heimat", pp. 1–9, 236–48.

[36] David Blackbourn, *The Conquest of Nature: Water, Landscape and the Making of Modern Germany* (London: Jonathan Cape, 2006), ch. 5. The quotation is from Erich Gierach, cited on p. 248.

The colonial imagination under National Socialism constitutes an important example of the ways in which the ostensibly non-political language and activities of heimat allowed, and even encouraged, National Socialism to become anchored in popular culture.[37]

The connections between heimat and National Socialism made it difficult to connect the former ideal to anti-fascism, but it was not impossible. The Cultural League's first secretary, Karl Kneschke, had been active in the workers' rambling movement in the Weimar period, had fought against the Nazis, and belonged to the group of émigrés in Britain who were committed to the cultural renewal of Germany. With impeccable anti-fascist credentials, Kneschke knew many prominent bourgeois Heimat activists in the GDR. This allowed him to relate to the leading enthusiasts among East German 'Friends of Nature and Heimat', while his activities were relatively undisturbed by Johannes R. Becher and the rest of the Cultural League leadership, who were only too happy to devote their attention to high culture.[38]

According to Kneschke, the love of heimat formed the basis of all desire for educational and cultural self-improvement. A person who truly loved his or her heimat could not tolerate its destruction through war.[39] The love of heimat was intimately related to a love of Germany that could not but respect all other peace-loving peoples who loved their heimat just as intensely. Heimat thus became intrinsically opposed to the nationalism that had characterized the ideal of 'homeland' in earlier periods.[40] Heimat described all of Germany, but a true love of heimat was possible only in socialism, whose love of peace contrasted sharply to the hostility and aggressiveness displayed by the Americanized western part of Germany.[41] Through socialism, a love of heimat became an instrument of moral regeneration.

In marked contrast to the continued appearance in public discourse of *völkisch* ideals amongst many West German heimat enthusiasts,[42] in the

---

[37] Applegate, *Nation*, ch. 7.   [38] Interview with Karl-Heinz Schulmeister, 11 November 2002.

[39] Karl Kneschke, 'Deutschland – unsere Heimat', *Natur und Heimat* (1952), no. 3, 1–2.

[40] Karl Kneschke, 'Vom Werden und Wachsen', *Natur und Heimat* (1952), no. 1, 2–3.

[41] Kneschke, 'Deutschland', 2.

[42] Museumsdorf Cloppenburg, Kulturamt der Stadt Oldenburg, Stadtmuseum Oldenburg (eds.), *Regionaler Fundamentalismus? Geschichte der Heimatbewegung in Stadt und Land Oldenburg* (Oldenburg: Isensee, 1999); Oberkrome, „*Deutsche* Heimat", pp. 437–57. By contrast, Celia Applegate has emphasized the ideological rupture of the early post-war period among heimat enthusiasts in the Palatinate. Applegate, *Nation*, esp. pp. 234–5. These differences should serve as a warning not to generalize 'the' connotations of 'the' West German heimat, but to differentiate by historical context.

GDR its *völkisch* undertones disappeared from public discourse from the late 1940s.[43] This also meant that the racial and *völkisch* connotations which heimat had acquired in the Third Reich were barely discussed in the GDR. Neither Kneschke nor other leading cultural functionaries in the Cultural League or the party itself chose to confront heimat enthusiasts with the past. Exceptionally, Georg Pniower addressed the relationship between heimat and the Third Reich by arguing that in the Nazi era, simplistic conceptions of the heimat landscape had served to lend weight to annexationist plans for eastern Europe.[44] Pniower did not pursue the implications of this insight – that heimat enthusiasts had contributed morally to German annexationist fantasies. Instead, he assured his readers that, amongst nature enthusiasts during the Third Reich, conceptions of nature and heimat had been less affected by Nazi ideology than one might have expected.[45]

Pniower's main charge against heimat enthusiasts during the Nazi period echoed a widespread accusation in socialist Germany: that the Third Reich had allowed them to retreat into the private sphere and encouraged them to look naïvely to the past.[46] This accusation related closely to the central charge made against heimat enthusiasts in the early GDR, encapsulated in the term 'heimatism' (*Heimattümelei*),[47] which meant idealizing the heimat while refusing to acknowledge the realities of the modern, socialist era. In other words, instead of charging the former Nazis among the heimat enthusiasts with supporting the Third Reich in ideology and practice, eastern Germany's cultural leaders accused them of the opposite: of disengaging from politics in search of a romantic, irretrievable past.[48]

In the absence of any debate in which the ideological connotations acquired by heimat during the Third Reich were clearly articulated, a remarkable continuity developed among active heimat enthusiasts in the GDR.

---

[43] Elements of *völkisch* terminology and concepts were still evident as late as 1948. LHA Schwerin, Ministerium für Volksbildung 2889/2: 'Niederschrift über die Naturschutztagung vom 6. bis 9. Mai 1948 in Kloster auf Hiddensee'.

[44] Pniower was the Director of the Institute for Garden and Landscape Cultivation (Institut für Garten- und Landeskultur) at the Humboldt University in Berlin.

[45] Georg Pniower, 'Naturschutz im Spiegel der Landeskultur', *Natur und Heimat* 1 (1952), no. 1, 4–7; no. 2, 4–8; here no. 2, 6–7.

[46] E.g. LHA Schwerin, Ministerium für Volksbildung 2865: Hermann Lachs to Regierungsrat Stiemke (10 April 1948). Lachs accused heimat enthusiasts in the Third Reich of being 'Blut- und Heubodenromantiker'.

[47] See, for instance, the charge against heimat as a source of 'chauvinist overbreeding [*Überzüchtung*] and romanticizing *heimattümelei*' in *Volks- und Heimatfeste, gestern, heute, morgen: Referat und Diskussionsbeiträge einer Beratung, die der Deutsche Kulturbund – Zentrale Kommission Natur- und Heimatfreunde – am 25. und 26. Oktober 1958 in Magdeburg veranstaltete* (Berlin: Deutscher Kulturbund Zentrale Kommission Natur- und Heimatfreunde, 1959), p. 19.

[48] See also e.g. Karl Kneschke, 'Volksbildende Vereine und Gruppen', *Die Aussprache* 4 (1949), no. 6/7, 9–10.

In many local heimat organizations within the Saxon Cultural League, up to 80 per cent of the membership consisted of former Nazi party members.[49] Saxony was by no means exceptional. In Mecklenburg, local council officials noted with consternation that former NSDAP (Nazi party) members could even advance into the local leadership of individual hobby or heimat groups.[50] The personal continuities among heimat enthusiasts and conservationists between the Third Reich and the GDR has been discussed in great detail elsewhere. Both Thomas Schaarschmidt and Willi Oberkrome have emphasized the inability of the Cultural League as well as the state cultural authorities to prevent this personal continuity. If the authorities wanted to promote heimat culture and encourage its quality, they needed the co-operation of activists who had developed their skills as conservationists, ornithologists and authors on local matters before 1945, even if the activists had been loyal supporters of the Third Reich.[51]

There is much to be said for this interpretation. Printed discussions and particularly internal reports bear witness to the frustration experienced by cultural functionaries faced with the continuing cultural activities of former Nazi party members. Yet this is only part of the picture. Heimat activities offered an innocuous way for former members of the Nazi party to engage with the new system.[52] As Karl Kneschke pointed out, if the Cultural League only worked with those who already sympathized with its aims, it could address only a very small circle. Since the moral regeneration of Germans had to include those not (yet) committed to socialism,[53] heimat could help transform the 'brains of our people'.[54]

In addition to anti-fascism, the ideal of class unity was equally central to the GDR's legitimacy. In practice, social cohesion was challenged not so much by class as by the presence of expellees. In the Soviet-occupied zone in 1949, around 4.4 million of the 18.5-million-strong population had been expelled from the Soviet Union, Poland or Czechoslovakia. Of all German states, Mecklenburg had by far the highest proportion of 'new citizens', who

---

[49] BArch-SAPMO, DY 27 226: 'Berichterstattung der Landesleitung des Kulturbundes Sachsen 1946–1951. Bericht Völzke, Lage Kulturbund 1946' (unpag.). The report refered to the large local organizations in Annaberg and Oberwiesenthal in the Saxon Erzgebirge.

[50] LHA Schwerin, Ministerium für Volksbildung 3176: 'Vom Rat des Kreises Demmin' (4 February 1948).

[51] Schaarschmidt, *Regionalkultur*, pp. 373–5. Oberkrome, „*Deutsche* Heimat", pp. 350–2.

[52] Schaarschmidt, *Regionalkultur*, p. 356. This point deserved much greater emphasis in an otherwise comprehensive study.

[53] BArch-SAPMO, DY27 481: 'Brief Heinz Willmann' (13 March 1948).

[54] BArch-SAPMO, DY27 919: 'Stenografisches Protokoll der Sitzung des Präsidialrates des Kulturbunds zur demokratischen Erneuerung Deutschlands' (4 November 1955), ff. 298–300.

formed a staggering 46.5 per cent of the state's total population by March 1949. The presence of such numbers of outsiders created tremendous divisions and conflicts in local communities between 'new' and 'old' citizens, and among new citizens from different backgrounds.[55] Forming the bulk of the landless labourers, the new citizens belonged to the poorest sections of the population, while those who had been lucky enough to receive small plots of land in the 1945 land reform often relied on the more established, wealthier farms for equipment.[56] The state tried to improve the lot of the new citizens by forcing the 'old citizens' to surrender some machinery and livestock, but this hardly benefited relations between the two groups.[57]

State and party claimed that, in contrast to the FRG, expellees in socialist Germany were fully integrated and no longer voiced any aggressive demands for a return to their old heimat.[58] In this context, heimat developed into a significant cultural strategy of integration,[59] as talks, hobby groups and local festivals could help newcomers understand their new heimat, engage with it and become part of it.[60] In practice, however, local heimat traditions, far from including new communities, did much to exclude them. This became particularly apparent in the use of local dialect. Heimat enthusiasts in Thuringia as elsewhere felt strongly about maintaining the use of dialect as an important mark of local specificity.[61] This also applied to literary culture which, they argued, expressed the soul, the concerns and the humour of working people, and formed an essential component of the country's 'high' literary heritage.[62]

---

[55] Michael Schwartz, *Vertriebene und „Umsiedlerpolitik": Integrationskonflikte in den deutschen Nachkriegs-Gesellschaften und die Assimilationsstrategien in der SBZ/DDR 1945 bis 1961* (Munich: Oldenbourg, 2004), pp. 478–9. Corey Ross, *Constructing Socialism at the Grass-Roots: The Transformation of East Germany, 1945–65* (Basingstoke: Macmillan, 2000), esp. pp. 23–30.

[56] Andreas Dix, *„Freies Land": Siedlungsplanung im ländlichen Raum der SBZ und der frühen DDR* (Cologne: Böhlau, 2002), pp. 314–15.

[57] Arnd Bauerkämper, 'Von der Bodenreform zur Kollektivierung: Zum Wandel der ländlichen Gesellschaft in der Sowjetischen Besatzungszone Deutschlands und DDR 1945–52', in Kaelble et al. (eds.), *Sozialgeschichte der DDR*, pp. 119–43.

[58] Johannes R. Becher, 'Frieden und nationale Einheit', in *Natur- und Heimat: Jahrbuch* (Dresden: Vereinigung Volkseigener Verlage, 1951), pp. 31–4; here p. 34.

[59] On other strategies of integration, see Arnd Bauerkämper, *Ländliche Gesellschaft in der kommunistischen Diktatur: Zwangsmodernisierung und Tradition in Brandenburg 1945–1963* (Cologne: Böhlau, 2002), here pp. 348–68, esp. 357–8.

[60] Palmowski, 'Building', pp. 384–5.

[61] See for example 'Die Altenburger Bauerntracht', *Altenburger Kulturspiegel* (May 1957), 88, and 'Ewos vun dor Karmsgons', *Altenburger Kulturspiegel* (November 1956), 245. See also E. Schmidt, 'Sprachforschung auf dem Thüringer Wald', *Kulturbund zur demokratischen Erneuerung Deutschlands Kreisleitung Ilmenau: Monatsprogramm Oktober 1955*, 12–13.

[62] Albert Zirkler, 'Von der Mundartdichtung', *Natur und Heimat* (1952), no. 8, 20.

In the 1951 Quedlinburg programme of Friends of Nature and Heimat, the organization announced that dialect culture was acceptable as long as it did not separate the heimat from the new citizens or the state.[63] This compromise might have been satisfactory to heimat enthusiasts, but it hardly solved the problem, which was particularly apparent in Mecklenburg and cis-Pomerania, the part of Pomerania now in the GDR. Not only did this region contain disproportionate numbers of 'new citizens', but everyday life was conducted in a widely spoken dialect, Low German. Emboldened by the large numbers of dialect speakers,[64] heimat enthusiasts were in no mood to compromise on the use of Low German as part of their local identity.[65] If new citizens could not understand Low German speakers, the latter insisted that there was no reason why the former should not learn the language and customs of the heimat.[66]

Clearly, the process of integration was more complex and cumbersome than the heimat ideal postulated by enthusiasts and cultural functionaries alike. Personal recollections of new citizens point to the stigmatization and exclusion they suffered, especially as children.[67] They were discriminated against in the allocation of scarce resources, in the provision of employment, and in political participation. In practice, differing – indeed, mutually exclusive – conceptions of heimat and its meanings (and geography) remained a touchstone of differentiation between new citizens, old citizens and the state.[68]

Ultimately, integration between new and old citizens was less a question of heimat than of generations. In the Mecklenburg border town of Boizenburg, two residents, Uwe Wieben and Karin Wulf, remember how

[63] For a different interpretation, which posits that the desire of the Cultural League's leadership to suppress regional dialects came up against the stubbornness of local groups in Saxony, see Schaarschmidt, *Regionalkultur*, pp. 393–5. Given Karl Kneschke's thorough knowledge of Saxony, however, it would be surprising if Kneschke really believed that the Cultural League in Berlin or at district level could actually do anything to suppress local dialects, even if he considered their complete eradication desirable.

[64] Their ubiquity among the indigenous population of Mecklenburg made Low German speakers a much more powerful lobby than the Sorbs in Lusitania, who were additionally disadvantaged by their distinctive ethnicity. As a result, Sorbs only received positive encouragement in the early years of the GDR, as a result of foreign pressures. Peter Barker, *Slavs in Germany: The Sorbian Minority and the German State since 1945* (Lampeter: Edward Mellon Press, 2000), esp. ch. 2.

[65] LHA Schwerin, Ministerium für Volkskultur 2866: 'Eröffnungsansprache zum niederdeutschen Bühnentag am 31.8.47 in Bad Doberan'.

[66] On the heimat enthusiasts' defence of Low German see Palmowski, 'Building', pp. 371, 373–4, 384–5.

[67] Edmund Käbisch, 'Die letzten Jahre der DDR: Mein Alltag als evangelischer Pfarrer in Zwickau', in Clemens Vollnhals and Jürgen Weber (eds.), *Der Schein der Normalität: Alltag und Herrschaft in der SED-Diktatur* (Munich: Olzog, 2002), pp. 373–416; here p. 374. Heiner Müller, *Krieg ohne Schlacht: Leben in zwei Diktaturen*, 2nd edn (Cologne: Kiepenheuer & Witsch, 1994), p. 27.

[68] Schwartz, *Vertriebene*, esp. pp. 482–509.

the immigrant (Catholic) Silesian community and the (Protestant) 'old' citizens remained divided for decades. Not until the 1970s did it become possible for members of the generation raised in the 1950s to attend each other's parties, but even then the community boundaries remained significant. These boundaries were defined precisely by the markers of heimat: first and foremost, the new citizens were Catholic, and thus remained culturally distinctive. The confessional distinction was reinforced by geography. The old citizens lived in the old town around the historic church and market square, while the new citizens lived in a separate, newly built area around the railway station (the whole area became known as the 'Catholic station'). From the 1950s, many children were no longer raised speaking Low German, but even with high German speakers, the regional northern intonations of the old citizens remained distinct from the Silesian intonations of the new citizens.[69] The culture of heimat was highly exclusive to those considered outsiders.

Beyond the ideal of social unity, the party justified the existence of the GDR by invoking historical inevitability and the socialist transformation of the economy. In this context, heimat was represented as an arena in which the fruits of socialism would become manifest for all. Photographs in newspapers and magazines of new houses, new cultural facilities constructed in the villages, and new schools all evidenced a heimat on its way to overcoming its intrinsic poverty and backwardness, one in which a better life beckoned.[70] Regional newspapers such as the *Freies Wort* (Suhl district) showed through local examples how the heimat was being transformed in its landscape and through the plan, demonstrating how, through the plan, 'people had changed'.[71] Here a new type of community was arising in which workers and peasants, and 'their' political and state authorities, worked together for the benefit of all. Through socialist reconstruction, the heimat was becoming better and more beautiful than ever before.[72]

In countless local yearbooks, journals and calendars, enthusiasts wrote about their heimat, just as they had done before 1945. Now, by approving what could be published the party and the Cultural League had the chance to influence the representations of heimat, and help both authors and

---

[69] Interview with Karin Wulf and Uwe Wieben, 16 June 2003.

[70] *NBI*, 12/1949, 14–15: 'Der Neulehrer von Etterwinden'; *NBI* 8/1949, 4–5: 'Vision 1950'. Paul Körner-Schrader, 'Wir blättern in einer Dorfchronik', *Natur und Heimat* (1952), no. 6, 10–13.

[71] *Freies Wort* (Suhl edition) (hereafter: *Freies Wort*) (29 April 1953): 'Bibra, ein altes Dorf mit neuen Menschen'.

[72] *Freies Wort* (30 April 1953): 'Auch über der Rhön liegt Sonnenschein'. See also *Freies Wort* (21 April 1956): 'Kaltenwestheim – damals und jetzt'; '18 Westdeutsche Frauen erlebten unseren Bezirk'.

readers to understand how socialism could develop beyond clichéd assumptions. As referees, Cultural League officials urged authors to show in detail just how socialism improved local economic and social conditions.[73] Cultural functionaries trusted that by reflecting on their locality as heimat, producers and consumers of culture could appropriate the benefits of socialism.[74]

Unfortunately, a disproportionate number of those interested in folklore and heimat activities such as ornithology or dendrology (the study of trees) did not, in fact, come from the working classes. For that reason, cultural functionaries emphasized that engagement with the heimat could lead the bourgeoisie towards a better understanding of socialism and the working class. Collectors, local museums and particularly historians were encouraged to focus their attention on local working-class traditions,[75] while ornithologists and other enthusiasts were urged to welcome workers into their midst.[76] More importantly, the party emphasized Heimat as a working-class concern. Folklore, after all, was the original occupation of the working classes and peasants: thus heimat themes in song, dance, play and dress helped workers and peasants express their own culture.[77] Hence the Zwickau Plan of 1952, which endeavoured to turn the mining area around the town into a model socialist community, emphasized that it was the workers themselves who were demanding to know more local history. Using Zwickau as an example, the party argued that local workers recognized the value of Thomas Müntzer's revolutionary legacy in that particular town. Furthermore, according to the party local workers appreciated the significance of the fact that Robert Blum, the hero of the 1848 revolution, had been their local deputy, and they demanded to know more.[78] Heimat allowed workers to reclaim the history and culture that for so long had been defined by the self-interested perspectives of the bourgeoisie.

By linking the workers' cultural and social empowerment to the idea of heimat, rather than simply to their geographical, social and economic context, the party attempted to root socialism in popular culture and to

---

[73] See e.g. BArch-SAPMO, DY27 2615: Gutachten für das Manuskript 'Bockauer Neujahrsbüchlein 1954–1955' (28 December 1956); 'Bemerkungen zu einem Manuskript der Broschüre zum 10. Jahrestag der DDR' (3 June 1959).

[74] On the difficult process of 'appropriating' (*aneignen*) the meanings intended by the party, see Eschenbach, 'Zur Umcodierung', *passim*.

[75] BArch-SAPMO, DY27 919: 'Erweiterte Tagung des Präsidialrats des Kulturbunds' (4 November 1955), ff. 256–8.

[76] K. Sämisch, 'Sektion Philatelie', *Die Aussprache* 4 (1949), nos. 6/7, 11–12; 'Debria', *Die Aussprache* 5 (1950), no. 2, 14; 'Ornithologen mit neuen Zielen', *Die Aussprache* 5 (1950), no. 11, 12.

[77] 'Die Folklore ist die wahre Geschichte des werktätigen Volkes', *Natur und Heimat* (1952), no. 6, 21–4.

[78] BArch-SAPMO, DY27 915: Erich Wendt in the 'Erweiterte Tagung des Präsidialrats des Kulturbunds' (3–4 November 1952), ff. 211–14. See also Schaarschmidt, *Regionalkultur*, pp. 380–3.

refashion popular memory. Important in this endeavour were heimat museums. In 1946, the Schwerin folklore museum (*Volksmuseum*) was reopened as a model institution for other museums to follow. According to its directors, the museum aimed no longer simply to collect treasures of deceased cultures, but instead to link the past to the present, specifically to the working people (*werkenden Menschen*). 'The visitor', the directors argued, 'should recognize the cultural development of his heimat and find confirmation of his inner connectedness to it. He should appreciate the eternal values that work could create, and he should learn to understand the context which allowed developments to merge, albeit with many detours, inevitably into the present.'[79] Much of the display represented the development of regional trades and crafts. Contemporary transformations also acquired disproportionate significance, with depictions of the 1945 land reforms already on prominent display. Socialist heimat museums aspired to encourage a new sensual understanding of past and present, encouraging visitors to touch objects, and to experience heimat in field excursions.[80]

The SED's pedagogic endeavours were severely constrained by financial realities on the ground. The Schwerin Folklore Museum was clearly conceived as a regional model for all other heimat museums in Mecklenburg – but the Schwerin museum received disproportionate levels of funding. In 1955, it received 83 per cent of the total funding for heimat museums in the Schwerin district, leaving barely enough for the district's thirteen other heimat museums to cover staff costs. Museum directors outside Schwerin found it impossible to change their collections or create new displays, even if they wished to.[81] Given that most of Mecklenburg's population could travel to Schwerin only with great difficulty, the educational impact of the Schwerin museum was relatively limited.[82] In short, although at the level of representation the party proved surprisingly adept at appropriating heimat, at the level of popular practice it did not have the means to transform popular attitudes.

---

[79] LHA Schwerin, Ministerium für Volksbildung 2903: 'An die Landesregierung Mecklenburg' (18 January 1948).

[80] *NBI* 16/1954, 8–9: 'Alte Schätze – neu erschlossen: Wir besuchten das Torgauer Heimatmuseum. Schloß Hartenfels: ein vorbildliches Beispiel neuzeitlicher Museumsgestaltung'. See also Heinz Knorr, 'Und die Heimatmuseen?', *Natur und Heimat* (1952), no. 6, 6–9.

[81] LHA Schwerin, Rat des Bezirks 4681: 'An die Fachstelle für Heimatmuseen (Halle/Saale)' (24 September 1954).

[82] LHA Schwerin, Ministerium für Volksbildung 2881: 'Rat des Kreises Demmin – Arbeitsbericht zum Referat Museum' (29 February 1952). See also *Monatsberichte des Heimatmuseums Demmin* (1951).

SOCIALIST REALISM

Neither the party nor heimat enthusiasts knew quite how to reconcile the party's aspirations for a society based on new values and principles with the persistence of heimat practices and ideals. This emerged particularly clearly in the so-called formalism debate. In 1950, the Third Party Congress of the SED condemned the apparent influence of 'cosmopolitanism' and 'American cultural barbarism' on GDR culture, demanding that the latter become more representative of the interests and conditions of working people. Responding to cultural developments in the Soviet Union, in which socialist realism emphasized the development of a 'humanist' classical canon that was 'national in form, socialist in content', the party endeavoured to create a 'realist' socialist culture to uplift the worker.[83] In March 1951 the Fifth Conference of the SED's Central Committee demanded a culture reflecting the realism of present conditions, which were all too often hidden by formal elements in culture and art ('formalism'). What was criticized, in other words, was cultural expressions in which the form was more important than the content. This led, in turn, to a revaluation of Germany's classical tradition, whereby proponents of formalism responded by attacking indifference to form, which they considered integral to content.[84]

The fight against formalism was waged through art and culture in general. Heimat folklore provided an important arena for the anti-formalist campaign, as socialist realism aspired to *Volkstümlichkeit*, a culture that arose from, could be understood by, and was intended for the people.[85] In early 1952, the SED created the Centre for Amateur Art (Zentralhaus für Laienkunst) in Leipzig, which in 1954 was renamed the Centre for Folklore (Zentralhaus für Volkskunst). The newly created Centre lost little time in issuing a set of instructions to all the country's districts and counties. 'A folklore based on realism', it advised, 'will strengthen our working people with energy, confidence, joy and enthusiasm and make a crucial contribution to forming a socialist consciousness. Folklore is a source of power for our people in its fight against the old, for the victory of socialism.'[86] 'True

---

[83] Thomas Lahusen, 'Socialist Realism in search of its shores: some historical remarks on the historically open aesthetic system of the truthful representation of life', in Lahusen and Dobrenko (eds.), *Socialist Realism*, pp. 5–26; here pp. 6–11.

[84] Haase *et al.*, *Die SED*, p. 206. Hermann Weber, *Geschichte der DDR*, 2nd edn (Munich: DTV, 1999), pp. 156–7. Dietrich Staritz, *Geschichte der DDR* (Frankfurt: Suhrkamp, 1996), pp. 71–4.

[85] Kleßmann, *Staatsgründung*, p. 289.

[86] LHA Schwerin, Ministerium für Volksbildung 2982: 'Arbeitsrichtlinien der Volkskunstkabinette' (15 October 1952).

folklore', the Centre approvingly quoted Walter Ulbricht, 'is essentially realist.'[87]

One way the party sought to redefine local culture to reflect the conditions of socialism was through amateur dramatics.[88] One interesting example in this regard is a play written by Hans and Hannelore Wienke, performed at the 1952 German agricultural fair at Markleeberg (Leipzig district). 'The Deed Must Follow' featured conversations on stage between ears of good wheat and ears of bad wheat, with the bad wheat bewailing its fate. Eventually, the farmer of the bad wheat comes along, and the voice of fertility, the echo, the wind, and a talking fat cabbage from a good field nearby convince him that he should apply the agricultural laws of the Soviet agronomist Mitschurin so that the farmer, too, can feed his family and fulfil the plan at the same time.[89]

It would be difficult to invent a more perfect caricature of socialist realism than 'The Deed Must Follow'. The problem was, however, that realism could be used to argue precisely against the type of plays written by the Wienkes. For example, one play presented to the Mecklenburg Cultural Ministry for approval dealt with a central issue in socialist agriculture, the voluntary pledge to increase production. It showed how a lazy farmer, Karst, was eventually persuaded by his neighbour, Lining, to double his milk production. But the censors rejected the play as unrealistic, not least because they judged personal pride to be an insufficient motive for increasing one's milk quota by as much as 100 per cent. In addition, they rejected the dialogue as being too artificial. Lining's jovial teasing ('When I consider the little sins you as a farmer have committed against the people') and the intimate promptings of Karst's wife ('What matters is our share in the supply') did not reflect the way Mecklenburg farmers talked, even under socialism.[90] For the Ministry, realism related to the play's effect: a play should have an implied message, a realistic plot and tension.[91] For this reason, officials commended the 'new farmer' Zimmermann for the natural representation of new farmers in his play 'The Pigsty' (*Dei Swienhütt*). The characters spoke without any artificiality, while the author had succeeded in

---

[87] Walter Ulbricht, cited in BArch-SAPMO, DY30 (Sozialistische Einheitspartei Deutschlands) IV 2/9.06 156, f. 220: 'Abschlußbericht der Abteilung Veranstaltungen im Organisation-Komitee der Deutschen Festspiele der Volkskunst 1952'.

[88] *Wochenpost* 13/1954, 5: 'Mit Onkel Bräsig im Thelpiskarren durch Mecklenburg: Die Fritz-Reuter-Bühne des mecklenburgischen Staatstheaters'.

[89] *Bauern-Echo* (7 June 1952): 'Die Tat muß folgen'.

[90] LHA Schwerin, Deutsche Volksbühne 1: 'Buer Karst un de Sülvstverpflichtung'.

[91] LHA Schwerin, Deutsche Volksbühne 1: 'An die Kulturgruppe des Energie-Bezirkes Nord Parchim' (12 March 1952).

resolving realistic conflicts and difficulties in a non-didactic fashion.[92] Mecklenburg officials thus had a very different conception to the Wienkes of how realism in folklore could be achieved.

Critiques of formalism targeted not only the content of heimat folklore but also the forms in which heimat traditions were presented, notably in community festivals. Years after the formalist campaign began, a Cultural League conference complained that many heimat festivals still paid scant or no attention to representations of the present or the transformations of the recent past. Realism barely featured in the folklore presented at such festivals. Instead, conference participants argued, the essence of most heimat festivals appeared to be excessive eating and drinking, to the detriment of cultural transformation.[93]

The anti-formalist campaign put heimat enthusiasts on the defensive. How could they possibly justify their pastimes against functionaries' charges that in relation to the goal of social, economic and cultural transformation, traditional community activities that related to the heimat were redundant at best, and wasteful at worst?[94]

The Cultural League's praesidium did its best to link heimat-related hobby activities to the pursuit of socialism, arguing that, since communism presented an objective historical development, exploring heimat under the conditions of socialism entailed a discovery of the scientific laws that governed both.[95] The Cultural League's first secretary, Karl Kneschke, emphasized that the scientific work which heimat enthusiasts carried out as part of their hobby was conducive to the greater good and could strengthen communism ideologically and economically.[96] One of the GDR's leading aquarists urged enthusiasts to spend less time on the tropical fish that graced many an aquarium, and focus their energy instead on native fish. These were less popular and little known, but a better understanding of native fish was much more important for the heimat and the economy.[97] Aquarists also justified themselves by highlighting their hobby's scientific value. Careful study of the aquarium revealed the dialectical laws of nature to which fish and water were subject. This, in turn, led to a new understanding of the developmental laws of nature and

---

[92] LHA Schwerin, Deutsche Volksbühne I: 'An den Neubauern P. Zimmermann' (18 February 1952).
[93] *Volks- und Heimatfeste*, pp. 7–32.   [94] Palmowski, 'Building', 371–2.
[95] BArch-SAPMO, DY27 915: 'Erweiterte Tagung des Präsidialrats des Kulturbunds' (3–4 November 1952), f. 169, contribution by Johannes R. Becher.
[96] Kneschke, 'Werden und Wachsen'. Karl Kneschke, 'Von der Wissenschaft zur Tat', *Natur und Heimat* (1952), no. 6, 1–3.
[97] Gerhard Busch, 'Einige Anregungen für unsere Arbeitsgemeinschaften', in *Aquarien- und Terrarien-Jahrbuch 1953*, 9–12.

society.[98] As a member of the Cultural League praesidium asserted, even 'from the perspective of a beetle the world can be understood in our sense, if one looks at the beetle in the right way'.[99] By pursuing their own passions on behalf of the heimat, individuals could verify for themselves the scientific laws on which socialism – and the plan – were based.[100]

Even if socialist realism did not oppose folklore as such,[101] but prescribed that it be filled with new content reflecting socialist realities, that was precisely the problem. There is something artificial and laboured in the protestations of heimat enthusiasts that their activities were closely related to socialism. In practice the anti-formalist debates neatly encapsulate why the party found it so difficult to relate to heimat practices and influence their nature.

To begin with, the application of realism was not just limited by different – and often contrasting – concepts of how the term could be defined.[102] Folklore also limited the application of realism through its essence, its local-ness. Devising folklore plays, songs and dances took time, and it could only be done by a very limited pool of authors from the local area. Moreover, for local folklore to be realistic it had to reflect communal relations, local accents and folk custom. This reflection of the local environment made folk plays and songs more popular (and thus, arguably, more effective), but this also limited their ideological content.

Moreover, formalist critiques failed to respond to popular desires, and this is shown by the formalist campaign against Herbert Roth and his ensemble. In 1951, Roth composed the Rennsteig Song, which celebrated a wanderer's joy at the sight of the Thuringian Forest's streams and valleys. Based on the success of this song, Roth and his ensemble became the most popular and enduring heimat music group in the GDR. During the 1950s, led by the Centre for Folklore, regional newspapers and local publications subjected Roth to harsh criticism on formalist grounds.[103] In May 1956, for instance, the cultural monthly journal of Altenburg county (Leipzig district)

[98] Reimar Gilsenbach, 'Liebhaberei oder Wissenschaft? Zum Geleit', *Aquarien- und Terrarien-Jahrbuch* 1954, 7–8.
[99] BArch-SAPMO, DY27 915: Ms. Langen-Koffler in 'Protokoll über die Präsidialratssitzung des Kulturbunds zur demokratischen Erneuerung Deutschlands' (15 July 1952).
[100] BArch-SAPMO, DY27 919, ff. 168/72: Erich Wendt in 'Stenografisches Protokoll der Präsidialratssitzung vom 14.10.1955'.
[101] Svetlana Boym, 'Paradoxes of unified culture: From Stalin's fairy tale to Molotov's lacquer box', in Lahusen and Dobrenko (eds.), *Socialist Realism*, pp. 120–34.
[102] Staritz, *Geschichte der DDR*, p. 72. This criticism was extensively formulated by the East German publication of 1986, *Die SED und das kulturelle Erbe*, pp. 197–205. For the case of music, see Toby Thacker, *Music after Hitler, 1945–1955* (Aldershot: Ashgate, 2007), esp. pp. 115–18, 189–90, 198–9.
[103] Karl Müller, *Erinnerungen an meinen Freund Herbert Roth* (Suhl: WOG-Verlag, 1996), p. 61.

invited a debate amongst its readers as to why Roth's music was harmful. The only contribution it could print, however, was from a reader who welcomed his music as a genuine expression of the Thuringian heimat.[104] Evidently there was no reader interest in supporting the motion against Roth, and the journal ended the debate as abruptly as it had begun. Anti-formalism failed to resonate among a population and local elites wedded to traditional conceptions of heimat.[105]

The unpopularity of formalist critiques was not confined to heimat traditions; it also affected youth culture, notably the party's inability to curb jazz.[106] This suggests a third problem, namely that in its formalist criticisms against all forms of culture, the SED was battling on too many fronts at once. A TV documentary made in 1957, 'Everywhere is Gnome Country', voiced sharp criticism against garden gnomes, kitschy porcelain statues and kitschy music (*Schnulzenmusik*). This programme would appear to be a perfect contribution to the anti-formalist campaign. In fact, it was fiercely criticized in the Artistic Council of the Documentary Film Studio by the SED's representative, Rutsch. He asserted that 'We are leading a fight against Americanism in dance music, and cannot take on a fight against musical kitsch at the same time ... Americanisms are much more harmful to us than musical kitsch.' Underlining his argument with thinly veiled racial metaphors, he claimed that it was far better for the radio to broadcast a kitschy heimat song like 'White Elderberry' than songs containing the 'sounds of the jungle'.[107] Rutsch reiterated the arguments of heimat and folklore enthusiasts themselves – that their activities kept the population from drinking and excessive dancing, and encouraged people in the 'sensible use of free time'.[108] Evidently, the SED had realized that it could not take on both rock'n'roll and heimat at the same time. If the party wanted to overcome 'lecherousness, pornography, obscenity, filth and trash' in music,[109] then music and lyrics celebrating the beauty of heimat had to be central to that objective.

---

[104] Helmut Böhme, 'Was ist wahre Volksmusik?', *Altenburger Kulturspiegel* (June 1956), 159.

[105] For a more detailed discussion of Herbert Roth, see Jan Palmowski, 'Regional identities and the limits of democratic centralism in the GDR', *Journal of Contemporary History* 41 (2006), 503–26; here 505–9.

[106] Thacker, *Music after Hitler*, ch. 7. Formalism makes a remarkably peripheral appearance in Poiger, *Jazz*, pp. 151–4.

[107] BArch-SAPMO, DY30 VI 2/9.02, 37, f. 26: 'Aktennotiz. Sektor Rundfunk und Fernsehen' (3 July 1957). On the racial dimensions of (East and West) German debates on jazz, see Poiger, *Jazz*, esp. pp. 85–91.

[108] Palmowski, 'Building', 382–4.

[109] See a report to the Ministry of Culture from 1954 reprinted in Thacker, *Music after Hitler*, p. 191.

Like its attempt to create a new historical narrative of heimat, the SED's struggle to create socialist cultural practices was constrained by the country's economic difficulties. New plays, songs, and even texts for heimat recital evenings were very hard to come by.[110] Paper was extremely scarce,[111] so that even where new 'socialist' material was available, its print run was usually insufficient as inadequate and declining amounts of paper were allocated to the printing of folklore material.[112] Throughout the 1950s, the supply of good amateur plays was unable to satisfy the demand, especially for plays in dialect.[113]

There was a fifth reason why the impact of state and party functionaries on heimat practices remained limited. At a time when consumer goods were in short supply, heimat offered an opportunity for individuals to spend more and reduce the money supply in circulation. In August 1954, the head of the Schwerin district council urged all county officials to organize festivals as well as popular cultural entertainment 'of any kind', in order to reduce the purchasing power of the population. 'The fact is', he explained, 'that there is indeed an excess supply of money among the population. Our cultural events must help this supply get moving and integrated back into the economy.'[114] What better way to achieve this goal than through the organization of popular festivals offering the sausages, beer and kitsch so dreaded by the anti-formalist movement? Little wonder that the state-run wholesale organization ('Deutsche Handelszentrale') purchased – and in this way encouraged – precisely the kind of kitsch and pseudo-art by the woodcutters of the Rhön and Erzgebirge regions which anti-formalists were so keen to overcome.[115] The party was thus constrained not simply by the tenacity of existing practices, but also by its own unwillingness and structural inability to transform those practices decisively.

---

[110] BArch-SAPMO, DY30 VI 2/9.02 154, ff. 153–4: Herbert Klecha, Ifa Metallwerk Gera, an das Zentralkomitee der SED (12 January 1953).

[111] Thacker, *Music after Hitler*, p. 191.

[112] BArch-SAPMO, DY30 VI 2/9.02 154, ff. 17–32: 'Ein Jahr Arbeit auf dem Gebiete der Laienkunst [1950]'. For an overview of the paper quota available to the GDR's publishers, see Bettina Hinterthür, *Noten nach Plan: Die Musikverlage in der SBZ/DDR – Zensursystem, zentrale Planwirtschaft und deutsch–deutsche Beziehungen bis Anfang der 1960er Jahre* (Stuttgart: Franz Steiner, 2006), pp. 217–18.

[113] LHA Schwerin, Rat des Bezirks. Abteilung Kultur 4607a. Bezirkshaus für Volkskunst, Schwerin: 'Analyse des künstlerischen Volksschaffens' (5 February 1960).

[114] LHA Schwerin, Rat des Bezirks. Abteilung Kultur 4595b: 'Gez. Meiritz, Abteilungsleiter' (31 August 1954). LHA Schwerin, Rat des Bezirks. Abteilung Kultur 4595b: 'Persönlich! An alle Vorsitzenden des Rates des Kreises. gez. Vorsitzender des Rates des Bezirkes Schwerin' (31 August 1954).

[115] BArch-SAPMO, DY30 VI 2/9.02 154, f. 40: 'Einschätzung des Entwicklungsstandes einiger Hauptfachgebiete des künstlerischen Volksschaffens' (no date, late 1953/early 1954).

The party accepted heimat enthusiasts, but offered little practical support. The one GDR-wide journal published for heimat enthusiasts, created in 1952, was limited to a print run of 30,000, which was barely enough for the almost 50,000 registered members of the Friends of Nature and Heimat associations. Meanwhile, discussions to merge the Friends of Nature and Heimat with the rambling association (attached to the German Sports League) came to naught.[116] Functionaries in Berlin had no interest in creating a strong, united voice for the practical concerns of heimat enthusiasts.

In the late 1940s and early 1950s, then, a gap opened up between the ways in which heimat became a forum for the representation of socialism, and the ability of socialist ideology to accommodate heimat at the level of popular practice. At the level of representation, heimat constituted a sphere in which the progress of socialism could be gauged. In theory at least, heimat served as a framework for integration, in which new citizens could be included, the bourgeoisie reconciled to working-class culture, and former sympathizers of National Socialism could relate to the new order. Indeed, economic improvements acquired particular significance from local memories of hardship suffered not just during the war, but for centuries beforehand. Heimat reinforced representations of anti-fascism and the plan, but at the level of popular practice the SED socialist leaders found it difficult to relate traditional heimat practices to the new cultural beginnings desired by socialism. Nonetheless, during the 1950s, heimat did acquire a central importance for the party. As the division of Germany continued, heimat became indispensable for the construction of a cultural identity specific to the GDR.

THE INVENTION OF 'NATIONAL' IDENTITY

The first attempts to construct distinctive territorial identities took place in the GDR's five component states. When, in 1948, artists from the Ore Mountains (Erzgebirge) exhibited their work to the workers and citizens of Freiberg (Saxony), the audience was presented mostly with paintings of heimat. The heimat on display was Saxony, whose landscapes and cities were depicted in the vast majority of paintings. One painting showed Ahrenshoop, on the Baltic coast, and a couple were set in France and Italy.

---

[116] According to Erik Hühns, section leader of the Friends of Nature and Heimat, both his organization and the ramblers repeatedly expressed their wish to unite throughout the 1950s and the 1960s, but this was never accepted. Interview with Erik Hühns, 3 December 2002. For written evidence from the late 1950s, see BArch-SAPMO, DY27 3307: 'An Erich Honecker, Mitglied des Politbüros des ZK der SED Berlin' (Letter from Heinrich Gemkow and Karl-Heinz Schulmeister, 26 June 1959).

West German landscapes and/or cityscapes were not featured at all, nor were those of neighbouring Thuringia or Saxony-Anhalt.[117] In Mecklenburg, too, heimat exhibitions at the local and regional levels referred the visitor first and foremost to the boundaries and the images of the new state.[118] By calling the visitor's attention to the heimat, the imagination of the individual state did, of course, also invoke an unspecified German nation. Nevertheless, at a time when the German question was wide open, common identifications could be represented most immediately and most plausibly at regional and state levels.

The significance of the emerging states in the representation of heimat is also apparent in election and propaganda posters. Here, the differences between GDR-wide and state-specific representations of heimat are striking. At the GDR level, depictions of heimat were essentially generic, owing to the lack of sites of memory that related to this particular territory. By contrast, in the context of states or localities, official propaganda used concrete images. In 1946, the CDU printed an election poster assuring voters that 'You, too, carry a responsibility for the fate of your heimat', below an image of three distinctive hills (Figure 1). This was not simply a generic iconography of heimat.[119] Rather, these three hills represented the 'Drei Gleichen', three castles standing upon three isolated hills in the Thuringian basin, the geographic heart of the state and a location that would be recognized by every Thuringian as a site of memory. Similarly, in appealing, in the same state elections, 'for peace, justice and heimat' (Figure 2), the SED depicted a woman in folk costume looking out over the mountains. It could have been a depiction of any mountainous landscape, and that was no accident: the Thuringian Forest did not have distinctively shaped mountains that every Thuringian could have recognized. But the woman in the folk dress placed this scene unambiguously in the Thuringian Forest, as folk costume was recognizably rooted in place. In these posters, heimat was used specifically to appeal to – and help reinvent – the regional consciousness of Thuringians.

The construction of state identity was much more complex in other states, since it was not at all clear how a place like Saxony-Anhalt could be

---

[117] BArch-SAPMO, DY27 4813: 'Ausstellungskatalog erzgebirgischer Künstler'.

[118] LHA Schwerin. Ministerium für Volksbildung 3237: Aufstellung der im letzten Vierteljahr 1948 in Schwerin durchgeführten Ausstellungen. *Führer durch die I. Mecklenburgische Rassehunde-Ausstellung* [1948].

[119] Alon Confino asks about these posters: 'Who could tell without reading the caption whether … [these figures] represented Thuringia, Saxony, or perhaps Württemberg?' The answer is: every Thuringian, precisely those for whom these posters were designed. Confino, *Germany*, p. 99.

1. 'Keiner fehle, jeder wähle!' (Let nobody be absent – everyone to the polls!). CDU election poster, Thuringia, 1947. Beneath the drawing of the three hills, the caption reads: 'You, too, carry a responsibility for the fate of your heimat.' The hills represent the 'Drei Gleichen', a trio of hills whose ruined castles stand out in the otherwise flat landscape of the Thuringian basin, between Erfurt and Gotha.

defined, and what its sites of memory were – if it had any. In Mecklenburg, the construction of identity was also highly problematic. The state included a small part of Pomerania, whose territory was mostly occupied by Poland and whose cultural distinctiveness was subsequently suppressed. Moreover, in striving for the construction of a state identity officials could not ignore

2. 'Für Frieden Recht und Heimat. Thüringen wählt SED' (For peace, justice and heimat. Thuringia votes SED). SED election poster, Thuringia, 1947. Every folk costume was specific to the locality, and would have been recognized by Thuringians immediately after the war.

the Low German dialect, even if it was far from exclusive to the state. As Low German speakers kept reminding the state's cultural authorities, Low German and the flat landscape linked Mecklenburgers to north Germans west of the border.[120] Nonetheless it was possible, at this level, to mould regional identities sufficiently to express the new state of Mecklenburg. Linking the state to its customs, an official of the Ministry of Culture asserted that he was part of a 'wholly and utterly Low German government', thus firmly rooting it in local traditions without specifying Mecklenburg too distinctly.[121] Constructing a common identity for a state as heterogeneous as Mecklenburg became crucial precisely because only a minority of residents were actually native to it, against a majority of expellees and Cis-Pomeranians. As cultural functionaries emphasized, through heimat and its

[120] LHA Schwerin, Ministerium für Volksbildung 2866: Eröffnungsansprache zum niederdeutschen Bühnentag am 31.8.47 in Bad Doberan.
[121] LHA Schwerin, Ministerium für Volksbildung 2865: 'Protokoll Volkstumstagung in Schöberg am 16./17. Nov. 1948'; here p. 8.

language all residents should be rooted in the land and identify with the territory, just as Low Germans did in other parts of the north.[122]

There is not the space in this book to explore the attempted constructions of state identities in depth. It is worth pointing out, however, that such attempts were short-lived. To be sure, many cultural references to the former states remained during the 1950s, not least because the states were not formally abolished until 1958. As late as 1957, Friends of Nature and Heimat in the districts of Halle and Magdeburg joined forces to publish *Mitteldeutsches Land*, a heimat journal designed to express the 'diverse historical, economic and cultural development of the state of Saxony-Anhalt'.[123] In general, however, the lack of official encouragement from 1952 onwards made it difficult for state identities to be actively encouraged and constructed. The demise of the states greatly aggravated the problems facing the party, notably how to relate the GDR to popular notions of culture and place at a time when most Germans had not yet accepted the division of Germany as permanent or desirable.

In the first years after the GDR's creation, one of the most important opportunities to represent the country in terms of heimat was tourism. Illustrated journals and newspapers were always busy reporting on heimat at vacation time, emphasizing the diversity of the country and the fact that every worker now had access to new parts of the heimat, courtesy of the vacation homes sponsored by the Free Trade Union.[124] In the late 1940s and early 1950s, heimat distinguished the GDR not through a sense of place, but through accessibility: here, the party suggested, the heimat can be enjoyed by all.

Heimat also featured prominently in what holiday-makers saw and experienced. Trade-union-sponsored vacationers on the Baltic coast and in the Thuringian Forest were presented with talks on local history, geography, customs and dialect, as well as heimat evenings with regional songs and dances. Among the entertainments organized in the seaside resort of Kühlungsborn in July 1951, for instance, were Mecklenburg folklore concerts and talks on 'Mecklenburg: its land and people', designed to firmly root visitors in the Mecklenburg heimat, and the country at large.[125] Officials hoped that heimat presentations would protect vacationers from

[122] LHA Schwerin, Ministerium für Volksbildung 2865: 'Die niederdeutschen Bühnen vor neuen Aufgaben. Aus der Eröffnungsansprache zum niederdeutschen Bühnentag am 31.8.47 in Bad Doberan'; here p. 3.
[123] *Mitteldeutsches Land* 1 (1957), i. 'Vorwort'.
[124] *Zeit im Bild* 4 (1954), 2–3. '2 Brettel und 1 Ferienscheck'.
[125] LHA Schwerin, Rat des Bezirks 3024: 'Veranstaltungs-Vorschau des Ostseebades Kühlungsborn Juli 1951'.

American musical 'unculture' while providing 'genuine' relaxation and entertainment.[126] Information on local history, meanwhile, allowed the holiday-maker to form a new understanding of how the histories and cultures of the GDR's regions were interlinked – and how they differed from those of Germans in the West.[127] Finally, regional songs and dances entertained the workers while allowing them to understand a new region of the heimat and become part of it.[128] The party hoped that by being enabled to access the heimat in its rich history and culture, vacationers would feel part of a distinctive community that included both themselves and their hosts: one that pointed towards socialism and the GDR.

Beneath every representation of heimat in relation to the GDR lurked one crucial issue, the division of Germany. After all, heimat and its emotional associations of protectedness, community and familiarity were understood by Germans in both East and West. For this reason, heimat became a quintessential motif in relation to the FRG. The SED tried to show in various ways that, even though the ideal of heimat was familiar to all Germans, in the FRG the heimat was being destroyed by American culture and Allied militarism. In the GDR, by contrast, folk customs could be reconnected to their cultural, humanist origins. Here, heimat was safe from the perversions of American 'cultural barbarism'.[129]

To demonstrate to all Germans the vibrancy of heimat in socialism, cultural functionaries organized a 'German Folklore Festival' (Fest der deutschen Volkskunst), held in July 1952 in East Berlin.[130] In fact, internal reports from both the SED and the Centre for Amateur Art were scathing about the event: it had been badly organized, average audience figures were too low, and the quality of most of the performances was poor.[131] Naturally, GDR newspapers put a very different gloss on the event, especially regarding the intrinsic link between heimat and socialism. The *Bauern-Echo* applauded the Mecklenburg choir of Kaliß, whose folklore presentation

---

[126] LHA Schwerin, Rat des Bezirks 3024: 'Bericht über den Ablauf der Badesaison und der Bäderbetreuung 1951' (Rügen, 25 September 1951); 'Entwurf: Feriendienst der Gewerkschaften beim Bundesvorstand des FDGB' (25 April 19[51?]).

[127] BArch-SAPMO, DY27 915, ff. 104–5: 'Präsidialratssitzung des Kulturbundes zur demokratischen Erneuerung Deutschlands, 19.9.1952'.

[128] On the 'existential' importance of this, see Prof. Franck in BArch-SAPMO, DY27 915, f. 107: 'Präsidialratssitzung des Kulturbunds' (19 September 1952).

[129] BArch-SAPMO, DY30 IV 2/9.06 158, ff. 2–9. 'Entwurf. Arbeitsaufgaben, Strukturplan und Stellenplan für das zukünftige Zentralhaus für Laienkunst'.

[130] BArch-SAPMO, DY30 IV 2/9.06 157, f. 154: *Tägliche Rundschau* (6 July 1952).

[131] BArch-SAPMO, DY30 IV 2/9.06 156, ff. 220–31; 276–342: 'Abschlußbericht der Abteilung Veranstaltungen im Organisation-Komitee der Deutschen Festspiele der Volkskunst 1952. Hauptabteilung Laienkunst. Auswertung der Wettbewerbe der deutschen Volkskunst' (29 July 1952).

derived from its members' own toil in the fields. So genuine was this display of the peasants' love of heimat that it brought tears to the eyes of the audience of Berlin workers. One worker was so moved that he even vowed to give up his vacation in order to help the farmers bring in their harvest.[132] Countless newspaper reports praised the various performances as genuine expressions of German culture which could not but touch the West Germans who had come as participants or onlookers. One article described the performance of the Potsdam Pedagogical Polytechnic Folklore Ensemble in the Potsdamer Platz. In contrast to the glaring billboards advertising bloodthirsty Western movies across the square in the British and US sectors, the ensemble presented yet further evidence of the 'blossoming of genuine German folklore' in the GDR.[133]

The German Folklore Festival illustrated the potential of heimat to express the essence of socialism: workers could truly celebrate the heimat because they owned its means of production; it stood for the transformation of the people and their environment, and it provided the framework for a new historic beginning. The festival thus reflected a dominant theme in the official representation of heimat in the early 1950s: the ideal of a 'genuine' heimat, possible only under the conditions of socialism, which would act as a bulwark against consumerism and Americanization.[134] Americanization meant the destruction of German national culture, which every song, every dance and every woodcarving produced in the GDR helped to prevent.[135]

The folklore festival was not the only occasion on which the theme of anti-Americanism was developed. Travel reports on the Western heimat abounded in illustrated journals and magazines. In the series 'The Beautiful German Heimat', Heinz Mildner published articles in the popular weekly journal, the *Wochenpost*. At the end of his trip through Swabia he arrived in Stuttgart, which he described thus:

Even if the town spares no effort to act like a world metropolis, putting on shrill neon-lights like a vain prostitute and attempting with band-aid and frippery to conceal the dirty-grey scars of war, it remains a Swabian town through and through.[136]

---

[132] BArch-SAPMO, DY30 IV 2/9.06 157, f. 143: *Bauern-Echo* (10 July 1952).

[133] BArch-SAPMO, DY30 IV 2/9.06 157, f. 164: *Märkische Volksstimme* (18 July 1952), 'Heute lacht Brandenburg'.

[134] BArch-SAPMO, DY30 IV 2/9.06 158, ff. 2–9: 'Entwurf. Arbeitsaufgaben, Strukturplan und Stellenplan für das zukünftige Zentralhaus für Laienkunst'.

[135] BArch-SAPMO, DY30 IV 2/9.06 156, ff. 259–60: annotated speech given at the German folklore festival, 'Mückenberger mit Dank zurück'.

[136] Heinz Mildner, 'Schöne deutsche Heimat: Schwäbische Rhapsodie', *Wochenpost* 15 (1954), 3.

This official imagery of the West German heimat became universal. On a trip to the northern town of Braunschweig, Heinz Keil reported:

In the largest cinema they are showing a film about [Nazi field marshal] Rommel. The passers-by don't take any of this seriously: the advertisements, the flood of neon lights, the shows put on in night bars, the end-of-summer sale for which there is no money ... and the number of shoe shops there are! ... Braunschweigers do not answer if one asks them about this. 'The English, especially the Americans, simply have a view of culture that is different from ours. But our mayor, Bennemann, and the other ones responsible don't speak against it ...' an old builder told me, hesitating whether he dare speak out.[137]

These passages depict many of the major themes through which the Americanization of the West German heimat was presented, not just in print but also, for instance, in GDR heimat films.[138] Although essentially the same as in the GDR, in West Germany the heimat was adulterated by capitalism and its harbingers, neon signs and overflowing shops. This heimat could be enjoyed by the English, by foreign students and by German shareholders and bankers. Workers, by contrast, could not afford to travel there, nor could they afford the goods in the shops. Reminiscent of the Weimar era, this constituted a state of affairs in which militarism and fascism might be rekindled.

Consumerism (the cinema, the neon signs and the shoe shops) was completely foreign, and contrasted sharply with the quintessential earthiness, the community and the familiarity, of the heimat.[139] In 1952, the Friends of Nature and Heimat journal *Natur und Heimat* depicted the success of new farmers (*Neubauern*) in the Brandenburg village of Gebersdorf. Here, the author found a harmonious ensemble of new and old farmers' houses, surrounded by fields 'smelling like fresh bread'. Joy at the transformation of the village combined with the rich smell of resin emanating from the surrounding Brandenburg forest.[140] Rational and emotional faculties combined to allow the inner meaning of heimat to become manifest. Socialism allowed the heimat to be truly comprehended.

The contrast with Americanization was reinforced by the 'natural' links which the party constructed between heimat traditions in the GDR and those in other socialist states. Reports on the reconstruction of Poland, for instance, served as evidence of how tradition and reconstruction went hand

---

[137] Heinz Keil, 'Braunschweig – Notizen einer Westdeutschlandreise', *Natur und Heimat* (1952), no. 8, 10–12.
[138] Lindenberger, 'Home, sweet home'.
[139] Heinz Keil, 'Deutscher Schwarzwald', *Natur und Heimat* (1952), no. 6, 14–16. Keil, 'Braunschweig'.
[140] Körner-Schrader, 'Dorfchronik'.

in hand under socialism.[141] Similarly, Hungary was a favoured site for illustrated journals to depict the richness of folklore in socialism.[142] Meanwhile, the Soviet Union was represented not only as merging modernity and tradition to perfection, but also as containing an expansiveness, a diversity of landscape and tradition, that could not be found in the GDR.[143] Heimat, then, needed no shoe shops or neon signs. Socialism enabled a perfect balance between social transformation and the preservation of heimat traditions, while the socialist community of states more than made up for the traditions and landscapes west of the demarcation line, to which East Germans no longer had access.

The authenticity of heimat in the GDR became a common theme in visual representations. In 1955, the cultural league of Sömmerda county (Erfurt district) organized a photography exhibition on the 'beautiful German heimat'. The winning photograph, which was printed in the county's heimat journal, featured a boy looking out into the distance over a gently sloping landscape with grazing cows, from which he was separated by a brook. The image was almost entirely self-contained except for a bicycle, half of which could be seen in the foreground leaning against a stone pillar. There were no houses in sight, and nothing that could identify the landscape as East or West German. Here no destruction had taken place, and no reconstruction was necessary (Figure 3).[144] As late as September 1959, the monthly heimat journal appeared with a picture of a village in Thuringia that could have come from anywhere in Germany: there were no monuments or other markers which anchored the half-timbered houses and the church steeple in any particular region. The picture of an all-German village was a particularly striking choice for an issue that discussed the close relationship between heimat and socialism (Figure 4).[145] Such images were common in representations of heimat during the 1950s,[146] and they found their way into SED election propaganda

---

[141] *NBI* 31 (1949), 15: 'Freude am Alten und am Neuen: vom dörflichen Leben in Mala bei Warschau'.

[142] *NBI* 19/1954, 3: 'Katalin und Janos heiraten: Bauernhochzeit im ungarischen Dorf Szentistvan'. *Zeit im Bild* 16 (1954), 6–7: 'In der Puszta klingt eine neue Melodie'.

[143] *NBI* 29 (1954), 'Hohe Schule des Muts – Eine der schönsten sowjetischen Urlaubsfreuden: die Alpinistenlager in der herrlichen Bergwelt des Kaukasus', 8–9. Archie Johnstone (USA) [sic!], 'Alma Ata: Stadt der Äpfel', *Wochenpost* 14 (1954), 13. *Wochenpost* 13 (1954), 'Sagenumwobene Krim', 13.

[144] Kulturbund zur Demokratischen Erneuerung Deutschlands, Kreisleitung Sömmerda, *Der Bote aus Thüringen: Monatsprogramm, Januar 1956* (Sömmerda: Kulturbund), p. i.

[145] *Aus der Arbeit der Natur- und Heimatfreunde* (September 1959), no. 9.

[146] See, for instance, *Aus der Arbeit der Natur- und Heimatfreunde* (March 1956), no. 3: 'Winter morning'. This image had represented the GDR at that year's Third International Photography Exhibition in Périgueux (France).

3. Winning photo in the competition 'The Beautiful German Heimat', in Sömmerda county (Thuringia). Kulturbund zur Demokratischen Erneuerung Deutschlands, Kreisleitung Sömmerda, *Der Bote aus Thüringen: Monatsprogramm, Januar 1956* (Sömmerda: Kulturbund), p. i.

for district elections in the mid-1950s (Figure 5).[147] To Alon Confino, the poetic, 'traditional' nature of such images of heimat pointed to a central problem for the party: they were incompatible with the political imagery of socialist transformation.[148] But these 'poetic' images in themselves carried an acutely political message: they were incontrovertible 'evidence' that in

---

[147] Confino, *Germany*, p. 107, and figure 23, p. 137.   [148] Ibid., p. 107.

4. Cover page of *Aus der Arbeit der Natur- und Heimatfreunde* (September 1959). The picture shows the south Thuringian village of Ummerstadt, but the collection of half-timbered houses could represent any town in the German heimat.

the GDR, the authenticity of the heimat was safeguarded from the encroachments of consumerism. The 'poetic' representation of heimat was pure politics.

The party invented heimat as a metaphor for the GDR, so that invocations of patriotism related to heimat rather than explicitly to the GDR. Through heimat, the socialist fatherland could be experienced through all the senses – smell, touch, taste, hearing and sight. By creating a true, 'inner' sensation of heimat, socialism on German soil acquired a natural quality and timelessness which it passed on to its quintessential creation, the

5. 'Wer die Heimat liebt...' (Whoever loves the heimat will vote for the National Front on 23 June). National Front election poster for local and district elections in 1957.

GDR.[149] Through heimat, the socialist part of Germany – in explicit contrast to the FRG – was presented as anchored in primeval articulations of Germanness in time, place and popular culture.

Socialist leaders used heimat to express emotional distinctiveness because it allowed them to publicly maintain a commitment to German unity, while actually reinforcing Germany's division. Following the rejection of the Stalin Note in April 1952, the GDR announced on 8 May 1952 that it planned to create a garrisoned, militarized police force, the *Kasernierte Volkspolizei*. Later in the month the GDR followed this up by cordoning off the border between itself and the FRG, creating a five-kilometre exclusion zone along the eastern side. This put the party into an extremely difficult position, because it had to persuade sufficient numbers of volunteers to become border guards along the internal German frontier. It even had to persuade these guards, as well as the garrisoned police recruits, to be willing to fight and die for their country, if necessary, defending it against encroachments from the FRG. Under these conditions, heimat became the keynote for representations of military service and the 'protection' of the border: individuals were there not so much to defend the GDR as to defend the heimat.

'Whoever feels the beauty of his heimat truly inside himself', wrote Johannes R. Becher in the introduction to a collection of his heimat poems, 'cannot but undertake everything in his power to protect this beautiful heimat from peril and destruction.'[150] A contribution to the journal *Die Aussprache* noted that true patriotism was founded in the love of heimat. And although patriots did not like to reach for their guns, 'we have to do what is necessary if there is no other way', the article asserted.[151] The primary uses of heimat and folklore were to educate working people to become upright patriots,[152] ready to defend the GDR as necessary.

At a meeting of the Cultural League's praesidium in July 1952, Lothar Bolz, the deputy prime minister, drew attention to the significance of the 'national' armed forces for the heimat. Now that such forces were being created, it was 'crucial that people be filled with love, loyalty, pride and respect for the state and the social order which had to be defended'. This could not be achieved through a mere intellectual understanding of history:

[149] On the vocabulary of the home(land), see Benedict Anderson, *Imagined Communities: Reflections on the Origin and Spread of Nationalism*, revised edn (London: Verso, 1991), pp. 143–4.
[150] Johannes R. Becher, *Schöne Deutsche* Heimat (Berlin: Aufbau-Verlag, 1952), p. 5.
[151] Paul Kaiser, 'Eine Diskussionsrede', *Die Aussprache* 7 (1952), no. 12, 10–11.
[152] BArch-SAPMO, DY30 IV 2/9.06 158, f. 184: Zentralhaus für Laienkunst, Fachgebiet Tanz, 'Thesen zur Diskussion über das Thema: Die künstlerische Gestaltung der Volkstänze [1954]'.

individuals must be inspired by an appreciation of national tradition and culture. Through poetry, music and dance, people's hearts must be renewed and filled with a desire to defend the heimat.[153]

Propaganda material visually linked images of military hardware to symbols of heimat and peace.[154] This was not the first time that a German state had used the ideal of heimat for military propaganda.[155] Yet, as the present chapter has shown, this was a German state that derived its legitimacy from the plan, from social transformation, and from anti-fascism. However, since the party was fully aware that most Germans would be most reluctant to die for any of those ideals, it had no option but to try to construct the GDR as the authentic heimat.

The martial significance of heimat was even more apparent in relation to the internal German border. After all, Germany's division cut across historic heimat regions, from Hanover and the Harz mountains in the north to the Rhön and Vogtland mountains in the south.[156] This presented the party with a dilemma: if it wanted to construct an identity within, it had to clearly define its borders, and doing so through heimat did not make the task any easier.[157] Moreover, at the border the same difficulties applied as with the military: it was extremely difficult to recruit border guards, so that young men had to be enticed into service. Even after 1961, when military service became compulsory, it was necessary to somehow legitimize the border in a way that related to popular culture. To this end, regional and GDR-wide newspapers were filled with 'adventure' reports about border guards, written almost uniformly through the imagery of heimat, in order to justify the border and make service in the border guards appealing to young recruits.[158]

Writing in *Neues Deutschland*, Olaf Badstübner contrasted the peaceful, wintry landscape of the Thuringian Forest with the threats to this idyll from the nearby border. The troops he met there were workers and peasants of all kinds, from all over the republic: these patriots had come together to defend

[153] BArch-SAPMO, DY27 915, ff. 34–6: 'Protokoll über die Präsidialratssitzung des Kulturbunds zur demokratischen Erneuerung Deutschlands' (15 July 1952).

[154] Confino, *Germany*, figures 22, 24–7, pp. 137–9.   [155] Confino, *Nation*, figures 9–16, pp. 194–201.

[156] In the north, the GDR came to incorporate the Hanoverian community of Neuhaus, which lay on the right bank of the River Elbe, because the British found this territory too difficult to access for lack of a bridge.

[157] That common identifications require external boundaries has become a commonplace in debates on identity. See, for instance, Franz C. Mayer and Jan Palmowski, 'European identities and the EU – the ties that bind the peoples of Europe', *Journal of Common Market Studies* 42 (2004), 573–98; here 577.

[158] *Freier Bauer*, 'Bei unseren Grenzern' (26 January 1958). On the difficulties of recruitment, see Stephan Fingerle, *Waffen in Arbeiterhand? Die Rekrutierung des Offizierkorps der NVA und ihrer Vorläufer* (Berlin: Links, 2001); here pp. 108–11.

what was theirs, the GDR and its socialist order.[159] The solidarity between GDR citizens and their guardians was reinforced by reports on soldiers helping the local community. The border troops helped overcome natural and industrial emergencies,[160] but they could also be relied on to help bring in the harvest.[161] They participated in the cultural life of the village, through their hobby groups or by participating in the village dance, to the delight of the local girls.[162] Many reports also noted how the inhabitants of the border villages, in return, thanked the border guards by acting as voluntary helpers and informants for them.[163]

These depictions employed different registers of heimat. There was the solidarity and the familiarity of the 'insider' community, which was threatened by the intruding outsider. Every Christmas, newspapers abounded with stories about the border guards' sacrifice, which alone made sure that everyone else could celebrate in peace. These stories were accompanied by traditional images of the topography of heimat in the deep midwinter, its tranquillity guaranteed by the border guards (Figure 6). No other occasion was more suitable, in the eyes of the GDR's press, to underline the relationship between the border and the safeguarding of heimat traditions. In addition, nature featured prominently, presenting life-threatening challenges to coastal patrols facing high, stormy seas, while border patrols in the mountains battled against outside temperatures of forty degrees below zero. Nature was a force that was respected, understood and overcome, and nobody was able to do this better than the border guards.[164] Moreover, the heimat portrayed was never static, but was one of ordered change. In these reports, the socialist transformations in the surroundings, as well as the troops' efficiency, perfectly complemented the landscapes and picturesque villages which the soldiers were called upon to protect. Just as in other periods and contexts of German history,[165] heimat was used to harmonize transformation and tradition. Through the modernity of the border the traditions of the border communities were able to thrive.

The border helped define the GDR not merely by delimiting and defining the communities within: it also separated the heimat from the FRG.

---

[159] Olaf Badstübner, 'Unsere Grenzpolizei wacht', *Neues Deutschland* (10 February 1953).

[160] *Berliner Zeitung*, 'Unermüdlich auf Wacht am Berliner Ring' (15 March 1958).

[161] K. H. Walther, 'Wo eine Wanderfahne weht', *Neues Deutschland* (11 April 1956).

[162] Walther, 'Wanderfahne'. *Freier Bauer*, 'Grenzern'. *National-Zeitung*, 'Fährtenhund „Cäsar" hat die beste Nase' (14 March 1958).

[163] Werner Schmoll, 'Nachts auf Streife an der Westgrenze', *Vorwärts* (18 November 1957).

[164] H. G. Strauch, 'Alarm im Kommando в', parts i–iii, *B.Z. am Abend* (22–4 March 1956). *Junge Welt*, 'Sturmfahrt zum Einsatzhafen' (14 March 1956).

[165] Boa and Palfreyman, Heimat; here pp. 23–4.

6. Soldiers patrol the hilltops so that the villages nestled in the valleys (here depicted in the background) can have a peaceful Christmas. 'Auf Friedenswacht' (On guard for peace), *Tribüne*, 24 December 1955.

Foreigners were characterized as possible intruders, disturbing the heimat. During the 1950s they were most commonly portrayed as Americans, or dark, shadowy smugglers whose links with West Germany were always implicit, but rarely stated explicitly. The frontier's inter-German divisiveness was never clearly articulated. The GDR was imagined and reconstituted as heimat by relating its borders to the communities inside these boundaries, but without explicitly expressing the exclusion of West Germany (and West Germans).

Heimat represented, in the first decade of the GDR's existence, a space of unspoilt villages, rich pastures and historic monuments, but was also a sphere of industrial, urban and spiritual renewal. Crucially, heimat retained a pointed ambiguity during the GDR's founding decade. Throughout the 1950s, it could be used to mean the 'German heimat', which included East and West Germany. This reflected the party's priority, from 1950, of ensuring the GDR's economic and ideological consolidation while maintaining a public commitment towards unification and hoping that the GDR would act as a beacon to West German workers.[166] For this reason, the growing political divisions were often popularized by showing how the heimat common to East and West Germans was being betrayed by the divisive actions of the West German government.[167] At the same time, the public connotations which heimat came to acquire from the late 1940s pointed unequivocally to a socialist cultural, political and social order. By relating patriotism and military defence to the heimat, political and cultural leaders could claim not to betray the ideal of German unity while doing precisely that. By setting traditional images of the heimat in new contexts, the Cultural League could pay homage to German tradition and legitimize the socialist experiment. By intertwining heimat and the socialist order, heimat was developed into a Trojan horse for early constructions of a specific GDR identity that could be articulated more openly from the late 1950s.

CONCLUSION

Heimat developed into an integral part of popular culture in socialist Germany, and the socialist authorities were deeply involved in this development. This was by no means inevitable, given that socialists were primarily interested in providing individuals with the educational and financial means to thrive on classical literature, music and art. The regret uttered by officials at the low popularity of classical concerts, as well as the tremendous subsidies with which the state continued to sponsor the high arts, leave

---

[166] Dirk Spilker, *The East German Leadership and the Division of Germany: Patriotism and Propaganda, 1945–1953* (Oxford University Press, 2006), pp. 196–245.

[167] *Zeit im Bild* 9, 'Rhein und Elbe fließen durch Deutschland' (1954), 10–11. *Zeit im Bild* 2, 'Es geht um unser Vaterland' (1954), 10–11. *Wochenpost* 20 (1954), 1 (title image: 'Rothenburg ob der Tauber').

little doubt as to the persistence of the socialist utopia in which the individual worker was inspired by the legacy of classical humanism. Nevertheless, the party came to accept cultural practices relating to heimat, for three reasons. First, the party could not ignore the popularity of heimat. Hobby groups, exhibitions of local collections, choirs, amateur theatre and folklore dancers all provided cultural activity that was cheap, available and popular. Given the party's commitment to cultural provision, particularly in the countryside, it was difficult for cultural functionaries on the ground to ignore this mainstay of local cultural activity.

Secondly, the ideal of heimat could help the party to reinforce its major ideological concerns. By linking the plan, social transformation, anti-fascism and moral regeneration to the theme of heimat, the party attempted to legitimize its ideological concerns and root them in popular culture. The ideal of heimat, whose longevity in German history has rested precisely on its adaptability to the disparate political concerns of Germans since the nineteenth century, proved sufficiently elastic to be connected to the goals of socialism.

Thirdly, in the GDR's foundational period, heimat as such was not a central *ideological* concern for the party. It developed, however, into a defining *national* concern. Its value lay precisely in its ambiguity vis-à-vis the two Germanies: the party attempted to construct a national community and identity which notionally included the 'West' of the heimat, the FRG. However, in the eyes of the party the true German heimat was inimical to Americanization, capitalism and consumerism. Heimat could only flourish under conditions of socialism, and under these conditions it could shape feelings of community and patriotism that related specifically to the GDR. During the mid-1950s, heimat became central to the construction of nationhood in the GDR.

In the foundational period of the GDR, there were limits to the attempts to fuse it with heimat and with socialism. A relatively traditional definition of heimat could reconcile long-established heimat enthusiasts to the status quo, but had little value for workers. By contrast, a more innovative and inclusive conception of heimat might have allowed the integration of new social groups, but this would have aroused the hostility of traditional local activists. Unable to achieve both in equal measure, the party prioritized the integration of enthusiasts formerly active during the Third Reich.

At the level of popular practice, a tension developed between the preservation of tradition implicit in the ideal of heimat, and the socialist emphasis on reconstruction and transformation. This tension also introduced a degree of unpredictability and incoherence into the party's approach to heimat, with local cultural officials often contradicting party policy in their eagerness to overcome what they considered to be outdated heimat practices. Indeed, many of the socio-economic transformations planned by the party destroyed local communities and cultures – as the GDR's one ethnic minority, the Sorbs in Lusitania, were to find out in this period.[168] There was a fundamental contradiction between the party's reliance on heimat for the construction of national identity, and its lack of interest in heimat as cultural practice.

Finally, the construction of heimat to refer specifically to the GDR was limited, since no landscape, no memorial yet existed that constituted a popularly accepted *lieu de mémoire* for the GDR. Whereas before 1952 its component states had begun to invent such sites of public memory, this was evidently much more difficult for the GDR as a whole. The party constructed the heimat to endow socialist Germany, its borders and its culture with distinctive meanings. As such, the party attempted to construct heimat as a metaphor for the GDR; yet, crucially, this metaphor remained imperfect so long as it lacked specific and popular sites of memory, and a distinctive imagination of place.

Evidently the appropriation of heimat for the construction of national identity was highly problematic. Still, in linking heimat to socialism and the GDR, the party had shown itself to be remarkably sensitive and responsive to popular culture. The success of this strategy could only be measured in the long run. For as long as state and party were forced to admit the existence of the 'western' part of the heimat, the concept of heimat was particularly vulnerable to rival interpretations in popular practice. This changed, however, from the late 1950s, as the prospect of unification receded – apparently irrevocably – into the background. In the second decade of the GDR's existence, the party could go either way: it could accelerate the construction of socialism and reinforce the GDR's identification through class and anti-fascism; or it could define the GDR unambiguously in terms of nationhood. In the second decade of the GDR's existence, the party began by attempting the former, only to end up pursuing the latter policy: the construction of the GDR as the socialist heimat.

---

[168] Barker, *Slavs*, passim.

CHAPTER 3

Traces of stones

INTRODUCTION

Hannes Balla feared nobody and no one. Yet he was moved by a longing which he could not define.[1] Leading a group of carpenters, the energetic Balla worked, for several months at a time, on various construction projects, from the deep-water harbour in Rostock to Hoyerswerda in Saxony, until he became restless and moved on to a new site. Eventually, he arrived at the vast construction site at Schkona, an experience that would change his life. Here the carpenter was challenged by the new party secretary, Horrath, and encouraged by his affection for the new engineer, Katrin Klee. Through these encounters, Balla realized that his restlessness had been futile, he could not run away: the traces of stones which his work had left all over the Republic remained as silent witness to his presence long after he had left. He joined the SED. Whereas before he had worked purely for himself and his men, he now surrendered his services to the party and his country, the GDR. Balla had turned 'from the I to the We'.

The novel *Traces of Stones*, which describes Balla's conversion at Schkona, a fictionalized town strongly resembling Bitterfeld, perfectly represents the ideal to which the party aspired from 1958: the socialist transformation of the individual. The book won its author, Erik Neutsch, the GDR's highest honour, the National Prize, in 1964, the year of the book's publication.[2] Balla's discovery about his own 'traces' not only reflected his conversion to socialism, but was intimately related to his discovery of the socialist heimat.[3]

---

[1] For a key passage in which the yearning is described, see Erik Neutsch, *Spur der Steine*, new edn (Munich: DTV, 1995), pp. 98–101.

[2] See, for instance, 'Erik Neutsch „Spur der Steine": Bedeutendes Werk unserer sozialistischen Nationalliteratur', *Kulturspiegel Altenburg Schmölln* (October 1964), 304.

[3] Strangely, historians have been almost solely interested in the controversial film, ignoring the book. The film focuses much less on Balla's own conversion, and instead concentrates on the relationship between Horrath and Klee. See, for instance, Joshua Feinstein, '*Spur der Steine*: Zum Verhältnis von Gegenwart und Geschichte im DEFA-Spielfilm der sechziger Jahre', in Martin Sabrow (ed.), *Verwaltete*

For he recognized that the work he had left behind throughout the country had transformed the whole GDR into his heimat. His restlessness and alienation were over. The novel ends with Balla leaving Schkona, a place he had come to love. This time, he left not in his own interests, but in those of his party. He no longer desired, or needed, to escape. Balla had come to realize that 'the heimat had become larger than he had previously thought'. 'Balla', the book ends, 'left a world which also awaited him. There were no more goodbyes. Everywhere is the heimat.'[4]

The prominence of heimat in the representation of the socialist transformation of the individual is striking because when the party embarked on this goal in the late 1950s, the idea of heimat was far from the minds of the party leadership. In 1958, as soon as Walter Ulbricht had reasserted his political authority in the wake of Khrushchev's destalinization drive of 1956,[5] the SED reignited a process of economic and social transformation. The seven-year plan, introduced at the SED's Fifth Party Congress on 10–16 July 1958, was to 'lead socialism to victory by 1965' by which time average consumption levels of basic consumer goods would surpass West German standards. This was to be achieved by renewed collectivization efforts in industry and especially in agriculture. Crucially, the desired completion of socialism through the plan was to be accompanied by a commensurate cultural transformation. State and party aimed at the creation of a 'socialist national culture' (*sozialistische Nationalkultur*), which entailed raising the cultural appreciation of the working class, and educating socialist cultural leaders (artists, directors of cultural groups) and opinion formers.

The close relationship between economic and cultural socialist transformation was encapsulated by the 'Bitterfeld Path' of 1959. Guided by the SED and its youth organization, the Free German Youth, Bitterfeld workers called on all workers to 'work, learn, and live in a socialist way'. With the slogan: 'Take up a pen, mate! The socialist national culture needs you!', the first Bitterfeld Conference, held on 24 April 1959, popularized the idea that in socialism, culture was open to all.[6] What was at stake, Walter Ulbricht explained to the SED's Cultural Conference in 1960, was nothing short of

Vergangenheit: Geschichtskultur und Herrschaftslegitimation in der DDR (Leipzig: Akademische Verlagsanstalt, 1997), pp. 217–36. Thomas Reichel, 'Die durchherrschte Arbeitsgesellschaft: Zu den Herrschaftsstrukturen und Machtverhältnissen in DDR-Betrieben', in Renate Hürtgen and Thomas Reichel (eds.), *Der Schein der Stabilität: DDR-Betriebsalltag in der Ära Honecker* (Berlin: Metropol, 2001), pp. 85–110; here pp. 87–9.

[4] 'Die Heimat ist überall': Neutsch, *Spur der Steine*, pp. 774, 778.
[5] Peter Grieder, *The East German Leadership, 1946–1973* (Manchester University Press, 1999), ch. 3.
[6] Staritz, *Geschichte der DDR*, pp. 173–84: Haase *et al.*, *Die SED*, pp. 255–6.

the creation of the socialist individual who could overcome the cultural and economic legacies of capitalism.[7]

Political and cultural functionaries set out to transform the country in great haste. Between 1959 and 1960, private agriculture was almost eliminated as the percentage of collectivized farms rose from 43.5% (1959) to 83.6% (1960).[8] The state repression necessary to achieve this goal, as well as the economic problems caused by the ensuing shortfalls in agricultural production, led to a dramatic rise in the number of East Germans leaving the country for West Berlin, from an annual total of 77,071 (1959) to 157,841 in 1960 and 179,635 by the first half of 1961. The practical consequences of the Fifth Party Congress led directly to the construction of the Berlin Wall starting on 13 August 1961.

The Wall reinforced the GDR's claim to distinctiveness,[9] which had been postulated unambiguously at the Fifth Party Congress. The ideal of creating a new socialist individual was inaugurated in 1958, and was maintained even after the failure of the 'New Economic System' in 1963. The goal of individual transformation continued to be decisive in socialist ideology even after 1967, when the ideal of a socialist national culture was replaced by that of the 'socialist community of people', a proposition that remained central throughout the twentieth anniversary celebrations of the GDR in 1969.

Arguably, then, the decade after 1958/59 marks the apogee of the party's ambitions for realizing socialism in economics, society and culture. This had serious implications for the theory and practices of heimat, which were forced to relate much more closely to socialism. However, as the ideal of the socialist national culture espoused by the SED failed to be translated into popular practices, the party became all the more reliant on existing cultural practices. From the mid-1960s, heimat developed as a principal expression of socialist transformation and achievement. By the time the GDR celebrated its twentieth 'anniversary' in 1969, heimat had become pivotal to the GDR's self-definition and representation.

---

[7] *Kulturkonferenz 1960: Protokoll der vom Zentralkomitee der SED, dem Ministerium für Kultur und dem Deutschen Kulturbund vom 27. bis 29. April 1960 im VEB Elektrokohle, Berlin, abgehaltenen Konferenz* (Berlin: Dietz, 1960), pp. 265–6.

[8] Steiner, *Plan*, pp. 92, 115–22.

[9] The extent to which the Wall represented a caesura is discussed in Dorothee Wierling, *Geboren im Jahr Eins. Der Jahrgang 1949 in der DDR: Versuch einer Kollektivbiographie* (Berlin: Links, 2002), esp. pp. 171–88. Patrick Major, 'Vor und nach dem 13. August 1961: Reaktionen der DDR-Bevölkerung auf den Bau der Berliner Mauer', *Archiv für Sozialgeschichte* 39 (1999), 325–54.

DEFINING THE SOCIALIST HEIMAT

In 1955, the year when both German states were granted formal sovereignty, heimat became a subject on the GDR's school curriculum. Taught in the third and fourth years, heimat lessons would introduce pupils to their immediate surroundings. Through heimat pupils would gain a better understanding of Germany's historical and cultural development, and its current division.[10] Since heimat was formally taught to all children, it was no longer enough to present it as the sphere in which the promises of socialism could be gauged. Instead, it became necessary to define how heimat related to socialist ideology as such, and to spell out how it helped define the GDR in the context of a divided Germany. In response, Sigrid Schwarz wrote perhaps the first academic study of this issue, arguing that people possess an innate emotional sense of heimat. The purpose of socialist education, she argued, was to channel this sense towards a connectedness to the socialist community, and a love of working people.[11]

At a time of rapidly worsening relations between the two German states, the Cultural League began to consider more systematically how the ambiguity of the relationship between heimat and the GDR could be overcome. In 1958, the organization hosted a conference which launched the concept of the 'socialist' heimat. At this conference Erik Hühns, deputy director of the Märkisches [Heimat] Museum in Berlin and the Cultural League's leading protagonist in the debate, argued that heimat was intrinsically linked to class.[12] According to Marxist-Leninist historical materialism, the means of production were the central factor that determined every social development in history.[13] If, in West Germany and elsewhere, 'heimat' involved bourgeois exploitation of the working class, it followed that the socialist heimat was characterized by the end of class inequalities. Under socialism, the heimat was owned by the workers and peasants, who had full power to transform it in accordance with their wishes and needs.[14] In this way, the socialist heimat entailed a new sense of aesthetics. 'The beautiful landscapes

---

[10] Werner Bastine, 'Zur Beziehung zwischen Heimatkunde und Geschichtsunterricht', in *Die Heimat im Geschichtsunterricht: Materialien zur Verwirklichung des heimatkundlichen Prinzips im Geschichtsunterricht* (Berlin: Volk und Wissen, 1957), pp. 24–30.

[11] Sigrid Schwarz, 'Die Liebe zur Heimat, ein wesentliches Ziel unserer patriotischen Erziehung', 2 vols., PhD thesis, Humboldt University Berlin (1956), vol. II, pp. 419–48.

[12] *Um unsere sozialistische* Heimat: *Referat und Diskussionsbeiträge einer Tagung am 20. Juni 1958 in Berlin* (Berlin: DKB, Zentrale Kommission Natur- und Heimatfreunde, 1958), pp. 9–11.

[13] Hubert Mohr and Erik Hühns (eds.), *Einführung in die Heimatgeschichte* (Berlin: Deutscher Verlag der Wissenschaften, 1959), p. 18.

[14] Ibid., pp. 7–8.

of our heimat', Hühns declared in 1968, 'are a part of our life. We do not distinguish between nature, the old settlements and new blocks of flats, cultural monuments and factories owned by the people.'[15] Industrial complexes and other achievements of socialist transformation formed part of the emotive impact of the socialist heimat.

Cultural League leaders argued that heimat derived its particular emotional value from the fact that everyone could actively participate in it.[16] Crucially, this meant that Hühns and his co-protagonist in the debate, Willibald Gutsche, disagreed with Schwarz's argument that socialist heimat was acquired through education. Instead, they held that it was distinguished by popular ownership and by its forward-looking nature. Heimat in the GDR was inherently about its own transformation,[17] and not, as allegedly in the FRG, about a passive clinging to the past.

Heimat enabled individuals to understand the socialist transformations of the late 1950s, and discouraged them from leaving. If so many young people left the GDR every year, Gutsche argued, this was because the country still harboured too many remnants of traditional bourgeois notions of heimat. Only a modern, socialist conception of heimat could convince the young of the emotional and practical superiority of socialism, and provide them with sufficient reasons to love their country and stay in it.[18] The problem, in other words, was not the socialist policies (such as the collectivization drive) in themselves, but the inability of citizens to realize what was good for them. Culture and heimat festivals could help by imparting 'to our farmers the joy of belonging to an agricultural co-operative'.[19]

This definition of the socialist heimat had fundamental implications for the conceptions of fatherland and nation. Erik Hühns distinguished between the 'immediate' heimat, defined by a person's local surroundings, and the 'wider' heimat which was determined by familiar customs, language and social conditions. The wider heimat was synonymous with the fatherland, which was always synonymous with the state, and this in turn

---

[15] BArch-SAPMO, DY27 331: 'Diskussionsgrundlage zum Wissenschaftlichen [*sic*] Colloquium über „*Nation – Vaterland – Heimat*" ausgearbeitet von Dr Erik Hühns und Artur Hockauf im Auftrage des Arbeitsausschusses der Zentralen Kommission Natur und Heimat des Präsidialrates des Deutschen Kulturbundes' (6 March 1968), here pp. 8, 10.

[16] 'Gedanken zum Begriff „sozialistische Heimat"', pt 14, *Um unsere sozialistische* Heimat, pp. 9–11.

[17] See also Herbert Bauer, 'Heimat – Vaterland – Sozialismus', in *Zur Unterstützung des heimatkundlichen Unterrichtes* (Suhl: Deutscher Kulturbund, 1962), pp. 10–35; here p. 26.

[18] *Um unsere sozialistische* Heimat, pp. 65–8.

[19] BArch-SAPMO, DY27 926: 'Tagung des Präsidialrates in Mestlin. Der Beitrag des Kulturbunds zur Entwicklung eines sozialistischen Kulturlebens auf dem Lande' (26 September 1958).

distinguished it – in principle – from the nation.[20] Under the peculiar
conditions of contemporary Germany the nation was as yet incomplete, for
only under socialism could a nation exist for all.[21] The western part of
Germany could only become a nation to the working class once workers
were no longer exploited there, and capitalism had been overcome. Until
that time, the German nation remained confined to the GDR.[22] Over time,
Hühns observed, the 'immediate' heimat would merge with the 'wider'
heimat, as individuals recognized that they had one heimat, the GDR,
which was also their fatherland.[23] The GDR would then be heimat, fatherland and nation all in one.[24]

Hühns' concept of heimat did not go unchallenged. Friedrich Donath
rejected Hühns' distinction between the 'immediate' and 'wider' heimat as
diffuse and impractical.[25] In a paper presented to the [East] German
Historians' Society, Max Steinmetz agreed that heimat stood in a close
relationship to the fatherland, the socialist state, since the love of heimat
necessarily implied love of the fatherland. However, they were differentiated
by size: heimat was more limited in its geographic extent than the fatherland,
and this was a fundamental, insurmountable difference. Steinmetz also disagreed with Hühns' dismissal of birthplace as unimportant: it is true that
many people had found their true heimat in regions of the GDR in which
they had not been born; nevertheless, for the majority of the population birth
was still the major factor in their feelings of heimat.[26] Steinmetz and Friedrich
Donath did find themselves in agreement with Hühns over the idea that, for
as long as Germany was divided into capitalism and socialism, only the GDR
could be the true German nation. However, for Donath and Steinmetz the
identity between the GDR and the German nation was all the more reason
not to confuse the GDR and heimat. Equating heimat with the nation, they
argued, rendered the heimat concept pointless and absurd.[27]

[20] Erik Hühns, 'Nation – Vaterland – Heimat', *Aus der Arbeit der Natur- und Heimatfreunde* (1959),
      no. 8, 169–79.
[21] See also Stefan Berger, 'National paradigm and legitimacy: uses of academic history writing in the
      1960s', in Major and Osmond (eds.), *The Workers' and Peasants' State*, pp. 244–61; here p. 253.
[22] Erik Hühns, 'Das Volk gestaltet seine Heimat', *Aus der Arbeit der Natur- und Heimatfreunde* (1960),
      no. 4, 67–9.
[23] For a similar argument, see Heinrich Gemkow, 'Über Wert und Mißbrauch der Heimatliebe:
      Gedanken zu Inhalt und Funktion des Heimatbegriffs', *Beiträge zur Geschichte der deutschen
      Arbeiterbewegung* (1962), no. 3/4, 657–70; here 669–70.
[24] Hühns, 'Nation – Vaterland – Heimat', 178–9.
[25] Friedrich Donath, 'Bürgerliche oder sozialistische Heimat?', *Sächsische Heimatblätter* 6 (1960), 258–60.
[26] Max Steinmetz, 'Die Aufgaben der Regionalgeschichtsforschung in der DDR bei der Ausarbeitung
      eines nationalen Geschichtsbildes', *Zeitschrift für Geschichtswissenschaft* 9 (1961), 1735–73, esp. 1754–8.
[27] Friedrich Donath, 'Bermerkungen zur Diskussion um die Begriffe Heimat – Vaterland – Nation',
      Aus der Arbeit der Natur- und Heimatfreunde (1959), no. 9, 226–8.

In response to these criticisms, Hühns accepted that there were conceptual differences between heimat, fatherland and nation, but he continued to insist on the dynamic whereby under the conditions of socialism, the individual's perception of heimat would become broader until it encompassed the entire GDR.[28] In fact, Hühns' approach contained greater ideological consistency. It accommodated more easily the official line that, in contrast to the FRG, in the socialist GDR the 'new citizens' had found their heimat, even if they had been born and raised elsewhere.[29] More significantly, if heimat was distinguished principally by the ownership of the means of production, and if heimat was about its own transformation, then it was only logical that, ultimately, heimat must extend to the entire GDR.[30]

The role of the birthplace, and the relationship between the immediate and the wider heimat, were never fully resolved. Hühns reaffirmed his position in 1969, in a book which subsequently acted as an important point of reference within the Cultural League.[31] By contrast, the official cultural-political dictionary, of which the first edition was published in 1970, carefully defined heimat as the 'territorial unity of the natural, social and cultural milieu, in which a person experiences the first crucial formation of his or her personality'.[32] Avoiding the main bone of contention – the relationship between heimat and birthplace – the dictionary endowed the location in which an individual grew up with particular significance. Crucially, it asserted that one's experience of heimat, of feeling at home ('sich heimisch fühlen') could only occur in socialism, irrespective of the individual's place of origin.

While some disagreements remained, the central tenets of heimat in the GDR were remarkably clear. The socialist heimat was owned by the working class, which could transform it according to its wishes. Bearing the workers' imprint, every region in the socialist fatherland enabled workers to belong. Heimat induced the most emotional feelings of attachment to the GDR, and just as the individual instinctively and rationally appreciated,

---

[28] Erik Hühns, 'Noch einmal: Nation – Vaterland – Heimat. Antwort an Dr Donath, Leipzig', *Aus der Arbeit der Natur- und Heimatfreunde* (1959), no. 9, 228–9. Erik Hühns, 'Zum Stand der Diskussion um den sozialistischen Heimatbegriff', *Aus der Arbeit der Natur- und Heimatfreunde* (1960), no. 10, 229–33.

[29] Hühns, 'Nation – Vaterland – Heimat', 175–7.

[30] See also Gemkow, 'Heimatliebe', here esp. 668–9.

[31] Erik Hühns, Heimat, *Vaterland, Nation* (Berlin: Tribüne/Deutscher Kulturbund, 1969).

[32] *Kulturpolitisches Wörterbuch*, 1st edn (Berlin: Dietz, 1970,), p. 206. The definition remained virtually unchanged until the end of the GDR. *Kulturpolitisches Wörterbuch*, 5th edn (Berlin: Dietz, 1989), pp. 388–9.

loved and stood up for his socialist heimat, so he would love and defend his fatherland, the GDR.[33]

By guiding individuals to a higher level of morality in dealings with each other and with the state,[34] the socialist heimat related closely to the 'Bitterfeld Path' and the 'socialist national culture'. At the heart of the socialist heimat and the socialist national culture lay a concern for *Volksverbundenheit*, for culture to be connected to the character of the people. On this basis, workers and artists could join forces to enable a transition 'from the I to the We', from the self to the collective.[35]

Since the cultural initiatives of the late 1950s embraced the ideal of individual artistic activity (*künstlerische Selbstbetätigung*), the Ministry of Culture urged the Centre for Folklore Art in Leipzig to develop and promote new popular dances, inspired by German tradition and that of the GDR's socialist neighbours. Such folklore should express the life, joy, adroitness and wealth of the new socialist person. More generally, the Ministry urged that folklore represent the treasures of the progressive heritage of past centuries, as well as the artistic traditions of the working class.[36] Since folklore could be appropriated by all, the Ministry of Culture urged folklore ensembles and institutions to do their part in promoting workers' artistic creativity, by inspiring them to sing, act, compose and paint, and by guiding workers' writing circles (*Zirkel schreibender Arbeiter*).[37]

This acknowledgement of the significance of folklore does not mean that the SED lost sight of its long-term goal, a population of workers engaging with high art and the classics. Yet, given the state of popular culture in practice,[38] the party clearly recognized that if socialist national culture was to have any chance of success, socialist heimat engagements would have to feature prominently. Ten years after the Bitterfeld Path had inaugurated a new socialist national culture, only around 250 workers' writing circles with 4,000 members existed in the whole of the GDR.[39] Only by including activities related to folklore in the widest sense (*Volkskunst*) could the Ministry of Culture claim that between 800,000

---

[33] Hühns, Heimat, *Vaterland, Nation*, p. 96.
[34] BArch-SAPMO, DY27 3385: Untitled [Entwurf über die Tätigkeit der Klub- und Kulturhäuser], Punkt 5 (3 August 1967).
[35] LHA Schwerin, Rat des Bezirks Schwerin 4627: 'Die kulturelle Entwicklung in unserer Republik [1958]'.
[36] LHA Schwerin, Rat des Bezirks Schwerin 4576: 'Entwurf der Programmerklärung des Ministeriums für Kultur der DDR über die Entwicklung der sozialistischen Nationalkultur' (19 November 1959).
[37] Ibid., pp. 82–3.   [38] Erna Sander in *Kulturkonferenz 1960*, pp. 147–51.
[39] Christoph Kleßmann, *Zwei Staaten – Eine Nation. Deutsche Geschichte 1955–1970* (Göttingen: Vandenhoeck und Ruprecht, 1988), p. 383.

and a million working people were culturally active. Even though the term 'working people' indicates that many of those active in folklore were not actual workers, at least the sheer numbers of culturally active citizens relating to heimat allowed the party to claim a lasting impact from its Bitterfeld conferences.[40]

It is too simplistic to consider the socialist construction of heimat and its significance as a typical instance in which 'the party' (i.e. the SED) appropriated and abused an otherwise innocent concept.[41] The debate was promoted by individual actors for very personal reasons. Hühns had been born in Charlottenburg (later to become part of Berlin's British sector), the son of divorced parents, one Jewish and one non-Jewish. Having survived the war thanks to luck and cunning, he studied with Alfred Meusel at the Humboldt University, and soon moved to the Soviet sector. After working with Meusel in the German Historical Museum, Hühns became director of the Märkisches [Heimat] Museum in Berlin. His personal background explains his passionate commitment to constructing a 'better' Germany, and the centrality of heimat in this endeavour.[42] Hühns' life story also explains his uncompromising stance on the relationship between heimat and birthplace. For him and for others who had been born outside the territory that now comprised the GDR, the emphasis on the socialist heimat open to all was a question of their own belonging.[43]

The heimat debate had been led by the generation following that of the 'Weimar Communists',[44] those born in the 1920s who were nevertheless deeply influenced by that older generation, notably Kneschke (who died in 1959), Meusel and, of course, Becher himself. By the late 1950s, this young generation had become extremely well connected. In 1954, Hühns and

---

[40] BArch-SAPMO, DY27 3385: 'Volkskunstkonferenz 5–7 December 1968 in Cottbus. Genosse Rudi Raupach: Probleme und Aufgaben der sozialistischen Volkskunst nach dem VII. Parteitag'. For this reason, this study disagrees with Sandrine Kott's point that the SED did not 'broaden' its definition of popular culture until the 1970s. A broad conception of *Volkskunst* was always present in the GDR, and became more widespread from the 1960s onwards.

[41] Karlheinz Blaschke, 'Die marxistische Regionalgeschichte: Ideologischer Zwang und Wirklichkeitsferne', in Georg G. Iggers *et al.* (eds.), *Die DDR-Geschichtswissenschaft als Forschungsproblem*, Internationale Tagung über Geschichtswissenschaft in der DDR (Munich: Oldenbourg, 1998), pp. 341–68; here pp. 354–5.

[42] These observations are based on an interview with Erik Hühns, 3 December 2002.

[43] A similar argument has been advanced by Judith Kretzschmar for the construction of the heimat image in the reportages of Karl-Eduard von Schnitzler: Tilo Prase and Judith Kretzschmar, *Propagandist und Heimatfilmer: Die Dokumentarfilme des Karl-Eduard von Schnitzler* (Leipzig: Leipziger Universitätsverlag, 2003), pp. 121–72, esp. pp. 107–10.

[44] Catherine Epstein, *The Last Revolutionaries: German Communists and their Century* (Cambridge, MA: Harvard University Press, 2003).

Heinrich Gemkow, a fellow student of Meusel and a member of the Institute for Marxism-Leninism, were charged with approving all heimat publications which were not submitted to an established publishing house. This brought them into contact with many heimat activists on the ground. Friedrich Donath, meanwhile, taught at Leipzig University and led the district organization of the Friends of Nature and Heimat. Although regional history chairs had not yet been established in the GDR, the socialist heimat had been conceived in close association with the professional historical establishment, as well as the SED, the Cultural League leadership, and its grass roots.[45]

Most importantly, in 1958 the Cultural League was still in a very fragile position after having been accused, in 1956–7, of constituting a centre of opposition to Ulbricht. The League's eagerness, at a central level, to remove any ideological ambiguity from the heimat concept enabled its praesidium to present the organization in a more conformist light. Proactively tying the idea of heimat to the socialist transformation of the individual enabled the Cultural League to move from the margins of ideology to its centre.

Even though heimat had been defined in relation to the nation and the locality with remarkable precision, the socialist heimat ideal remained sufficiently adaptable to various socialist ideological currents. The notion of the 'socialist heimat' was used with remarkable consistency while other ideological notions proposed by the SED within that one decade – the Bitterfeld Path, the socialist national culture, the socialist community of people – came and went. As each of these initiatives was redefined, the socialist heimat moved further towards the core of the party's ideological goals. In fact it encapsulated the essence of the party's different initiatives: the creation of a new, moral, socialist human being transforming and enjoying life in the GDR.

'FROM THE I TO THE WE' – LOCAL FESTIVALS AND THE JOY OF SOCIALISM

The cultural initiatives launched by the Fifth Party Congress in 1958 entailed the creation of a centralized cultural network so that a cultural centre, village club or culture house would exist in every village and town in

---

[45] Interestingly, following Donath's move to Rostock, he was succeeded in 1962 as the guiding spirit of the Leipzig district Friends of Nature and Heimat by Carl Czok, who had just finished his habilitation thesis (which qualified him for professorial rank) and advanced to become perhaps the GDR's leading regional historian.

the GDR. These grass-roots cultural institutions were to be supported by a dense network of professionally run culture houses that were either attached to industrial co-operatives or sponsored directly by the county. These culture houses received direction from the district and the Centre for Folklore in Leipzig, which in turn were guided by the Ministry of Culture in Berlin. In Schwerin district, for instance, between 1958 and 1960, sixty-two village clubs were founded, and by 1963, as many as 377 village clubs and sixty-six workers' clubs (*Klub der Werktätigen*) had been created.[46] By then a centralized cultural infrastructure had been established that reached every part of the GDR, north and south.[47]

The importance of village clubs for the creation of socialist national culture was explained by Herbert Krebs, deputy chairman of Worbis county council, at the SED Cultural Conference in 1960. Under the guidance of the culture house of Worbis county, individual village clubs co-ordinated the programme of cultural providers such as the Cultural League and the local cinema. This, said Krebs, had allowed the creation of an entirely new and genuinely popular culture which found its expression in the staging of the 'Eichsfeld Festival', on behalf of which 1,300 people had become active through their local village club.[48] How much truth there was in Krebs' assertions is secondary to the assumptions implicit in his report. Worbis county included some of the country's most intransigent Roman Catholic communities (including the village of Holungen, discussed in Chapter 7). If village clubs could transform cultural life there, they could do the same anywhere in the land.

In practice, it was extremely difficult for village clubs to launch the socialist national culture. Many village clubs existed on paper only and organized no activities after their creation. Moreover, despite the official assumption that activists and culture houses would be delighted to work together, in practice cultural work was often marred by personal or institutional rivalries, or a general lack of interest. Trade union as well as party functionaries were frequently uninterested in culture, doing little to promote the local culture centre and village club.[49] Worse, instead of engaging in the cumbersome business of promoting new cultural activities, many

---

[46] LHA Schwerin, Rat des Bezirks 4627: 'Material für die Festansprache am 8. Mai 1963' (3 May 1963).

[47] LHA Schwerin, Rat des Bezirks Schwerin 15108: 'Programm zur Entwicklung sozialistischer Kulturarbeit 1962/63 Kreis Ludwigslust'.

[48] Herbert Krebs in *Kulturkonferenz 1960*, pp. 100–6.

[49] LHA Schwerin, Rat des Bezirks Schwerin 4600: 'Auswertung des Einsatzes am 25.7.1962 der Arbeitsgruppe kulturelle Massenarbeit im Kreis Lübz', p. 2. LHA Schwerin, Rat des Bezirks Schwerin 4598: 'Bericht über die bisherige Realisierung des Perspektivplanes im Kreis Hagenow und die noch vorgesehenen Maßnahmen' (10 August 1957), p. 10.

mass organizations competed against each other for the sponsorship of existing groups. The Cultural League often complained that hobby groups were lured away by the trade union with promises of generous financial assistance.[50] Finally, pressure to produce the desired statistics led to superficial compliance with directives.[51] In many respects, then, the Bitterfeld programme obstructed itself. By setting unrealistic targets it encouraged the formulation of cultural commitments that became formulaic and devoid of content. Cultural initiative remained the province of the few, not the many.[52]

A new cultural infrastructure could create the preconditions for cultural renewal, but could not in itself generate practices that were popular. Herein lay the core problem, because promoting a socialist culture at a time of deep social and economic upheaval proved far from straightforward. For instance, to mark the socialist transformation of the countryside, cultural authorities throughout the GDR instituted a 'Festival of the Fully Collectivized Village'. Owing to the divisiveness and unpopularity of the collectivization drives,[53] these festivals proved an unmitigated failure. In Schwerin district, so few people were prepared to contribute to the celebrations in 1959 that local authorities were forced to hire professional artists, at a total cost of 400,000 DM. In Deibow, farmers told officials that they could not think of any reason why they should celebrate on this day, while in Niendorf-Weselsdorf villagers refused to 'celebrate their own funeral'.[54]

As farmers had not overcome their reservations by 1962, the authorities instituted a 'Festival of the Collectivized County', which allowed better control by the district cultural authorities.[55] These festivals were unremitting in their ideological content. In the county of Schwerin-Land, the programme included readings of speeches by Khrushchev and Ulbricht,

---

[50] BArch-SAPMO, DY27 3513: 'Bericht des Vorsitzenden des Zentralen Fachausschusses Aquarien- und Terrarienkunde auf der VII. Zentralen Tagung vom 10. bis 12. September 1965 in Berlin', pp. 28–30.

[51] LHA Schwerin, Rat des Bezirks 7720/7721: 'Bericht über die Verwirklichung der Beschlüsse des VIII. Deutschen Bauernkongresses im Hinblick auf die Entwicklung eines vielseitigen und interessanten geistigen und kulturellen Lebens auf dem Lande' (19 September 1964), p. 7.

[52] For Thuringia, see BArch-SAPMO, DY27 1975: 'Zusammenarbeit mit der Bezirksleitung des Kulturbundes Erfurt 1959–62. Bericht über die Finanzrevision 1961'. For Mecklenburg, see LHA Schwerin, Rat des Bezirks 4600: 'Einschätzung zum Röblinger-Programm und zu den Jahresendabrechnungen in den LPG'n im Kreis Gadebusch' (date pencilled in: 30 September [196]2).

[53] Bauerkämper, *Ländliche Gesellschaft*, here esp. pp. 447–58. See also Ross, *Constructing Socialism*, pp. 113–20, and McDougall, *Youth Politics*, pp. 112–15.

[54] LHA Schwerin, Rat des Bezirks Schwerin 4607b: 'Bericht an den Rat über die Bildung von Kreiskulturzentren und die Arbeit der Dorfklubs [*c.* 1960]'.

[55] LHA Schwerin, Rat des Bezirks Schwerin 4575: 'Informationsbericht, Schwerin' (4 April 1962). LHA Schwerin, Rat des Bezirks Schwerin 4582: 'An den Sekretär des Rates des Bezirkes, Gen. Lehmann' (24 November 1962).

recitations of 'The Collective' and 'The New Beginning', and performances of agitprop sketches.[56] Whereas heimat festivals in the 1950s had usually combined traditional songs and sketches with a few ideological representations, the Festival of the Collectivized County did the reverse by offering the occasional heimat song in an essentially ideological programme. Unsurprisingly, popular participation in the collectivization celebrations of 1962 declined even from its previous low levels.[57] Recalling expropriation was not a good way to celebrate the joys of socialism.

Of all the new festivals invented in the 1960s, perhaps the most ubiquitous was the 'Festival of the Joy of Life'. In 1963, the county cultural centre at Parchim (Schwerin district), which in 1961 had won the competition for the GDR's best cultural centre, successfully organized seven events, attended by a total of 2,700 visitors, to mark the 'Festival of Socialist Joy'.[58] The week's most popular event by far was a Low German evening with Mecklenburg dances and poems, which drew a crowd of 1,000 people. An evening for pensioners was also well attended, though the ideological impact of folk songs like 'Must I Go and Leave for Town?' ('Muss i denn') and 'Goodbye, my Beloved Homeland' ('Nun ade du mein lieb Heimatland') was doubtful at best. A youth dance evening was also popular, though it proved difficult to arouse enthusiasm for the latest socialist dance invention, the 'Orion'. When a few couples finally agreed to perform the dance, they were accompanied by heckles and whistles from the audience, leaving an exasperated organizer to complain to the authorities that this was not the first time the dance had been disrupted. She would never promote the Orion again.[59]

At one of the GDR's most successful county cultural centres, in other words, it may have been possible to celebrate the 'Festival of Socialist Joy' with events that were genuinely popular. However, the popularity of the events was based on their traditional nature (folklore evenings for the local public, a local dance for the young, etc.). Indeed, the participants filled the evenings with their own meanings. The heckling of the Orion dancers and the songs sung at the pensioners' evening are indicative of individual and collective demarcations of space, of 'Eigen-Sinn' (Lüdtke), against the

---

[56] LHA Schwerin, Rat des Bezirks Schwerin 4602: 'Festprogramm – vollgenossenschaftlicher Kreis Kreisensemble Schwerin-Land. Programm des Kreisensembles Güstrow, „Der Mensch ist des Menschen Freund"'.

[57] Ibid., 'Erfahrungsaustausch der Kreise Ludwigslust – Perleberg – Hagenow' (7 March 1962).

[58] LHA Schwerin, Rat des Bezirks Schwerin 15108: 'Bericht des Kreiskulturhauses „Kurt Bürger" Parchim für die Zeit vom 1.8. bis 10.10.1963'.

[59] Ibid., 'Einschätzung der Veranstaltungen am 5., 6. und 7. Oktober 1963 im Kreiskulturhaus "Kurt Bürger" Parchim'.

state. Whatever the meanings of the 'Eigen-Sinn' displayed here, they certainly did not reflect the joys of socialism.

The problems facing the party in its desire to mould new traditions were as much structural as ideological. In 1963, the local authorities of Eisenach created the 'Festival of Light and Joy of Life'. The festival was, on the surface, no different from heimat festivals anywhere else: it was centred on the 'Prince's Lake' in the heart of the city and locals celebrated with sausages and beer, while – a particular local touch – hundreds of floating candles lit up the lake. Nevertheless the festival proved a flop. It had been intended as a socialist counterpart to the *Sommergewinn*, the GDR's largest spring festival, which Eisenachers celebrated with gusto.[60] However, whereas the *Sommergewinn* was organized through traditional community structures, the 'Festival' was intended to strengthen state-sponsored neighbourhood districts, and formed part of the economic-cultural competition which the party encouraged among residential groups. For this reason, local authorities had great trouble in generating the requisite enthusiasm amongst the intended organizers. Given the persistent lack of response among residents, which left much of the work and sponsorship to the local authorities, the festival was abandoned in 1972.[61]

In many ways, the party's inability to harness local festivals to the construction of a socialist festival culture is not particularly surprising. The work of Victor Turner and others has shown that local festivals served as an expression of *communitas*, of states of cultural and social desire which were antithetical to the structuredness of ordinary life.[62] Rituals and cultural performances such as 'spectacles', i.e. public displays of a society's central meanings, always contained inherent challenges to existing power relations.[63] The anti-structural elements in local festivals, whether in rituals of reversal like carnival or in cultural performances, were inimical to the ordered nature of the socialist festivals which state and party tried to invent. The party wanted nothing left to chance. Since culture was to express socialism and socialist relationships, socialist festivals and performances were ordered and calculable, and precluded precisely the unpredictable nature of traditional festivals. Unless the party allowed some anti-structure

---

[60] See also Chapter 4.

[61] Stadtarchiv Eisenach 12 – 2005: Fest der 1000 Lichter, 1963–71. Here: 'Protokoll über die Beratung zur Vorbereitung des Festes der 1000 Lichter 7.4.71' and 'Niederschrift über die Beratung am 5.8.71 betr. Fest der 1000 Lichter. Eisenach, den 12.8.71. Referat Kultur, gez. Strohmeyer'.

[62] Turner, *Dramas*, pp. 54–5. Turner, *The Ritual Process*, esp. ch. 4.

[63] Charlotte Aull Davies, 'A oes heddwch? Contested meanings and identities in the Welsh National Eisteddfod', in Felicia Hughes-Freeland (ed.), *Ritual, Performance, Media* (London: Routledge, 1998), pp. 141–59.

to be expressed, festivals lost their essence as expressions of local community and cultural identification. Requiring that local festivals mirror the laws of socialist transformation was simply a contradiction in terms.

From the middle of the 1950s to the early 1960s, popular cultural activity appears to have declined before levelling off during the rest of the latter decade. In the district of Schwerin, the number of people engaged in folklore groups fell from around 15,000 in 1952 to around 9,700 in 1961, with the decline of amateur theatre performances in dialect being especially striking.[64] The number of choirs also declined disproportionately. Overall, public cultural activity diminished not just in counties across the northern GDR.[65] In Altenburg county (Leipzig district), for instance, fifty-eight cultural groups existed between 1952 and 1956, but only twenty-three by 1962, at least on paper.[66] A qualitative study of the Thuringian village of Niederzimmern has also shown that the 1950s were a golden age for a village culture whose integrative influence declined sharply during the 1960s.[67] The downturn in organized cultural activity was evident in the workplace,[68] but it also manifested itself in the closure of social spaces: the number of rooms available for youth events declined by half between 1954 and 1960,[69] and the number of pubs, which often constituted the only communal meeting places in a locality, also dropped. In the district of Leipzig alone, 160 pubs were closed in the years before 1962.[70] In the light of this decline, the creation of one culture house per county was hardly impressive, especially as the more controlled atmosphere of a culture house could hardly make up for the loss of the informal sociability of a pub. Unless alternative meeting places could be provided, it would be impossible, the Cultural League warned, to revive local culture in the district.[71]

---

[64] LHA Schwerin, Rat des Bezirks Schwerin 4595a: 'Bericht über die bisher geleistete Arbeit und den Stand der Kultureinrichtungen und der Kulturarbeit im Bezirk Schwerin. Bezirkskabinett für Kulturarbeit [1952]'. LHA Schwerin, Rat des Bezirks Schwerin 4609: 'Angeforderte statistische Meldung vom Ministerium für Kultur vom 14. November 1961' (1 December 1961). Of the 9,706 participants, 3,279 were active in choirs, 926 in fanfare groups, 873 in agitprop groups, 706 in folkdance groups, 673 in instrumental groups, 626 in amateur dancing circles and 496 in amateur theatre.

[65] This was the case, for instance, in Goldberg (Schwerin district) and Malchin (Neubrandenburg district). LHA Schwerin, Rat des Bezirks 4600: 'Auswertung des Einsatzes am 25.7.1962 der Arbeitsgruppe kulturelle Massenarbeit im Kreis Lübz'. LHA Schwerin, Kulturbund Neubrandenburg 52 (1960), *passim.*

[66] 'LPG sind Kulturträger auf dem Land', *Kulturspiegel Altenburg Schmölln* (September 1962), 271–2.

[67] Antonia Maria Humm, *Auf dem Weg zum sozialistischen Dorf? Zum Wandel der dörflichen Lebenswelt in der DDR und der Bundesrepublik Deutschland 1952–69* (Göttingen: Vandenhoek & Ruprecht, 1999); here p. 266.

[68] Kott, 'Geschichte', p. 188.   [69] Fenemore, 'Youth policy', p. 181.

[70] Helmut Häußler, *Kulturbund und Wohngebiet* (Leipzig: Bezirksleitung des Kulturbundes, 1963), p. 12.

[71] Ibid.

It is extremely difficult to conclude from these figures to what extent heimat activity actually declined during the 1960s. Given the advent of television – which, by the end of the 1960s, had become the citizens' most popular pastime – and the decreasing availability of adequate facilities, it would be surprising if the decline noted by the Cultural League and the party did not correspond substantially with reality. However, it is also likely that some of the apparent drop in heimat activity was a result of individuals no longer reporting their doings. For instance, in 1965, the leader of the aquarists, a group which constituted a sub-organization of the Friends of Nature and Heimat, lamented that, of around 50–80,000 aquarists in the country, only 3,500 chose to belong to organized associations. (This number represented a decline from 5,000 in 1957.)[72] The pursuit of heimat activities may have been far less apparent to the authorities in the 1960s, but that does not mean that they no longer existed.

In fact, regional folklore and other traditional pastimes continued to be in evidence throughout the 1960s, albeit at lower levels than in the 1950s. Throughout these decades, for instance, the *Treckfiedel*, a simplified version of the accordion, was regularly played in Mecklenburg villages, at celebrations and in public meeting spaces in the evenings.[73] Over and above the maintenance of folkloric practices at an individual level, culture houses maintained some demand for performances by local choirs, amateur actors and other folklore groups, because they attracted good audiences. Folklore groups also continued to be welcome performers at the holiday centres run mostly by the trade union, introducing visitors to the sounds and dances of the local heimat. The trade union was committed to socialist national culture, but it could hardly ignore either the demand of holidaymakers or the local supply of cultural fare.[74] Since village clubs and culture houses continued to rely on traditional popular culture, at the zenith of socialist national culture demand for traditional folklore groups was reduced, but not eliminated.

The party's push for a new socialist culture led to a decline in popular cultural practices at the grass roots, as enthusiasts either failed to register for heimat activities or stopped engaging in them altogether. However, most citizens failed to take up new 'socialist' practices instead. The 'socialist

---

[72] BArch-SAPMO, DY27 3513: 'Bericht des Vorsitzenden des Zentralen Fachausschusses Aquarien- und Terrarienkunde auf der VII. Zentralen Tagung vom 10.-12. September 1965 in Berlin'.

[73] Dabel villagers had very clear recollections of this. Interviews with Helga Böhnke, Rosemarie Bartelt, Wolfgang Cords and Karl-Heinz Schwabe, 5 July 2003.

[74] BArch-SAPMO, DY27 2953: 'Vorläufige Übersicht über die Tätigkeit des Deutschen Kulturbundes auf dem Gebiet der Volkskunst im Bezirk Erfurt' (14 July 1967).

national culture' so desired by Walter Ulbricht never became truly popular.[75] Nor did the party succeed in creating a synthesis between the socialist national culture and heimat-related practices. There was one level, however, at which the party did succeed in constructing an ideal of the socialist heimat: the level of representation. Here the party redefined the GDR, its districts and its localities. In so doing, the SED attempted to endow socialism with the emotionality of heimat, and construct a sense of attachment, optimism and pride in the socialist GDR.

HEIMAT AS A 'NATIONAL' METAPHOR

If functionaries worried about the decline of traditional cultural practices in their localities owing to the growth of television, there was one consolation: television offered unprecedented potential for reaching GDR citizens. In 1960, 16.7 per cent of households owned a television set. Only five years later just under half of all households had purchased a set, and this figure rose to nearly 100 per cent by 1975.[76] In this decade the number of TV hours broadcast also doubled, from fifty-eight to 116 hours per week.[77] Television became widely available, and constituted the citizens' most popular pastime. In 1967, watching TV was the favourite weekend leisure activity of 68 per cent of the population,[78] and it remained the citizens' favourite pastime for two decades.[79] East Germans loved TV.

If the party wanted to create a socialist sense of heimat, and achieve its aim for a 'socialist national culture', it needed to do so not least through television. In fact, the late Ulbricht years saw formative developments in this field which had an impact well beyond 1971. Beginning in 1964, East German television (Deutscher Fernsehfunk, DFF) broadcast an entertainment series entitled 'Songs of a Small Town', moderated by the popular presenter Heinz Florian Oertel. Produced at great expense, the show featured instrumental music written by Walter Kubiczek, a composer better

---

[75] For the failure of the Bitterfeld Path amongst workers in Berlin, see Kott, 'Geschichte', pp. 178–84.

[76] *Statistisches Jahrbuch der Deutschen Demokratischen Republik 1978*, Staatliche Zentralverwaltung für Statistik (Berlin: Staatsverlag der DDR 1978), p. 274, table 10. The precise figures are unclear, as they differ depending on the yearbook. The statistical yearbook for 1978 puts the proportion of households owning a TV set (as opposed to households holding a licence) in 1970 at 81.7 per cent, and at 82.7 per cent in 1976. In the statistical yearbook for 1988, by contrast, the figures are 89.4 per cent and 102.3 per cent respectively: *Statistisches Jahrbuch der Deutschen Demokratischen Republik 1988*, Staatliche Zentralverwaltung für Statistik (Berlin: Staatsverlag der DDR, 1988), p. 291.

[77] *Statistisches Jahrbuch 1978*, p. 311, table 41. [78] Weber, *Geschichte der DDR*.

[79] BArch-SAPMO, DY30 IV/B2 9.06 85: Abteilung Kultur, 'Ergebnisse der Umfrage zu einigen Fragen von Geselligkeit und Unterhaltung', pp. 3–4. These findings are also discussed in Chapter 4.

known for his score for the DEFA spy series 'The Invisible Lens'. This was the first entertainment programme to be recorded outside the studio, in order to capture a town's characteristic features, its people and its culture.[80] Scenes with nationally renowned singers performing songs in local settings would be interspersed with reports by Oertel on local factories, shops and cultural facilities.

The sixth programme, broadcast in 1966, featured the county town of Müritz, situated on the GDR's largest lake, halfway between Berlin and the Baltic coast. The show presented interviews with local townsfolk to show 'new' socialist people enjoying their socialist heimat, and depicted happy holidaymakers making themselves feel at home. One feature introduced the local foundry, which produced steel for the entire country, while another presented an ocean-going vessel named *Waren*, which now sailed the seven seas in the name of the town and of the entire GDR. As in all programmes in the series, the episode not only showed a local peculiarity or tradition but also related it to the country as a whole. The town and its inhabitants had, according to the programme-makers, manifested a new, socialist way of life and a new socialist feeling of community.[81]

The show combined the construction of socialism with a redefinition of the socialist heimat. At the end of the reportage on the foundry Oertel interviewed the foreman, Dieter Karow, who mentioned his passion for singing. True to the Bitterfeld Path, in the following scene he delighted viewers with the song 'Tonight or Never' (first performed by the Comedian Harmonists in 1932). There is an odd dissonance in this scene. In the song, Karow begs his beloved to say whether she loves him or not; yet Karow does not sing the song in a romantic setting. Rather he moves inside the foundry, apparently addressing his tools and his all-male working-class colleagues on a cigarette break, who exchange encouraging glances with him. Instances of such disconnections are numerous. One scene features the Enzo Trio singing the popular song 'Weekend and Sunshine', which again was first performed by the Comedian Harmonists in the 1930s, in a café overlooking Lake Müritz. Nothing odd about this, except that the Trio sing the tune in Bavarian *Lederhosen*, Alpine hiking boots and Bavarian hats.

By merging popular tunes that had no socialist connotations with unfamiliar images and settings, the programme integrated the familiar, the

---

[80] Peter Hoff, 'Von „Da lacht der Bär" über „Ein Kessel Buntes" – ins „Aus". Politische Geschichte der DDR in Unterhaltungssendungen des DDR-Fernsehens', in Heide Riedel (ed.), *Mit uns zieht die neue Zeit ... 40 Jahre DDR-Medien. Eine Ausstellung des Deutschen Rundfunk-Museums* (Berlin: VISTAS, 1993), pp. 89–90.

[81] Palmowski, 'Regional identities'.

known and the comfortable into socialist settings, thus lending them new meanings. The Enzo Trio's Bavarian outfits in deepest Mecklenburg suggested that local culture was separable from its geographic origins. This homeland, a place in the GDR, combined the cultural richness of all of Germany. Gender relations were ordered, and popular love songs from all ages could still be sung. The show employed homeland motifs to evoke emotions of love, security, familiarity and excitement, and relate them to the construction of socialism.[82]

'Songs of a Small Town' represented the central ideological aim of the Ulbricht era: the creation of a socialist community of people. This aim found its way almost without dilution into the yearly planning documents of the DFF, including the entertainment section. In contrast to entertainment programmes in the FRG, which to the DFF were distinguished by sentimentality, inhumanity and brutality,[83] socialist entertainment was to be based on realism, but it was also designed to help shape socialist aesthetic values characteristic of the socialist community.[84] Television programmes should therefore represent the changed socialist individual and make the nature of this transformation visible in individual thought and action, in relationships with the state, and in relationships of people with each other.[85] Television was to act as an important conduit for socialism in everyday life.[86]

In response to viewers' desire for light entertainment and variety shows, the DFF launched further programmes including, in 1966, a show entitled 'Winter Season'. This was a variety show on a maritime theme, produced by the regional studio in Rostock. Filmed inside a studio that was decorated with maritime motifs, the dress of the presenters and of the guests, as well as the sketches and the songs, all conformed to this marine theme. In 1967, the theme became more explicit in the show's new title, expressed in seafarers' slang: *Klock 8, achtern Strom* ('At 8 o'clock, behind the river').

[82] Deutsches Rundfunkarchiv Babelsberg (DRA), Deutscher Fernsehfunk – HA Unterhaltung, Alt UH B 33: 'Drehbuch zu Schlager einer kleinen Stadt', 6. Folge: Waren/Müritz. DFF1, 'Schlager einer kleinen Stadt', broadcast 22 October 1966 at 8 p.m.

[83] DRA, Vorbereitende Planmaterialien Unterhaltung, 'Referat zur ersten Bereichsparteiaktivtagung der APO Unterhaltung am 6.12.1968'; here pp. 1–18, esp. pp. 4–5 (unfortunately, the name of the author is not recorded).

[84] DRA, Vorbereitende Planmaterialien Unterhaltung: 'Stichworte für die Wahlversammlung der Hauptabteilung (HA) Unterhaltung [1968]'.

[85] DRA, Schriftgutbestand Fernsehen: 'Endgültiger Plan 1969. Vorgabe für die Programmtätigkeit des Deutschen Fernsehfunks 1969', pp. 37–9.

[86] DRA, Vorbereitende Planmaterialien Unterhaltung: 'Planangebot der HA Unterhaltung zum Beschluss der Intendanz über die Vorgabe 1968' (Berlin, 9 August 1967), Part I, p. 7.

The show introduced singers from abroad, particularly from other socialist countries and from the non-socialist Baltic states. It also focused on presenting new material from domestic artists, notably songs about Rostock, about the sea, and about going out into the world. New dances were also presented, and sometimes even premiered.[87] The fifteenth show, for instance, recorded on 30 September 1969, featured local shipbuilding as its theme. Following the opening credits, to pictures of a new ship being launched, the presenter, Horst Köbbert, sang his first contribution: 'Yes, here ships are built, their mother is Rostock, their father are we.' 'A ship leaves the yard', a choir responded, 'and again forms a new bridge over the sea.' 'Whenever a ship left the yard', the presenter continued, 'into the foaming, rising floods, a small part of our heart went along with it: goodbye, proud vessel, and farewell!' A further song was presented by Köbbert, his co-presenter Rica Deus, and the choir, on the town of Rostock. 'Let's go for a stroll ... where there is always something new ... we are in love with Rostock, our town.' Horst Köbbert added that here 'life is pulsating, much is happening', so that anyone who left would 'take this certainty across the sea: the town is younger and more beautiful than ever!' One leitmotif of this particular show was a globe that linked many of the acts, and which featured drawings of the GDR's shipping routes all over the world. This globe was also presented to viewers between songs, thus constantly underlining the town's (and the country's) internationalism. The message about Rostock's transformation was brought home in relaxed conversations among the commentators, as another presenter, Peter Borgelt, mused on the feat of constructing a shipyard where twenty years before there had been potato fields.[88]

Klock 8 presented almost a textbook entertainment version of the socialist heimat by emphasizing its transformation, and inviting all viewers to relate to this achievement. From the middle of the 1960s to the early 1970s, the show acquired added significance, giving cultural expression to 'Baltic Week', a showcase event in which the GDR presented itself and its achievements to the world as part of its efforts to gain international recognition.[89]

---

[87] In 1969, for instance, the show introduced the 'Koka-Nova' to the GDR audiences, a dance that originated in Bulgaria. *Norddeutsche Neueste Nachrichten* (Rostock) (22 February 1969).

[88] DRA, Schriftgutbestand Fernsehen: 'Deutscher Fernsehfunk. Alt Ostseestudio Rostock B417. Sendemanuskript „Klock 8, achtern Strom"' (21 July 1969). Deutscher Fernsehfunk (DFF): 'Klock 8, achtern Strom' (25 October 1969). Peter Borgelt, of course, is also well known as one of the leads in one of the GDR's most popular TV series, *Polizeiruf 110*.

[89] A cartoon in *Neues Deutschland* summarized this perfectly. It featured the Baltic Week's emblem, two seagulls with the letters 'DDR' on their wings, flying past a spectator whose circular head represented the globe. As the spectator watched the seagulls and a dove of peace fly by, a speech bubble came out of the globe/head containing the word: 'Recognition!' *Neues Deutschland* (14 July 1968).

Second only to the Leipzig Fair, Baltic Week was an international event for which the GDR tried hard to entice representatives from the other Baltic nations (especially Scandinavia and Finland) to come to the GDR and see the socialist Germany.[90] This reinforced the symbolic importance of Rostock and its maritime environment. Rostock's international harbour in Warnemünde, its shipyards, and the overseas trade passing through the city were all creations of the past twenty years. *Klock 8* represented Rostock and its invented traditions; its achievements presented a metaphor for the entire GDR and its place in the world.[91]

In 1968, the DFF defined a number of key themes that should be the subject of journalistic endeavour in the forthcoming months, but which also represented the broadcaster's aims more generally. 'The months leading up to the twentieth anniversary of the GDR', one of the aims read,

> are a time in which the image of our Republic is experiencing a drastic trans-formation. On the great building sites in the town centres of Berlin, Leipzig, Halle and Magdeburg we can detect the contours of new departures ... Local people are giving their towns and villages a more beautiful, colourful, festive appearance. A devastated country is giving way to a beautiful heimat for its inhabitants, and through their ambitions for a more beautiful heimat the country is giving an important boost to social life and the communal work of the citizens.

One of the central challenges, the DFF concluded, was to capture and represent the breadth and beauty of the heimat and the GDR – especially in colour.[92] Representing and strengthening the love of the socialist heimat became a central task for GDR television, through programmes devoted to politics, entertainment and culture.[93]

These priorities were reflected in the programme 'Songs of a Big City', which was based on the idea of 'Songs of a Small Town'. From 1968 until 1972, shows presented portraits of Berlin, Dresden, Rostock and

---

[90] Lu Seegers, '"Die Zukunft unserer Stadt ist bereits projektiert." Die 750-Jahrfeier Rostocks im Rahmen der Ostseewoche 1968', in Adelheid von Saldern (ed.), *Inszenierte Einigkeit: Herrschaftsrepräsentationen in DDR-Städten* (Stuttgart: Steiner, 2003), pp. 61–106.

[91] This message was underlined by the *Klock 8* shows that were broadcast during Baltic Week. See, for instance, DRA, Schriftgutbestand Fernsehen: 'Deutscher Fernsehfunk Ostseestudio Rostock am 20.4.1970' (number 18 in the series, broadcast on 4 July 1970). This programme was broadcast in five other socialist countries: the Soviet Union, Poland, Hungary, the CSSR and Bulgaria. *Mitteldeutsche Neueste Nachrichten* (Leipzig), '"Klock acht" in der Hafenbar' (21 December 1970). See also Eckart Kroneberg, 'Seefahrt', *Der Tagesspiegel* (7 July 1970).

[92] DRA, Schriftgutbestand Fernsehen, Vorbereitende Planmaterialien Unterhaltung: 'Programmspiegel zur Planverteidigung im Koordinierungszentrum Unterhaltung (dem Plan 1969 nachgestellt): „Die Parteibeschlüsse verpflichten uns."' (2 July 1968), p. 39.

[93] DRA, Schriftgutbestand Fernsehen, Vorbereitende Planmaterialien, HA Unterhaltung: 'Die Programmtätigkeit des Deutschen Fernsehfunks 1969, Teil 1' (25 October 1968).

Karl-Marx-Stadt, as well as Warsaw, Budapest, Moscow, Cracow and Prague. As one of the first entertainment shows broadcast in colour from 1969, each show presented, as in the preceding series, the socialist transformation of the local heimat, its citizens, and the changes in work and leisure. Unlike its predecessor, however, the emphasis in this series was not on the combination of small-town idyll and economic and cultural progress. 'Songs of a Big City' emphasized bustling urbanity, the fulfilment of consumer desires, modern living and nightlife, and the sensuality of urban life.

On 17 April 1971, the DFF broadcast 'Songs of a Big City – Karl-Marx-Stadt'. The show was generously advertised in the television journal *FF Dabei*, whose front cover featured an image of the 'Street of Nations', the town's newly built centre. A three-page article, richly illustrated with stills from the film, advertised the programme and its main themes. The article directed readers' attention to the producers' declared intentions: to highlight the transformation from a working-class 'city of soot' to a modern socialist metropolis, which attested to the development and growth of the socialist human being disconnected from the fascist past.[94] The old 'Saxon Manchester' had been left behind, and the proletariat had needed only twenty-five years to overcome the city's past and create one of 'Europe's most modern and most beautiful industrial cities'.[95] Its 'traces of stones' bore witness to the socialist heimat for all citizens.

The programme itself enjoyed good (though not spectacular) audience ratings, and was disproportionately popular among workers.[96] The first and penultimate scenes featured skydivers, who, followed by the camera, approached the city from the air, displaying the city's expansive modern architecture, the linear, structured layout of its streets, and the factories within it. The city's architectural modernity constituted a major theme. In one scene, for instance, Heinz-Florian Oertel interviewed the city's director of construction standing behind a model of the centre's construction plan. The scene was followed by a montage, featuring close-ups of models of particular buildings from the director's plan, historic film showing the building's construction, and images of the completed building. Another central theme was working life, especially in the city's modern, innovative

[94] DRA, Schriftgutbestand Fernsehen, Vorbereitende Planmaterialien, HA Unterhaltung: UH B 68. 'Szenarium „Schlager einer Großen Stadt", Karl-Marx-Stadt' (hereafter 'Szenarium KMS'), p. 3.

[95] *FF Dabei* 16 (1971), 'Schlager einer Großen Stadt' 4–7, 28, and title page.

[96] The programme gained 40.9 per cent of the audience figures. This was an average rating for a large entertainment programme, but an excellent one given its informative content. DRA, Schriftgutbestand Fernsehen: 'Abteilung Zuschauerforschung. H081-03-02/0062, Ergebnisse der 9. Sofortresonanz vom 20.4.1971', pp. 6–9.

industries and places of learning. One reportage, for instance, featured the director of the Malimo plant. Malimo was a synthetic fibre used for clothing which, the programme informed its viewers, had been invented in Karl-Marx-Stadt and was exported throughout the world.

If in the 1950s heimat had defined itself against consumerism, this was decidedly no longer the case by the late 1960s. Consumerism was omnipresent in Karl-Marx-Stadt. To the swing of Kubiczek's music, the opening credits were shown against pictures of the pulsating city by night, with fuzzy shots of moving headlights, and a battery of individual and superimposed shots of neon advertisements which changed so fast that the viewer could not possibly see – let alone remember – them all. In the programme, shoppers were frequently seen coming out of shops or walking past richly decorated shop windows. At night, the city offered every kind of entertainment imaginable, including bars and cafés. This reflected another main theme, the leisure opportunities offered by the town and its environment to a deserving workforce. The programme repeatedly highlighted the international sporting achievements of the town's citizens, and showed clips of the beautiful heimat surrounding the city. Against images of the nearby hills, the Kriebstein dam and Augustus Castle, the popular duo Monika Hauff and Klaus-Dieter Henkler sang joyfully and admiringly: 'Everything around me I like very much.'[97]

Just as in other shows, the locality served as a metaphor for the GDR. The city's sporting successes, its export achievements, and its offers of consumption and leisure were the achievements not just of the town's citizens but of the entire GDR. If the construction master plan was being faithfully and effectively realized in this town, this was evidence that it would yield similarly rich results for the entire country. The message was underlined by the metaphor of spring and of flowers. In one musical offering, Helga Zerrens sang against a background showing everyday scenes of happy children playing and grown-ups laughing, much of it filmed in soft focus. 'Spring', she sang, 'the town breathes again, and differently than ever before.' Zerrens sang about the light and the flower-scented air in the backyards of the freshly painted houses, bringing smiles to every child's face. The roses planted in front of the houses were particularly significant, so Oertel informed the viewers, for they had been planted by children from Maidanek, Lidice, Auschwitz and Coventry. 'Songs of a Big City' was a feel-good film, about the youthful socialist community of people that had already been created, and which had left its grey, inhumane past behind.

---

[97] 'Alles um mich her, gefällt mir sehr.'

'Songs of a Big City' tried to appeal to the viewer not simply through evidence, but also through the senses. The TV journal left viewers in no doubt as to why these were crucial to the film: 'Whenever there is talk of change, of the transformation of the individual, then if you want to comprehend it completely and feel it you should go through the streets of this town and look its citizens in the eye.'[98] This sentiment was repeated almost verbatim in the film's voiceover introducing a series of shots of socialist individuals in the 'Street of Nations' going about their business in bright sunshine. The sensuousness of this experience was further encouraged by frequent references to smells, and the suggested abundance of culinary delights available in the city and its environs. Most importantly, the senses were mobilized by the use of bright colours. Helga Zerrenz, for instance, sang her song in a bright yellow outfit, with many of the children playing around her in jumpers of similarly strong colours. Frequent shots of roses or bushes against a backdrop of modern architecture presented a metaphor for a blossoming GDR, but they also provided strong colours to enliven camera shots of monochrome buildings. The abundance and promise of the socialist heimat were not just to be seen, they were to be felt and experienced by every viewer.[99]

In the 1960s, most television programmes were not related to the theme of heimat. However, at a time when it was common for prime-time entertainment shows to attract ratings of 22 per cent or less,[100] the DFF discovered the popularity of heimat. With 23.2 per cent regular and 55.3 per cent occasional viewers, 'Songs' had a well above average reach of almost 80 per cent of all viewers. Remarkably (and unusually), the programme's quality ratings were relatively unaffected by viewers' ability to receive Western television. In the mid-1960s, 'Songs' was the GDR's fourth most popular entertainment show.[101] Meanwhile, *Klock 8* received even higher ratings, and became the longest-running entertainment show on GDR television.

The popularity of entertainment shows related to heimat does not necessarily mean that the messages which television producers 'encoded'

---

[98] *FF Dabei* 16 (1971), 'Schlager einer Großen Stadt', 7.
[99] Szenarium KMS, pp. 3–3a.
[100] These ratings were recorded for shows such as 'Melodic Meanderings' (*Melodie auf Abwegen*), which was watched by only 11 per cent of those able to receive West German television! DRA H074-00-02/0015, Deutscher Fernsehfunk, methodisches Kabinett. Berlin, im November 1965: Das Unterhaltungsprogramm des DFF im Urteil seiner Zuschauer im September 1965 (hereafter 'DFF Survey 1965'), pp. 41–2.
[101] DFF Survey 1965, pp. 80–3.

were 'decoded' by viewers in the same ways.[102] Viewers could enjoy the socialist messages of community, but they could also watch 'Songs' simply because it was well made and featured good music. Nevertheless, through television the socialist heimat became part of most people's everyday activity, as most people, in town and in the countryside, watched these shows either regularly or occasionally, or read about them in their newspapers and TV guides.

Television was not the only means of constructing the socialist nation. Illustrated journals, magazines and newspapers also represented the transformations of the GDR and its citizens. With a print run of over 700,000 copies per week, the *Neue Berliner Illustrierte* (*NBI*) was one of the GDR's most popular illustrated journals. For the GDR's twentieth anniversary in 1969 it printed a collage of pictures entitled 'The beauty of my heimat' (Figure 7).[103] The two-page spread contained four colour photographs, the largest of which depicted the new Schwedt oil refinery. The development of the small community of Schwedt into a major industrial centre had been one of the key initiatives of the Fifth Party Congress in 1958. Schwedt symbolized the country's economic transformation as few other sites did.[104] To the left of this picture was one of Halle-Neustadt. This new town not only represented all the advances of socialist living: it was built for commuters to the nearby chemical works, hence the picture also contained associations with Bitterfeld and Leuna. Below these two images were photos of Rügen Island off the Baltic coast, and of Meissen on the Elbe in Saxony. The spread thus contained images from the north, south, east and west; it defined the country by the sea and its major river, through socialist transformation and historical continuity, modern production and traditional crafts (Meissen porcelain), work and recreation. The annotation at the bottom left of the page reinforced the pictures' message still further: 'Our love of the Heimat's beauty urges us towards necessary, creative changes to the landscape and its people, and embraces our concern for the peaceful development of our heimat, the GDR.'[105]

---

[102] Stuart Hall, 'Encoding/decoding', in Stuart Hall *et al.* (eds.), *Culture, Media, Language: Working Papers in Cultural Studies, 1972–79* (London: Hutchinson/The Centre for Contemporary Cultural Studies, University of Birmingham, 1980), pp. 128–38.

[103] *NBI* 40 (1969), 12–13. Its subtitle read 'The GDR – this is the heimat place ['heimstatt'] of the entire people. It is the socialist fatherland of us all.'

[104] See the excellent article by Arnulf Siebeneicker, 'Kulturarbeit in der Industrieprovinz: Entstehung und Rezeption bildender Kunst im VEB Petrolchemisches Kombinat 1960–1990', *Historische Anthropologie* 5 (1997), 435–53.

[105] *NBI* 40 (1969), 12–13.

7. 'Meiner Heimat Schönheit' ('The beauty of my heimat'), *NBI* 40 (1969), pp. 12–13. Pictures: top right: Schwedt (oil refinery); bottom right: Meißen; bottom left: the shallow waters of the Mecklenburg coast; top left: the New Town of Halle. Beneath the caption are lines by Johannes R. Becher: 'And should I praise the beauty of my heimat / I feel disquiet – how many lives long would I have to praise you in thousands of ways, an eternal hymn.'

The text on the bottom left explains: 'Johannes R. Becher wrote these lines for his, for our, heimat. However, he began the collection of poems from which these lines stem with the admonition: "The beauty of nature is not the only beauty within a country … The essence of beauty is harmony. The whole beauty of a country is also composed of a 'beautiful' history, 'beautiful' people, 'beautiful' human effort, the beauty of art and of language, and a 'beautiful' human order." When the poet Johannes R. Becher wrote this, our GDR, whose first minister of culture he was, was only a few years old. He was just able to experience the beginnings of this, our beautiful human order, our developing socialist community of people. Our love for the beauty of the heimat urges the active, creative transformation of the landscape and its people, encompassing concern for the peaceful development of our heimat, the GDR.'

By linking the sites of socialism with sites of history and memory, the party was not only constructing the GDR, but also attempting to endow sites of memory with new meanings.[106] The Schwedt oil refinery thus became more than a major part of the plan: it was also a part of the landscape that had been transformed for the benefit of all. Crucially, the *lieu de mémoire* of socialist construction also endowed the historic site of Meissen with new meanings: this represented a history which was brought to its fulfilment by the socialist transformation as exemplified by Schwedt, and could only be appreciated in its full glory in this new, socialist heimat. By representing Meissen in relation to socialist reconstruction, the city was transformed from a site of German memory into a site specific to the GDR.

A related way of redefining the GDR consisted in the iconographic representation of the socialist heimat. In the run-up to the GDR's twentieth anniversary, the *NBI* contained a series entitled 'Atlas DDR', to testify to the achievements of the past two decades and present a 'snapshot' of the present in a context of continuing dramatic transformation.[107] Every two weeks a different theme was represented and discussed, such as industrial output, agricultural production or trade with the Soviet Union. The two pages that formed the centrefold of the magazine portrayed the theme on a map of the GDR, while the pages before and after the map contained factual information and tables. In the map on the theme of culture, for instance, iconic images of theatres dotted throughout the land allowed readers to verify visually the cultural density and diversity of their country which were explained further at the back of the map. Other themes mapping the GDR heimat included recreational areas for weekend travel, vacation spots and folklore festivals.

The series started off with a general map of the GDR (Figure 8). Jostling for space on this map were icons of industrial plants (such as Bitterfeld), products (the Trabant at Zwickau, a doll representing Sonneberg), beauty spots (the Thuringian mountains), transport (shipyards in the north, an Interflug plane over Berlin), socialist monuments (the Berlin television tower, the Neubrandenburg house of culture), recreation (holidaymakers in the north, a rock climber in the Elbian Sandstone mountains) and historic monuments at Bauzen and Nordhausen: the GDR was the composite of all these local representations. So rich, colourful and dense were

---

[106] On buildings as sites of memory, see Rudy Koshar, *Germany's Transient Pasts: Preservation and National Memory in the Twentieth Century* (Chapel Hill: University of North Carolina Press, 1998), pp. 6–11.

[107] *NBI* 37 (1968), 18–19.

8. Atlas DDR, *NBI* 38 (1968), pp. 18–19.

these maps that they invited the eye to keep roaming over them, simulating an endless visual and sensuous discovery that could but hint at the diversity that was only symbolized upon these maps, the actual GDR heimat.[108]

The maps featured in *NBI* related to a tradition of heimat representation that had emerged in the nineteenth century. Alon Confino referred to them as 'identity maps', because even in their variety, iconographic representations provided a common denominator understood by all Germans.[109] The assertiveness with which heimat icons specific to the GDR were depicted represents a striking departure from the 1950s.[110]

'Atlas DDR' also featured iconic maps of each district, in relation to the rest of the country. The specific traits of each district were related closely to the GDR, with the nature of the icons on each district map carefully reflecting local sensitivities. For instance, Altenburg could have been represented by its imposing castle, a number of historic churches and the impressive Lindenau museum. But in the map for Leipzig district, Altenburg was symbolized by two playing cards, and this image struck a chord.[111] Altenburgers staked their local pride first and foremost on the claim that Altenburg was the home of Germany's most popular card game, Skat.[112] Icons that confirmed readers' own vision of their particular community in turn 'authenticated' the vast majority of icons and images of which readers had no first-hand experience. 'Atlas DDR' highlighted the richness and diversity of locality, region and district, and related them unambiguously to the greater whole, the GDR heimat.

Attention to local identities did not mean that all representations of the socialist heimat were equally popular. The depiction of Berlin as the cosmopolitan centre of the heimat that lacked for nothing might have induced pride in the GDR, but it might also have heightened feelings of jealousy in other parts of the country for the advantages enjoyed by the

---

[108] As the editors were careful to note: 'The problems and contentions of millions of consciously acting individuals, the diversity of the creative spirit that permeates the life of an entire people, this balance sheet of values created, cannot be made visible in this form of a purely factual representation.' *NBI* 38 (1968), 19.

[109] Confino, *Germany*, pp. 114–24.

[110] Confino, *Germany*, p. 141, figures 31 and 32. In these maps, the GDR's distinctiveness was asserted through sites of industrial production, while the historic icons in figure 32, such as the 'Völkerschlachtsdenkmal' in Leipzig, had an all-German significance.

[111] *NBI* 26 (1969), 20–1.

[112] Jan Palmowski, 'Local activists and renegotiations of heimat in the GDR, 1949–90', in Mary Fulbrook (ed.), *Power and Society in the GDR, 1961–1979. The 'Normalisation of Rule?'* (New York: Berghahn, 2009).

city.[113] Moreover, it is not clear that citizens accepted the new aesthetic of
the socialist heimat. In the issue celebrating the GDR's twentieth 'birthday',
for instance, the *NBI* included an image of a brown-coal mine in its images
of the heimat (Figure 9).[114] The ideal of beauty was underlined by the two
other images on the page, which depicted the Baltic Sea and its surf in
glistening sunshine. Associations of beauty and fulfilment contrasted
sharply with a photograph printed a few years earlier by the Altenburg
Friends of Nature and Heimat. Entitled 'Not the Sahara, but desolate land
near Lucka [in Altenburg county]', the image depicted the wasteland of an
exhausted brown-coal mine, palpably expressing the Friends' frustration at
the environmental scars left behind by lignite mining, which had turned
heimat landscapes into veritable deserts.[115] The aesthetics of the socialist
heimat were clearly not shared by all.

Taken as a whole, the representations are striking not just for the
consistency with which the national heimat was constructed from its
composite, different parts, but also for the sheer repetitiveness of these
depictions. In 1971, the *NBI* featured a weekly competition entitled 'Do
you know your heimat?', in which readers were invited to do a multiple-
choice quiz on different parts of the heimat which were also represented in
large centrefold images, including Rostock harbour, the brown-coal energy
plant at Boxberg in Lusitania, the Leuna chemical works, and Berlin.[116]
Once again, what is striking here is not simply the fact that industrial sites
and cities were represented as part of the GDR heimat, but the sheer
repetitiveness. Just from reading the *NBI* between 1969 and 1971, readers
would have learnt about Rostock's new economic function as the country's
major international port in general maps, maps of trade, maps introducing
Rostock district, maps of GDR traditions, amateur photographs, cross-
words, and write-in competitions. Radio shows reinforced these themes,

---

[113] The examples of resentment against Berlin are plentiful, and existed throughout the GDR's existence
(interview with Uwe Wieben and Karin Wulf, Boizenburg, 16 June 2003). The resentment of the
'provinces' was often articulated openly: see Eva Fleischer's statement at the Third Party Congress,
1956. Protesting against the 'lack of connections between the Ministry of Culture and the provinces',
she continued: 'But the province is the Republic! Do we not sometimes create the impression that the
Ministry of Culture is – I want to express myself very carefully here – to some extent, the cultural
department of Greater Berlin?' *Leipziger Volkszeitung*, 4 April 1956. ('Eva Fleischer, Hochschule für
Musik auf der 3. Parteikonferenz: Die Kunst – Waffe für den Sieg unserer großen Idee'.)

[114] *NBI* 40 (1969), 15.

[115] Horst Grosse, 'Der „Wartburg" und die Pleiße', *Kulturspiegel Altenburg Schmölln* (May 1962), 134–5.
Some of these discussions are recorded in ThStA, Deutscher Kulturbund Ortsgruppe Altenburg,
No. 23–1. Kulturbund Kreiskommission Natur- und Heimatfreunde Altenburg 1962–4.

[116] *NBI* 21–26 (1971), 24–6.

9. Collection of images showing 'The beauty of my heimat'. The ensemble of images was taken from the documentary 'You are mine', shot by Annelie and Andrew Thorndike for DEFA in 1969. These images celebrate the beauty of the heimat, a beauty that was to be found as much in the surf off Rügen Island as in the brown-coal mine at Klettwitz. *NBI* 40 (1969), 15.

with *Klock 8* and other television programmes adding to Rostock's socialist definition visually and acoustically.

The clarity with which individual towns, monuments and landscapes were endowed with particular meanings contrasts sharply with the previous absence of such meanings; given Germany's fragmented past, no state had been able to construct unambiguous sites of memory for the German nation.[117] By the late 1960s, citizens could be in no doubt about how Rostock, Berlin or Oberhof related to the GDR. Of course, this does not mean that individuals were unable to develop alternative, private meanings for these sites and how they related to the GDR and the German nation. The repetitiveness of the pictorial and graphic images, and the unidimensionality of their intended meanings, resulted in a deluge of images which created new spaces for individual selection, generating contexts for the construction of alternative meanings by the readership.[118]

The representation of the GDR as the socialist heimat contained a remarkable shift from representations of heimat in the first decade of the country's existence. The FRG no longer served as a direct or indirect reference point from which the heimat in East Germany was derived. Through its localities and its districts, the socialist heimat was a land of diversity, comfort and community. It transformed the GDR into a distinctive nation, with its own history, its own culture and its own trajectory into the future.

IMAGINING THE LOCAL SPHERE

If the party tried to create new festivals, this was not simply to popularize socialism, it was also to redefine the nature of the locality and region and invent their traditions. The GDR's regions and localities were redefined in close relation to the 'heimat GDR', as distinctive components of it. The very best the new socialist culture had to offer was presented annually at the national level, in the workers' festivals (*Arbeiterfestspiele*), inaugurated in 1959 as part of the Bitterfeld Path. Highlights of this showcase for the new socialist national culture included a joint performance by the Leipzig

---

[117] Etienne François and Hagen Schulze (eds.), *Deutsche Erinnerungsorte I–III*. Vol. 1, 4th edn (2003); vols. 2, 3, 2nd edn (2002) (Munich: C. H. Beck). See also Andreas Fahrmeir, 'Discussion', *German History* 23 (2005), 405–11.

[118] Bernd Weisbrod, 'Medien als symbolische Form der Massengesellschaft: Die medialen Bedingungen von Öffentlichkeit im 20. Jahrhundert', *Historische Anthropologie* 9 (2001), 270–83; here 275. Weisbrod wrote this article with the Federal Republic in mind, but it is also particularly relevant to the GDR.

Gewandhaus orchestra and the workers' choir of the Riesa steelworks (1959), the first conference of worker writers (1960), and the first performances of workers' operas (1961).[119] The festivals also acted as a national folklore competition. The Fourth Workers' Festival at Erfurt, for instance, included competitions for amateur film, choral music, wind orchestras, folk dance, classical dance, amateur dance orchestras, amateur painting, workers' theatre, cabaret and agitprop groups, and new cultural creations.[120] National festivals encouraged districts to assume a cultural identity in their own right. District finals selected those who would go on to represent the district at the 'national' workers' festivals. Participating in these district events became an achievement in itself, as individuals represented 'their' village, town or county and could be seen to do so by other participants, live or in local newspaper reports.[121]

Amateur sports developed into a further forum through which heimat was expressed. The 'spartakiadic games' (*Spartakiaden*), for instance, were developed as a GDR-wide youth athletics competition in which every county organized a sports festival to select its best young athletes to compete at district level. A further competition in the district selected representatives for the GDR-wide finals.[122] The spartakiadic games were much more than sports competitions; they were enriched by folklore and other cultural presentations, especially at the district and national levels.

The district emerged as an intermediary between the 'immediate' and the 'wider' heimat, as the widest forum for local culture. At the same time, the district developed into a cultural arena in its own right. The highlight of popular culture in every district was the annual 'Press Festival', sponsored by the respective SED district newspaper. Over a weekend in late June the choirs, folklore ensembles and hobby groups of the district would gather in the district capital to present a rich programme of concerts and exhibitions. District culture came alive for every resident to witness, while being linked to the socialist nation through the appearance of 'national' stars as seen and heard on TV.[123]

---

[119] *Kulturpolitisches Wörterbuch* (1970), pp. 22–5. See also Bundesvorstand des FDGB (ed.), *Geschichte des Freien Deutschen Gewerkschaftsbundes* (Berlin: Tribüne, 1982), pp. 463–7.

[120] LHA Schwerin, Rat des Bezirks Schwerin 4609: 'Entwurf Arbeitsplan 1962 des Bezirkskabinetts für Kulturarbeit Schwerin'.

[121] BArch-SAPMO, DY27 2953: leaflet 'Jüterboger Heimatspiele. Theater der Werktätigen im Deutschen Kulturbund im Zeichen der 8. Arbeiterfestspiele 1966'.

[122] See, for instance, *Freie Presse* (Karl-Marx-Stadt edition) (hereafter: *Freie Presse*), 'Kinder- und Jugendspartakiaden' (14 June 1965), 8.

[123] See, for instance, the programme of the Press Festival in Karl-Marx-Stadt in *Freie Presse* ('Heute für Morgen' supplement), 'Das sind unsere Pressefest-Programme' (19 June 1965).

Districts also became crucial to the ways in which local society and culture were publicized. In response to a chronic shortage of paper, in 1962 the licences of the Cultural League's GDR-wide heimat journals were withdrawn. Subsequently, there existed no GDR-wide journal directed at heimat enthusiasts. To make things worse, most local weekly heimat newspapers or journals, which had been abundant in the 1950s, had by now ceased publication. Local councils often reduced or refused subsidies which they had paid previously, and following collectivization local journals found it difficult to attract advertisers.[124] By 1965, most local publications had been abandoned,[125] leaving one single outlet for the representation of the locality: the back page of the district newspaper, which was produced in a separate edition for each of the district's counties, with local news and announcements.[126]

Reading the news of the local heimat in their district paper connected the majority of East German households during the 1960s and beyond. In 1965, a representative survey conducted in Rostock district found that 71.4 per cent read the district newspaper, with 27.8 per cent reading *Neues Deutschland*, and 52.9 per cent a different newspaper.[127] A different survey found that of all readers of district newspapers, 77.9 per cent turned first to the local news, with local classified ads constituting the second largest area of interest (57.9 per cent). Since two-thirds of men and three-quarters of women spent only half an hour per day reading the paper, readers scarcely had time to turn to other sections.[128] In a survey of the *Leipziger Volkszeitung*, 90 per cent of all respondents said they took a particular interest in the local news.[129] Most readers and households obtained most of their written news by keeping up to date with local events as reported in the district newspaper.

---

[124] BArch-SAPMO, DY27 1975. 'Zusammenarbeit mit der Bezirksleitung des Kulturbundes Erfurt 1959–62. Bericht über die Finanzrevision 1961', pp. 4–5.

[125] Dorothee Harbers, *Die Bezirkspresse der DDR (unter besonderer Berücksichtigung der SED-Bezirkszeitungen): Lokalzeitungen im Spannungsfeld zwischen Parteiauftrag und Leserinteresse* (Marburg: Tectum, 2003), pp. 123–30.

[126] In fact, many local papers ceased publication to avoid presenting a rival outlet to the district newspaper. *Strasburger Kreisecho* (24 December 1965).

[127] DRA, Schriftgutbestand Fernsehen, Programmanalysen: 'Auszüge aus dem vertraulichen Material des DFF der Umfrage im Stadt- und Landkreis Rostock in der Zeit vom 4.3.-9.3.1965'. As the survey was taken in and around Rostock, the proportion of those reading the district newspaper would have been under-represented relative to the district as a whole.

[128] Institut für Theorie und Praxis des Journalismus an der Karl-Marx-Universität (ed.), 'Analyse der Informationsgewohnheiten der Bürger der DDR durch die Massenmedien Presse, Rundfunk und Fernsehen' (4 September 1967), in BArch-SAPMO, Staatliches Rundfunkkomitee, DR 6 658: 'Vorschläge zur Erarbeitung einer Prognose für den Journalismus der DDR'. This is also quoted in Harbers, *Bezirkspresse*, p. 187.

[129] Ibid., pp. 178–9.

The interconnectedness between the district and the local heimat was further reinforced through guidebooks. The first GDR travel guide was issued in 1961,[130] and it was followed by a wave of regional guides that focused on the districts. In 1963, a hiking guide was published for the Thuringian district of Gera. Making their case for a guide to just one district, the authors argued that Thuringia had been riven by particularism in the past, a tradition which had extended even to the (unified) state of Thuringia after 1945. The break-up of Thuringia in the district reform of 1952 had thus overcome Thuringian particularism. The district of Gera (and, by implication, Suhl and Erfurt) represented a natural climax to Thuringia's fraught history.[131] Gera was endowed with historical legitimacy through Marxist dialectic, even if it is highly doubtful that many shared the guide's interpretation of Gera district as the culmination of Thuringian history.[132]

The Gera hiking guide reshaped the heimat not just through history, but, more importantly, by redirecting the wanderer's gaze. This is illustrated by the section guiding the hiker on the long-distance path between Zittau and Wernigerode. After the path entered the district near the Buchhübel, hikers' attention was drawn to the most challenging terrains of Germany's oldest race track. Moving on, they could then admire the Young Pioneer camp 'Mitchurin', a holiday resort catering, as the guide explained, at any one time for 800 children from the district and the Soviet Union. Walking past the 'stone rose', a natural phenomenon of 'rare perfection', they would eventually arrive at Saalburg. The guidebook explained the history of the local castle and the memorial to those murdered in 1945 on their trek from Buchenwald concentration camp. Eventually, wanderers would reach Burgk castle, the 'best example of medieval castle construction', engulfed by an agricultural co-operative located in front of it, and a children's home behind. A little further on, the Hohenwarte dam was a 'special expression of the socialist will to construct (*Aufbauwillen*)'; it would become Germany's largest dam and serve many of the GDR districts' electricity needs. In Bad Blankenburg, hikers could admire the town's newly constructed 'socialist suburb' as well as the ruins of Greifenstein castle.[133]

---

[130] *Reiseführer Deutsche Demokratische Republik* (Leipzig: VEB, 1961).
[131] Komitee für Touristik und Wandern des Bezirkes Gera/Deutscher Kulturbund, Bezirkskommission Gera der Natur- und Heimatfreunde, *Wanderungen im Bezirk Gera* (Leipzig: Brockhaus, 1963), pp. 6–10.
[132] On the evolution of Thuringian regional identities, see Palmowski, 'Regional identities'.
[133] Komitee/Deutscher Kulturbund, *Wanderungen*, pp. 18–26.

It is not surprising that a guidebook should praise the objects it describes,[134] but the frequency of the unqualified claim that a particular site is the best, oldest or most unique is striking. At times this could perhaps be proved, as in the case of the Buchhübel's race tracks. Other claims, however, were more dubious, such as the assertion that Burgk was Germany's best medieval castle. Gera, the guidebook implied, was a district which, though geographically the smallest after Berlin and Suhl, was rich with a diversity of sites of the highest quality, in not only the GDR but also (by implication) the FRG. By association, this increased the prestige of sites for which a distinctive claim could not be made but which were praised as being equally significant to the traveller. The guidebook, then, sought to endow the socialist heimat with an authenticity accessible only to the traveller able to 'discover' and 'verify' the uniqueness and beauty of the district's castles, furnaces, children's homes and construction sites.[135]

Images of the heimat were also presented in coffee-table books depicting individual districts in large-format photographs. With titles like 'Land between [the rivers] Saale and Elster' (for Gera district) or 'Between the Rennsteig [mountain-path] and the Rhön [mountains]', these books suggested – in fact invented – a natural specificity for the districts.[136] The latter publication, on the Suhl district, included pictures of factories producing internationally desirable goods, as well as Europe's largest potash works. The book also presented snow-capped mountains, theatrical productions at Meiningen and students at Ilmenau University. One photograph foregrounded two large crags (Figure 10). The Thuringian Forest was a landscape of gentle hills and valleys, but this picture suggested a landscape closer to the Alps, an image supported by its caption that the Forest was a site of 'glorious hikes and climbing outings in the mountainous heights of the Rennsteig [path]'.[137] When Herbert Roth and his ensemble began, in the 1960s, to 'Have a go at yodelling' ('Probier's mal mit Jodeln') in their songs, this no longer looked out of place in the Thuringian context.

[134] Jan Palmowski, 'Travels with Baedeker: the guidebook and the middle classes in Victorian and Edwardian England', in Rudy Koshar (ed.), *Histories of Leisure* (Oxford: Berg, 2002), pp. 105–31.
[135] On the guidebook's ability to offer distinctive meanings and authenticity, see Rudy Koshar, '„What ought to be seen": tourists' guidebooks and national identities in Germany and modern Europe', *Journal of Contemporary History* 33 (1998), 323–40.
[136] *Land zwischen Saale und Elster*, introduced by Armin Müller (Leipzig: Brockhaus, 1963). *Zwischen Rennsteig und Rhön*, introduced by Waltern Werner and Rolf Tröstrum (Suhl: Deutscher Kulturbund, Bezirksleitung Suhl, 1966). For another interesting example see Oskar Schwär and Karl Czok, *Oberlausitz* (Dresden: Sachsenverlag, 1961). This described a region within Dresden district, and thus articulated the point that Dresden was not simply a 'Saxon' district, but had become something new and different, founded upon but separate from its historical roots.
[137] *Zwischen Rennsteig*, p. 29.

10. The Thuringian Forest, presented through an image in a coffee-table book on the Suhl district. The caption reads '[Zalla-Mehlis is] a base for glorious hikes and climbing outings in the mountainous heights of the Rennsteig.' *Zwischen Rennsteig und Rhön*, introduced by Waltern Werner and Rolf Tröstrum (Suhl: Deutscher Kulturbund, Bezirksleitung Suhl, 1966), p. 29.

A cultural, geographic and economic diversity was thus invented for districts which were demographically and geographically quite small. This was crucial in the years immediately following the construction of the Berlin Wall in 1961. Here was a heimat, these representations suggested, whose consumer goods, whose landscapes and whose culture left no wish unfulfilled. Not only did this link the districts to leisure pursuits regularly undertaken by citizens, from athletics to choral singing: it also assumed a practical significance for those who wanted to 'escape' through travel. By integrating what people saw when they left their familiar environment into the ideal of socialist transformation, guidebooks sought to relate the unusual and the superlative to readers' everyday experiences of socialism.[138] This enhanced the everyday, while the diversity and the spectacular sights of the

[138] For further reflections on the relationship between travel and everyday activities, see Rudy Koshar, *German Travel Cultures* (Oxford: Berg, 2000), pp. 6–9.

districts made international travel redundant. Why travel further afield when unsuspected riches could be enjoyed in the heimat?

At the levels of the GDR and its districts, socialist transformations could be represented, but not necessarily verified. This was different at local level, where the nature of heimat and the transformation of its inhabitants could be gauged. Gerhard Gillmeister was one such inhabitant. He had just come fifth in the national competition for milking cows held at the Markkleeberg agricultural fair. His local newspaper, the *Strasburger Kreisecho* (Neubrandenburg district) printed, on the front page, a picture of Gillmeister and his dog, with a herd of cows grazing in the local landscape in the background. In a further article inside the newspaper, Gillmeister was portrayed as a member of his agricultural collective. Here, the emphasis was not on his outstanding achievement, but on his normality. 'This is Gerhard Gillmeister', the article concluded, 'a young person who knows his path in life. He is progressing in our socialist society ... does exemplary work and is fulfilled in his job. He is a young person of our society.'[139]

The locality became an important forum not just for the representation of workers, but also of women in socialism. In 1967, the Erfurt district branch of the Cultural League conducted a survey of its cultural groups. Among the district's heimat groups the only ones deemed to be particularly deficient in their ideological stance towards the socialist heimat happened to be those run by *Hausfrauen*.[140] If housewives were considered to be out of tune with the idea of the socialist heimat, the opposite was the case for Irma Forberg from Grossbrettbach (Gotha county). She was featured on the cover page of her local newspaper as someone who not only worked in her local agricultural co-operative, but also did her work in the pigsties with joy and love ('Lust und Liebe'). Irma contributed to her socialist community and was rewarded by it. She and her husband owned a car, a Trabant, and for her dedicated work she had been awarded a trip to Prague.[141]

Local news tended to be quite unambiguous in defining gender roles in relation to the heimat. The reason why Irma Forberg, according to the local newspaper, enjoyed a Sunday drive was that she could go out for a meal in the Thuringian Forest, so that for once she did not have to cook. In the summer of 1965, the Gotha county newspaper reported on the local Women's League's day-trip to the Unstrut river. Such trips, the article

[139] 'Einer der besten Melker', *Strasburger Kreisecho: Heimatzeitung für den Kreis Strasburg* (29 October 1965).
[140] BArch-SAPMO, DY27 2953: 'Vorläufige Übersicht über die Tätigkeit des Deutschen Kulturbundes auf dem Gebiet der Volkskunst im Bezirk Erfurt' (14 July 1967).
[141] 'Auf die Liebe kommt es an! Gruß u. Glückwunsch zum 8. März', *GHZ* (3 March 1965).

observed, gave great joy to the participants because they got to know 'our beautiful heimat'. All participating women, the story continued, worked full time, and in the evening they cooked and cleaned the house. Heimat offered respite for women so that they could continue to fulfil their multiple roles as domestic cleaners, cooks and workers. The notion was not used to influence gender relations and attitudes beyond the workplace.[142]

The heimat community was not defined solely by model characters like Gerhard Gillmeister or Irma Forberg; it was also characterized by its deviants, a point that was brought home by extensive reports in local and district newspapers about court proceedings. True to the ideal of socialist law, the articles focused on the socio-psychological factors that had moved the perpetrator to become deviant. Those convicted were usually people who either refused to work or had a tendency to excessive alcohol consumption, or both. These were people, in other words, who took no active part in the transformation of the socialist heimat, who did not use their free time 'sensibly', and who had refused to lead a proper (*ordentlich*) life.[143]

Stories about Irma Forberg, Gerhard Gillmeister or alcoholic deviants appear to relate to the heimat only in its socialist definition, according to which it was shared by all who took part in its transformation. There was little about these stories in themselves that pointed to a specific sense of place, or a distinct expression of tradition and local-ness. However, the ensemble of local stories like these, consumed day after day, invited readers to imagine their specific community through the individuals that formed it. Furthermore, Benedict Anderson has pointed to the ceremonial aspect of newspaper reading. Locals read these stories in the knowledge that only they did so, and that the narratives could be shared between them.[144] These were mostly private acts; hence it would be misleading to ascribe to these moments the capacity to build *communitas* in Victor Turner's sense, a term that is linked to the social experience of liminality and anti-structure.[145] Reading local news was not so much performance as ritual – a non-intentional way of acting that is not related to the actors' opinions,

---

[142] 'Burgenfahrt durchs Unstruttal', *GHZ*, (10 July 1965).

[143] See, for instance, 'Im Gerichtssaal notiert: Vier Monate Gefängnis', *Strasburger Kreisecho* (29 October 1965); 'Im Gerichtssaal notiert: Trauriges Heldentum', *Strasburger Kreisecho* (10 December 1965); 'Unser aktueller Gerichtsbericht: Rein äußerlich zwei Gentleman [*sic*]', *GHZ* (7 April 1965); 'Unser aktueller Gerichtsbericht: Die Rechnung ging nicht auf', *GHZ* (23 September 1965). Three out of these four cases were linked to excessive alcohol consumption.

[144] Anderson, *Imagined Communities*, passim, esp. pp. 32–6.

[145] Victor Turner, *From Ritual to Theatre. The Human Seriousness of Play* (New York: PAJ Publications, 1982), pp. 38–47.

but nonetheless manifests community and belonging.[146] By providing commonly shared narratives about individuals within the locality, the series of stories consumed in the local press on a regular basis did have an important capacity to affect the imagination of heimat, community and a sense of place, irrespective of the actual meanings which readers ascribed to these narratives.

The immediacy of the locality suggested that here, stories about socialist achievements could be verified; equally, however, at this level the problems that stood in the way of the ideal of the socialist heimat were manifest for all to see. In response, local newspapers encouraged controlled debate, in which individual failings could be exposed and those responsible could be challenged to justify themselves. One important source of irritation, throughout the country, was inadequate local availability of consumer goods and acceptable restaurant facilities.[147] Readers' letters and regular editorial columns in the local pages addressed issues such as uncollected rubbish in the streets (often referred to as *Schandflecken*, eyesores), or unacceptable waste produced by local companies. The local pages of the *Freie Presse* in Karl-Marx-Stadt, for instance, ran a regular feature called 'At Home', in which readers were encouraged to send in complaints about their own housing community. The newspaper reprinted these complaints about the state of individual houses, adding its own suggestions for improvements.[148]

The controlled nature of local debate was underlined by the frequently used metaphor of the house or the family. Reflecting on the first Altenburg pond festival (*Teichfest*), the mayor, Frank Grimm, noted that 'we Altenburgers celebrated with our guests as one big family our successes in the construction of socialism in the GDR'.[149] When the community of Ehrenhain, also in Altenburg county, celebrated its forest and park festival, the local newspaper reported that the villagers had been keen to prepare the village for the event, for, the paper noted, 'when one receives guests, one

---

[146] Susanna Rostas, 'From ritualization to performativity. The concheros of Mexico', in Felicia Hughes-Freeland (ed.), *Ritual, Performance, Media* (London: Routledge, 1998), pp. 85–103, here pp. 88–90.

[147] Complaints about hygiene standards, service and the quality of food in restaurants were commonplace, but perhaps the most striking complaint concerned one of the Altenburg restaurants which had booked in a wedding party and a funeral reception for the same room. *Leipziger Volkszeitung* (Altenburg), 'Post an uns – Post für Sie' (22 April 1966).

[148] 'Bei uns zu Haus', *Freie Presse* (Karl-Marx-Stadt, local section) (13 May 1965). See also, on the same page: 'Post an uns', which included complaints about vandalism, unfinished public works, and the existence of 'Schandflecken' (eyesores).

[149] 'Liebe Altenburger', *Leipziger Volkszeitung* (11 October 1966), in ThStA Altenburg, NL Kuno, Apel No. 765.

cleans the house particularly thoroughly'.[150] The socialist heimat provided for unprecedented intimacy. This allowed criticism to be understood as helpful and constructive, strengthening the family without ever challenging the unalterable fundamentals of kinship ties.

The immediate heimat, then, provided a context for individual behaviour, for putting things in order. It was also a sphere of community, emotion and intimacy, in which people loved their duties and cared for one another. In this loving context, the individual was also subjected to control: not by an anonymous state or its even more anonymous security services, but by the watchful – and loving – eye of the socialist community.

CONCLUSION

If it is true that the more modern the state and the more artificial its boundaries, the greater the state's need to invent 'national' traditions,[151] it is difficult to imagine a state that was in greater need of inventing 'national' traditions than the GDR after 1958. This was a state whose boundaries enjoyed little legitimacy and little popular support, especially after the construction of the Berlin Wall. It was governed by a political elite which its citizens had not chosen. Moreover, even if its designs for social and cultural transformations were not realized, the party's utopian ambitions to create the new socialist individual were real enough. The party desperately needed to invent traditions and identifications that were specific to the GDR.

To this end, the party initiated a comprehensive transformation of the cultural infrastructure and the creation of a new cultural language. Culture houses, 'spartakiads' and workers' festivals became an important part of the cultural calendar, well beyond the 1960s. Through such institutions, the GDR did acquire a specific cultural language and infrastructure with which millions engaged passively or actively, by attending events or participating in them. However, these institutions were a relative failure, since they were unable to generate voluntary activity. As socialist institutions devoted to prescribing the meanings of culture, it was difficult for them to accommodate the individual creativity which voluntary activity by its nature generated. Moreover, they were closely linked to the utopia of a new socialist society, a profoundly rational project. Assuming the inevitability of

[150] 'Ein Dorf rüstet zum Fest', *Leipziger Volkszeitung* (11 June 1966), in ThStA Altenburg, NL Kuno, Apel No. 765.

[151] On the proportionally greater need for newly constructed states to invent their traditions, see Eric Hobsbawm, 'Mass-producing traditions: Europe, 1890–1914', in Eric Hobsbawm and Terence Ranger (eds.), *The Invention of Tradition* (Cambridge University Press, 1983) pp. 263–308.

historical materialism, they simply could not generate a popular appeal that could entice the non-socialist majority of the population into cultural activity. To those affected by the social and economic dislocations of the late 1950s and the early 1960s, the idea that socialism was about to take hold of every individual was hardly appealing. Consequently, culture houses were normally only successful if they received substantial public funds, while press festivals and spartakiades also needed substantial financial and organizational resources. Judged by the SED's own ambitions, socialist national culture failed to become the mass phenomenon it was designed to be.[152]

The failure of successive cultural initiatives to realize socialism was the most important reason why the language and images of heimat became so central during the 1960s, and why they became pervasive in the representation of the GDR. Having discovered the emotional appeal of heimat in the early 1950s, political and cultural leaders embraced it as the sensuous vehicle through which the socialist utopia of the period could obtain greater popularity. The socialist heimat linked the limitless prospect of socialist change to the boundedness of the locality; it connected the harsh economic transformations of a rapidly industrializing society to the intimacy of the local, and provided the vocabulary for dissatisfaction and grievances produced by socialism to be expressed in the familiarity of the local environment. Heimat endowed the socialist design with a vocabulary and imagery of rootedness and 'primordiality' that was indispensable if citizens were to develop a love for their country.[153]

The contrast with the representation of heimat in the 1950s is striking. Whereas at that time the relationship between heimat and the GDR could only be alluded to, by the late 1960s heimat had become closely related to the representation of the state, and of the GDR as a whole. By the late 1960s, the party had constructed sites of memory that became universally recognizable and which described the GDR, and only the GDR. By 1965 the heimat had changed fundamentally in essence. It remained a source of authenticity, but had surrendered its ascetic connotations. In the socialist heimat, citizens lacked for nothing.

Naturally, the GDR never presented itself exclusively through the heimat. Throughout the period, the ideal of the GDR as a workers' and

[152] See also Esther Eugénie von Richthofen, 'Bringing culture to the masses: control, compromise and participation in the GDR. A case study of the *Bezirk* Potsdam', PhD thesis, University of London (2006), parts II and III.
[153] On the vocabulary of patriotism, see Anderson, *Imagined Communities*, pp. 141–5.

peasants' state continued to be prominent in image and text. The GDR also continued to derive its legitimacy and distinctiveness from the ideal of anti-fascism. The rose bushes from Auschwitz planted in Karl-Marx-Stadt not only featured prominently in 'Songs' but were also highlighted in the TV guide introducing the programme, thus directing the viewer's attention further to this item. But the relationship between heimat and anti-fascism had changed. Whereas in the 1950s heimat had reinforced the themes of anti-fascism and socialism, now socialism and anti-fascism reinforced the essence of the socialist heimat, the GDR.[154]

Twenty years after its creation, the GDR defined itself principally, though never exclusively, through the homeland and the national community. In this it resembled other maturing socialist states in which the appeal of a socialist utopia gave way to constructions of identity through nationhood. There was a crucial difference between the GDR and other socialist nations, however. The GDR's 'nationhood' had come to be defined not through humanist culture, but through heimat. Given that the GDR's cultural and historical peculiarities did not lie in its high culture but in the locality, this outcome was probably inevitable. It did mean, however, that the country's intelligentsia had comparatively little involvement in the construction of the socialist nation, in marked contrast to Romania or the Ukraine. Until the 1970s at least, the socialist heimat ideal could not be related to the cultural heritage of Goethe, Schiller or other German classics. Instead it was reflected in the contemporary work of Erik Neutsch, Erwin Strittmater and Bernhard Steeger, but in this canon 'Traces of Stones' was, perhaps, unique in its literary significance.[155] The socialist heimat invited few dissident literary works. When Stephan Heym or Christa Wolf engaged with socialism, they did so on many fronts – but hardly at the level of the socialist heimat. In the GDR, the homeland and the socialist nation never became a running theme of intellectual discourse as did the place of the homeland elsewhere in Eastern Europe.[156]

---

[154] This is apparent even in the portrayal of heimat in children's literature: Mareike Vorsatz, 'Unsere Heimat, die schöne – Agitation und Propaganda der „ABZ-Zeitung"', in Christoph Lüth and Klaus Pecher (eds.), *Kinderzeitschriften in der DDR* (Bad Heilbrunn: Klinkhardt, 2007), pp. 90–120.

[155] Whereas Neutsch's *Spur der Steine* reflected the changed aesthetics of heimat, which now included building sites and chemical plants, Strittmater's *Ole Bienkopp* focused on the transformation of the rural heimat. The same is true of Bernhard Steeger's novel *Menschenwege*, a highly popular heimat novel that never made it into the literary canon outside the GDR, but was the basis for Steeger's own TV adaptation, the popular drama *Märkische Chronik*, discussed in Chapter 4. Bernhard Steeger, *Menschenwege* (Halle: Mitteldeutscher Verlag, 1974); Erwin Strittmater, *Ole Bienkopp* (Berlin: Aufbau Verlag, new edn, 2005).

[156] Verdery, *National Ideology*. Farmer, *Ukrainian Nationalism*, pp. 101–14.

PART 2

Public and private transcripts

In 1971, Erich Honecker succeeded Walter Ulbricht as head of the Socialist Unity Party (SED), promising to be more mindful of the needs of the population. Under Honecker's rule, which lasted until 1989, the party continued to define 'national' identity through the socialist heimat. The party's emphasis on the population's well-being and contentment meant that the dichotomy between the socialist heimat ideal and the party's disrespect for popular heimat practices became untenable. Subsequently, heimat practices were welcomed as expressions of the country's diversity, the richness of its heritage and the joy of living in the GDR. Consequently, the Honecker period was characterized by a veritable boom in heimat practices. Local festivals celebrating the heimat abounded, local historians received unprecedented outlets for the dissemination of their work, and people concerned with the environment were encouraged to see to specific projects. Not only were the dedicated few encouraged in their heimat practices; through the GDR-wide annual participatory campaign 'Join In!', every individual was urged to express her or his love for the heimat through action. Heimat no longer simply represented the socialist nation, it became constitutive of socialist citizenship.

The party's diverse attempts not only to appropriate the representation of heimat, but also to affect popular practices and their meanings, raise questions fundamental to GDR scholarship. To what extent was the party able to realize its ambitions, and affect individual behaviour and values? Conversely, from the citizens' perspective, what did participation in state-sponsored activities – in socialist heimat festivals, the watching of heimat television shows and the participation of millions in 'Join In!' – indicate about popular acceptance of the regime? Could such activities constitute evidence of a 'normalization' (Fulbrook) of life in the GDR and a stabilization of the regime? Part 2 examines these questions about the relationship between the party and the citizens by focusing on aspects of wide popular participation in state-sponsored activities related to the socialist heimat. It complements this perspective with a focus on an area of significant tension, the environment, to see how citizens expressed their growing disillusionment with the physical well-being of the heimat, and how the party responded to this. In sum, this part of the book explores how state and party continued to develop and popularize the socialist ideal of heimat, and how citizens engaged in the heimat developed their own meanings, which differed from, and often sharply contrasted with, those of the party.

James C. Scott has investigated how the 'dominant' (in this case the party) had an impact upon the 'subalterns' (here, those active in relation to the heimat), and what strategies subalterns employ to avoid the demands of the dominant. With close reference to Scott's work, I shall argue that the socialist heimat is best understood as part of the public transcript of social- ism to which citizens had to subscribe. In expressing their activities through the language of the socialist heimat, individuals did not necessarily accept its meanings and identify with socialism and the GDR. The 'subalterns' developed meanings that were quite separate from the party, connotations which reinforced the identity of the locality and region against the state.

The socialist heimat ideal became important in masking the party's power. By relating its ideal of the socialist heimat to wide areas of popular practice, the party reinforced its message that its power reached every aspect of life; that socialism was there to stay. Through the transcript of the socialist heimat, the party provided a language through which practices, individual initiatives and wider concerns could be articulated, albeit within confines set by the party. This form of communication functioned remark- ably well under duress, even when environmental destruction gave rise to increasingly widespread frustration. Remarkably, most of those concerned about the environment continued to express their concerns through the official language of the socialist heimat. However, the party's use of heimat to mask its power came at the cost of the original goal of the socialist heimat: the creation of popular identifications with socialism and the GDR. Providing the opportunity for individuals to pursue their interests did little to over- come frustration over the state's inability to address core concerns. Moreover, the ability of individuals to develop their private meanings beneath their public acclamations of the socialist identity undermined precisely the 'national' identity which the socialist heimat was intended to generate. Thus, the socialist heimat helped maintain socialist rule by asserting that the party's domination was unavoidable. However, in theory and practice the socialist heimat remained sufficiently flexible for citizens to develop subjectivities and engage in practices that were distinct from the party's ideals of patriotism and nationhood.

CHAPTER 4

Heimat and identity in the Honecker era

INTRODUCTION

Whereas in the 1960s the socialist heimat became central to the party at the level of representation, in the Honecker era the party tied the socialist heimat closely to popular culture. State and party endorsed a proliferation of heimat-related activities, including local history research, folklore, the organization of local festivals and conservation. The socialist heimat also became a leitmotif in television, illustrated journals, and district as well as GDR-wide newspapers. Local activities, regional diversity and tradition were encouraged as goods in themselves, as increasing the GDR's cultural riches. The socialist heimat became an important part of the 'public tran-script' between state and party on the one hand, and the citizens on the other.

James C. Scott has employed the concept of the public transcript to refer to an 'open interaction between subordinates and those who dominate'.[1] It is predicated on the communication between these groups, which can be verbal, written or symbolic. The public transcript is complemented by the 'offstage' behaviour of groups, the 'hidden' transcript, in which subordi-nates develop meanings that are obscured from the dominant. In following the public transcript while also developing hidden transcripts, especially where there is a strong imbalance of power, subordinates create import-ant levels of agency for themselves. Subordinates' compliance with the public transcript enables resistance at the level of the hidden transcript. The two levels are never entirely separate, according to Scott; rather, there is a constant conflict between 'onstage' and 'offstage' behaviour at the level he termed 'infrapolitics'. This is the level at which subordinate groups try to test the limits of the authorities' control, evading the public transcript as far as possible without openly challenging it.[2]

---

[1] Scott, *Domination*, p. 2.   [2] Ibid., chs. 1 and 7; Scott, *Weapons*, Introduction and ch. 1.

During the Honecker era, the party's ideal of the socialist heimat as forming a space in which citizens could identify with the GDR is best analysed in terms of the public transcript, since the notion of the socialist heimat reached far beyond ideology to include a range of popular discourses and practices. The term is also useful because these discourses were never 'free': they were not open-ended debates, but interactions whose parameters were always set by the party. Through the public transcript of the socialist heimat, the party sought to determine how heimat was represented and discussed in public and private discourse, and how it should be reflected in popular practice.

The practical significance of heimat activities changed in the late 1960s and the early 1970s. In 1966, workers were given every second Saturday off, and in the following year, the five-day working week was introduced.[3] As a result, the popular demand for recreational facilities and cultural provisions – especially for regional weekend tourism – increased sharply. Previously, traditional heimat activities had been sponsored mainly by the vacation centres along the north coast, the Thuringian Forest, the Harz mountains, and southern Saxony. Now, as demand for the provision of leisure opportunities that allowed citizens to use their free time 'sensibly' rose in absolute numbers, holidaymakers travelled across all fourteen districts outside Berlin. In response to the pressure on lakes and forests by weekend excursionists, district authorities became acutely aware that they needed to provide educational facilities as well as excursions to the immediate heimat. Hiking enthusiasts were encouraged to put up signposts along footpaths, ornithologists provided information on the local bird population, and local aquarists presented facts on the fish in surrounding rivers and lakes. Even local monuments and castles, long eschewed as memorials to a feudal past, came to be appreciated as tourist destinations.[4] The growth of leisure time increased both the demand for and the supply of local heimat activities.

At the Eighth Party Congress on 15–19 June 1971 the SED's new General Secretary, Erich Honecker, asserted that the GDR was now on a course towards a 'developed socialist society', the ultimate realization of communism in social, economic and cultural relations. Honecker emphasized that at the heart of these developments stood the individual, since the purpose of

---

[3] Staritz, *Geschichte der DDR*, p. 232. On the impact of the introduction of the five-day working week on popular culture more generally, see von Richthofen, 'Bridging culture', pp. 193–201.

[4] BArch-SAPMO, DY27 3639: 'Konzeption: Vorschlag zur Entwicklung des Naherholungsgebietes Kohrener Land [*c.* 1966]'. BArch-SAPMO, DY27 3696: 'Protokoll der Arbeitsausschußsitzung vom 15.3.1967 in Waren, Weinbergschloß' (on the proposed creation of the Müritz Lakes Nature Reserve).

socialism was to serve the well-being and joy of the people. On this basis, the Eighth Party Congress directed the party's attention to 'the people's material and cultural standard of living'.[5] Scholars have commented widely on the party's subsequent efforts to improve the supply of consumer goods, the provision of housing and the quality of social provisions. Just as important, however, was the Congress's emphasis on the cultural fulfilment of the individual. Individual cultural engagement was subsequently promoted less in an attempt to create a uniform 'national culture', than to promote individual tastes and desires.

Endorsed by the party, cultural practices inspired by heimat became central to popular culture as never before. Heimat constituted a principal framework of reference for television shows, allowing the party to construct an ideal type of the socialist homeland, which it also tried to convey in the press. The uniqueness of the socialist homeland also served as a reference point for other pastimes, such as folklore, local history research and festivals. The party's attempts to link the socialist heimat to popular practices defined the public transcript in a variety of ways, and this makes it particularly important to ask what meanings individuals attributed to their own practices. Only by exploring such meanings can we ascertain whether the party was successful in realizing its ultimate goal: using heimat to awaken in the socialist citizen a love for the GDR.

This chapter begins by investigating the ideological construction of the socialist heimat during the 1970s and 1980s. The following section shows, through the example of television, how the party's ideal of heimat entered the public transcript. I shall then summarize a variety of other ways in which the socialist heimat became part of popular culture. Finally, I shall examine some of the meanings which the party attempted to promote at the grass roots, and how individuals in turn related to the public transcript of the socialist heimat. I shall argue that, although the proliferation of heimat culture was predicated on encouragement by state and party, the motivations for heimat activities were essentially locally based. Citizens and communities developed their own meanings for heimat, which they expressed – only thinly disguised – in the language of the party's official transcript.

---

[5] 'Entschließung des VIII. Parteitages der Sozialistischen Einheitspartei Deutschlands', in *Protokoll der Verhandlungen des VIII. Parteitages der Sozialistischen Einheitspartei Deutschlands, 15.-19. Juni 1971 in der Werner-Sellenbinder-Halle zu Berlin*, vol. II (Berlin, 1971), p. 296. For GDR accounts of the Eighth Party Congress, see Gerhard Roßman *et al.*, *Geschichte der Sozialistischen Einheitspartei Deutschlands: Abriß*, Institut für Marxismus-Leninismus, (Berlin: Dietz, 1978), pp. 555–64. Heinz Heitzer *et al.*, *DDR: Werden und Wachsen. Zur Geschichte der Deutschen Demokratischen Republik*, Akademie der Wissenschaften der DDR/Zentralinstitut für Geschichte (Berlin: Dietz, 1974), pp. 518–21.

HEIMAT AND HERITAGE

At the Eighth Party Congress in 1971, the new SED secretary, Erich Honecker, reaffirmed the party's commitment to raise both material and cultural standards of living. At the Congress itself Honecker offered few details about how this was to be achieved. Nevertheless he broke new ground in his emphasis on individual welfare as the ultimate object of socialism in ideology and practice, a focus which would be retained in the SED's political programmes for the 1970s and 1980s. Honecker committed the party to wide-ranging social welfare policies and improvements in the provision of consumer goods. Since under Ulbricht the construction of housing had lagged behind every other industrialized country east and west of the Iron Curtain,[6] the party put particular emphasis on the construction of new flats. Honecker promised in 1971 that 500,000 new flats would be built by 1975, in which year he announced that the housing shortage would be eliminated once and for all by 1990.[7]

Whereas the party's social policy priorities had been established by the end of 1971, it took the SED a few years to flesh out the implications of its cultural ambitions. At the party congress Honecker had advocated a new diversity of cultural expression to reflect the richness and variety of life in the developed socialist community.[8] It was soon apparent that the party's new priorities, as announced at the Congress, had fundamental implications. In a speech to the Cultural League's praesidial council, Hans-Joachim Hoffmann, the head of the SED Central Committee's cultural section, confirmed that art needed to represent the new complexity of life under socialism. It must reflect new socialist relations, but also the relationship between the individual, society and nature. According to Hoffmann, culture should represent the richness of the GDR's 'developed socialist society' in any variety of appropriate artistic genres and on the basis of the GDR's 'heritage' (*Erbe*).[9]

---

[6] Jay Rowell, 'Wohnungspolitik', in Dierk Hoffmann and Michael Schwartz (eds.), *Geschichte der Sozialpolitik in Deutschland seit 1945* (Baden-Baden: Nomos, 2004), vol. VIII, *1949–61: Deutsche Demokratische Republik*, pp. 699–726; here p. 702.

[7] Staritz, *Geschichte der DDR*, pp. 282–7.

[8] Rüdiger Thomas, 'Kulturpolitik und Künstlerbewußtsein seit dem VIII. Parteitag der SED', in Gert-Joachim Glaeßner (ed.), *Die DDR in der Ära Honecker: Politik, Kultur, Gesellschaft* (Opladen: Westdeutscher Verlag, 1988), pp. 589–608; here p. 591.

[9] BArch-SAPMO, DY27 952, ff. 45–9: 'Stenografisches Protokoll der Tagung des Präsidialrates des Deutschen Kulturbundes am 24. März 1972' ('On the development of culture following the Eighth Party Congress'). Opening statement by Joachim Hoffmann.

The Cultural League was quick to seize on the implications of the party's changed cultural attitudes. If Honecker wanted to address the individual in all his or her concerns, the immediate socialist heimat would become crucial. As Heinrich Gemkow, one of the Cultural League's vice-presidents, argued, this was the sphere in which social developments and the transformation of individual relationships under socialism were most immediately apparent. Only if individuals knew their heimat could the dialectical process between economic and social change on the one hand, and the continuity of the natural surroundings on the other, be truly appreciated.[10]

The party's desire to relate culture more closely to present cultural needs challenged the party's traditional preference for the humanist classics. As Dr Kahla, a member of the Cultural League's praesidium, noted, the Thuringian landscape could be experienced through a poem of world literature; but it could also be accessed through 'undemanding little heimat songs and the popular songs that we warble as we roam through forests and meadows'.[11] Both Herbert Roth and Johann Sebastian Bach were now part of the kaleidoscopic heritage of the socialist heimat of Thuringia. Karl-Heinz Schulmeister, First Secretary of the Cultural League, vigorously defended this new line: 'It seems to me that we have to put our main emphasis on tapping the rich possibilities [of cultural activity] which are presenting themselves for large numbers of people, and for this it is absolutely essential that we take individual activity seriously in all its diversity and stop belittling it ... For if I have understood the Eighth Party Congress correctly, what matters is the well-being of all citizens, hence it is important that they can pursue their inclinations.'[12] Whether it was a matter of 'high' or 'low' culture, individual passions and interests, and the culture of each locality, had to be taken much more seriously.[13]

The new aesthetic and cultural appreciation of the heimat had a further, 'high political' dimension. In response to the negotiations between the GDR and FRG governments leading up to the Basic Treaty of 1972, the party expected an influx of hundreds of thousands of West German visitors. This made it crucial that GDR citizens be firm in their socialist convictions,

---

[10] BArch-SAPMO, DY27 952, ff. 228–43: 'Sitzung des Präsidialrates des Deutschen Kulturbundes am 12. Mai 1972'. (The contribution of the Cultural League to knowledge of the socialist heimat and landscape.) Opening statement by Heinrich Gemkow.

[11] BArch-SAPMO, DY27 952, ff. 272–4: 'Sitzung des Präsidialrates des Deutschen Kulturbundes am 12. Mai 1972', comment by Dr Kahla.

[12] BArch-SAPMO, DY27 952, ff. 280–6: 'Sitzung des Präsidialrates des Deutschen Kulturbundes am 22. September 1972', opening statement by Karl-Heinz Schulmeister.

[13] BArch-SAPMO, DY27 952, f. 243: 'Sitzung des Präsidialrates des Deutschen Kulturbundes am 12. Mai 1972', opening statement by Heinrich Gemkow.

always conscious of how different they were from West Germans.[14] Encouraging individuals' private hobbies promoted their emotional attachment to the immediate socialist heimat, and also helped them realize their connectedness with the heimat of other socialist states. Hence citizens could not be led astray by misleading 'imperialist' arguments,[15] and they could also overcome nationalist stereotypes as millions availed themselves of visa-free travel to Poland and Czechoslovakia from 1972.[16] Although differences among these socialist nations would always remain,[17] the individual who was conscious of his or her socialist heimat would feel at home in, and identify with, any socialist society.[18] The socialist heimat provided for GDR patriotism and socialist internationalism in equal measure.

The widening of spheres through which the socialist heritage of the heimat could be appreciated was related to debates in literature and art. The heritage ideal had been important in the high arts since the late 1940s, as musical and literary scholars had argued with each other, and with their peers in West Germany, about the influence of the humanist classics on the arts in the GDR.[19] Honecker's demand in 1971 for art to relate more closely to the developed socialist society and its cultural aspirations aroused a new debate among literary elites.

In 1973, the influential cultural magazine *Sinn und Form* initiated a discussion in the course of which it became clear that the 'heritage' of the GDR related to all forms of classical literature, which, if understood correctly, could provide a new understanding of the present.[20] As one scholar put it, 'What socialism is and what it means for the individual … can only be fully grasped by those who know the experiences and evidence of history.' Indeed, all literature was significant inasmuch as it related to the present: 'Through its conscious, sensuous and immediate indebtedness to the heritage, literature relates to a sheer limitless spectrum of general, yet

---

[14] BArch-SAPMO, DY27 952, ff. 92–3: 'Stenografisches Protokoll der Tagung des Präsidialrates des Deutschen Kulturbundes am 24. März 1972', comment by Dr Müller, Premnitz.

[15] BArch-SAPMO, DY27 952, f. 245: 'Sitzung des Präsidialrates des Deutschen Kulturbundes am 12. Mai 1972', opening statement by Heinrich Gemkow.

[16] Staritz, *Geschichte der DDR*, p. 292. Roßman *et al.*, *Geschichte der Sozialistischen Einheitspartei Deutschlands: Abriß*, pp. 567–8. On the alarm raised by GDR citizens' behaviour abroad, see BArch-SAPMO, DY27 952, f. 107: 'Stenografisches Protokoll der Tagung des Präsidialrates des Deutschen Kulturbundes am 24. März 1972', comment by Klaus Gysi. BArch-SAPMO, DY27 952, f. 394: 'Sitzung des Präsidialrates des Deutschen Kulturbundes am 22. September 1972', opening statement by Karl-Heinz Schulmeister.

[17] Günter Lange, Heimat – *Realität und Aufgabe: Zur marxistischen Auffassung des Heimatbegriffs*, 2nd edn (Berlin: Akademie-Verlag, 1975), pp. 118–22.

[18] BArch-SAPMO, DY27 952, ff. 245–50: 'Sitzung des Präsidialrates des Deutschen Kulturbundes am 12. Mai 1972', opening statement by Heinrich Gemkow.

[19] Schlenker, *Das „kulturelle Erbe"*, passim.   [20] Haase *et al.*, *Die SED*, pp. 398–404.

historically determinable human actions and attitudes.'[21] From here it was but a small step for the party to determine that all culture and history contributed to the richness of the GDR's heritage.[22] Even traditions that appeared to have no link to socialism could be interpreted through socialist dialectic, whereby the relationship between historically determined processes and individual action could not be understood properly without an awareness of the complex interaction of material and social processes in the present.[23] All of the GDR's traditions, understood in the right way, pointed to socialism.

Once the heritage concept had been broadened and transformed into the party's central cultural strategy, it did not require a great conceptual leap to link the GDR's heritage to an expanded understanding of the value of heimat pursuits. In 1975, Horst Haase, section head at the Institute for Social Sciences at the SED's Central Committee, emphasized that the 'national' heritage included not just Bach and Caspar David Friedrich but also the GDR's buildings and monuments, its landscape and its relationship with other socialist societies.[24] Hans Koch, Chair of Cultural Sciences at the SED's Central Committee's Institute for Social Sciences, was pleased to observe that the new definition of heritage already mirrored the Cultural League's activities in practice. From coin collectors to heimat historians, the Friends of Nature and Heimat related history and culture in all its varying facets to every aspect of everyday life in the context of the social and political realities of the GDR.[25] As Kurt Hager, the Politbüro's chief ideologue, put it, 'The German Democratic Republic has a particularly rich endowment of cultural treasures of many epochs and peoples … It is an urgent political priority to ensure more than ever before that the knowledge, respect and love of this cultural wealth will become a deep fountain of socialist heimat-connectedness and proletarian internationalism.'[26] Broadening and

---

[21] Robert Weimann, 'Diskussion um Plenzdorf: Goethe in der Figurenperspektive', *Sinn und Form* 25 (1973), vol. 1, 222–38; here 235–6.

[22] BArch-SAPMO, DY27 423, f. 5: 'Die weitere Entwicklung der Denkmalpflege in der DDR und die Aufgaben des Kulturbundes' (1976), opening speech by Manfred Fiedler.

[23] Werner Kahle, 'Zur Einheit von Historischem und Aktuellem beim Aneignen des Erbes', in *Sozialistische Lebensweise und kulturelles Erbe: Auszüge aus einer Diskussion* (Berlin: Kulturbund der DDR, 1976), pp. 57–63.

[24] *Sozialistische Lebensweise und kulturelles Erbe: Auszüge aus einer Diskussion* (Berlin: Kulturbund der DDR, 1976), pp. 9, 11–23.

[25] BArch-SAPMO, DY27 957, ff. 254–353; here ff. 263–6: 'Stenografisches Protokoll der Sitzung des Präsidialrates des Kulturbundes der DDR am 18. April 1975', introductory remarks by Hans Koch. Koch's lecture is also printed in Hans Koch, 'Kulturbund und kulturelles Erbe', *Mitteilungsblatt des Kulturbundes der DDR* 2 (1975), 2–20.

[26] Kurt Hager, *Ergebnisse und Aufgaben unserer sozialistischen Kulturpolitik* (Berlin: Dietz, 1975), p. 39.

popularizing heimat pursuits became central to fulfilling the SED's principal cultural strategy from the mid-1970s, namely the realization of the GDR's cultural heritage.

Paradoxically, the emphasis on its own specific heritage created more, not less, ambiguity in the GDR's cultural relations with West Germany. Both countries now competed for the historical legacy of Prussia, Luther and the Reformation. In 1977, Dietrich Stobbe, governing Mayor of West Berlin, proposed to create an exhibition on Prussia's legacy in West Berlin. In response, GDR historians and cultural leaders openly laid claim to the legacy of Prussian history, which was no longer derided as purely negative.[27] Frederick the Great was now lauded for encouraging progressive traditions in art and literature,[28] and the Prussian reformers of the early nineteenth century because their bourgeois reforms accelerated a historical process that led to socialism.[29]

The emphasis placed on local history and local traditions was reinforced by a growing feeling, during the 1980s, that the GDR had come of age. Historians and ethnographers therefore called for research into the development of the country's popular traditions,[30] while historians also debated the importance of the regions in the historical development of the GDR since 1949.[31] Consequently, traditions were debated that had previously been avoided in public discussion. From the mid-1980s, for instance, the regional traditions of cis-Pomerania (the westernmost part of Pomerania that became part of the GDR) could be discussed openly; evidently, the party no longer feared that reflecting on Pomeranian traditions would stir desires

[27] Edgar Wolfrum, 'Die Preußen-Renaissance: Geschichtspolitik im deutsch–deutschen Konflikt', in Martin Sabrow (ed.), *Verwaltete Vergangenheit: Geschichtskultur und Herrschaftslegitimation in der DDR* (Leipzig: Akademische Verlagsanstalt, 1997), pp. 145–66.

[28] Günther Vogler, 'Staatsgedanke und Staatsrealität im absolutistischen Preußen', in *Preußen in der Geschichte des deutschen Volkes: Beiträge aus der Veranstaltung der Zentralen Kommission Wissenschaft des Präsidialrates und der Bezirksleitung Potsdam des Kulturbundes der DDR am 5. und 6. Juni 1980 in Potsdam* (Berlin: Kulturbund der DDR, 1981), pp. 31–8.

[29] Helmut Bock, 'Es gibt kein historisches „Niemandsland": Zu aktuellen Problemen des Erbes und der Tradition im Sozialismus von heute', in Helmut Meier and Walter Schmidt (eds.), *Erbe und Tradition in der DDR: Die Diskussion der Historiker* (Cologne: Pahl-Rugenstein, 1989), pp. 218–39; here p. 235.

[30] Ute Mohrmann, 'Sitten und Bräuche im Lebenszyklus der DDR-Bürger – eine volkskundliche Forschungsaufgabe', in *Zur Formierung der sozialistischen Nation: Forschungsbeiträge* (Berlin: Akademie für Gesellschaftswissenschaften beim ZK der SED, 1984), pp. 110–17. Willibald Gutsche, 'Platz und Aufgaben der Ortschronik in der geschichtswissenschaftlichen und geschichtspropagandistischen Arbeit in der DDR', *Heimatgeschichte* 11 (1981), 35–54; here 40.

[31] BArch-SAPMO, DY27 451: 'Konferenz der Gesellschaft für Heimatgeschichte zum Thema „Der Beitrag der Heimat- und Regionalgeschichte zur DDR-Geschichte 1945–61" am 11. und 12.11.1986 in Dresden'.

for lands now occupied by Poland.[32] During the 1980s, discussions of what constituted the GDR's 'heritage' became ever broader and more nuanced.

At an ideological level, however, the 1980s failed to provide new impulses to the heritage debate. In 1988, Horst Haase reaffirmed the significance of the GDR's local and regional traditions for an appropriation of the country's heritage. The GDR's heritage, he argued, was always related to the laws of socialist development in the present and future. This heritage gained its significance through the interrelationship between local diversity and love for the heimat on the one hand, and the socialist nation's position in the international community on the other.[33] The nexus between heimat, its heritage, and the love of socialism and the GDR persisted throughout the Honecker era.

The core ideals of the socialist heimat, and its relationship to state, fatherland and nation, remained intact from the late 1950s to the 1980s. Under Honecker, however, the party declared regional diversity to be a good in itself. Individuals no longer needed to pursue particular hobbies with a view to the way they expressed socialism – the very fact that they engaged with their heimat now served as evidence for the 'real existing' socialist community.

Moreover, the significance of the ideological confrontation characterized by the 'Prussian revival' does not lie in what this reveals about the GDR's appropriation of German history for its own legitimacy.[34] As previous chapters have shown, the GDR had defined and legitimated itself through local, regional and national historical traditions since its creation. The significance of the 'Prussian revival', and the heritage debate more generally, lay in the ambiguity it reintroduced into the consideration of the locality. The attention which West Germans paid to the appropriation of local traditions in the GDR moved heimat-related activities into the ideological front line.[35] Through the proliferation of their activities, folklorists, local

---

[32] It is striking, for instance, that the First Mecklenburg Folklore Festival of 1980 was held in the Pomeranian town of Stralsund. On the traditions of Pomerania, see Ulrich Bentzien, 'Probleme regionaler Volkskultur: Einleitendes Referat zum Thema des Symposiums', *JbVkKg* 29. Deutsche Akademie der Wissenschaften (Berlin: Akademie-Verlag, 1986), pp. 17–36; here p. 35.

[33] Horst Haase, *Erben für unsere Zeit: Tagung des Präsidialrates des Kulturbundes der DDR am 21. Januar 1988* (Berlin: Kulturbund der DDR, 1988), esp. pp. 9–11.

[34] Irma Hanke, 'Heimat DDR', in Hans-Georg Wehling (ed.), *Politische Kultur in der DDR* (Stuttgart: Kohlhammer, 1989), pp. 180–93; here p. 184.

[35] Paul Lauerwald, 'Notwendigkeit und Möglichkeiten der propagandistischen Nutzung der Ortschroniken', in *Platz und Aufgaben der Ortschronik bei der geschichtswissenschaftlichen und geschichtspropagandistischen Arbeit in der Deutschen Demokratischen Republik*, Heimatgeschichte 11 (Berlin: Zentrale Ortschronisten Konferenz der DDR, 1981), pp. 68–76. Gutsche, 'Platz und Aufgaben', p. 39.

historians, stamp collectors and other enthusiasts acquired an enhanced significance as guardians (and exemplars) of the GDR's distinctiveness. No longer just the preserve of local enthusiasts and cultural league activists, individual heimat practices became a central concern of the party.

'THE REPUBLIC OF GOOD HUMOUR'

If Honecker articulated new ideological priorities and concerns, these had to be communicated through television, whose popularity until the late 1980s endowed it with outstanding potential to affect the values and mentalities of its consumers.[36] According to Walter Fischer, all forms of human communication are narrative. We assess both fiction and non-fiction as stories, evaluating them for their coherence against the older stories that define our experience. Stories give order to human experience. They offer symbolic interpretations of aspects of the world shaped by history and culture, and in this way establish common ways of living and communicating.[37] From the 1960s, it was television that told stories to the majority of citizens in the GDR.

In the GDR as elsewhere television became a primary object of private consumption and leisure, and acted as a central reference point of social and cultural communication.[38] It had the potential to connect the individual to cultural codes that could be shared more widely.[39] The medium thus helped shape the symbolic worlds of GDR citizens and offered narratives that helped them order their social reality.[40] Television programmes formed a crucial part of everyday life, not just by defining what citizens did, but also by helping to shape how they saw and interpreted the GDR. If the party wanted to construct the GDR through the diversity of its heritage, it had to do so not least through television.

Entertainment programmes during the 1970s aimed principally at spreading 'good humour, happiness, relaxation, joy and sociability, well-being

---

[36] BArch-SAPMO, DY30 IV/B2 9.06 85: Abteilung Kultur, 'Ergebnisse der Umfrage zu einigen Fragen von Geselligkeit und Unterhaltung', pp. 3–4. These findings are also discussed in Chapter 3. Television remained the citizens' most popular leisure activity until 1987.

[37] Walter R. Fischer, *Human Communication as Narration: Toward a Philosophy of Reason, Value and Action* (Columbia: University of South Carolina Press, 1987), esp. pp. xi, 48–66.

[38] Thomas Lindenberger, 'Einleitung', in Thomas Lindenberger (ed.), *Massenmedien im Kalten Krieg: Akteure, Bilder, Resonanzen* (Cologne: Böhlau, 2006), p. 13.

[39] John Fiske and John Hartley, *Reading Television*, 2nd edn with a new foreword by John Hartley (London: Routledge, 2003), here pp. 60, 103.

[40] On these general points, see James Shanahan and Michael Morgan, *Television and its Viewers: Cultivation Theory and Research* (Cambridge University Press, 1999), pp. 192–4.

and good atmosphere'. In this way, entertainment on television could contribute to promoting and imprinting 'the socialist way of life, the socialist feeling of heimat, socialist internationalism and the moral values of the socialist community'.[41] Heimat became a crucial framework for fulfilling GDR TV's central ideological aims during the 1970s and beyond – to represent a 'republic of good humour' ('Republik der guten Laune').[42]

Emphasizing the role of heimat in television's offerings was a reaction to the low ratings of GDR TV. In the early 1970s, more than 80 per cent of viewers could receive West Germany's first television channel. This exerted a decisive influence on what East Germans wanted to see and how they saw it.[43] The fact that most potential viewers failed to tune in to GDR TV on any given night was particularly troublesome since the GDR sought to distinguish itself from the FRG in cultural terms. As a result, the director of GDR television, Heinrich Adameck, urged that programmes should become more diverse, popular and simple, and relate more closely to the wishes and experiences of the population.[44] In a word, television producers decided to respond to the Eighth Party Congress by making entertainment programmes more folksy (*volkstümlich*).[45]

Putting more emphasis on heimat as a framework for programmes killed several birds with one stone. Heimat culture was popular, while also responding to the party's emphasis on traditions that were specific to the GDR. Heimat programmes allowed the party to appeal to individual emotions and sentiments. The public could be influenced much more easily through entertainment shows than through political programmes, as entertainment shows could enter the subconscious and affect the individual much more deeply.[46] Moreover, heimat programmes were relatively inexpensive, and they were in plentiful supply. If the television makers were already burdened by the high cost of programmes that too few people watched,[47] this financial

[41] DRA Schriftgutbestand Fernsehen: Vorbereitende Planmaterialien 'Planangebot 1976', p. 1.
[42] DRA Schriftgutbestand Fernsehen: 'Deutscher Fernsehfunk Bereich Unterhaltung. Planangebot 1971' (Berlin, 5 July 1971). This quotation refers to a central theme (*Grundthematik*) of the DFF, and not just the entertainment section.
[43] DFF Survey 1965, pp. 10–16, 23–6, 72, 75.
[44] DRA Schriftgutbestand Fernsehen: Vorbereitende Planmaterialien Unterhaltung, 'Einige wesentliche Auszüge aus dem Protokoll der Komiteesitzung in Friedrichshagen zum Thema Unterhaltung (Nachtrag zum 12.11.70)'.
[45] DRA Schriftgutbestand Fernsehen: 'Programmspiegel zur Planverteidigung im Koordinierungszentrum Unterhaltung (dem Plan 1969 nachgestellt)'.
[46] DRA Babelsberg, DFF HA Unterhaltung, DDR-F Vorbereitende Planmaterialien: 'Referat zur ersten Bereichsparteiaktivtagung der APO Unterhaltung am 6.12.68', pp. 5–6.
[47] DRA Schriftgutbestand Fernsehen, Vorbereitende Planmaterialien Unterhaltung: 'Einige wesentliche Auszüge aus dem Protokoll der Komiteesitzung in Friedrichshagen zum Thema Unterhaltung (Nachtrag zum 12.11.70)'.

dilemma increased still further after the launch of the second television channel in 1969, and the steady increase in broadcasting time for both channels.[48] GDR TV desperately needed cheap, home-grown entertainment that was popular. For both ideological and pragmatic reasons, heimat became essential to television programming.

In 1973, GDR TV devised a new programme inspired by the farmers' market held at the Interhotel Panorama in Oberhof, one of the GDR's prestigious hotels built in the country's top mountain resort. The hotel welcomed nine hundred guests per week, including prominent artists and other celebrities as well as trade-union sponsored, working-class holiday-makers. Inside this vast hotel, guests were treated to a weekly Thuringian folklore evening. The event inspired programme-makers to develop an entertainment show on vacationing in the GDR. In a series of hour-long programmes to be broadcast in 1974, GDR TV aimed to show 'unobtrusively' the benefits of holidays in the GDR, which could be enjoyed and afforded by all. The show presented a land of plenty where guests could help themselves to traditional, hearty regional specialities, notably Thuringian sausage, ham and cold meats, served with beer in rustic steins, by staff in traditional folk dress. The stage was thus set for artists from the GDR and other socialist countries to perform songs about their heimat.[49]

First broadcast on Saturday lunchtime, when audiences rarely tuned in to television, the 'Oberhof Farmers' Market' immediately attracted such good ratings that it was moved, first to Sunday evening and then to the prime-time Sunday afternoon slot of 4.30 p.m.[50] So popular was the show that television producers abandoned plans to move it to other vacation resorts in the GDR.[51] What made the show popular was not the happy workers in the audience, but, as the show's producers found, the representation of

---

[48] By 1967, total number of hours broadcast had increased to 4,515 per year (up from 3,007 in 1960); that figure rose to 6,028 in 1970, 7,704 in 1980 and 8,706 in 1987. *Statistisches Jahrbuch 1988*, p. 325. Cf. *Statistisches Jahrbuch der Deutschen Demokratischen Republik 1968*, Staatliche Zentralverwaltung für Statistik (Berlin: Staatsverlag der DDR, 1968), p. 479.

[49] DRA Schriftgutbestand Fernsehen, Vorbereitende Planmaterialien Unterhaltung: 'Planangebot des Bereiches Musik für 1975. Berlin, den 15.6.73. Vorlage Nr. H. 52–73-3'.

[50] On 9 March 1974 it was broadcast in the difficult Saturday slot of 2.10 p.m., attracting a remarkable 7.6 per cent of the potential audience which gave the show a very good quality rating of 2.26. DRA Schriftgutbestand Fernsehen, Programmdirektion Zuschauerforschung, H081-03-02/0054: 'Ergebnisse der 11. repräsentativen Umfrage', p. 3. On Saturday, 2 November 1974, when the show had been moved to 4.30 p.m., it was watched by 30.4 per cent of viewers (and 40.6 per cent of SED members). DRA Schriftgutbestand Fernsehen, Programmdirektion Zuschauerforschung: H081-03-02/0054, 'Sehbeteiligung und Bewertung der Sendungen der 44. Woche', p. 3.

[51] DRA Schriftgutbestand Fernsehen, Vorbereitende Planmaterialien Unterhaltung: 'Jahresplan 1975 Annotationen: Samstagnachmittagsprogramm 1975'. DRA Babelsberg, HA Unterhaltung, Vorbereitende Planmaterialien: 'Programmangebot 1976', p. 31 ('Oberhofer Bauernmarkt').

'sociability, the socialist heimat and the socialist way of life'.[52] The 'Farmers' Market' continued as a heimat show, with a 'rustic' Thuringian decor, and the studio audience enjoying Thuringia's culinary delicacies. The show's geographical reach increased beyond the Thuringian Forest to encompass all of Thuringia, with each episode presenting a theme on the region's heritage, including Thuringian crafts, industries, and folklore.[53] Of the six annual programmes, one consisted of an outside broadcast from a particular place of interest, such as the long-distance walking path, the Rennsteig, along the heights of the Thuringian Forest (1978), or the Thuringian open-air farming museum in Rudolstadt (1979).[54] The 'Farmers' Market' represented, and thus helped recreate, the beauty of the Thuringian heimat for all viewers in the GDR, rendering Thuringia visually and emotionally accessible to all citizens.

The 'Farmers' Market' was one of a number of new entertainment programmes created in the early 1970s. 'Musik und Snacks' (Music and Talk), for instance, constituted a northern equivalent to the 'Farmers' Market', since it was originally conceived to make one of the GDR's major tourist destinations, the Baltic coast, available to all. First broadcast in the difficult Sunday morning slot at 11 a. m., the show's audience grew from 300,000 in 1973 to 1.5 million in 1975. As a result, it was rescheduled to the more popular Sunday afternoon slot, and this brought a further increase, to three million viewers.[55] In its new slot, 'Music and Talk' alternated with 'Berlin Original', also broadcast once a month, which aimed to 'entertainingly inform' on the capital as a city open to the world (*Weltoffenheit*). This was intended 'not to be a regional show, but a series from the capital about the capital for all viewers throughout the Republic'.[56] GDR TV was thus careful to strike a balance in its construction of GDR heimat traditions between north and south, while never forgetting the unpopular capital, Berlin.

---

52 The full quotation is: 'Das Grundmodell der Sendung hat sich beim Zuschauer bewährt. Die Absicht, auf anregende Weise sozialistisches Lebens- und Heimatgefühl zu vermitteln und Geselligkeit zu pflegen, bleibt erhalten.' DRA Schriftgutbestand Fernsehen: 'Programmplanung Prof. Dr Glatzer. Planangebot des Bereichs Unterhaltung/Musik 1976', f. 31.

53 DRA Schriftgutbestand Fernsehen, Vorbereitende Planmaterialien Unterhaltung. 'Planangebot 1976. Auskunftsblatt für Einzelsendungen', f. 31 ('Oberhofer Bauernmarkt').

54 'Oberhofer Bauernmarkt', *FF Dabei* 23 (July 1979).

55 Roman Brenner, 'Journalistische Unterhaltung – unterhaltender Journalismus', *Neue Deutsche Presse* (2 February 1978). See also Roman Brenner, 'Musik und Snacks: Eine 15-jährige Fernsehreihe und ihre Perspektive', *Neue Deutsche Presse* (11 November 1988). This was equivalent to a 21.7 per cent audience share for its episode broadcast on 21 December 1975. This was not an overwhelming figure, but it exceeded the drama in the prime-time evening slot, *Die Überlebende*, a GDR–Polish production, which attracted 17.9 per cent. (*Aktuelle Kamera* that evening was watched by 14.2 per cent.)

56 DRA Schriftgutbestand Fernsehen, Vorbereitende Planmaterialien: 'Planangebot 1976'.

Similarly, despite the declining importance of the 'Baltic Week' after 1971, GDR TV continued to air the popular variety show *Klock 8*, but complemented it with a variety show from Berlin ('A Potful of Colours', *Ein Kessel Buntes*), which presented the city's cosmopolitanism and openness.

Based on the popularity of heimat shows in the early 1970s, new programmes were developed in the second half of the decade which revealed the GDR's diversity beyond the traditional vacation spots. 'Everything Sings', broadcast four times a year from 1976, was a studio show in which lay choirs and folklore ensembles performed folk songs to varying images of the heimat. 'Travelling by Foot' (*Auf Schusters Rappen*), broadcast five times a year from 1978, used rambling as its central motif, as the presenter walked through the countryside to introduce the 'hidden charms' of areas that had not yet been discovered by the guidebooks.[57] Television 'verified' the heimat and influenced the popular imagination of the GDR in its regional diversity.

These programmes portrayed the GDR in rich and colourful variety, and aimed at providing plenty of diversions for a population desperate to travel further afield than Thuringia or the Baltic coast. With its folk songs and images from all parts of the homeland, 'Travelling by Foot' offered a 'televisual vacation' amidst the beauties of the heimat.[58] As one television critic noted, 'Why seek distant horizons when so much beauty lies on one's doorstep?'[59] Nevertheless, in these programmes one theme featured less and less until it disappeared almost completely from the spectator's view: socialism and its goal of formulating the new human being. There was little in the 'republic of good humour' that was specifically socialist.

Heimat shows were popular, and attracted disproportionately large audiences across the GDR. For instance, *Klock 8* was watched on 27 December 1975 by 54.4 per cent of viewers, with 49.5 per cent of those able to receive West German TV still tuning in on that day.[60] On 7 August 1976, the show attracted an audience share of 54.2 per cent, including 70.5 per cent of agricultural workers and 79.5 per cent of those unable to receive Western TV (against 47.6 per cent of those who could) watching it. Viewing figures were disproportionately low among the intelligentsia (29.2 per cent) and

[57] *Sächsische Neueste Nachrichten* (10 May 1989).
[58] Horst Pöhle, 'Eine erfrischende Landpartie zwischen Ostsee und Erzgebirge', *Freiheit* (Halle) (27 July 1988).
[59] Anni Geisler, 'Tele-Sicht: Schönheiten vor der Haustür', *Neuer Tag* (Frankfurt an der Oder) (7 September 1983). See also Peter-Michael Jachmann, 'Tele-Sicht: Ein Stück Heimat mit Herz nahegebracht', *Neuer Tag* (Frankfurt an der Oder) (3 September 1988).
[60] DRA Schriftgutbestand Fernsehen, Programmdirektion Zuschauerforschung, H081-03-02/0056: 'Sehbeteiligung und Bewertung der Sendungen der 52. Woche' (1975), p. 5 (x/1/52/75/11/6).

those aged between 14 and 25 (40.2 per cent). They were disproportionately high among those aged between 46 and 65 (62 per cent).[61] The 'Farmer's Market' received an audience for its 19 September 1976 show of 39.2 per cent. Broken down by viewer groups, above-average figures were recorded for those living in communities with fewer than 10,000 inhabitants (45.4 per cent against 33.6 per cent in larger towns), viewers aged over 65 (54.5 per cent), and viewers between 46 and 65 years of age (45.4 per cent). Predictably, audience figures were below average where Western TV could be received, but at 34.0 per cent the difference was relatively small. On a quality rating from 1 (outstanding) to 6 (bad), viewers awarded the show an outstandingly high 2.02,[62] with viewers of the intelligentsia and young viewers between 14 and 17 years of age giving it below-average marks (3.18 and 2.68 respectively), while working-class viewers awarded it an outstanding average rating of 1.72.[63]

In the mid-1970s, therefore, heimat shows were disproportionately popular among farmers and workers, those aged over forty-five, and those living in communities with fewer than 10,000 inhabitants.[64] But these shows also attracted viewers of all generations and classes, and they did comparatively well in areas with Western TV reception;[65] even there, the GDR's major heimat shows in the 1970s succeeded in attracting the majority of those who actually switched on the television set. Heimat programmes even appealed to the younger and urban population in remarkable numbers. To be sure, they did not appeal to a majority of these groups, but even among these viewers ratings were still above average for the afternoon slots when these

---

[61] DRA Schriftgutbestand Fernsehen, Programmdirektion Zuschauerforschung, H081-03-02/0056. 'Angaben zur Resonanz auf das Programm der 32. Woche', p. 6 (VIII/2/32/76/21/6).

[62] The high rating can be appreciated by relating it to the average ratings of the outstandingly popular *Polizeiruf 110*, which had uniquely high audience figures (1973: 53.1 per cent; 1974: 56.4 per cent; 1975: 56.5 per cent; 1976: 57.2 per cent), but whose quality ratings, at between 2.72 and 2.82, were well below those of *Oberhofer Bauernmarkt*. DRA Schriftgutbestand Fernsehen, Programmdirektion Zuschauerforschung, H081-03-02/0056, 'Angaben zur Resonanz auf das Programm der 36. Woche', p. 1a (VIII/2/36/76/21/6).

[63] DRA Schriftgutbestand Fernsehen, Programmdirektion Zuschauerforschung, H081-03-02/0056, 'Angaben zur Resonanz auf das Programm der 38. Woche', p. 7 (VIII/2/38/76/21/7).

[64] These trends can be generalized for the mid-1970s more generally, though the precise audience composition varied with each programme. On 2 March 1974, for instance, *Klock 8* received an outstanding rating of 61.9 per cent overall and 69.2 per cent among workers. DRA Schriftgutbestand Fernsehen, Programmdirektion Zuschauerforschung, H081-03-02/0054. 'Ergebnisse der 10. repräsentativen Umfrage', p. 24.

[65] At 34.0 per cent, audiences in areas with Western TV reception were not significantly below the overall average for *Oberhofer Bauernmarkt* on 19 September 1979. DRA Schriftgutbestand Fernsehen, Programmdirektion Zuschauerforschung, H081-03-02/0056: 'Angaben zur Resonanz auf das Programm der 38. Woche', p. 7 (VIII/2/38/76/21/7).

programmes were broadcast, and overall they were not far below the national average for GDR TV as a whole.[66]

Heimat shows were truly popular, in part because the optimism with which the heimat was portrayed appeared to correspond to viewers' expectations. In 1983, the television magazine *FF Dabei* printed a series of readers' comments about 'Travelling by Foot'. Viewers complained if they felt that too few pictures captured the beauty of the landscape, and praised the show if they considered the heimat to have been represented in all its splendour. Viewers who lived in the areas shown, or who had been there, had particularly high expectations that 'their' heimat must be positively portrayed.[67] The televised image of heimat needed to be beautiful while corresponding to individual memory. When the show presented Bad Lobenstein in the Gera district, the district newspaper expressed irritation that the programme had 'borrowed' images from a town 100 kilometres away, thus implying that the original was not sufficiently interesting on its own.[68] Viewers had come to expect the visual beauty and optimism that these shows had been designed to convey. Heimat shows resonated with the population's local pride and attachment. Individuals might have grown tired of socialist politics or economics constantly being presented in an overly positive light, but of their heimat they expected nothing less.

Heimat became an important framework for more than light entertainment shows. An important measure of this development is the major drama series which GDR TV produced to mark major political occasions. 'The Dolles' Family Album', broadcast on the GDR's twentieth anniversary in October 1969, showed how the Dolle family from Berlin learned, over a period of twenty years, to appreciate and enjoy the fruits of socialism. In this mini-series, heimat featured mainly through the regional humour of the characters, but otherwise its significance was barely apparent as the episodes focused on how national events impacted upon the family.[69] Ten years later, by contrast, heimat assumed a central role in 'The Long Street', the drama series produced for the GDR's thirtieth 'birthday'.[70] The drama depicted the transformation of the socialist homeland through the experiences of the Hollmann family in Grafenberg, a fictitious community

---

[66] On average, 38.1 per cent of the viewing population watched GDR TV at 8 p.m. prime time in 1974, and 34.8 per cent at 8 p.m. prime time in 1975. DRA Schriftgutbestand Fernsehen, Programmdirektion Zuschauerforschung VIII/2/52/76/21 [1976].

[67] Readers' letters ('Land und Leute kamen zu kurz'), *FF Dabei* 7 (1981). Readers' letters ('Wanderziel leicht verfehlt'), *FF Dabei* 13 (1981).

[68] *Volkswacht* (Gera-Stadt), 'Mit Volksliedern zwischen Burgk und Bürgel' (19 February 1981).

[69] On the programme, see also Palmowski, 'Citizenship', esp. pp. 73–4.

[70] In socialist parlance, the anniversary of the GDR's foundation was celebrated as the country's 'birthday'.

somewhere in the Mark Brandenburg region. Written by Gerhard Bengsch, it showed how milestones in GDR history, such as the construction of the Berlin Wall or collectivization, impacted upon the family and benefited the whole community, in the context of heimat. The final episode even featured a heimat festival which was filmed on location at the actual 'blossom' spring festival in Werder, near Potsdam. The drama's producers were quite clear that because heimat related to individual experience, it enabled the film to present everyday concerns realistically and with singular authenticity.[71]

Arguably the most comprehensive, and successful, dramatic representation of the socialist heimat was 'Chronicle of the Mark', based on a book by Bernhard Steeger (who also wrote the script), broadcast in January and February 1983, on the fiftieth anniversary of Hitler's coming to power. Just as West German television presented contemporary German history through the villagers of Schabbach in Edgar Reitz's Heimat series, broadcast a year later, so the villagers of (the fictional) Güterlohe in the Mark Brandenburg presented a 'complex mirror of the whole population' between 1939 and 1946.[72] While historians have studied Reitz's Heimat as a 'film about the identity of Germans in the twentieth century',[73] little attention has been devoted to the 'Chronicle', which constructed an ideal-type of Germans assuming true freedom and nationhood as socialists.

The story is centred on the friendship of Hannes Trostberg and Jupp Keuner. Trostberg, from Güterlohe, meets and befriends Keuner, a communist from the nearby county town. For his acts of resistance Keuner is imprisoned by the local Nazi leader, Grauling. At the beginning of the Second World War, Hannes has to join the Wehrmacht, and ends up on the Eastern Front. In these turbulent times, three villagers, postman Dreibrot and servants Wilm and Anna, maintain their decency and honesty through difficult times and prove to be convincing and receptive candidates for conversion to communism upon the village's liberation. Until that day arrives, however, Güterlohe is dominated by a widowed estate owner, Sieglinde Zahn, for whom both Wilm and Anna work. She falls in love with Grauling, and through her weakness of character she betrays Hannes' wife, Janne, to him. Janne is imprisoned for listening to Radio Moscow just after receiving a coded message from Hannes that he is alive and serving in the Red Army. Janne is killed by the Nazis before Hannes returns

---

[71] See the press cuttings and press information on the series in Deutsches Rundfunkarchiv (Babelsberg), 'Die lange Straße'.

[72] DRA Schriftgutbestand Fernsehen: 'Märkische Chronik. Abnahmeprotokoll' (Berlin, 19 November 1982).

[73] Confino, *Germany*, p. 57.

triumphant when the Red Army liberates the village. Zahn flees and the village is reorganized, with Wilm becoming mayor; the final episodes chronicle the early post-war years as the villagers cope with land reform, reconstruction and capitalist sabotage. 'Chronicle of the Mark' focuses the viewer's attention closely upon the village and its characters. Outside events are never shown, and wider historical developments only become apparent through the fates and the attitudes of the villagers themselves.

Each programme in the series was advertised extensively in the TV journal *FF Dabei*, with one photograph chosen to represent the series as a whole: a wide landscape at dawn, featuring a large lime tree at the centre, with a village steeple in the distance. The image underlined the author's intentions in making the Brandenburg landscape central to the story and the characters.[74] When those responsible for GDR TV's drama section reviewed the programmes, the committee was particularly pleased with how this intention had been realized, noting the 'poetic camerawork which shows the regional Brandenburg (*märkisch*) landscape in its beauty and diversity: all seasons and their moods are captured to support and reinforce the effectiveness of the relevant scenes'. The music was designed to enhance both the action and the landscape, and the dialect supported further the unity between villagers and their region. All this allowed the viewers to 'empathize with characters moved by a love of, and an intimate relationship with, the heimat'.[75]

'Chronicle of the Mark' depicted the socialist heimat in ideal type: this was a place in which the heroes were not free from personal weakness, but they stayed true to their class, except for Zahn. Those who, like postman Dreibrot, overcame their reservations and followed their working-class instincts could participate fully in the socialist heimat. The local framework provided the characters with an authenticity and familiarity that they would otherwise have lacked. In the use of accents, of the landscape, of colour, and the close-up of village society, 'Chronicle of the Mark' represented the apogee of socialist heimat articulation in GDR drama.

The show proved to be an outstanding success. It attracted a disproportionate number of viewers above forty-five years of age, and of those in small-town and rural areas. In marked contrast to heimat entertainment shows, the popularity of *Märkische Chronik* increased with educational attainment, with around 50 per cent of the country's intelligentsia watching

---

[74] DRA Schriftgutbestand Fernsehen: 'Märkische Chronik. Abnahmeprotokoll' (Berlin, 13 April 1982).
[75] DRA Schriftgutbestand Fernsehen: 'Märkische Chronik. Abnahmeprotokoll' (Berlin, 10 June 1982, 11 and 19 November 1982). 'Märkische Chronik – Regiekonzeption' (5 January 1981).

the series.[76] Its viewing figures increased steadily, from 22 per cent for the first episode to between 26 and 29 per cent for episodes 2–4, and to around 40 per cent for episodes 10–12. What made these figures truly remarkable was that the programme faced tough competition from the second GDR channel, which featured a French crime series and a series of Alain Delon films in competition to the 'Chronicle'. Together, the two channels reached between 50 and 60 per cent of the GDR's viewing audience.[77] When the 'Chronicle' was broadcast, a majority of viewers switched on GDR television.

'Chronicle of the Mark' was based on a good script: the story was internally consistent and visually appealing. Moreover, the characters were convincing and mostly avoided the appearance of one-dimensionality. The owner of the local estate, for instance, was not portrayed as a ruthless capitalist, but as an arriviste (she had married into wealth) who was uncertain of her social position and who was emotionally manipulated by Grauling. The story was deeply ideological, but by linking it to the local setting, in the geographical heart of the GDR, the characters' convictions and conversions became verifiable and credible. Through its historical setting, the show responded to the idealized visions of heimat that were popular with viewers, without necessarily clashing with the experience of the socialist heimat in the present. This was good drama.[78]

Drama productions allowed problematic issues such as individual hardship or communal tensions to be raised. But the overall message of such productions was very similar to the more clichéd representations of heimat in light entertainment shows. In drama, too, heimat served as a framework of reassurance, as the familiar setting of the locality served to resolve conflicts in the socialist way. This was an idealized image of heimat, which corresponded to what viewers expected to see, and which did not change fundamentally during the GDR's existence.

In important respects, then, the party constructed and exercised power by relating to, and in turn affecting, viewers' expectations and images of the homeland. This perspective would lend support to Adorno's critique of

---

[76] On 30 January, for instance, 51.4 per cent of viewers from the intelligentsia (and 42.6 per cent of civil servants) watched the series, whose average viewership was 35.0 per cent. On 1 February, the programme was seen by 50.0 per cent of viewers from the intelligentsia, in contrast to an average viewing share of 32.4 per cent. By comparison, on 5 February 1983, *Klock 8* attracted 39.3 per cent of total viewers, but 48.5 per cent of working-class viewers. DRA Schriftgutbestand Fernsehen, H081-03-02 0117: 'Sehbeteiligungen 1983. 8. Programmwoche' (x/3/8/83/32/3).

[77] DRA Schriftgutbestand Fernsehen, H081-03-02 0117: 'Sehbeteiligungen 1983'.

[78] For the principle of 'narrative fidelity' on which this evaluation is based, see Fischer, *Human Communication*, pp. 47–8, 108–10.

television on the grounds that its clichéd, simplistic representations dull the senses and in this way streamline and involve viewers. Accordingly, viewers rely on televised stereotypes to bring order to an increasingly complex, 'modern' world, which in turn makes television an effective tool of power for those who control it.[79] The problem with this view is that it assumes that viewers are passively subjected to the images that they see. GDR television producers were fully aware that viewers were not passive recipients of their offerings. If viewers did not like a programme, they could simply switch off. Even worse for the party, most viewers could (and did) tune in to Western television.

To date, there is no agreement among cultural studies scholars on how television influences viewers.[80] There appears to be widespread agreement that media reality and social reality are intertwined and impossible to separate.[81] This view is supported by cultivation theory, which proposes that television exercises an influence not through individual programmes or specific messages, but through the mass production of messages and the construction of a symbolic environment.[82] Indeed, scholars have gone so far as to suggest that there is no qualitative difference between fictional and non-fictional narratives; we do not experience fictional narratives by suspending our disbelief, but by relating these narratives to our pre-existing knowledge and experiences. Consequently, we reject fictional (and non-fictional) narratives only if they clash with our individual experience and thus require conscious scrutiny. Just as the film *Jaws* changed people's experience of swimming, so any fictional account that corresponds to viewers' experiences is likely to have an effect on viewers even if they know the story to be invented or even false.[83] In this way, televised heimat narratives affected the social imagination and fantasies relating to heimat, and helped shape the cultural memory of East German citizens.[84] Just as

---

[79] Theodor W. Adorno, 'How to look at television', *Hollywood Quarterly* 6, no. 3 (1952), 222–40.

[80] For a discussion of the latest research on television and its cultural impact, see Horace Newcomb (ed.), *Television: The Critical View*, 7th edn (Oxford University Press, 2007).

[81] Inge Marßolek and Adelheid von Saldern, 'Einführung', in Inge Marßolek and Adelheid von Saldern (eds.), *Zuhören und Gehörtwerden. Radio im Nationalsozialismus und Radio in der DDR der fünfziger Jahre*, 2 vols. (Tübingen: edition diskord, 1998), vol. I, pp. 11–45, here pp. 38–9.

[82] Shanahan and Morgan, *Television*, pp. 11–15.

[83] Richard J. Gerrig, *Experiencing Narrative Worlds: On the Psychological Activities of Reading* (New Haven/London: Yale University Press, 1993).

[84] In general, see Ernst Hanisch, 'Die linguistische Wende: Geschichtswissenschaft und Literatur', in Wolfgang Hardtwig and Hans-Ulrich Wehler (eds.), *Kulturgeschichte heute* (Göttingen: Vandenhoeck & Ruprecht, 1996), pp. 212–31.

narrative more generally constitutes a primary source for 'building and updating models for understanding the world',[85] the televisual narrative of the socialist heimat, its colours and its emotions formed part of the experience of heimat in the everyday.

GDR TV's commitment to the production of historical drama formed part of a wider emphasis among functionaries on the importance of history for an understanding of the socialist heimat. In 1988, Helmut Sakowski, vice-president of the Cultural League, opened an address to its Praesidium on a very personal note. He had just returned from a trip to Saxony, and he felt moved to profess how this experience had rekindled his 'love for our beautiful country GDR and its people':

> It was the beginning of May, blue skies, sunshine. Saxony was in bloom, and the rhododendron blooms … were superabundant. Villages and towns displayed their best side. I was enchanted by Dresden, and stunned at the golden gate of Freiberg cathedral. Here I was a thoroughly happy person.
> A few observations impressed me particularly. There was in particular the lively interest of GDR citizens, especially the young ones, in locating themselves in relation to the history of their immediate heimat region, evident particularly in Dresden, but also in Freiberg … Everywhere … people want to immerse themselves in the well of history, in order to confirm their own identity, that of GDR citizens.[86]

By immersing themselves in the 'well' of local history and traditions, GDR citizens would appreciate that the GDR was on the winning side of history.[87] The significance of local history and tradition was not just evident to Cultural League functionaries. As Erich Honecker declared in 1980, the citizens' well-being was greatly 'influenced by how they related to their locality and its history. This, too, affects their consciousness, their readiness to protect and preserve what our fathers fought for, and what we have all created.'[88] Socialist patriotism was based on pride in, and consciousness of, the historical achievements of the GDR made evident through the heimat.

[85] David Herman, 'Stories as a tool for thinking', in David Herman (ed.), *Narrative Theory and the Cognitive Sciences* (Stanford: CSLI, 2003), pp. 163–92; here p. 185.
[86] BArch-SAPMO, DY27 976, ff. 226–7: 'Stenografische Abnahme vom Band. Tagung des Präsidialrates des Kulturbundes der DDR am 17.5. 1988'.
[87] BArch-SAPMO, DY27 960, ff. 225–8: 'Sitzung des Präsidialrates am 8. Juni 1977', comment by Heinrich Gemkow, vice-president of the Cultural League.
[88] Horst Bartel, 'Aufgaben und Probleme der regionalgeschichtlichen Forschung und Propaganda in der DDR', in *Aufgaben und Probleme der regionalgeschichtlichen Forschung und Propaganda in der DDR* (Berlin: Gesellschaft für Heimatgeschichte im Kulturbund der DDR, 1978), pp. 27–39; here p. 33. Bartel spoke as director of the Central Institute of History at the GDR's Academy of Sciences.

The party's awareness of local history as a central instrument in the creation of socialist patriotism led the party to sponsor the writing of regional history by academic historians.[89] Shadowing this development, the Cultural League broke up the disparate and unwieldy 'Friends of Nature and Heimat' into three streamlined 'societies': the Society for Heimat History (created in 1979),[90] the Society for Conservation (1977), and the Society for Nature and the Environment (1980). In doing so, cultural functionaries hoped to provide better support for (and control of) the members of each organization, not least by bringing together enthusiasts and professionals. Through professional and ideological guidance, amateurs could learn to relate their interests to the GDR, and to master the dialectic between socialist patriotism and proletarian internationalism as a whole.[91]

The young were particularly encouraged to develop an interest in the history and nature of their locality. The 1970s witnessed the coming-of-age of the first generation raised entirely under the conditions of the GDR. By the early 1980s, 60 per cent of the population had no recollection of the GDR's foundation in 1949, and 44 per cent had no memory of 13 August 1961.[92] Owing to the poor knowledge many teenagers had of their heimat,[93] pedagogues and the Cultural League increased their efforts to improve the teaching of heimat in schools.[94] The ideal of love for the socialist heimat also featured prominently in the 'Baptism of Youth', a ritual most teenagers underwent at the age of sixteen.[95] In addition, the Society for Heimat

---

[89] Blaschke, 'Regionalgeschichte', pp. 362–6.

[90] The society's membership increased from just over 20,000 at its creation to 30,000 in 1989. Helmut Meier, *Der Kulturbund im politischen System der DDR in den siebziger Jahren*, Hefte zur DDR Geschichte 62 (Berlin: Helle Panke/Gesellschaftswiss. Forum, 2000), pp. 50, 54.

[91] Willibald Gutsche, 'Aufgaben und Probleme der marxistisch-leninistischen Regionalgeschichtsforschung und -propaganda in der DDR', in *Aufgaben und Probleme der regionalgeschichtlichen Forschung und Propaganda in der DDR* (Berlin: Gesellschaft für Heimatgeschichte im Kulturbund der DDR, 1978), pp. 9–25; here pp. 14–15.

[92] Max Unterlauf, 'Die Nutzung der Ortschronik Leuenberg in der Geschichtspropaganda', in *Heimatgeschichtliche Arbeit – Positionen, Probleme, Erfahrungen*, Arbeitsmaterial für die Fachgruppen Heimatgeschichte/Ortschroniken des Kulturbundes der DDR (Berlin: Kulturbund der DDR, 1985), pp. 49–53; here p. 49.

[93] As inspectors noted from their visit to Werningerode county in December 1974, the fact that pupils named their local mayor as Erich Honecker or even Henry Kissinger 'gave food for thought'. BArch-SAPMO, Ministerium für Volksbildung DR 2 A 6658 HA Unterricht, Abt. Unterstufe: 'Informationsberichte, Heimatkunde 1971–4'.

[94] See, for instance, *Heimatgeschichte und Geschichtsunterricht: 3. Gemeinsames Kolloquium der Ernst-Moritz-Arndt-Universität Greifswald, des Rates des Bezirkes Neubrandenburg und der Gesellschaft für Heimatgeschichte im Kulturbund der DDR am 22. Oktober 1987 in Neubrandenburg* (Greifswald: Universität Greifswald/Neubrandenburg Bezirk/Gesellschaft für Heimatgeschichte, 1989).

[95] Zentraler Ausschuß für Jugendweihe in der Deutschen Demokratischen Republik, *Vom Sinn unseres Lebens*, 4th edn (Berlin: Verlag Neues Leben, 1986). This book was presented to all participants at the 'Baptism of Youth' ceremony.

History tried to encourage the young to engage in history research themselves in their own spare time. By guiding extra-curricular activities in schools, youth camps and the Free German Youth, the Society strove to encourage among the young an interest in the history of their school, their village and local sites of historical interest.[96] Through local history and local traditions, the younger generation would acquire respect for the achievements of the old, develop patriotism and learn to love the socialist nation.[97]

Individuals were encouraged not just to enjoy their history but to record current events for posterity. As early as 1955, the Politbüro had issued a decree whereby every locality was to keep a record of local developments. Once the history of the GDR itself had become the focus of the party's attention, it became doubly important that every locality kept a chronicle of events to deepen popular 'historical consciousness and socialist patriotism'.[98] A new decree of 26 November 1981 re-emphasized every community's duty to select individuals to keep a record of local events and transformations, not just for posterity, but also to provide experts on local history.[99]

The resources released by the party and, to a lesser extent, the Society for Heimat History ensured that publications available to enthusiasts as authors and consumers increased exponentially. The Society for Heimat History alone published a series of journals including 'Heimat History' (from 1980) and 'Culture and Way of Life' (on folklore, from 1981), while also printing proceedings from countless national and regional conferences. Moreover, districts and increasingly counties began to publish their own history chronicles, history yearbooks and periodicals: by 1989, there was hardly a county in the GDR that did not publish its own history journal.

Clearly, there was much more to heimat than met the eye. In any locality it was possible not just to look at the 'peaks and valleys' of history, but also at the 'toil of the plain countryside', the lives of the 'many'.[100] Thanks to a new interest in the history of the everyday, professional and amateur historians

---

[96] *Heimatgeschichte und Jugend*, Heimatgeschichte 13 (Berlin: Kulturbund der DDR, 1982).

[97] BArch-SAPMO, DY27 963, ff. 114–17: 'Tagung des Präsidialrates der DDR zum Thema „Kulturbund und Volksbildung" am 5. Juli 1979', comment by Hans-Georg Quadt, Demmin.

[98] Reiner Breuer, Friedrich Donath, Wolfgang Jacobeit and Karl-Heinz Moeller (eds.), *Unsere Ortschronik: Hinweise und Anregungen zu ihrer Führung*, Arbeitsmaterial für die Fachgruppen Heimatgeschichte/Ortschroniken des Kulturbundes der DDR 4 (Berlin, 1978); here p. 8.

[99] *Ortschroniken in Vergangenheit und Gegenwart*, Heimatgeschichte 14, Arbeitsmaterial für die Fachgruppen Heimatgeschichte, Ortschroniken des Kulturbundes der DDR (Berlin, 1982).

[100] Gutsche, 'Aufgaben und Probleme', p. 16.

sponsored research on folk history and folk culture.[101] Folk tales, myths and folk practices now became the subject of investigation, with publications on myths and local tales of supernatural goblins, gnomes and mermaids enticing new interest in the locality.[102] Folklore allowed a much richer understanding of the country's past through a greater emotional and sensuous appreciation of the GDR's local heritage.[103]

Naturally, the party not only sponsored publications on folklore, it also encouraged folkloric practices. In support of popular folkloristic occupations, from crafts to the manufacture of folk costumes, the state instituted a GDR-wide folk-art campaign ('Initiative des künstlerischen Volksschaffens'), from 1973 to 1975. Communities were encouraged to compete by creating folklore ensembles, by instituting village festivals and by beautifying their localities in their spare time. Despite the party's confident claims of success,[104] it is unclear whether the campaign spurred the creation of new local initiatives, or whether it simply recorded existing ones.[105] Nonetheless, the campaign signalled to enthusiasts on the ground that the party now welcomed local initiative and expressions of local identity in all its diverse forms.

During the 1970s, the party sponsored a kaleidoscope of events, such as the Festival of Sorbic Culture and the Festival of Folklore in Socialist Countries. In addition to the encouragement of local ensembles, participation by folklore groups from other countries also underlined the connection

---

[101] Interest in folklore had been sustained by the Centre for Folklore in the 1950s, but had received little encouragement since. Ute Mohrmann, 'Ergebnisse und Grenzen praxisbezogener Volkskunstforschung der DDR in den fünfziger Jahren', *Volkskunst als Kulturgeschichte: Kultur und Lebensweise* 1 (1981), 53–65.

[102] Rudolf Schramm, *Die Wunderblumen vom Röschnitzgrund: Sagen und sagenhafte Erzählungen des mittleren Elstertals aus den Kreisen Greiz und Zeulenroda*, 2nd edn (Greiz: Kulturbund der DDR Kreissekretariat Greiz, 1981), vol. 1, p. 2. See also Rudolf Schramm, *Das Liebschwitzer Ranzenmärchen: Volkssagen und sagenhafte Erzählungen des mittleren Elstertals vorwiegend aus den Kreisen Gera-Stadt und Gera-Land* (Greiz: Kulturbund der DDR Kreissekretariat Greiz, 1980), vol. II, p. 2. Waltraud Woeller, *Berliner Sagen* (Berlin: Interessengemeinschaft für Denkmalpflege, Kultur und Geschichte der Hauptstadt Berlin im Kulturbund der DDR, 1980), p. 3.

[103] Hermann Strobach, 'Methodologische Probleme bei der historischen Erforschung und Darstellung der Volksdichtung', *Beiträge zur historischen Erforschung der Volksdichtung: Kultur und Lebensweise* 2 (1980), 71–85.

[104] One report noted that 2,500 local festivals were 'enriched' as a result of the movement, with 3,000 hobby groups competing for the title 'outstanding folklore collective' (*hervorragendes Volkskunstkollektiv*).

[105] Of over forty respondents in personal interviews, all of whom were asked about the origins of their heimat concerns, not one mentioned this initiative as a reason or at least an encouragement for their activities.

between local, socialist patriotism and proletarian internationalism.[106] Folklore also acquired greater prominence at workers' festivals. The 1978 festival in Suhl district featured a large folklore exhibition entitled 'Our Life is Rich and Beautiful'. The exhibition featured 1,300 folkloristic items chosen from over 10,000 contributions from all over the GDR, and bore witness, as the party put it, to 'joy of life, optimism [and] love of nature and heimat'.[107] From the 1970s, folklore ensembles received unprecedented material, logistical and motivational support.

No part of the GDR was exempt from the folklore revival. In 1977, the SED instituted the 'Folklore Festival' ('Tage der Volkskunst'), which was to be held over a whole weekend once or twice a year in Berlin's Palace of the Republic. At each festival, a different district presented itself to the capital (and hence to the socialist nation) through its folklore. The district of Gera, charged with organizing the first folklore festival from 17 to 19 November 1978, organized thirty different events in which 1,600 folklore enthusiasts from the district performed in choirs, wind bands, fashion shows with products from Gera, and dance groups.[108] The festival gave folklore enthusiasts a chance to perform in Berlin, and brought regional folklore to the metropolis. Opening up the GDR's most prestigious cultural site for events to folklore enthusiasts marked a 'coming-of-age' for the genre, manifesting the party's espousal of heimat and folklore as integral to the 'nation's' cultural canon.

Folklore came to be featured not just in Berlin, but also in the GDR's regional centres. In 1988, the eleven large palaces of culture across the GDR together attracted 19.3 per cent of the total audience of all culture houses throughout the country (including county and village clubs), a total of over 6 million visitors. This in itself represented a record figure, but the Ministry of Culture noted with particular satisfaction that this success was due to an increase in popular home-grown productions. Among these, folklore events were highly significant. Such events included the popular choir festivals in

---

[106] BArch-SAPMO, DY30 IV/B2 9.06 85, SED Abteilung Kultur: 'Information über den Stand der Vorbereitung des V. Festivals der Sorbische Kultur' (Berlin, am 4.12.1979). 'Information über den Stand der Vorbereitung des „11. Festivals des künstlerischen Volksschaffens sozialistischer Länder". Berlin, 8.4.1980'.

[107] BArch-SAPMO, DY30 IV/B2 9.06 85, SED Abteilung Kultur: 'Information über die Ausstellungen des bildnerischen Volksschaffens und der betrieblichen Fotogruppe der DDR in Suhl (Berlin am 20.6.1978)'.

[108] BArch-SAPMO, DY30 IV/B2 9.06 85, SED Abteilung Kultur: 'Information über die Durchführung der „Tage der Volkskunst" des Bezirkes Gera vom 17. bis 19. November 1978 im Palast der Republik' (27 November 1978).

Dresden and Magdeburg, dance festivals in Gera, and folklore days in Karl-Marx-Stadt.[109]

At the district level the party promoted folklore in other ways: at press festivals and through creating district-wide festivals related to music, agriculture and sports.[110] Further opportunities for presenting folklore, and the associated subsidies, existed at the local level. The party greatly encouraged villages and towns to celebrate annual heimat festivals, as well as the major anniversaries of the locality's foundation, not least because such celebrations were extremely popular. In 1977, a poll by the SED's Institute of Opinion Research found that visiting heimat, folklore and press festivals ranked third among the citizens' favourite forms of entertainment. It was not nearly as popular as watching television and spending time with friends, but observers from the party were struck by the fact that these periodic events were more popular than more regular pastimes such as cinema and listening to the radio.[111] By the 1980s, folklore and heimat traditions constituted a popular feature of everyday culture throughout the GDR.

It is difficult to see how the revival of local history and folklore could have proceeded without the transformation of heimat reporting in the press. From the early 1970s, district newspapers provided extensive coverage of folklore and heimat traditions.[112] In weekend supplements, readers received advice on short excursions and information on distinctive features in surrounding localities.[113] Local anniversary celebrations were reported as

[109] LHA Schwerin, Rat des Bezirks Neubrandenburg 26994: 'Vorlage Nr. 63/89 für die Dienstbesprechung des Ministers am 24.4.89'.
[110] On the origins of this festival, see BArch-SAPMO, DY30 IV/B2 9.06 86, SED Abteilung Kultur: 'Aktennotiz mit dem Stellvertreter des Ministers für Kultur, Genossen Siegfried Wagner, am 18.7.1974'. See also LHA Schwerin, Rat des Bezirks Neubrandenburg 19943: 'Zuarbeit an [die] Pressestelle beim Vorsitzenden des Rates des Bezirkes „Volkskünstler bereichern das Kulturangebot". Neubrandenburg, den 3. Dezember 1981'. LHA Schwerin, Rat des Bezirks Neubrandenburg 19943: 'Bericht über die in der Zeit vom 15.3. bis 18.3.1977 im Bezirk Neubrandenburg durchgeführten Untersuchunge-n [sic] zu [sic] Verwirklichung des Ministerratsbeschlusses vom 9.8.1973' (Berlin, 29 March 1977).
[111] BArch-SAPMO, DY30 IV/B2 9.06 85, SED Abteilung Kultur: 'Ergebnisse der Umfrage zu einigen Fragen von Geselligkeit und Unterhaltung', pp. 3–4 (poll conducted around 1977). In the survey, a representative group of almost 3,000 citizens were asked what they liked best to do in their free time. Of these, 71.8 per cent enjoyed watching TV, 64.7 per cent enjoyed socializing with friends and family, and 33.6 per cent enjoyed going to heimat, folklore and press festivals, with listening to the radio in fifth place (favoured by 29.1 per cent), and going to the cinema in eighth place (23.7 per cent).
[112] See, for instance, 'Mecklenburger Folklore – humorvoll und lebendig', *SVZ* (22 June 1976). 'Mehr als 120 Solisten wetteifern im Musikwinkel der DDR', *FP* (12 May 1975).
[113] 'Denkmalpflege in Ludwigslust', '... dem Rat der Stadt ist's schimpflich. Eine ergebnislose Beschwerde von 1688', *SVZ* (18 June 1976). 'Ein Projekt um tausendfache Ferienfreuden', *SVZ* (2 July 1976). 'Es müssen ja nicht gleich 58 Kilometer sein ...' *FP*, 'Heute für Morgen' supplement (16 May 1975).

evidence of the joy and transformations of socialism,[114] while educational pieces regularly popularized the history of local sites, advertised newly published books on heimat, and explained local coats of arms.[115] District newspapers were also increasingly attentive to heimat features in other parts of the country, particularly in neighbouring districts.

Led by *Neues Deutschland*, GDR national newspapers also emphasized the country's local heritage and cultural diversity.[116] They often ran a series on a theme that linked different heimat locations, for instance the 'fountains of the GDR'.[117] Such newspapers also contained stories about mythical and other unusual features of the heimat: evidently there was always more to the heimat than met the eye.[118] Reporters also never tired of introducing individual heimat activists and their work.[119] Whether through regional and national newspapers, magazines or popular books, heimat transferred part of everyday living to the printed page.

The GDR was far from being the only country which experienced a growth of local and regional consciousness during the 1970s. However, in the GDR the revival of local history and tradition was distinctive: the diversity of tradition and the sensations inherent in the homeland were related to a persistent theme specific to the country – the difficulty involved in travelling abroad. As citizens acquired more free time and more money, it became more important than ever to divert the growing demand to the mysteries of the homeland that awaited discovery. For Hugo Weinitschke,

---

[114] 'Ein Höhepunkt der Festwoche – der historische Umzug. 750 Jahre Parchim', *SVZ* (28 May 1976). 'Mecklenburgische Städte verändern ihr Gesicht: Wittenburg, Crivitz und Ludwigslust feiern ihr Stadtjubiläum', *SVZ* (18 June 1976).

[115] 'FP-Serie über Stadtwappen (10): Auerbach im Vogtland', *FP* (14 May 1975). 'Schriftsteller unseres Bezirkes über Werke ihrer Kollegen', *FP*, 'Heute für Morgen' supplement (23 May 1975).

[116] 'Zum Lachen und Nachdenken anregend', *Neues Deutschland* (28 December 1978). 'Pferderitt und Plapperwasser', *Neues Deutschland* (18/19 April 1987). 'Ostara gab dem Fest den Namen: Von Bräuchen, Sitten und Aberglauben zum Osterfest in Mecklenburg', *Ostseezeitung* (Rostock) (6 April 1985). 'Saatreiten und Sommergewinn', *Neuer Tag* (Frankfurt an der Oder) (29 March 1975).

[117] See, for instance, 'Ein Hecht mit Glocke', *Junge Welt* (13 September 1979) and 'Edelheilsame Quelle', *Junge Welt* (20 September 1979). 'Schöne Brunnen unserer Republik', *National-Zeitung* (3 October 1986); 'Brunnen unserer Heimat', *Das Volk* (Weekend supplement) (3 March 1989).

[118] '„Wer da kumet nach dem Hon Steyne …": Geschichte und Gegenwart der Feste in der Sächsischen Schweiz', *Neues Deutschland* (29 July 1978). 'Liebe auf Raubritterart: Geheimnisse um den Arnstein in der Sächsischen Schweiz', *Der Morgen* (20 January 1982). 'Landschaften in der DDR: Uralte Felsen und die Jugend bunter Täler. Der Harz: Bizarre Wirklichkeit gestern und heute', *Berliner Zeitung* (23/24 February 1985). 'Die Ostersuppe löffeln', *Der Morgen* (17 April 1984).

[119] See, for instance, the coverage of the restorer of Güstrow's historic doors, Hans-Jürgen Klug: BArch-SAPMO, DY27 963, ff. 101–6: 'Tagung des Präsidialrates der DDR zum Thema „Kulturbund und Volksbildung" am 5. Juli 1979', comment by Hans-Jürgen Klug. 'Die Türen meiner Stadt', *SVZ* (6 July 1977). 'Von Tür zu Tür', *SVZ* (13 May 1979). 'Wie historische Türen in gute Hände kamen', *Neues Deutschland* (7 August 1979). 'Die Türen einer alten Stadt', *Sonntag* (24 February 1980).

head of the Cultural League in Halle, there was simply no need for the population to occupy itself with distant lands. 'The GDR, our beautiful heimat, also offers treasures and sites worth seeing, which are hidden to many people because of their ignorance.'[120] As in the 1960s, functionaries tried to channel citizens' wanderlust to the discovery of the heimat.

Moreover, the resources which the party made available for the promotion of local culture were designed to compensate for the shortages in other areas of life. Socialist culture, both in its classical and in its heimat manifestations, allowed individuals to better appreciate the dialectic in socialism between material and cultural changes.[121] The significance of this increased exponentially during the 1980s. With reference to new consumer developments in the FRG, notably video recorders and the advent of private television, Hans-Joachim Hoffmann, the Minister of Culture, urged that culture should impart an 'indigenous feeling of heimat, an individual relationship to the state, sensations of everyday life, and joy'. Only when equipped with such emotions could citizens, and especially the young, resist the ever more 'alluring and tempting colours' of the West.[122]

The important political and ideological functions which heimat practices acquired beg the question of how citizens at the grass roots responded to this. Given the growth in heimat activities at all levels, it is clear that the politics of the socialist heimat did not turn off the rising numbers of activists. Such increasing levels of popular participation allowed the party, and subsequent scholars, to argue that citizens accepted, and in this way sustained, the political conditions of their everyday life. However, participation in itself says little about individual motivations and meanings. What did the practices encouraged by the party from the 1970s indicate about the motivations, meanings, and political commitment of individual actors?

LOCAL FESTIVALS AND THE PUBLIC TRANSCRIPT

Local festivals allowed the party to present itself, its achievements and the GDR more generally, through the prism of the locality. No heimat festival was complete without reference to the party and the mass organizations, and

---

[120] BArch-SAPMO, DY27 958, f. 227: 'Beratung des Präsidialrates über Probleme und Erfahrungen der Förderung des geistig-kulturellen Lebens der jungen Generation am 19. September 1975 im CdK Berlin', speech by Hugo Weinitschke.

[121] BArch-SAPMO, DY27 692: 'Stenografisches Protokoll der Tagung des Präsidialrates des Kulturbundes der DDR' (19 January 1979). See esp. the comments by Willibald Gutsche, Arno Hochmuth and Werner Kahle.

[122] BArch-SAPMO, DY27 976, ff. 261–75: 'Tagung des Präsidialrates des Kulturbundes der DDR am 17.5.1988', comment by Hans-Joachim Hofmann.

no pageant could do without floats dedicated to the GDR. When the Thuringian village of Neustadt on the Rennsteig celebrated its 500th anniversary in 1989, the pageant illustrated the village's history and the local economy, with motifs symbolizing the German communist party's foundation in 1920, the SED's creation in 1946, the mass organizations, the achievements of the health system, and so on.[123] Similarly, when the nearby city of Eisenach celebrated its annual spring festival, individual motifs in the pageant were devoted to the party. Moreover, the event's programme regularly contained articles on the socialist transformation of the town's environment.[124] Local festivals allowed the party to bring ideology and the plan into the local fabric, while also enabling it to claim such events as an expression of joy in socialism.[125]

This raises the question of why the party was so successful at stimulating local activity on behalf of the heimat. After all, as we have seen, the party had tried to stimulate socialist heimat festivals in the late 1950s and early 1960s, with much less success. Why were individuals keen to be involved on behalf of their locality from the 1970s, and how did they respond to the party's appropriation of the homeland for socialism and the joy of living in the GDR? The remainder of this chapter will address these questions for the case of local, 'socialist' heimat festivals in three different locations, two in Thuringia and one in Mecklenburg. These were chosen because they complement each other and collectively illustrate a number of features which were also representative of heimat activity beyond these particular localities.

In Eisenach, a town of some 50,000 inhabitants at the foot of the historic Wartburg castle, near the inner-German border, locals celebrated, every year, the 'onset of summer' (*Sommergewinn*), which was the GDR's largest spring festival. Of the festivals discussed here, this was by far the most elaborate. In the three months before the event, a group of women met

---

[123] *500 Jahre Neustadt am Rennsteig 1489–1989: Eine Ortschronik in den Bildern des historischen Festumzugs* (Neustadt am Rennsteig: Rat der Gemeinde, 1989), p. 1.

[124] See, for instance, *Sommergewinn: Heimatliches Volksfest in der Wartburgstadt Eisenach*, ed. Fachgruppe Sommergewinn der Arbeitsgemeinschaft der Natur- und Heimatfreunde im Deutschen Kulturbund (1973), 2. *Sommergewinn: Heimatliches Volksfest in der Wartburgstadt Eisenach*, ed. Fachgruppe Sommergewinn der Arbeitsgemeinschaft der Natur- und Heimatfreunde im Deutschen Kulturbund (1974), 6. 'Eisenachs Wohnungsbau bis 1990', *Natur- und Heimatfreunde im deutschen Kulturbund* (1974), no.6; 29–31.

[125] See, for instance, comments on the meanings of a folklore exhibition in BArch-SAPMO, DY30 IV/B2 9.06 85, SED Abteilung Kultur: 'Information über die Ausstellungen des bildnerischen Volksschaffens und der betrieblichen Fotogruppe der DDR in Suhl. Berlin am 20.6.1978'.

every night to produce over 200,000 paper flowers that were then used to embellish the floats in the pageant, and to decorate individual houses in their part of town. Their husbands, meanwhile, organized and built the floats, and directed the festival overall. The *Sommergewinn* was an intensely local festival whose organizational core lay in a small area to the west of the centre, which had not been incorporated into the town until the middle of the nineteenth century. Here, around the Ehrensteig street, had lived the families who worked as servants in the castle and had been considered socially inferior to the Eisenach merchants. Locally known as the 'Stiegker' (derived from the 'Ehrensteig'), their homes had been passed down through generations, so that residents spoke a dialect different to that spoken elsewhere in town. The *Sommergewinn* was, at its heart, a Stiegker festival. These residents formed the core of the organizing team, while its most popular characters, 'Henner' and 'Frieder', provided local humour in Stiegker dialect.

Each *Sommergewinn* articulated a specific theme, usually based on local features. The 1967 festival, for instance, emphasized the 900th anniversary of Wartburg castle. The main organizers received special leave from their employers in the weeks leading up to the event. Local businesses provided the vehicles to pull the floats, while teachers encouraged their pupils to sell commemorative tokens and provide staffing for the pageant. The party's emphasis on the socialist heritage from the 1970s did not have a pivotal significance for the festival, whose origins went back to the imperial era, but it did enable the *Sommergewinn* to become increasingly elaborate. The festival reached a climax in 1987, when, to the theme of Eisenach as a railway hub, the pageant featured a giant low-loader truck carrying a locomotive through the streets of the city.

However important the support of state and party, the festival existed through the Stiegker community, for whom the countless evenings of preparation were not just work, but also opportunities to have a beer with childhood friends and talk to them in their own local dialect. Asked what motivated the members of the community to become involved in the organization, Peter Apel, himself a Stiegker, explained:

Even if you say: I'm fed up, I don't want to participate, like I did at one stage - you have to participate, you come from the Stieg and there is no other way, we are from the western part of town. If we don't do it, this will collapse ... People met, they met in the Waldschlösschen pub for example. In the club room the women sat together, and the men, and we played skat, and the women brought food from home ... you know, in GDR times if you wanted to build a house or whatever, without a community you could not do anything. One person needed the other, helping each other was essential. And this community was there. In all sorts of ways. No matter what you did, we helped each other.[126]

In Eisenach, the *Sommergewinn* worked because it constituted a crucial part of the identity and self-worth of the Stiegker community, whose sense of belonging and mutual dependability was reinforced by the conditions of scarcity that prevailed in the GDR. Local festivals and traditions may have been made easier by the party's material encouragement, but they expressed local identities honed by the lack of wider opportunities for personal fulfilment.

While the *Sommergewinn* was a festival unique to the city of Eisenach, the anniversary celebrations of Wechmar were far more typical of local festivals. Wechmar lies in the Thuringian basin, equidistant from Gotha and Erfurt. In 1982, the sixteen-year-old Knut Kreuch conducted research on his home village of Wechmar as part of a school project. In the process, he traced his village's origins to a document signed in AD 986. To prepare for Wechmar's 1,200th anniversary due in 1986, Kreuch founded a local branch of the Society for Heimat History. In the four years leading up to the anniversary celebrations, Kreuch oversaw a veritable renaissance of heimat culture in which village tradition was reinvented. Several generations of the Bach family had lived in the village. Under Kreuch's direction, the villagers renovated the façade of the house in which the Bach family had lived, in time for the 300th birthday of Johann Sebastian Bach (who himself had never lived there) in 1985. The village's traditions were also represented in a new heimat museum. Villagers referred with pride to the 'Bach-community' of Wechmar.

Celebrating and inventing their tradition allowed individuals to shine. Internally, the community could be rallied to beautify the village and

---

[126] 'Auch wenn die gesagt ham du ich hab die Schnauze voll ich will da nicht mitmachen. Bei mir war's ja ähnlich, so. Und da musste mitmachen, du stammst von Stieg und das geht nicht anders und wir sind Weststädter usw. Wenn wir das nicht machen dann geht's in die Brüche und so ne? ... Die Leute die ham sich ja getroffen. Verstehen se die ham sich zum Beispiel im Waldschlösschen getroffen da hinten. Im Vereinszimmer da saßen die Frauen zusammen, die Männer, da wurde auch Skat gespielt usw. Wobei die Frauen die ham von daheim das Essen gebracht ... Wissen se und dieses ganze Gemeinschaftsgefüge, zu DDR-Zeiten wars ja auch teilweise so, wenn se nen Haus gebaut haben wissens es ja auch, wenn Sie nicht gemeinschaftlich was bewegt ham – da war nicht viel. Einer brauchte den anderen. Ja, die Hilfe untereinander war erforderlich. Und diese Gemeinschaft die war ja vorhanden. Ja, in vielfältiger Form. Ganz egal was Sie da gemacht ham. Einer hat dem anderen geholfen.' Interview with Peter Apel, 18 June 2003. When I interviewed Jürgen Klapczynski, the former mayor, Dieter Kuhla (who participated in the *Sommergewinn* as a non-Stiegker) and Jürgen Brunner (the head archivist in Eisenach), all pointed to the community of the Stiegker as the principal driving force of the festival.

improve facilities,[127] while also earning external recognition. This was important because, as one organizer of a local anniversary festival put it, 'if you were a small village, you were redundant like a spare wheel on a car'.[128] For Kreuch all this had tangible personal benefits. After reneging on his commitment to serve as a volunteer in the army, Kreuch became persona non grata with the village's party hierarchy – but only until the district newspaper printed a full-page interview with him, holding him up as a model inhabitant of the socialist heimat.[129] Local festivals showed what individuals and village communities could do to put themselves on the regional map, at least in the minds of the villagers themselves.

Local festivals relied on individuals taking the initiative, but they also worked because they could tap into enormous reserves of local pride. This was no different in the north of the country. Uwe Wieben, then director of the local heimat museum, remembers the 725th anniversary of Boizenburg, a small Mecklenburgian town of some 15,000 inhabitants on the banks of the river Elbe:

So many people became active, really in this 725-year anniversary people discovered things, every shop remembered its traditions ... You know, sometimes as the museum director I looked with envy into the shop windows. Why had we not known about these things, all of a sudden some shopkeepers or businesses were looking back on their tradition. That was a mass movement, in such a town.[130]

Reflecting on why people got so involved, Wieben's successor at the museum, Karin Wulf (a native of the town who also attended the interview) explained: 'perhaps it was this unusual occasion, they soon noticed that here at last was something out of the ordinary, and something very diverse'.[131] In Boizenburg as elsewhere, a local anniversary inspired particular local action that was by no means unique to the GDR. Although the practical circumstances of organization were specific to the GDR, the driving force for such events was local, not ideological.

What, then, of the party? How did people celebrating local festivals respond to the party's protestations that these festivals represented GDR tradition and the joy of life in socialism? Participants who were interviewed agreed with hindsight that the festivals were not overly political, even if certain themes had to be included. According to Wieben,

---

[127] Interview with Knut Kreuch, 19 May 2003.
[128] 'Biste kleine Gemeinde, bist du immer 5. Rad am Wagen.' Interview with Manfred Kastner, Neustadt am Rennsteig, 29 March 2003.
[129] *Das Volk*, 'Heimatgeschichte und Heimatliebe' (26 September 1987).
[130] Interview with Uwe Wieben and Karin Wulf, 16 June 2003.   [131] Ibid.

The influence of politics was relatively limited, except perhaps for the barriers which one had in one's own head, the self-censorship, which you carried permanently as GDR citizen and which nobody had to tell you. Of course one knew: the foundation of the local branch of the KPD, that had to be represented [in the pageant], as a key event ... the foundation of the local branch of the SPD perhaps did not have to be a topic.[132]

Other interviewees confirmed this for the *Sommergewinn* in Eisenach. Here, the pageant overwhelmingly presented themes of animals, flowers, the seasons, and historical figures. The pageant always included floats highlighting wider political themes. It was not so much that the party dictated openly how socialism should be presented in the pageant; one simply knew that, if 1969 marked the hundredth anniversary of the creation of the German socialist workers' party in Eisenach, this had to be displayed in that year's pageant. And since that year also marked the GDR's twentieth anniversary, this also needed to be a theme. As festivals constituted part of everyday life, one paid one's dues to state and party, and one knew how this had to be done.

In important respects, specific heimat festivals came to resemble the annual political festivities on 1 May (Labour Day) and 7 October (the 'birthday' of the GDR). Naturally, these were not events in which local themes dominated the festivities. Nevertheless, the meanings of these political occasions were localized in ways that were very similar to local heimat festivals. In Boizenburg, Uwe Wieben and Karin Wulf remembered that on 1 May, workers from the two factories marched towards the market square. Many workers found excuses not to turn up, but among those that did appear, carrying the banners was particularly unpopular. Wieben remembered: 'goodness gracious: "Long live the GDR" – I had to carry it once, with one of the town's porters, so we always looked away to the side.' While the speeches were being given on the market square, the crowd would begin to disperse, though as head of the local national democratic party Wieben was unable to 'piss off', as he put it, too early. At some stage, one dumped the banner in a corner and disappeared from the official proceedings: the women and children went through the streets to amuse themselves, and the men gathered to get drunk on the traditional Mayday outing. This was repeated on 7 October, except that on the night before the event, trade unions and other organizations held special festivities. According to Wieben:

---

[132] Ibid.

This was a social event, you celebrated. You were not forced to go, you could have left after an hour … Yes, and then there were medals. It could be that you had become an activist of socialist labour. You got a small medal, and 300 Marks. [These were] Aluminium chips [i.e. GDR currency] … But the 300 Marks were 600 beers. And that was something. And if one got 300 Marks and brought 250 home, then the wife was also happy.[133]

The unpopularity of having to carry the banner is highly reminiscent of Apel's account of the *Sommergewinn*, where manning the floats dedicated to socialism was unpopular, and represented a poor deal for those whose lot it was that year. The example of Boizenburg further demonstrates how 'nationwide' party celebrations were filled with local meanings: socialist decorations were integrated into local culture, with those stuck with carrying the banner, or being decorated, subjected to local teasing and made to buy a round of drinks. Socialist rituals were thus localized, strengthening the local community rather than socialism.

Even if socialist rituals and the socialist heimat ideal did not influence the locality in the way the party had hoped, they nevertheless had a crucial political function. This is best explored through the 'public transcript', practices that involve rituals of subordination which act as euphemisms for the power of elites.[134] From this perspective, the public transcript of the socialist heimat, i.e. practices whereby citizens publicly related their local traditions to the socialist heimat and 'localized' socialist rituals, constituted a regular affirmation of the party's power. With each festival, the party helped reinforce local community and tradition, in return for the citizens' public affirmation of the authority of socialism and the party. Carrying the banner may have become a subject for local jesting, but it was carried nevertheless. The party's socialist labels and rituals thus became an important part of everyday life: for the party, it meant that its authority remained unchallenged, while for the local community such festivals provided further opportunities to strengthen its bonds. In appearing simply to serve the cultural interests of the population, the rituals and practices of the socialist

---

[133] 'Also, am Vorabend fanden ja immer so staatliche Feiern statt, von der Gewerkschaft. Und da ging man dann auch hin … Also, da war es gesellig. Da wurde gefeiert. Da wurde man nicht mit dem Knüppel hingetrieben, da wurde man auch nicht überzeugt, man hätte auch nach einer Stunde gehen können, keiner hat einen gezwungen … Ja, doch, dann gab's noch Auszeichnungen. Da konnte es sein, daß Sie mal Aktivist der sozialistischen Arbeit geworden sind. Dann haben Sie so einen kleinen Orden gekriegt, und dann gab es noch 300 Mark. Hier, Aluchips … aber 300 DDR-Mark, waren 600 Bier… Also, das war schon was. Und wenn man denn 300 Mark gekriegt hat und brachte noch 250 Mark mit nach Hause hat die Frau sich auch gefreut.'

[134] Scott, *Domination*, esp. pp. 3–5, 13–14.

heimat varnished the party's power, which required constant popular affirmations of current power relations in everyday life.

One typical example of the public transcript concerned the festival brochure for local anniversaries. Knut Kreuch described the brochure written for Wechmar's 1,200th anniversary:

We received permission to print our history in five pages, but four of these had to deal with the history of the workers since 1945. We said, 'There is absolutely no way.' So I went to my friend HW in [Gera, the county] town, and I said to him: 'Listen, you have to arrange it so that at the meeting of the control commission [at which the publication would be approved] they won't look at our programme.' So he said: 'OK, you have to write it in such-and-such a way'. So we wrote it exactly in the way he suggested: [for instance,] 'the working peasantry participated in the peasants' war'. As a result, they complimented us on how beautifully written this programme was.[135]

By learning and adopting the language of the party, the villagers were able to write their history in the way they chose to, devoting most of the brochure to the 'Bach community's' pre-1945 history as that of the village's working-class peasantry. By writing about what they wanted in the terms of the socialist struggle between workers and peasants, individuals could encode their own meanings in the socialist heimat ideal. This experience is not at all untypical, as memories of how villagers insisted on their own meanings in the face of the party's transcript abound.[136] In the GDR, the key was not so much what one said, but how one phrased it, and who said it.[137]

Villagers learned, in other words, to articulate their own meanings of heimat in the public transcript. This strategy became part of an arsenal of 'tricks' that locals played upon the authorities, tricks through which communities were able to keep their distance from socialism and the state. Such stories of local cunning could be hidden from the dominant, as Scott had argued, but they did not always have to be. For Eisenach's *Sommergewinn* celebrations, for instance, Peter Apel explained how it was possible to delay the construction of the occasional float dedicated to socialism so that it was not ready for the procession. For this reason, it is more helpful to speak of 'private' rather than 'hidden' transcripts, as these communications and

---

[135] Interview with Knut Kreuch, 19 May 2003.
[136] Much the same thing happened, for instance, at the 500th anniversary of Neustadt am Rennsteig. Interview with Manfred Kastner, 29 March 2003.
[137] 'Man konnte auch schon 1986 was sagen, und damit aneggen oder nicht aneggen. Es kam dann immer wieder darauf an, wie war die Verpackung? Und WER sagte es?' Interview with Knut Kreuch, 19 May 2003.

meanings developed away from the dominant, without necessarily being obscured from their view. For, strikingly, much of the local 'trickery' occurred in full view of the party. What could be more effective than fooling the party by its own methods, by expressing private meanings in the party's own language? As the Wechmar example shows, the public transcript of the socialist heimat was sufficiently flexible to allow actors to express alternative, intensely localist meanings.

CONCLUSION

In the Honecker era, heimat became an important arena for the satisfaction of desires for leisure and culture. It provided a successful, popular and relatively inexpensive framework for the production of television programmes. In turn, this reinforced the significance of the socialist heimat in the everyday lives of the population, through what they watched and how this helped them interpret their daily lives. Moreover, the diversity of the heimat served to render the GDR more attractive for domestic tourism, a particularly important endeavour given the difficulty of foreign travel. Finally, heimat provided a framework for social interaction, through hobbies as well as festivals. Heimat thus helped achieve the party's central goal, formulated at the Eighth Party Congress: to fulfil individual desires. Heimat came to constitute an important cultural and social reference point across the GDR, as citizens became aware of, and for the most part also connected to, the cultural traditions and social relations connoted by the heimat ideal.

In important respects, this invention of a localized identity through heimat was neither unrealistic nor unsuccessful. For television as for newspapers, the socialist heimat offered a framework for the construction of stories that were genuinely popular, and which created new emotional dimensions for socialism and GDR citizenship. Moreover, the proliferation of heimat festivals, the promotion of local tourism and the growth of folklore all found a popular response. A local tourism infrastructure developed through the creation of footpaths, the regeneration of local parks and stately homes, and the activities of heimat museums. The proliferation of heimat not only affected the self-representation of state and party in the public transcript, it also became more important than ever in the everyday lives of GDR citizens.

Citizens gained increased opportunities for personal cultural fulfilment, as long as they subscribed to the public transcript of the socialist heimat. They could not watch shows invoking the heimat without acknowledging this transcript. Local historians and archaeologists could not publish their findings without referring to the achievements of socialism, while newspapers were always careful to link local particularities to the GDR's heritage. Similarly, no local festival was complete without references to the achievements of state, party and the Soviet Union. Subscribing to the public transcript of the socialist heimat was the price citizens had to pay for indulging their cultural desires.

The fact that the party and the citizens could converge on a public transcript of heimat distinguishes the Honecker era from the first twenty years of the GDR. In the 1950s, the party had difficulties in linking heimat practices to socialism and the GDR; for much of the 1960s citizens resisted the ideological appropriation of heimat through the Bitterfeld Path. After 1971, the party no longer tried to fit local popular practices into its ideological mould, but instead adapted its cultural aspirations to existing popular practices. The party's desire to overcome the dichotomy between representations of the socialist heimat and popular cultural practices constituted the decisive shift of the Honecker era. Welcoming popular practices in this way came at a price: popular culture may have been distinctive to the GDR's regions, and it was related to what citizens actually enjoyed, but it was increasingly unclear how it related to socialism as such.

As its representation on television demonstrates, heimat became compatible with socialism without ever becoming uniquely socialist. This reconciliation of the socialist GDR with older heimat narratives resonated deeply among the population, as viewing figures indicate. It is also highly likely that these shows did constitute an important part of people's everyday lives. According to Jerome Bruner, stories are influential precisely when distinguished by 'narrative banality', whereby stories conform exactly to our expectations of them.[138] By linking socialist achievements to relatively traditional tropes of the heimat, the party had found a way of construing the GDR as part of everyday reality that was relatively effective and popular. Paradoxically, this could also undermine the GDR's particular features. Local anniversary festivals or television shows were generically quite similar to the festivals and shows enjoyed in West Germany. The 'Farmers' Market' is a good case in point. Despite attempting, not without success, to articulate a distinctive Thuringian identity, the show developed as a mirror image of the West German heimat show focused on neighbouring Hesse, the 'Blue Goat'. By appealing to intrinsic regional traditions, the party emphasized regional distinctiveness, forgetting that regional distinctiveness had been the essence of an all-German culture for centuries.

---

[138] Jerome Bruner, 'The narrative construction of reality', *Critical Inquiry* 18 (1991), 5–9.

Many if not most citizens did not share the meanings the party gave to the public transcript of the socialist heimat. What emerges in relation to Scott's work is the elasticity of the public transcript in a state like the GDR. Here, citizens did not necessarily need to express divergent meanings outside the public transcript. By learning and appropriating the language of the socialist heimat, individuals could insert nuances that were clear to all those for whom they were intended, and in this way mark their own distance and differentiation. While the Wechmar Friends of the Heimat emphasized the village's history before 1945 through the language of the party, local readers were quite clear on how to read that language. Moments of *Eigen-Sinn*, like looking away from the banner one carried, allowed one to provide alternative meanings without leaving the public transcript. Activists learned how to 'encode' their meanings in the language of the party, while spectators knew how to 'decode' what they read and saw. Contrary to the party's intentions, it was possible for individuals and communities to engage publicly in the socialist heimat without assuming the identity of GDR citizens.

The ability of individuals to appropriate the public transcript for their own individual or local meanings indicates the main weakness, but also the central strength, of the socialist heimat. If they wanted to engage in heimat-related activities, citizens had to appropriate the public transcript of the socialist heimat. Communities delighted in communicating their own meanings through the public transcript of heimat, and television viewers saw through the transcript to follow a good story. Yet in encoding and decoding through the public transcript, and by submitting to socialist rituals, for instance in local festivals, citizens continued to express their meanings within the constraints set by the party. By submitting to the public transcript, citizens did not necessarily accept the meanings of the socialist heimat. They did, however, submit to the unavoidability of socialism as the status quo.

CHAPTER 5

Citizenship and participation in the local community – 'Join in!'

INTRODUCTION

In the run-up to the SED's Tenth Party Congress in April 1981, GDR television broadcast a four-part documentary on how the socialist home-land had changed for the better under the party's leadership. Through images of the heimat, 'In the Tide of Time' showed how, ten years on, the promises of the Eighth Party Congress to provide protection, social welfare, and cultural riches for all had become reality.[1] One long scene featured Erfurt's historic city centre and its main square, the Anger. To these images, the voiceover declared:

Erfurt – the Anger. The feeling of comfort belongs to the home, to life, to work. The town, the village, the surroundings, they all fit as a joyfully worn piece of clothing. The beautiful towns and communities are also the work of their inhab-itants through 'Join in!'[2]

The homeland had not just been created under the party's direction. Through the 'Join in!' initiative, every citizen had made a distinct contri-bution to the socialist transformation of the environment. Through 'Join in!', party and citizens were one.

Under the name 'More beautiful our cities and communities – "Join in!"', all citizens were called to participate in maintaining and caring for their local surroundings. This annual campaign was founded in 1967 by the National Front (NF), which co-ordinated the contributions of the various mass organizations, from the women's league to the trade union. At the beginning of every year, collectives ranging from housing com-munities, hobby groups and workplace brigades had to commit them-selves to voluntary activity on behalf of their homeland. These projects

---

[1] 'Im Strom der Zeit', *FF Dabei* (24 March 1981).
[2] *Im Strom der Zeit, Teil Eins: Unser Land, DDR I* (24 March 1981).

were to be completed in time for the GDR's 'birthday' on 7 October, and constituted each citizen's 'gift' to the state. 'Join in!' constituted a demonstration of socialist patriotism.

Involvement in the 'Join in!' campaign related closely to the 1967 socialist law of citizenship, which postulated an identity between the state and its citizens. Accordingly, individual political action was largely directed at participation in local affairs.[3] 'Join in!' represented the ideal example of 'socialist democracy in action', because by submitting ideas and discussing them with local functionaries, every participant became involved in local decisions, from their inception to their execution.[4] Citizens were bound to raise local administrative shortcomings immediately. This, in turn, would lead to much more effective, responsive and imaginative local administration.[5] When Walter Ulbricht commended the 'Join in!' movement as a 'school of socialist democracy in the communities and in the residential districts',[6] this applied both to citizens and local officials.

The participatory campaign expressed the goals of the 1968 constitution, notably the existence of a socialist community (Art. 3) and the 'socialist national culture' (Art. 18). Participation helped each citizen to recognize his or her own responsibility towards society,[7] whereby each should contribute according to his means (§2) for the material benefit of all (§9).[8] According to the National Front's first secretary for the Erfurt district, Günter Zimmermann, even cleaning the streets brought society closer to attaining the constitutional reality (*Verfassungswirklichkeit*) of socialism.[9]

---

[3] Jan Palmowski, 'Citizenship, identity and community in the GDR', in Geoff Eley and Jan Palmowski (eds.), *Citizenship and National Identity in the GDR* (Stanford University Press, 2008), pp. 73–91.

[4] ThHStAWe, Nationale Front 133, f. 223. Address to National Front functionaries in Erfurt, 25 September 1968.

[5] BArch-SAPMO, DY30 IV/A2 9.02 196: 'Bericht über eine Beratung mit Genossen Albert Norden ... am 18. Mai 1968', p. 11.

[6] BArch-SAPMO, Nationalrat der Nationalen Front der DDR, DY6 2330. 'Nationales Aufbauwerk' (c.1968; old reference marked at the top: Akte 2300-420-000).

[7] BArch-SAPMO, DY6 2330: 'Beschluß: Maßnahmen zur Entwicklung und Führung des Wettbewerbs der Städte und Gemeinden zur Vorbereitung des 20. Jahrestages der DDR' (6 February 1968).

[8] ThHStAWe, Nationale Front 29; here ff. 52–3: 'Die Führung des Wettbewerbs der Städte und Gemeinden in Vorbereitung des 20. Jahrestages der Gründung der DDR' (Bezirkssekretär der Nationalen Front, Günter Zimmermann, 22.5.68). Zimmermann also related the movement to articles 5, 12, 15, 17, and 41–3. His speech took up ideas communicated from the centre, sometimes verbatim. See BArch-SAPMO, DY6 2330: 'Gedanken für die Beratung mit den Verantwortlichen der Bezirkssekretariate für den Wettbewerb der Städte und Gemeinden am 19.4.1968'.

[9] BArch-SAPMO, DY6 2330: 'Das Mitglied des Sekretariats des Nationalrats, Kollege Herbert Eichhorn, erklärte in einem Gespräch mit der Nachrichtenagentur Radio DDR...' (June 1968).

The party was certain that 'Join in!' would invigorate everyday life with a sense of patriotism, both actively and passively. Through the economic (and, by implication, moral) value created by joint voluntary work, citizens would experience the benefits of clean and beautiful public spaces and better cultural facilities.[10] In this virtuous circle, citizens would in turn be motivated to undertake renewed action on behalf of the community, rendering the locality yet more beautiful. 'Join in!' thus enabled a new quality of citizenship to emerge, which in turn led to a deeper love of heimat and the socialist fatherland.[11] Albert Norden, head of the Politbüro's propaganda department and member of the National Front's Praesidium, was adamant that the central objective of 'Join in!' was to instil a sense of heimat among citizens, whose labours formed the bedrock of the successful development of the entire state.[12] Werner Kirchhoff, first secretary of the National Front's Praesidium, wrote: 'When for the twentieth anniversary of our republic not only the large cities, but also the small towns and villages present themselves visibly in a new guise, our citizens' joy of life will increase; their feeling of heimat, their love of the socialist fatherland will be strengthened. They will say with pride: I am a citizen of the German Democratic Republic.'[13]

In the 'Join in!' movement the party sought to transform the citizens' widespread verbal commitment to the heimat into public action. Action on behalf of their heimat reinforced their 'state consciousness' (*Staatsbewußtsein*),[14] and distinguished GDR citizens from West Germans, whose society was characterized by 'pseudo-culture, criminality, horror, drug addiction and pornography'.[15] In contrast to such unhealthy individualism, the participatory movement in the GDR allowed citizens to demonstrate and develop their responsibility for society as a whole. Through 'Join in!' citizens learned to live and behave in socialist ways,[16]

---

[10] BArch-SAPMO, DY30IV/A2 9.02 196: *Neues Deutschland*, 'Städte und Dörfer werden schöner' (9 August 1968).

[11] BArch-SAPMO, DY6 2330: 'Hinweise für die Presseinformation am 27.6.1968 (Herbert Eichhorn). Grundlage: Beschluß des Sekretariats für Presseinformation'.

[12] BArch-SAPMO, DY30 IV/A2 9.02 196: 'Bericht über eine Beratung mit Genossen Albert Norden … am 18. Mai 1968', p. 6.

[13] BArch-SAPMO, DY6 2330: *Neue Zeit*, 'Fundament unserer Erfolge: Die Gemeinschaft in der Nationalen Front' (21 September 1968).

[14] BArch-SAPMO, DY6 2333: 'Gedanken für die Weiterführung des Wettbewerbs [1969]', pp. 2–3.

[15] BArch-SAPMO, DY6 2330: *Neue Zeit*, 'Fundament unserer Erfolge'.

[16] LHA Schwerin, Nationale Front Neubrandenburg 103: 'Erfahrungsaustausch am 12.9.1979 in Burg-Stargard mit Bürgermeistern über Probleme der Führung des Wettbewerbs '„Schöner unsere Städte und Gemeinden – Mach Mit!"'.

and to respect socialist law.[17] Socialist citizens were clean, orderly, respectful of property and mindful of each other's safety. While in West Germany, 'citizens' movements' (*Bürgerbewegungen*) formed in opposition to the state, in the GDR citizens kept streets and pavements free from litter, thus testifying to the bond between state, party and the socialist community.[18] Thanks to the 'Join in!' competition, Germans in the GDR had become fundamentally different from those in the West.

Through 'Join in!', the party sought to ensure that individual commitment to the socialist heimat went beyond the public transcript, and was appropriated in behaviour, thought, and attitude. This chapter explores how individuals responded to this agenda by state and party, and what meanings the citizens developed in turn. Since the National Front measured patriotic engagement in 'Join in!' principally in economic terms, I shall begin by exploring the competition's economic scope and limitations. The second section focuses on why individuals participated, and how their motivations related to the official construction of citizenship. Finally, the third part looks more closely at the campaign's private, intensely local meanings which this participatory competition engendered in practice. I shall argue that these local meanings encouraged a cohesion centred on the locality, which contrasted with official narratives of citizenship and socialist patriotism. 'Join in!' was successful in allowing individuals to respond creatively to some of the most actute problems of the socialist economy, but this undermined the party's endeavours to create a unique bond between socialism and the individual.

'JOIN IN!' – MORE BEAUTIFUL OUR CITIES AND COMMUNITIES[19]

From the GDR's creation in the late 1940s, the party tried to encourage voluntary participation in campaigns beyond the workplace as a sign of individual and collective commitment. The most important of these initiatives, the 'National Reconstruction Effort' (Nationales Aufbauwerk,

[17] LHA Schwerin, Nationale Front Neubrandenburg 103: 'Aktennotiz über eine Beratung mit Kreissekretären zur Grundorientierung des Nationalrates für die Führung des „Mach Mit!"-Wettbewerbs in den Jahren 1981/85' (14 August 1981).

[18] Werner Gramann, *Nationale Front und Bürgerinitiative: Die Rolle der Nationalen Front der DDR – das Zusammenwirken der Ausschüsse mit den Volksvertretungen bei der Organisierung des „Mach Mit!"-Wettbewerbes in den Städten und Gemeinden* (Berlin: Staatsverlag der Deutschen Demokratischen Republik, 1973), pp. 40–1, 55–6, 57–8, 60–1.

[19] The slogan was used interchangeably in two versions: '"Join in" – more beautiful our cities and communities', and 'More beautiful our cities and communities – "Join in!"'.

NAW), was launched by the SED's Central Committee on 25 November 1951. Directed by the National Front (NF), citizens were encouraged to devote some of their spare time to the reconstruction of East Berlin. A year later, the movement was extended to cover the entire GDR. As part of the NAW, citizens contributed to the construction of schools, museums, culture houses and roads. They helped bring in the harvest, and engaged in prestigious projects such as the development of Rostock harbour and the Sosa Dam. Although the NAW had considerable difficulty in enticing citizens to contribute to its campaigns in practice,[20] the National Front claimed that, over the fifteen years of its existence, the NAW pumped an extra 4 billion Marks (M) into the economy.[21]

Alongside the NAW, the Friends of Nature and Heimat organized their own participatory campaign, in which residents were called upon to clean up and beautify their villages and small towns in pursuit of the title 'The Beautiful Village'. Taking up an idea widely promoted during the early years of National Socialism, the campaign originated in Dresden district in 1955, before the Friends of Nature and Heimat transformed this into a GDR-wide participatory campaign the following year.[22] While the popular response to this campaign was extremely varied, in many villages and regions individuals actively engaged in cleaning up public spaces, mending and painting fences, and planting greenery.[23]

Almost immediately tensions arose between 'The Beautiful Village' and the NAW. The Cultural League's Friends of Nature and Heimat had originally initiated the campaign as their contribution to the NAW.[24] However, in many parts of the country National Front officials showed little enthusiasm for promoting the competition, fearing that this would deflect from the NAW's main goal of post-war reconstruction.[25] At the same time, the Cultural League's competition offered a rare opportunity to bring the NAW into villages and small towns, where it and the NF had thus far found it particularly difficult to establish their presence. Consequently, in 1958 the National Front took over the 'Beautiful Village' organization from the Cultural League. With this move, the NF hoped in part to appropriate the support of heimat activists for its own

---

[20] Port, *Conflict and Stability*, pp. 228–9.   [21] BArch-SAPMO, DY6 2330: 'Nationales Aufbauwerk'.
[22] Schaarschmidt, *Regionalkultur*, pp. 423–33.
[23] BArch-SAPMO, DY27 3164, Bezirk Halle, 'Protokoll über die Bezirkswettbewerbskommission „Das schöne Dorf"am 30. Oktober 1956'.
[24] Schaarschmidt, *Regionalkultur*, p. 430.
[25] Ibid., 'Bericht über den Stand des Wettbewerbs „Das schöne Dorf" in allen Bezirken der Deutschen Demokratischen Republik' (*c.* October/November 1956).

ends, to assert its control over their activities, and to integrate them better into the NAW in general.[26]

Under the National Front's direction, 'The Beautiful Village' was immediately adapted to respond to the decision of the Fifth Party Congress (1958) to increase economic production levels so that per capita consumption would exceed West German levels by 1961.[27] The communal voluntary tasks which villagers undertook for the competition were meant to testify to the creation of a socialist community marked not only by the collective ownership of land, but also by the transition from the 'small I to the large We' under socialism.[28] Since only a socialist [collectivized] village could be truly beautiful,[29] the central goal of 'The Beautiful Village' no longer consisted of beautifying the village, but rather in accelerating collectivization and increasing agricultural production. This was clearly summarized in the slogan for the 1960 competition: 'More Meat and Milk, More Fat and Eggs'.[30]

The National Front's appropriation of 'The Beautiful Village' led to a dramatic decline in participation rates among the Friends of Nature and Heimat. Most of the competition's original proponents in the Cultural League refused to participate in the new competition, which they no longer regarded as their own.[31] In Dippoldiswalde county (Dresden district), for instance, three villages participated in 1955, forty-six in 1956, and in 1957 all fifty-seven villages in the county took part. In 1958, when the NF took over the campaign, forty-eight villages participated, and in 1959, not a single one did.[32] Given widespread hostility to the collectivization of agriculture, and the general discontent with the economic situation, linking 'The Beautiful Village' competition to collectivization ensured that it was

---

[26] BArch-SAPMO, DY6 2318: 'Betr. Aktion „Das schöne Dorf"' (28 February 1958), item 6.

[27] BArch-SAPMO, DY6 2318: 'Büro des Präsidiums, H. Schnitzler, an Karl-Heinz Schulmeister. Betr. Wettbewerb „Das schöne Dorf"' (15 July 1958).

[28] Ibid., 'Um das schöne sozialistische Dorf' (letter from Rogowski, head of the National Front's press department, to the editors of *Der freie Bauer*, 25 April 1958).

[29] Ibid.,: pamphlet 'Worum geht es beim Wettbewerb Das schöne Dorf? An alle Freunde der Nationalen Front, die an der Verschönerung des Lebens in unseren Dörfern mitarbeiten' (November 1957).

[30] BArch-SAPMO, DY6 2307: 'Alle helfen mit bei der Steigerung der Marktproduktion in der Landwirtschaft', Entwurf (draft)(23 January 1960). On the changed character of the movement, see also BArch-SAPMO, DY6 2318: 'Einschätzung des Wettbewerbs „Das schöne Dorf" 1959' (signed Rogowski, December 1959). BArch-SAPMO, DY6 2307: 'Beschluß des Präsidiums des Nationalrats über die Verbesserung der Arbeit der Ausschüsse der Nationalen Front auf dem Lande' (3 March 1959).

[31] BArch-SAPMO, DY6 2307: 'Hausmitteilung Gen. Herr an Gen. Seigewasser' (9 October 1958).

[32] BArch-SAPMO, DY27 2817: 'Einschätzung „Das schöne sozialistische Dorf" im Kreis Dippoldiswalde' (signed Kurt Klaus, 11 November 1963).

doomed to failure. In late 1961 the NF discontinued the initiative. Although in the following years some members of the Friends of Nature and Heimat reappropriated the competition to try and energize local organizations on behalf of the heimat,[33] 'The Beautiful Village' had failed to establish itself as a mass participatory movement.

Just as the socialist national culture had been launched in 1959 with a carefully orchestrated call from the workers of Bitterfeld, so the NAW was replaced by 'spontaneous' calls from workers, under the careful guidance of the National Front. In the 'Torgau Initiative' of 1967, workers from that town urged all citizens to help in the construction and beautification of their residential areas, and to focus on culture and leisure projects that would improve the quality of life for all.[34] In response to this call from the provinces, workers in the Berlin district of Köpenick launched the initiative 'More beautiful our cities and communities – "Join in!"' on 28 February 1968. Mindful that the workers of Berlin had pioneered the GDR's reconstruction efforts ever since the War, they now called on the rest of the country to follow their example and donate their voluntary labour in honour of the GDR's twentieth birthday.[35]

In marked contrast to the NAW, 'Join in!' did focus on the outward beauty of the locality, at least officially. The movement's original goals consisted of beautifying towns and communities, improving conditions and facilities in residential areas, fostering the ideological and cultural advancement of the population not least through better leisure centres, and improving relations among citizens and between citizens and 'their' state.[36] This does not mean, of course, that the NF was not interested in the economic gains that resulted from voluntary work. On the contrary, renewed patriotism through 'Join in!' would produce a greater dedication of the individual to the fulfilment of the plan. More immediately, voluntary participation in the plan, even if it occurred mainly outside the workplace, led to additional economic benefits and thus strengthened the socialist economy.[37] Nevertheless, the National Front in Berlin was

---

[33] Ibid.   [34] BArch-SAPMO, DY6 2330: 'Nationales Aufbauwerk'.

[35] Ibid., 'Diskussionsbeitrag des Genossen Werner Kirchhoff … auf der Bürgervertretung in Berlin-Köpenick am 29.2.1969'.

[36] Ibid., 'Information über erste Ergebnisse und Erfahrungen des Wettbewerbs der Städte und Gemeinden zu Ehren des 20. Jahrestages der DDR' (Berlin, 2 May 1968), p. 2.

[37] In Ulbricht's words, 'The economic achievements brought about through the voluntary work of our population cannot be overestimated.' Walter Ulbricht, 'Durch schöpferische Initiative wird unsere Heimat schöner und reicher als je zuvor', in *Schöner unsere Städte und Gemeinden – Mach Mit! Zum 20. Jahrestag der DDR*, ed. Nationalrat der Nationalen Front (Berlin: Staatsverlag der Deutschen Demokratischen Republik, 1968), pp. 18–19.

at pains to emphasize to local officials that this really was primarily a participatory movement for the cultivation and care of the heimat.

To the Berlin central office, the district of Erfurt, and especially its district capital, showed how well this competition could work. During one weekend in April 1969, over 20,000 citizens participated in a spring-cleaning exercise, in which 15,000 pansies were planted, 100 km of streets cleaned, and tramlines cleared of rubbish. The NF headquarters in Berlin were particularly impressed that the spring-cleaning proved to be a testament to ongoing socialist integration, noting that citizens from other parts of the district, including the recalcitrant Eichsfeld, had helped tidy up 'their' district capital. Indeed, bands and food stalls had ensured that this was not a weekend of hard labour but a celebration of the socialist community in action.[38] The following weekend, on 26 April, it was the turn of nearby Mühlhausen to be cleaned up, with 6,700 citizens apparently helping out in the county town alone. Again, cultural groups performed while helpers cleaned up the town and contributed to economic projects that were part of the plan.[39]

Unfortunately, Erfurt appeared to be less an example than an exception to the rule. In May 1968, Albert Norden was appalled to find that in Karl-Marx-Stadt district, functionaries had tried to mobilize the population not to care for and tidy up their villages, but to complete construction projects that were lagging behind schedule. He was also aghast that throughout the country, functionaries had initiated costly projects while ignoring the beautification of town centres. Norden urged functionaries to focus on town centres, where the need was greatest, and where the effects of the volunteers' work could be verified by the greatest numbers of people. Citizens, he argued, needed to witness directly the fruits of their labour.[40]

Fifteen months into the campaign, Paula Acker, a member of the National Front's national council at the centre of the movement's organization, wrote a concerned note to Klaus Sorgenicht, head of the Central Committee's department for state and legal affairs. At a time when the competition was supposed to be reaching its climax, Acker wrote 'I am very concerned about the ['Join in!'] competition between towns and communities. To tell the truth, there is nothing happening up and down the country. Only a few examples stand out, a state of affairs that should

---

[38] BArch-SAPMO, DY30 IV/A2 9.02 196: 'Berlin, den 22.5.1969. Arbeitsmaterial. „Frühjahrsputz" in Erfurt-Stadt'.

[39] Ibid., 'Arbeitsmaterial! So muß gearbeitet werden! Bezirk Erfurt. Vorbereitung und Durchführung „Frühjahrsputz" am 26.4.1969 im Kreis Mühlhausen'.

[40] Ibid., 'Bericht über eine Beratung mit Genossen Albert Norden … am 18. Mai 1968'.

have been overcome. We need mass movements, not an example here and there.' Acker lamented that the only districts where 'Join in!' had developed satisfactorily were Erfurt and possibly also Gera.[41] According to the National Front's own internal communications, participation in the campaign of 1968–9 had fallen well below expectations.

Publicly, 'Join in!' was heralded as the resounding success that its close connection to the GDR's twentieth 'birthday' required it to be. By 15 June 1969, the NF was pointing to the creation, thanks to the citizens who had 'Joined in', of 34,042 places in kindergartens, and almost 80,000 in day-care centres. They had built 1,627 classrooms and renovated 17,361 flats. Towns and cities had been cleaned up, and citizens had engaged in more cultural activities, not least in preparation for the twentieth anniversary celebrations of the state on 7 October 1969.[42]

Although the 'Join in!' movement of 1968–9 had fallen short of expectations, Walter Ulbricht announced on 26 September 1969 that it was to become an annual event. Subsequently the National Front tried to increase its control over the movement, and to improve results by changing the ways in which the competition was organized. Whereas initially the NF had advocated joint projects that were undertaken over one weekend as highlights of communal engagement, from the early 1970s 'Join in!' was advocated as a continuous participatory activity. Individual highlights were still encouraged, but only if they complemented regular voluntary activities throughout the year.[43]

In response to the Eighth Party Congress,[44] six priorities were to determine popular 'Join in!' activities in the future:[45] beautifying and repairing existing housing; building additional housing; building private housing; tending green spaces in residential areas; cleaning up industrial waste; and gathering and recycling materials.[46] Of these six priorities, only one related exclusively to the original goal of making local

[41] Ibid., 'Genossen Klaus Sorgenicht. Abteilung Staat u. Recht, von Agitationskommission Paula Acker, 22.5.69'. 'Paula Acker an Genossen Norden, 22.5.69'.

[42] Ibid., 'Abschlußbericht Wettbewerb der Städte und Gemeinden am 20. Jahrestag der DDR' (4 September 1969).

[43] Gramann, *Nationale Front*, pp. 62–4.

[44] BArch-SAPMO, DY30 IV/A2 9.02 196: 'Werner Kirchhoff am 30. Juni 1971 an Gen. Prof. Albert Norden, Mitglied des Politbüros des ZK der SED. Anliegend kurze Information über Situation im Wettbewerb der Städte und Gemeinden nach VIII. Parteitag'.

[45] See, for instance, *Verbesserung der Wohnbedingungen – wichtigste Aufgabe im „Mach Mit!" Wettbewerb*, Gemeinsame Tagung des Sekretariats des Nationalrats der Nationalen Front der DDR und des Ministeriums für Bauwesen am 24. Okt. 1973 in Eberswalde-Finow (Berlin, 1973), a publication issued by the National Front in order to publicize and popularize this shift of emphasis.

[46] Gramann, *Nationale Front*, pp. 62–4.

spaces more beautiful, while clearly the emphasis now rested on economic improvement and the provision of better housing.

The competition could have very beneficial effects for citizens and the plan alike. In 1973, for instance, the local residential administration in the model new town of Halle-Neustadt had registered 3,000 complaints about the condition of the new flats.[47] To enable individual citizens to deal with such problems, the National Front founded lending stations where tools could be borrowed for the repair and refurbishment of houses.[48] According to the National Front's own figures, 960 lending stations existed throughout the GDR by 1975, and 1,450 by 1976. This enabled residents to undertake regular, preventive maintenance work of their own as a contribution to 'Join in!', with the aim of avoiding major repair work requiring skilled workers.[49]

Through 'Join in!', the National Front tried hard to encourage the formation of housing communities. The NF argued that through communal activities residents would work together and get to know each other, and this would provide the beginnings of new local connections. For this reason, the National Front also encouraged the organization of heimat festivals as part of 'Join in!' Just as in the 1960s the SED had promoted such festivals because they encouraged villagers to engage in communal cleaning activities, so the National Front hoped that preparing for local festivals would provide additional motivation for communal projects, especially in new towns.[50] Communal activity in the participatory movement thus helped, according to the NF's ideal, to overcome the alienation which many citizens were experiencing in the new towns, and to create bonds and identities characteristic of the homeland's smaller towns and villages. In sum, 'Join in!' became an important contributor to achieving Honecker's ambitions for the construction of new flats and entire new towns. Paradoxically, it was also designed to help overcome some of the social and cultural problems caused by this same rapid construction programme, by fostering the sense of protectedness so desired by Honecker.[51]

---

[47] BArch-SAPMO, Volkskammer der DDR, DAI 11813: Abg. Marta-Maria Böttcher: 'Bericht über die Beratungen, die ich zu Problemen des Wettbewerbs „Schöner unsere Städte und Gemeinden – Mach mit!" in meinem Wahlkreis Halle-Neustadt durchgeführt habe'.

[48] Erwin Bondzin, 'Wohnverhältnisse verbessern: Was kann die Nationale Front der DDR dazu tun?', *Mach mit: Zeitschrift für die Ausschüsse der Nationalen Front der DDR* 10 (1976), 4–9; here 8–9.

[49] Bondzin, 'Wohnverhältnisse', 9.

[50] Werner Seidel, 'Verbesserung der Wohnbedingungen – gemeinsames Anliegen der KWV und Nationaler Front', in *Verbesserung der Wohnbedingungen*, pp. 55–6. Kurt Heunemann, 'Gründliche Vorbereitung, exakte Planung, rechtzeitige Information', ibid., pp. 57–9.

[51] LHA Schwerin, Nationale Front Neubrandenburg 114: 'Referat für die Tagung mit den Hausgemeinschaften' (4 September 1974).

Throughout the 1970s and 1980s, the movement closely reflected the party's shifting economic and social concerns.[52] Through an ever-growing number of sub-competitions, the National Front sought to channel the environmental concerns of the population into concrete action. By 1988, 'Join in!' comprised competitions entitled 'Beautiful Railway Stations', 'The Cared-for Landscape – The Cared-for Environment', 'A Healthy Forest', and 'Our Waters – Cared-for Waters'. Not forgetting its commitment to neighbourhood communities, the National Front also created an annual competition for the 'Golden House Number', an award presented to model housing communities. In 1987, when the National Front claimed the citizens had contributed to the housing programme to the value of over 13 billion East German marks, it also noted that citizens had gathered 430,000 tonnes of scrap metal and 1.3 billion bottles and glasses. Citizens had planted 8.9 million trees through 'A Tree of Life for my Country'; they enthusiastically joined the initiative 'Our Waters – Cared-for Waters', and contributed to the initiative 'Beautiful Railway Stations' by cleaning 1,500 stations throughout the country.[53] Right up until the end of the GDR's existence, the National Front insisted on the economic significance of the participatory campaign, holding it up as evidence of the citizens' commitment to socialism.

Since the 'Join in!' campaign was linked closely to the exercise of citizenship and socialist patriotism, it is difficult to see how the National Front could have done anything other than postulate the campaign's growing success, year on year. But beneath these apparently impressive figures lurked a number of fundamental problems.

At the heart of the GDR's economic system was the centralised planning of input and output for each economic unit, whereby even minor disruptions to the plan in one unit directly affected economic production elsewhere. Perhaps the greatest challenges to economic planners consisted in gathering all the information necessary for effective central planning and finding mechanisms to prevent – or at least limit – disruptions to the plan.[54] By contrast, 'Join in!' aimed at creating economic values through improvements that were over and above the plan. This is undoubtedly why, in the

---

[52] LHA Schwerin, Nationale Front Neubrandenburg 103: 'Aktennotiz über eine Beratung mit Kreissekretären zur Grundorientierung des Nationalrates für die Führung des „Mach Mit!"-Wettbewerbs in den Jahren 1981/85' (14 August 1981).

[53] LHA Schwerin, Nationale Front Neubrandenburg 96: 'Ergebnisse der Bürgerinitiative „Schöner unsere Städte und Gemeinden – Mach mit!" im Jahre 1988' (pamphlet presenting results of the 'Join in!' movement for the entire GDR).

[54] Caldwell, *Dictatorship*, ch. 1.

initial phase of 'Join in!', Albert Norden, Paula Acker and others were so keen to emphasize cleaning activities over construction projects. It was always possible to clear away rubbish, tidy front gardens or weed local parks.[55] By contrast, construction projects that were not included in the plan raised the issue of finding extra resources (such as construction materials and expensive tools) whose supply was fixed and whose utilization would lead to shortages elsewhere within the plan.

By focusing on construction in the 1970s, and expanding the competition to cover other concerns such as the cultural life of the 'new towns' and the collection of recyclable materials, the National Front did try hard to better integrate the competition into the plan. Individual and collective contributions were anticipated by planners, and the NF's expectations were communicated to participants before they made their commitments at the beginning of the year. However, in an economy plagued by material shortages, particularly as the Honecker era progressed, this still left room for substantial shortfalls in supplies for individual projects. Moreover, individuals and communities continued to pursue projects that were not part of the plan. Citizens were keen to create assets like communal swimming pools, the costs of whose upkeep far exceeded any savings obtained through communal labour. Throughout the movement's existence, the party struggled to integrate 'Join in!' into the plan.[56]

The party's decision to direct the movement towards extra construction created additional problems. In many communities, it was difficult to gather the technology needed to carry out the construction projects. Agricultural or industrial co-operatives were not always willing to provide their expensive and already overused machinery for the 'Join in!' movement.[57] Moreover, many projects required skilled craftsmen. As the mayor of Sondershausen (Erfurt district) put it succinctly, 'What do I need all these citizens for? The skills of experts are what's needed.'[58] However, skilled craftsmen appeared to be particularly resistant to the National

---

[55] As stated in the original call to initiate 'Join in!' in Berlin, to beautify even the remotest corner of Berlin often required only 'water, soap and sponge, paint, shovel and brush, coupled with thought and dynamism'. *Schöner unsere Städte und Gemeinden*, p. 64.

[56] BArch-SAPMO, DY6 2331: 'Zwischenbericht: Über den Wettbewerb „Schöner unsere Städte und Gemeinden – Mach mit!" zu Ehren des 20. Jahrestages der Gründung der DDR' (22 May 1969).

[57] BArch-SAPMO, DY6 2337: 'Ergebnisse der in 19 Kleinstädten und Gemeinden durchgeführten Untersuchungen zur weiteren Entfaltung der „Mach Mit!"-Initiative zur Verbesserung der Arbeits- und Lebensbedingungen' (11 July 1973).

[58] 'Was brauche ich viele Bürger – Kapazitäten von Fachleuten sind notwendig'. ThHStAWe Nationale Front 133, f. 54: 'Einschätzung der Leistungstätigkeit des Kreissekretariats der Nationalen Front Sondershausen' (19 September 1969).

Front's participatory calls. Those not already working on construction sites were already poorly paid and highly dissatisfied,[59] while their colleagues working for construction co-operatives were used to extra pay for extra work, and often demanded up to 15 marks per hour for their services.[60] Without the skills of this group of labourers, however, the construction of new and the repair of old housing could not proceed. Evidently, not every citizen's participation was of equal value.

As well as resorting increasingly to paying participants, the National Front pursued other strategies to stimulate activity. Through the growing diversity of competitions, the organization hoped to prevent communities from becoming set in their ways as they registered their contributions, year in, year out.[61] In practice, however, the multiplication of competitions and honours led to a loss of control over individual contributions.

In Neubrandenburg district, the National Front introduced in 1980 'The Beautiful Village' and its urban counterpart, 'The Beautiful Residential District'. To acquire this title, villages or residential districts not only had to fulfil a range of criteria, such as providing an active cultural life and well-maintained public spaces, but also had to have already received the accolade of being an 'area of model orderliness, cleanliness and discipline'. By 1986, 61.2% of Neubrandenburg villages had been recognized as 'areas of model orderliness, cleanliness and discipline', but for the district leaders of the National Front, this was insufficient; functionaries could think of no reason why many more villages should not receive this accolade within a year.[62] By 30 June 1988, 90.5 per cent of villages had been recognized as 'areas of model orderliness, cleanliness and discipline', with 74.6% also counting as 'Beautiful Villages'. However, the contrast between these accolades and the grim, grey appearance of many localities was only too evident, and troubled even the National Front.

---

[59] ThHStAWe Nationale Front 13, ff. 114–18: 'Aktuelle Berichterstattung lt. Informationsplan des Sekretariats des Nationalrates für das 1. Quartal 1976 – Termin: 16.2.76' (13 February 1976).

[60] LHA Schwerin, Nationale Front Neubrandenburg 111: 'Aktennotiz über ein Informationsgespräch des Bezirkssekretärs mit den stellvertretenden Vorsitzenden des Bezirksausschusses der NF am 10.6.75'.

[61] This was a persistent problem identified by the National Front in Neubrandenburg district in 1981: 'Es steht die Frage der Routine, schon seit Jahren und auch jetzt'. LHA Schwerin, Nationale Front Neubrandenburg 103: 'Aktennotiz über eine Beratung mit Kreissekretären zur Grundorientierung des Nationalrates für die Führung des „Mach Mit!"-Wettbewerbs in den Jahren 1981/85' (14 August 1981).

[62] LHA Schwerin, Nationale Front Neubrandenburg 3906: 'Wertung der erreichten Ergebnisse in der Bärgerinitiative [sic!] „Schöner unsere Städte und Gemeinden – Mach Mit!" im Jahre 1986 und Aufgaben bei ihrer Weiterführung im Jahre 1987', p. 5.

Functionaries now raised concerns about the political effect of declaring the village to be beautiful when its inhabitants obviously did not think so.[63] Clearly, the NF had itself provided strong encouragement to inflate the reporting of local achievements.[64] If its awards were ineffective it had only itself to blame.

Even though the National Front used material gains as evidence of socialist citizenship, in private functionaries confessed they had no idea what values the citizens actually contributed.[65] To overcome this problem, the National Front continued to refine its methods for quantitatively measuring the value of completed projects. Every hour committed to 'Join in!' was given a monetary value; tables converted the most common activities, from painting fences to installing sanitary facilities in flats, into monetary values. This gave rise to a number of problems. The value created was often economically counterproductive. For instance, many individuals used the materials and even the small remuneration provided by the competition to construct private homes and garages. These were accounted for as value created, even though they diverted scarce resources away from public projects where they were needed most.[66]

The problem of inaccurate information was exacerbated by constant changes in the value given to particular activities. Between 1985 and 1986, for example, the value created by the citizens of Neubrandenburg jumped by over 60 per cent, from 336 marks per capita in the district in 1985 to 551.74 marks per capita in 1986. Yet over the same period there had been a decline in work carried out on a number of major projects, such as the number of façades renovated (down by 643) and the number of pensioners' flats renovated (down 176). That such spectacular increases in value were nevertheless achieved was thus largely the result of the more generous accounting practices introduced in 1986.[67]

---

[63] Ibid., 'Wertung der erreichten Ergebnisse in der Bürgerinitiative „Schöner unsere Städte und Gemeinden – Mach Mit!" im Jahre 1986 und Aufgaben bei ihrer Weiterführung im Jahre 1987. Erfahrungsaustausch zur Gestaltung schöner und produktiver Dörfer am 9.9.1988'.

[64] BArch-SAPMO, DY6 4994: 'Einschätzung der Ergebnisse des Wettbewerbs „Schöner unsere Städte und Gemeinden – Mach Mit!" in Vorbereitung auf den 30. Jahrestag der Befreiung vom Hitlerfaschismus. Nationale Front Bezirk Suhl' (Suhl, 11 April 1975).

[65] LHA Schwerin, Nationale Front Neubrandenburg 103: 'Aktennotiz über eine Beratung mit Kreissekretären zur Grundorientierung des Nationalrates für die Führung des „Mach Mit!"-Wettbewerbs in den Jahren 1981/85' (14 August 1981).

[66] BArch-SAPMO, DAI 11813: 'Teilbericht der Arbeitsgruppe des Volkskammerausschusses für Eingaben der Bürger über den Einsatz im Kreis Lobenstein, Bezirk Gera, am 18/19. Oktober 1973'.

[67] LHA Schwerin, Nationale Front Neubrandenburg 3906: 'Wertung der erreichten Ergebnisse in der Bürgerinitiative „Schöner unsere Städte und Gemeinden – Mach Mit!" im Jahre 1986 und Aufgaben bei ihrer Weiterführung im Jahre 1987'.

In part because of these constant changes and uncertainties in how values were computed, localities had considerable leeway in their reports. Functionaries in Röbel, one of the underperforming counties of Neubrandenburg district, noted that in 1981, the number of citizens involved in cleaning activities had almost doubled relative to 1980, with the total number of hours devoted to this task increasing by 18,460. And yet, when converted into value, functionaries were perplexed to find that the figure had actually declined, from 303,732 marks in 1980 to 273,282 marks in 1981. Functionaries concluded that even in this small county, accounting practices differed greatly between villages.[68] If one locality notched up twice as much value as its neighbour,[69] it was never clear whether this was the result of greater popular commitment, better organization, or simply more generous accounting practices.

Finally, creating new assets was one thing – but maintaining them was quite another. Many communities committed themselves to creating clean and green public spaces from one year to the next. However, there was no accountable value attached to maintaining such spaces in subsequent years. While counting on every citizen's activity, the NF persisted in the ideal of 'spontaneous' activism that should not be routinized and become part of the plan. But as a result of this approach, many of the assets created in one year were abandoned in the next.[70] Moreover, no account was taken of the depreciation of created assets. Between 1987 and 1989 the National Front in Neubrandenburg valued the installation of a bathroom at between 3,500 and 6,000 marks,[71] a span that in itself left much room for subjective interpretation. Yet in 1987 the GDR's sole domestic supplier of bathtubs had to cease production temporarily. For a year, all bathtubs were imported from Romania; these were of such poor quality that they often corroded after six months.[72] If fitted with such

[68] LHA Schwerin, Nationale Front Neubrandenburg 103: 'Analyse angewandter Führungsmethoden und erreichter Ergebnisse im „Mach Mit!" Wettbewerb des Kreises Röbel', p. 3.

[69] For instance, in 1986 Prenzlau county made almost the same contributions to the competition as another county with the same number of inhabitants, Pasewalk, but its results in value terms were twice as good. LHA Schwerin, Nationale Front Neubrandenburg 3906: 'Wertung der erreichten Ergebnisse in der Bürgerinitiative „Schöner unsere Städte und Gemeinden – Mach Mit!" im Jahre 1986 und Aufgaben bei ihrer Weiterführung im Jahre 1987', p. 3.

[70] LHA Schwerin, Nationale Front Neubrandenburg 103: Lektion 'Grundprobleme der Weiterführung des „Mach-mit!-Wettbewerbs"', p. 31.

[71] LHA Schwerin, Nationale Front Neubrandenburg 3906: 'Hinweise für die wertmäßige Umrechnung ausgewählter VMI-Leistungen'. This file from 1987 to 1989 contains two tables with identical titles.

[72] BArch-SAPMO, DAI 17301, ff. 31, 51: 'Stenografisches Protokoll. Sitzung des Ausschusses für Eingaben der Bürger vom 25. bis 27. Oktober 1988 in Dessau', comments by deputy Fehl, and Karl Schmiechen from the Ministry of Construction.

bathtubs, bathrooms renovated in this period would soon have declined considerably in value, but this never appeared in the NF's statistics. The values recorded each year thus said little about either the quality of what had been produced, or the permanence of the citizens' improvements.

The 'Join in!' campaign clearly represented a concerted attempt by the party to ensure that citizens appropriated socialism in their daily lives. Yet the party itself had to concede that citizens did not appear to have changed their behaviour significantly as a result of the competition. Why, then, did millions contribute to the campaign nonetheless, and what aspects of socialism, if any, did they appropriate? Moreover, how did citizens respond to the shortcomings of the campaign and the problems it was designed to alleviate? The following section asks what the campaign meant for individual appropriations of socialism.

DOMINATION AND THE PUBLIC TRANSCRIPT

Today, one is hard-pressed to find anyone, whether former SED member or not, who relates their activity in 'Join in!' to the party's public transcript: a sense of patriotism and a distinctive GDR citizenship.[73] One person who comes close to linking individual participation to the designs of state and party is Gertrud Glandt. Glandt had been county secretary for an active branch of the Cultural League in Rudolstadt, a small, historic Thuringian town in Gera district. Originally from the Rhineland, Glandt had been evacuated to the area during the war. After the war, she married a local, joined the party, and chose to stay. After confirming that 'Join in!' had worked well in her town, she considered the evidence that the movement worked less well elsewhere in the GDR:

I cannot judge this, though I can hardly believe it. I do not believe this. I ask you, which collective, which brigade would have dared not to participate? This reached all the way into the workplace.[74]

Here was an evident belief in the people's unquestioning response to the calls of the National Front, a belief which was not corroborated by any other respondent. Yet, when asked earlier why there had been so much activity on

[73] Of over forty people I interviewed about their activities in 'Join in!', not one related these to the purposes of the party.
[74] Interview with Gertrud Glandt, 30 April 2003. 'Kann ich nicht beurteilen, wobei ich das beinahe nicht glauben kann. Ich glaube das nicht. Aber ich bitte Sie, welches Kollektiv, welche Brigade, wer hätte sich denn erlaubt, da auszuscheren. Das ging doch rein bis in die Betriebe.'

behalf of the heimat in this area, Glandt emphasized that this could only come from individuals:

Many wonderful things were created … But why? Because we did not order these people around. I cannot go to them and say: 'At the Ninth Party Congress it was decided that you should do it this way or that way.' That does not work.[75]

Even Glandt agreed that individual or collective activity on behalf of the local heimat could not be imposed or dictated. It was born of individual passion and interest; invoking socialist patriotism would have been counterproductive.[76]

Jürgen Thormann, Cultural League secretary for Mühlhausen, made this point more explicitly:

Two or three times a year, our preservationists set out to clean the city walls. They did this out of their love for the town. I recorded this 'in the name of the National Front [Initiative]: Join in!' Or take the Reisa nature reserve. We had a group that worked there enthusiastically throughout the year, they would have done this even without the competition. We did nothing artificially, because that did not work, I'm telling you, people were already full up with the workplace, their jobs, public life, they were already in this hubbub. We did not decide 'now we will do something'. That was not on, they would have come back to me and said: 'you must be crazy, if I want to do that I can go to my workplace'. They said themselves what they wanted to do.[77]

Pointing to their contributions through the Cultural League allowed hobbyists to evade the 'Join in!' movement at the workplace or in their residential areas, which gave them important and rare opportunities to elude interference from the party. From this perspective, 'Join in!' worked

[75] Interview with Gertrud Glandt, 30 April 2003. 'Es wurde viel schönes geboren … Aber warum? Weil wir diesen Leuten keine Vorschriften gemacht haben. Da kann ich nicht hingehen und sagen, auf dem 9. Parteitag wurde beschlossen, ihr sollt das so und so machen. Geht nicht.'

[76] Glandt's observations were confirmed by Manfred Kastner in Neustadt am Rennsteig in an interview on 29 April 2003 (in response to the question whether his group participated in 'Join in!'), and Kurt Ludwig (25 March 2003), Erfurt district secretary of the Cultural League (in response to the question how far Cultural League members were prepared to be involved in 'Join in!', and the kinds of projects in which they were involved).

[77] Interview with Jürgen Thormann, 29 April 2003. 'die Denkmalpfleger haben Arbeitseinsatz an der Stadtmauer 2–3 Mal im Jahr gemacht. Das haben die gemacht zur Liebe ihrer Stadt. Ich habe das gemeldet „im Rahmen der Nationalen Front Mach Mit" … [oder das] Naturschutzgebiet Reisa: da hatten wir eine AG [*Arbeitsgemeinschaft*] die da idealistisch das ganze Jahr gearbeitet haben, die hätten das auch ohne den Wettbewerb gemacht. Wir haben nischt künstlich [gemacht], weil das nicht ging, ich sag doch, die Leute waren doch mit Betrieb, Arbeit, Gesellschaftsleben [ausgelastet], die waren doch sowieso schon in diesem Trubel … Wir haben das nicht beschlossen: wir machen jetzt irgendwas … Das ging gar nicht, da hätten die zu mir gesagt, „ja, du spinnst wohl, da kann ich auch in den Betrieb gehen". Die haben selber gesagt [was sie machen wollen] …'

not because it activated citizens, but because it was able to encompass activities that citizens were already engaged in anyway.

Even if many activities were conducted irrespective of 'Join in!', mass organizations were very keen to record activity levels as part of the competition. For the Cultural League, for instance, registering its members' contributions served as a strategy for accruing official credit with state and party which could be 'cashed in' on other occasions.[78] As Kurt Ludwig, district secretary in Erfurt, noted,

Once you realized how this worked, you got money, you got means, and so you said: 'Of course the Cultural League has to join in.' Otherwise the Cultural League always had this reputation as in: well, these are crazy, they have a language of their own, they do not speak the language of the *Neues Deutschland* [newspaper].[79]

Recording impressive 'Join in!' figures was important for the Cultural League to demonstrate its political and economic significance to the National Front, and to its own membership.

Many activists took part only indirectly; their labour would have been recorded, but they were not necessarily aware of, or interested in, how this was done. Despite his commitment to the homeland's environment, Hartmut Baade left no doubt that he had had no dealings with the 'Join in!' movement. When I persisted in asking whether the hours he devoted to his environmental activities were registered anywhere, Baade confirmed that his hours of activity were certainly compiled and converted into values for the National Front. But he considered this meaningless for his own motivation. The dishonest accounting methods invalidated the competition completely in his eyes.[80]

If individuals and communities did take on new projects, this was because the competition allowed them to fulfil some of their long-standing needs and wants. This was particularly the case in the GDR's small towns and villages. Owing to the plan's hierarchical system of allocation, scarce resources were disproportionately allocated to the administrative capitals, industrial centres and county towns. Many villagers realized that if they

---

[78] BArch-SAPMO, DY27 962. 'Stenografisches Protokoll der Tagung des Präsidialrates des Kulturbundes der DDR' (19 January 1979).

[79] 'Aber wenn man das erst mal mitgekriegt hatte, dann kriegte man Geld, dann kriegte man Förderung, und da sagt man, natürlich muß der Kulturbund mitmachen. Sonst war der Kulturbund immer so'n bisschen [verrufen wie:] „naja, das sind Spinner, die haben immer so 'ne eigene Sprache, die reden nicht die Sprache des *Neuen Deutschland* [*sic*] ...' Interview with Kurt Ludwig, 25 March 2003.

[80] Interview with Helmut Baade, 19 April 2005. 'Also ja, abgerechnet wurde durch den Kreisnaturschutzverantwortlichen dann sicherlich, aber wissen se das war so bedeutungslos und im Endeffekt wurden die Zahlen meistens von drei Institutionen gleichzeitig abgerechnet und dann noch mal addiert, also das war etwas formales, [da] kann ich nichts weiter dazu sagen.'

wanted their houses to benefit from running water and indoor toilets, they themselves would have to install local connections to the central water and sewage systems. Oberdorla is a good example of such improvements being made through 'Join in!' Along with its neighbouring villages of Langula and Niederdorla, Oberdorla formed part of the 'Vogtei', a microregion just north of Mühlhausen which is linguistically and historically distinct from its surroundings. The Vogtei's cohesion was reinforced through the local 'Thomas Müntzer' co-operative which acted as the major employer for the three villages. The successful co-operative donated materials and machinery for the construction of a gym, a village hall and the local sewage system. These projects had all been carried out through the participation campaign, and thus contributed to the high values which both the co-operative and the villages could report to the National Front. When I asked interviewees why they had engaged in these campaigns, once again neither the National Front nor socialist patriotism featured as factors. Rather, villagers had their own concrete and very local motivations: if the villagers themselves did not pursue these projects, nobody would.[81]

When looking at the range of motivations for individual engagement in 'Join in!', a number of preliminary conclusions stand out. First, the competition worked in many respects because it provided a commonsense answer to the problems of the GDR economy. Everyday life was characterized by constantly shifting but never-ending supply shortages. 'Join in!' allowed a localized discussion of these problems and a common search for practicable solutions in a collective effort to 'make do'. Some local solutions were more eccentric than others. In 1974, the Cultural League of Rudolstadt wanted to restore the house in which Goethe and Schiller had first met, and make it the seat of a new Goethe Society. One of the problems the members of the Cultural League faced was cleaning and renovating the dirty, tumbledown outside walls of the house without scaffolding, which was unavailable. The local caving society's finest hour had come. It organized collective days of action in which its members, tied to a rope fastened to the roof, used their agility to help renovate the house.[82] The unorthodox use of special skills in this case was not unique. In Dresden, the National Front overcame the lack of scaffolding by

---

[81] Interviews with Inge and Berthold Fritzlar and Armin Walter, Langula, 18 April 2005. When I asked them what kinds of 'Join in!' initiatives had been carried out in the village, none of them could name any. When I asked them about the local water and sewerage connections, however, they had much to tell about their communal activities.

[82] Interview with Gertrud Glandt, 30 April 2003.

employing a group of fifteen mountaineers who used their expertise to rid historic buildings of unwanted weeds and moss.[83] The party encouraged individuals and communities to accommodate themselves as best they could to the shortcomings of the plan.

'Join in!' also gave citizens the wherewithal to realize particular ambitions, provided these could be registered as part of the competition. In 1969, Horst Meyer, a biology teacher in Neubrandenburg district, launched an initiative with a group of his pupils which he realized through 'Join in!' Meyer had decided to renovate a dilapidated estate which had belonged to an early nineteenth-century agrarian reformer. Within three years, Meyer and his pupils had succeeded in renovating the country house and transforming it into a museum, which opened in 1972. In subsequent years, Meyer's group and other volunteers from the area helped in the continuing expansion of the museum, the restoration of the surrounding park, and the organization of a yearly open-air festival. It is difficult to see how Meyer could have succeeded without 'Join in!':

And what we did we could sell under the guise 'we are doing this ... for the "Join in!" competition' ... Of course that acquired a completely different gloss ... Certain things that we wanted to do ... if one packaged something .... that one could otherwise never have done, through the 'Join in!' competition or in honour of the GDR's jubilee [anniversary] ... under such an artificial pretext we made the impossible possible.[84]

By presenting his activities as acts of citizenship performed in honour of the party and the country, Meyer knew he could muster official support and encouragement which he would otherwise not have received. This was particularly crucial before the mid-1970s, when the 'heritage' debate had not yet affected local officials' often dismissive attitudes towards local history projects that were not related to the communist movement.

---

[83] *Mach Mit* 10, 'Aus unserer Leserpost' (1976), 46.

[84] The full quotation is: 'und man konnte damit unser Gemachtes dann auch verkaufen unter diesem Vorzeichen, wir machen das ... eben im Mach-Mit-Wettbewerb ... Das hatte dann natürlich nen ganz anderen Anstrich ... ja also und ich hats vorhin schon gesagt, wir warn da sehr pfiffig auch. Bestimmte Dinge die uns am Herzen lagen, denen [von der Partei] mit zu verkaufen, also einfach unter einem Vorzeichen wie jetzt ein Jubiläum. Also Jubiläum der DDR oder so steht bevor ja. Da mussten sich alle verpflichten irgendwas zu machen. Und wenn man dann geschichtlich was verpackte, was man [anders] überhaupt nicht machen konnte ... Der Mach-Mit-Wettbewerb oder hier zu Ehren des Jubiläums der DDR; na dann konnte man gute Sachen vielleicht auch ein bisschen schneller befördern ne. Und in der Hinsicht waren wir absolut pfiffig, das ham wir, dafür ham wir so nen 7. Sinn entwickelt. Um auf diese Weise auch das Unmögliche möglich zu machen, unter so einem Vorzeichen und so einem künstlichen...' Interview with Horst Meyer, 5 February 2003 [name changed].

Meyer alluded to an important ritual of public life. All major accomplishments, from construction projects to local heimat festivals, were dedicated to particular anniversaries related to state and party, as a manifestation of the unity between the party and the working class, and of popular patriotism.[85] But one could evidently turn the tables, as Meyer had done, by using such occasions to realize one's own ambitions.

Given the party's own awareness of the campaign's shortcomings, and the moral effect this might have on the citizens, it is difficult to believe that the SED seriously believed in the realization of the socialist individual through 'Join in!' Instead, the campaign served to reaffirm the public transcript, expand it, and thus confirm the party's domination. The fact that the widest possible range of activities was dedicated to the movement and to the state in a highly ritualized fashion, in particular language and through specific acts, affirmed the official transcript of the unity between state, party and citizens. The competition provided a language for individual initiative and a means of expressing communal frustration at shortcomings. This did not necessarily create identity with the party, but it did provide a growing number of rituals and practices that could be related to socialism, and through which individuals affirmed that party and state were 'stable, effective, and here to stay'.[86]

It would be misleading, however, to see the 'Join in!' movement solely in terms of domination, not least because those who participated often experienced the competition as invigorating and empowering. If the party was unable to realize the competition as it intended, clearly this means that individuals had considerable space to free themselves from the party's ambitions. The following section explores more closely how the nature of popular participation helps us understand how power was contested between state and party on the one hand, and the citizens and their communities on the other.

'THIS REALLY IS HEIMAT!'

When I asked Alfred Erck, who served as district president of the Cultural League in Suhl during the 1970s and the 1980s, how the

---

[85] 'Das war typisch für die DDR, es wurde alles in diese Pläne eingeordnet. Denn es geschah doch nichts in der DDR – und darüber habe ich mich immer fürchterlich aufgeregt – das nicht aus Anlaß geschah. Eine Autobahn war nötig zwischen Berlin und Rostock, die wurde aber nicht deshalb gebaut, sondern aus Anlaß des 20. Jahrestages der Gründung der DDR.' Interview with Kurt Ludwig, 25 March 2003.

[86] Scott, *Domination*, pp. 58–69; here p. 66.

Cultural League managed to entice so many people to become involved in the competition, he replied:

In this region, you have to get your hands dirty. It is different here to Mecklenburg. Here, when someone in the village paints a fence, the neighbour comes along, takes a look at it, and three days later he'll also have painted his fence. Try painting a fence in Mecklenburg. Nothing will happen. It is simply a different mentality. This really is heimat.[87]

As I shall demonstrate in Chapter 8, Mecklenburg villagers could and did make significant contributions to the 'Join in!' competition. Striking in this quotation, however, is the insight that participation was not solely a matter of individual motivation, as the previous section has shown. The degree and nature of popular participation owed much to the particular social and cultural complexion of the local community.

Taking the two model communities identified by the National Front in Berlin in 1969, Mühlhausen and Erfurt, there were particular reasons why the competition was successful there. When I asked Horst Benneckenstein, a former member of the Erfurt Cultural League, about the local spring-cleaning activities there, he responded:

Erfurt had become the host of the International Gardening Exhibition in 1961 ... people volunteered hours of their time to scrub: the army went, the police went, teachers went, but many volunteers also ... But this was not really so tragic and dogged. [We said to each other:] 'How about it? Say, Saturday, let's meet for four hours or so, from 8 a.m. to midday.' We'd have some bratwurst and beer on the side, well, and then we worked to prepare the exhibition ...Until 1989, Erfurt was always the 'city of flowers'.[88]

---

[87] 'Man muß mal die Hände in der Erde haben in dieser Region. Das ist auch hier anders als in Mecklenburg. Wenn hier drüben einer einen Zaun streicht, auf dem Dorf, dann kommt der Nachbar an, guckt sich das an, und drei Tage später hat der dann seinen Zaun auch gestrichen. Streichen Sie mal in Mecklenburg einen Zaun. Passiert überhaupt nichts. Das ist einfach eine andere Mentalität. Das ist nun wirklich Heimat.' Interview with Alfred Erck, 21 May 2003.

[88] H.B.: Na ja nun hing das mit Erfurt natürlich auch so zusammen: ... Erfurt hatte 1961 ja nun ... übernommen eine internationale Gartenbauausstellung ... Das wurde dann ausgebaut ... Was da freiwillige Arbeitsstunden geschrubbt wurde: da ist die Armee hingegangen, da ist die Polizei hingegangen, da sind die Lehrer hingegangen, aber [auch] viele Freiwillige ... Und das war ja alles nicht so tragisch und so verbissen. [Man sagte sich:] „Wie siehts aus nich? So Sonnabend, 4 Stunden [lang], da treffen wir uns morgen so um 8 bis um 12 ne?" Machten Bratwurst dazu, und Bier gabs dazu, na ja da wurde da oben eben die IGA vorbereitet ... Und Erfurt war immer so, es war bis zur Wende Blumenstadt.'

J.P.: 'Und aber warum hat das in Erfurt sagen wir mal geklappt aber in Oranienburg halt nicht ?'

H.B.: 'Na ja, weil die Leute natürlich auch drauf, na in gewissem Sinne warn se stolz auf ihre Blumenstadt. Da wurde eben geschmückt, und da wurden Blumen in die Fenster gestellt ... Na Erfurt war ne Zeit lang ... als sauberste Stadt in der DDR bezeichnet. Das lag an vielen Dingen. Das

In Erfurt, the spring-cleaning activities of 'Join in!' thus appealed directly to the citizens' local pride, a tradition of gardening and flowers that dated from the late nineteenth century.[89] Locals could be rallied on behalf of 'their' garden city, but the communal activity was not so much a personal sacrifice as a local event, complete with the culinary icons of Thuringian identity, 'Thuringian' sausage and beer.

'Join in!' was thus successful where it responded to (and so reinforced) previously existing local identities and traditions. Indeed, local authorities had a great interest in fostering such local sentiments of community. In Mühlhausen, the town celebrated its church fair every year in late August or early September. For the organization of this huge festival, the town's residential districts were traditionally divided into around forty church-fair communities (*Kirmesgemeinden*). Each community was presided over by a 'mayor', and all the mayors each year elected the 'lord mayor' of the church fair, who negotiated directly with the local council. The church fair itself was a week-long event that culminated in a pageant, to which each community contributed a themed float of its own. 'Join in!' worked well in Mühlhausen mainly because the church fair required intensive preparation by hundreds of locals, and all those hours spent preparing the fair were registered as 'values' created through the National Front's 'Join in!' competition.

The example of Mühlhausen suggests that successful contributions to 'Join in!' were often the result of careful compromises between citizens and the party. For instance, the local council could count on the communities to provide the manpower for spring-cleaning activities, provided that the council provided the money for sausages and beer.[90] More generally, the town council (and the party) needed the hours contributed by the communities to report to the National Front, while the communities required in turn the goodwill of the council. Not only did the communities need its financial generosity, but since at the annual pageant those floats

lag am Bürgermeister, wie der verstand mit den Leuten umzugehen. Und das lag aber [auch] an so gesellschaftlichen Organisationen … am Kulturbund auch. Interview with Horst Benneckenstein, 28 April 2003.

[89] The significance of flowers and the International Gardening Exhibition, as well as the local citizens' pride in their own contribution to this fair, is well documented (in much greater detail) in Alice von Plato, '„Gartenkunst und Blütenzauber"': Die Internationale Gartenbauausstellung als Erfurter Angelegenheit', in Adelheid von Saldern (ed.), *Inszenierte Einigkeit: Herrschaftsrepräsentationen in DDR-Städten* (Stuttgart: Steiner, 2003), pp. 183–234.

[90] Interview with Jürgen Thormann, 29 April 2003. The 'festival atmosphere' was also recognized by the National Front in 1969 and taken as an indicator as to why the spring-cleaning activities were successful there. BArch-SAPMO, DY30 IV/A2 202 196: 'Arbeitsmaterial! So muß gearbeitet werden! Bezirk Erfurt. Vorbereitung und Durchführung „Frühjahrsputz" am 26.4.1969 im Kreis Mühlhausen'.

were the most popular which provided most criticism of local affairs, the communities needed the council's political generosity to allow at least some of these to be displayed at the pageant.[91] Indeed, during the 1960s and early 1970s there were constant skirmishes about how this ritual of reversal related to socialism. The council opposed timing the festival in the middle of the harvest season, and it was unhappy at the festival's religious origins, insisting for years that the church fair be known as the 'Festival of Socialist Joy'. It was only once the church fair was firmly embedded in the 'Join in!' movement, from the mid-1970s, that the local council overcame its discomfort with the nature of the festival. The church fair no longer constituted a threat to the authorities if its participants accepted the ritual subordination to the transcript of socialist citizenship through 'Join in!'[92]

'Join in!' fed on, and in turn encouraged, expressions of local pride. In their recollections of what they had achieved through communal labour, the villagers of Langula and Oberdorla could not in the least share Berlin's adulation of the 'Join in!' initiative in Mühlhausen. From the point of view of villagers who had laid their own drainage pipes and built several communal buildings, the odd bit of spring cleaning in the county town simply could not compare.[93] Such perspectives from villages where the competition had sustained much communal activity were typical. In his recollections Knut Kreuch was adamant that in Wechmar the 'Join in!' movement found a response to which the nearby towns of Gotha and Erfurt did not come close. Kreuch was certain of this because in a village like Wechmar one knew that everybody participated, whereas in larger towns he had no doubt that the figures were doctored.[94] The citizens of Erfurt, by contrast, could claim success for their contributions not because they compared themselves to the outlying villages, but because here 'Join in!' was clearly more successful than in other district capitals, as well as Berlin.[95]

---

[91] This statement is based on an assessment by Günter Würfel, 'lord mayor' of the church fair from the mid-1970s to the present day (2005), about what kinds of themes were usually the most popular at pageants. Interview with Würfel, 21 April 2005.

[92] Scott, *Domination*, ch. 6.

[93] Interviews with Inge and Berthold Fritzlar and Armin Walter, Langula, 18 April 2005.

[94] Interview with Knut Kreuch, 19 May 2003.

[95] From his perspective in Meiningen (Suhl district), Alfred Erck, the Cultural League's district president for Suhl, felt strongly that voluntary engagement was possible in a particular way in Thuringia: 'das läuft eben am Besten im Thüringer Wald. Das läuft schon nicht mehr so gut in Erfurt. Und das läuft eben gar nicht in Berlin oder in einer anderen Großstadt.' Interview with Alfred Erck, 21 May 2003.

The example of Wechmar and the surrounding areas provides further important evidence as to why individuals participated. Motivating factors were not just local pride, but also considerable peer pressure. As Kreuch explained:

The small villages developed amazing ambitions. Every citizen planted his front garden, and if the neighbour had not yet planted his, he went across and said, 'Listen, you have three hours, and then your garden will look just the same.'[96]

In Wechmar, crucial for the competition's success was the regional, small-town setting in which one knew what one's neighbours were doing, and also what the surrounding villages were doing.

Peer pressure was often reinforced by informal 'encouragement' which worked particularly well in locations where everyone knew everyone else. As Kreuch explained, in neighbouring Güntersleben 100 per cent of villagers registered their activity in 'Join in!' Here the mayor refused to authorize the allocation of building materials to dodgers. Local co-operatives could also entice individual participation by refusing to allocate a vacation place, or by denying a bonus to the entire brigade if one member did not contribute his due to the competition. In this way, villagers who were already predisposed to participate in making their homeland beautiful were still more encouraged to undertake communal improvements. Of course, these private transcripts may not have reflected the respect for socialist law that the National Front expected. Within the framework of socialism, 'Join in!' provided a framework for local actors keen on improving the conditions of their locality, in the process reinforcing distinctly local and regional networks and meanings.

THE RENNSTEIG GARDEN

'Join in!' provides a prism through which we can better understand the complex interactions between individual actors in their specific cultural as well as political contexts. In the late 1960s, Otto Schwarz, head of the Cultural League in Jena (Gera district) and a botanist at the university, had the idea of creating an alpine garden in an area along the Rennsteig, a path along the ridge of the Thuringian Forest. Here, at an altitude of

---

[96] 'Die Zahlen stimmten, waren vielleicht noch untertrieben. Die kleinen Dörfer haben einen Ehrgeiz entwickelt, das war sagenhaft. Da hat jeder Bürger vor seiner Haustür gepflanzt, und wenn der Nachbar noch nicht gepflanzt hatte, ist er hingegangen und gesagt hör zu, du hast noch 3 Stunden Zeit, dann sieht's genauso aus wie hier.' Interview with Knut Kreuch, 19 May 2003.

868 metres, unusual climatic conditions provided an ideal home for plants that normally only grew in Alpine conditions at altitudes of 2,000 metres. Although the project was officially sponsored by the Suhl district Cultural League, the hours of voluntary labour were contributed by Cultural League members and volunteers from all three Thuringian districts, Gera, Erfurt and Suhl. By late 1973, the Rennsteig Garden had taken up 9,000 hours of voluntary work, and by 1976, 20,000 hours had been reported through 'Join in!' The activity clearly paid off: the garden was constantly expanded, and visitor numbers increased from 30,000 in 1976 to 180,000 in 1988.[97]

From the beginning, this was seen as a 'Thuringian' project by the Cultural League leaders of the three Thuringian districts, who met regularly and got on very well with each other. These meetings had been maintained ever since the creation of the districts. As Kurt Ludwig, former district secretary of the Erfurt Cultural League, explained:

> We always met to keep the concept of Thuringia in play. [We] said: 'We are not so stupid as to follow the example of the seven Thuringian dynasties': these borders had been removed, but in practice it was difficult to get over the new district borders. We just did not want to play along with that.[98]

This was confirmed by Alfred Erck, who, in response to the question whether people saw themselves as 'Suhlers' or 'Thuringians', responded (among other things) that the Cultural League had always tried to maintain a sense of regional Thuringian identity, from the regular meetings of its leaders to the landscape days and the Rennsteig Garden. When I asked him whether it would not have been much easier and less complicated to keep to the district level, he responded:

---

[97] 'Botanischer Garten auf dem Rennsteig: Einmalige Sammlung der Hochgebirgsflora aller Erdteile', *Neues Deutschland* (18 September 1973). 'Eine Idee wird am Rennsteig Wirklichkeit: Botanischer Garten Oberhof ist „Mach mit!"-Werk', *Der Morgen* (17 September 1975). 'Erholung und Bildung im Hochgebirgsklima', *Freies Wort* (8 August 1989).

[98] 'Wir waren spöttisch untereinander. „Selbständige Gebirgsrepublik Suhl" …[Ich] fühlte mich als Erfurter. Und [dann gab es] die „Gierschen Fettguschen", die Großschnauzen aus Gera, aus der Sicht der Erfurter. Aber generell waren wir drei: der Erck, Karl-Heinz Hahn, ich, und auch Prof. Werner in Jena: wir haben uns immer getroffen, um übergreifend den Begriff Thüringen im Spiel zu halten. [Wir] Haben gesagt, wir sind doch nicht so dumm, und machen das Gleiche, was die sieben Thüringer Fürstenhäuser gemacht haben: diese Grenzen waren zwar weg, aber über die neuen Bezirksgrenzen war es schwer zu kommen. Da haben wir nicht mitgemacht.' Interview with Kurt Ludwig, 25 March 2003.

Well, that was precisely the problem. Of course the political leaders were of the opinion that we had to think in terms of the whole region ... [but] there was this heimat orientation: to retain Thuringia as a unit, and that's what we did.[99]

When the idea of the Rennsteig Garden was born, it was just the sort of project that could express a sense of togetherness in Thuringia, and spur the Cultural League leaders into action.

In practice, the project would have been doomed without the dogged persistence of the Suhl district secretary of the Cultural League, Willi Opitz. A communist from the Weimar years and a concentration camp survivor, he was officially recognized as a 'victim of fascism', which allowed him (as his Cultural League chairman remembered) to 'get away with a lot' that others could not. Opitz had originally served as secretary to the district council in Suhl, until he fell from grace by maintaining links with the West, against the party line. Opitz, however, continued to have excellent connections to the party locally and regionally, and these became invaluable in generating official permissions, and in coordinating the logistical organization of building materials. According to Kurt Ludwig, district secretary of the Erfurt district Cultural League, if you had reached an impasse and 'you needed anything, you went to Willi, and he arranged it'.[100]

Opitz was the kind of person who had to be doing something practical all the time, who needed to create things with his own hands. The restless Cultural League secretary was determined to realize his ambition by hook or by crook. As the district president of the Cultural League, Prof. Alfred Erck, remembered: 'then Opitz began to get going. And even my wife and I were not exempt from being up there for a certain number of hours to carry rocks. He was like a maniac.'[101] Under Opitz's leadership, every Cultural League member was expected to do his or her bit, and if people needed the League's patronage – from stamp collectors to those who needed permits to catch songbirds in the Thuringian Forest – they first had to put in some hours at the Garden.[102]

The Garden was never at the top of the National Front's concerns, since it could scarcely be said to create better housing conditions or beautify existing villages. Opitz had to be creative about generating much-needed external support, which often came from the National People's Army

---

[99] 'Na ja, das war eben das Problem: natürlich war die politische Führung der Meinung, es muß bezirksweit gedacht werden ... Das war dieses Heimatorientierte: Thüringen als ganzes noch zu erhalten – das ist gemacht worden.' Interview with Alfred Erck, 21 May 2003.

[100] Interview with Kurt Ludwig, 25 March 2005. Interview with Alfred Erck, 21 May 2003.

[101] 'Und dann fing Opitz an, zu wirken. Und auch ich war nicht gut angesehen, wenn wir nicht so und so viel Stunden da oben waren, um Steine zu schleppen, meine Frau auch nicht. Der war wie ein Verrückter.' Interview with Alfred Erck, 21 May 2003.

[102] Ibid.

or the Red Army. Of the two, it was easier to enlist the help of the Red Army, which used its machinery to lay the pipes and cables connecting the garden to the water, electricity and telephone networks of Oberhof. The Red Army's willingness to help was probably not inspired by admiration for the Thuringian heimat (as a newspaper report implied).[103] Rather, the Soviets were suffering even severer supply shortages than the National People's Army, which made them more eager to help in exchange for the foodstuffs and everyday utensils which the Cultural League procured for them.[104]

Volunteers could not be enticed solely by cajoling and peer pressure. Hence the organizers did their best to create events and traditions which would make the Garden, and people's activity in it, part of Thuringian identity. In the early years, Herbert Roth, author of Thuringia's unofficial anthem (the Rennsteig Song), performed there repeatedly for the volunteers, helping to popularize the Garden and raise further funds. From 1979 the Garden hosted its own annual heimat festival, held on the first weekend in July. This 'Blossom Festival' drew large crowds through attractions like a special sale of plants and seeds, and the performance of heimat music. For the festival's tenth anniversary, held years after Roth's death, Roth's ensemble and his erstwhile partner, Waltraud Schulz, presented a song dedicated to the Rennsteig Garden, itself an expression of how much the Garden had become a 'natural' part of the Thuringian heimat.[105]

Interestingly, the Rennsteig Garden invoked an important aspect of the heimat which was also linked to 'Join in!' and the ideal of the socialist heimat: its international dimension. The movement was to serve not just to differentiate East German society vis-à-vis the FRG, but also to highlight East Germany's affinities with socialist societies further east and south, where such competitions were also held on a regular basis.[106] This is unlikely *per se* to have made any impression on the founders of the Rennsteig Garden. Yet to them, the linking of the heimat to the wider world, beyond even the wider German nation, would not have seemed out of place. Before the war, Otto Schwarz had lived in Turkey for a while, and he maintained excellent connections abroad after 1945. According to Erck, Schwarz had seen the world, and wanted to bring something of faraway regions into the homeland. The Rennsteig Garden exactly fulfilled

[103] '868 Meter über dem Meeresspiegel', *Wochenpost* (21 October 1977).
[104] Interview with Alfred Erck, 21 May 2003.
[105] '...und zum 10. Blütenfest Premiere für das Rennsteiggartenlied', *Freies Wort* (Suhl) (25 July 1988).
[106] Vaclav Kalous, 'Politische Aktivität des Bürgerkomitees – wichtige Vorbedingung für die „Aktion Z"', in *Verbesserung der Wohnbedingungen*, pp. 33–4. Jerzy Breitkopf, 'Masseninitiative der VR Polen', ibid., pp. 35–6.

this purpose. Its Siberian and Alpine flora was not just there to be admired; seedlings could also be purchased for planting in one's own private garden. Since under socialism, individuals could not easily venture from the heimat to explore the unknown, the garden allowed the unknown to be explored in the heimat.[107] 'Join in!' constituted an attempt to localize the citizens' energy and wanderlust, and transform them into innovation on behalf of the heimat.[108]

The example of the Rennsteig Garden shows with particular clarity how local, individual and regional factors combined towards the movement's ultimate success. Strikingly, this was not simply thanks to individual enthusiasm on the part of those who planned the activity or donated their voluntary labour. Success in 'Join in!' also depended crucially on the ability to identify and exploit informal, unofficial ways to attain one's goal, from penalizing those who did not 'volunteer' their labour to identifying individuals in the state, the party or even the army to whom one could offer favours. The example of the Rennsteig Garden challenges James C. Scott's sharp differentiation between the 'dominant' and the 'subalterns'. Those applying peer pressure and using informal channels of communication were often party members and officers at local or district level. The private transcripts that developed with 'Join in!' did not conform to the official ideals of citizenship and socialist patriotism, but it is clearly not the case that officials and party members had no idea of the meanings that developed beyond the public discourse. The party may not always have been informed about every aspect of the private transcript, but party members were rarely isolated from the communities they lived in.

LOCAL PARTICIPATION AND SOCIALIST PATRIOTISM

The final question to be asked is how the transcript of the socialist heimat affected individual identification with the state. Communities were always affected by their political and structural environment; private meanings could develop differently from, but never independently of,

---

[107] When I asked Kurt Ludwig why the Garden was created, he responded that it was to deepen people's love for nature. When I interjected that this was not really the nature of the heimat, he responded: 'Ja, aber Sie vergessen ja die Ursehnsüchte der Menschen die auch der Sozialismus nicht abschaffen konnte, in die Ferne, in die Weite zu gehen. Diese Sehnsucht ins Land zu holen ist ja auch etwas, das dazu [zum Rennsteiggarten] gehört.' Interview with Kurt Ludwig, 25 March 2003.

[108] Horst Meyer also noted that his energy on behalf of the homeland derived from an unfulfilled ambition to travel the world. Interview with Meyer, 5 February 2003.

the public transcript. This is illustrated by the Stiegker community of Eisenach. As I showed in Chapter 3, this community was central to the organization of the *Sommergewinn* festival, prepared over several months, evening after evening, at the Waldschlösschen pub. In the early 1970s, the Waldschlösschen was in such a state of disrepair that it was torn down. Outraged that 'their' pub had been torn down, the Stiegkers sent a petition to the district council. Rather than outlining the pub's importance for communal boozing, the Stiegkers were advised by F.O., a resident who had been decorated with the 'Fatherland Medal', to phrase their petition in the language of the public transcript. Consequently, they protested that this had been an important cultural venue which not only served for the preparations of the *Sommergewinn* festival but also was a meeting place for the local football team. The district decided that the Stiegkers had a case, and promised to support the construction of a new pub. In return, the Stiegkers called a residents' meeting and, given the scarcity of builders, pledged their own reconstruction efforts to the 'Join in!' initiative. The state was pleased at this manifestation of citizenship, the Stiegkers got their pub, and their community benefited because for every hour donated the state paid five marks, which the Stiegkers decided to put into the common kitty.

Just because the Stiegkers had donated their time to 'Join in!', the party could not assume that they had done so as socialist citizens who would henceforth accept the party's directions. Peter Apel, one of the Stiegkers in charge of the reconstruction, recalled one incident when the party tried to establish control over the community:

One day they sent M.S. to us to be in charge, he was the head of the residential district at the time … Suddenly this figure appeared, on Saturday morning, in this suit, we were in blue overalls working away back there. And he stood there and wanted to do the accounts. He didn't stand a chance. So I said, 'Boy, if you don't take a big hike, then there will be a huge bang here.' [He replied:] 'But I am the new head of the residential district.' … this guy was completely finished.

JP: But would it not have been good to have him, since he could have just written down the number of hours you did, and then you could have prided yourself on your efforts on behalf of the state?

PA: But what do you do with an idiot like that in a community like ours?[109]

---

[109] PA: Eines Tages haben die uns M.S. vorgesetzt, der war damals Wohnbezirks-Vorsitzender … Plötzlich stand diese Figur da, Samstag früh da in som Anzug, mir waren in blauen Arbeitsklamotten und haben da hinten gearbeitet. Und er stand da und wollte die Abrechnung machen. Ja, der hat doch gar keine Chance gehabt. Da hab ich gesagt: „Jung wenn Du nicht die große Flocke machst, dann tuts nen großen Schlag hier." „Ich bin der neue Wohnbezirks-Vorsitzende" … da war doch dieser der Wohnbezirks-Vorsitzende – war doch erledigt.

This incident shows clearly the demarcation of boundaries between the public and the private transcript. This was not principally about the party as such: after all, F.O., who was also a member of the party, had been accepted as part of the community, whereas M.S. clearly was not. What mattered was how individuals, irrespective of their relationship to the party, related to the community and accepted its codes. Whereas F.O. put his connections, his socialist reputation and his knowledge of the public transcript at the service of the community, M.S. patently did not. His intentions and even his outward appearance marked him as an outsider who had no business there. This was primarily a distinction not between community and politics, or even between the locality and the state, though it was closely related to both. Rather, this was a distinction between private and public transcripts, between the cultural codes and social meanings of the community on the one hand, and the socialist meanings of citizenship and community on the other.[110] Neither sphere existed independently of the other, yet both were clearly demarcated from each other.

If 'Join in!' reinforced pre-existing communal, local and regional ties, how did the ideal of socialist citizenship affect views of state and party? In interviews in which the participatory movement was discussed, no reference to the GDR as a culturally bounded country (for instance, through 'Join in!') was ever made. Respondents referred to the GDR as a geographical entity, as Thuringians compared themselves to Saxons or Mecklenburgers, and Mecklenburgers to Thuringians or Saxons (the central regions, from Anhaltine to the Mark, never appeared in this context). In each case, however, participation or non-participation in the contest was defined by the community, and respondents in Thuringia and Mecklenburg were quite clear about this. One did not participate in this movement as a citizen of the GDR.

References to socialism, the party or the National Front were quite common, albeit in a predominantly negative context. The National Front and the competition as such was seen as a systemic framework in which meaningless figures and phrases counted: one which one could appropriate to one's own, local needs. To Horst Meyer, himself an active and energetic participant (and SED party member), the National Front and 'Join in!' represented 'Aktionismus', a mind-numbing, impersonal interest in activity for its own sake.[111] Uwe Wieben, head of the heimat

---

JP: Aber es wär doch für Sie gut gewesen, der hätte die Stunden abrechnen können, und dann hätten se gleich melden können hier wir ham so viele Stunden Aufbau geleistet.
PA: Ja, aber was wollense denn mit sonem Spinner in unserer Gemeinschaft?
Interview with Peter Apel, 18 June 2003.
[110] Ibid. [111] Interview with Horst Meyer, 5 February 2003.

museum in Boizenburg (Mecklenburg), described the National Front as 'number jugglers' (*Zahlenjongleure*) who concerned themselves merely with their own reports and action plans.[112] And Jürgen Thormann summed up his recollection that the National Front was never interested in the actual, qualitative achievements of the heimat groups, but only in numbers and appearances, with the words attributed to socialist reformer Eduard Bernstein: 'The aim is nothing, the movement everything.' ('Das Ziel ist nichts, die Bewegung alles.')[113]

As shown above, one way in which the National Front had hoped to symbolize the link between individual and local engagement on the one hand, and the National Front on the other, was by giving out awards and prizes. Indeed, the National Front hoped that its medal for participation would unite all those who had contributed to 'Join in!', so that the display of the medal among the majority of the population would distinguish a new, GDR-wide community.[114] In his capacity as former county secretary of the Cultural League, Jürgen Thormann insisted that even if most awards did not carry cash prizes, their symbolic importance should not be dismissed:

Everyone in the GDR wanted his certificate, even if nobody wants to admit it today: there were never enough certificates to go round. We [in Mühlhausen] were always inventing new ones, so that we from the centre could in some way say 'thank you' to everyone.[115]

GDR-wide competition inflation thus contributed to a growing expectation that certificates be awarded, an expectation that was often met through local initiatives. Yet, whether the awards came from the locality or from the National Front at the district or GDR levels, they did not necessarily reinforce the bonds between the individual and the state and party. When I asked what they associated with the competition, the following exchange ensued between Uwe Wieben (U.W.) and Karin Wulf (K.W.) from Boizenburg in Mecklenburg:

KW: Oh God, once a year we swept [laughs].

UW: And then they got one of these 'Golden House Numbers'. When U.S. from Berlin, an old Boizenburger, calls me today, he says, 'Here is S. from the

---

[112] Interview with Uwe Wieben, 16 June 2003.   [113] Interview with Jürgen Thormann, 29 April 2003.
[114] BArch-SAPMO, DY6 2333: 'Probleme, die sich im Wettbewerb „Schöner unsere Städte und Gemeinden – Mach Mit!" ergaben und vor Beschlußfassung zur Weiterführung des Wettbewerbs 1971 Beachtung finden müssen' (6 November 1970), pp. 10–11.
[115] 'Und dafür mussten die ne Urkunde kriegen, denn jeder wollte in der DDR seine Urkunde und wenn der sagt, auch wenn se heute keiner haben wollte, so viele Auszeichnungen gabs gar nicht. Wir ham immer welche erfunden, damit wir bei den Zentralen jedem irgendwie Danke sagen konnten.' Interview with Jürgen Thormann, 22 April 2005.

infamous "Rise of Youth Path, 26'", that's where he lived. I always used to tease him: 'Aren't you the Golden House Number?' Hmm, why did they get this? Because they pulled up a few weeds and maintained the area in front of their new apartment block ...

KW: perhaps they officially took a green space into their care ...

UW: and because they reported: our block even celebrates twice a year.

KW[amused]: 'house community' ...

UW: 'We meet in the cellar!' They would have done this anyway [laughs]. But like this it could even be counted as contributions.[116]

Awards may have been expected, but they did not necessarily lead to gratitude vis-à-vis the state or its mass organizations. The value of awards derived from their local meanings. More interestingly, official certificates represented another element of ritualization in the relationship between the National Front and the participants, but one that expressed the expect-ations not of the National Front, but of the participants themselves. What becomes evident here is a double euphemism of power at work: the party expected participation in 'Join in!' as an act of citizenship, though individuals clearly developed their own local and regional transcript from their participation. However, in return for their acquiescence in the public transcript, individuals expected from the National Front an official acknowledgement that their actions did indeed constitute a dem-onstration of patriotism. Citizens pretended that they were subscribing to the public transcript of citizenship, expecting in return that local func-tionaries would pretend to believe them.

CONCLUSION

'Join in!' became an important factor of everyday life across the GDR. During the twenty-two years of its existence, there were probably few, if any, towns and villages which had not seen the creation of a garden, a pavement, a flat, a community hall, a swimming pool or an open-air theatre

---

[116] Karin Wulf (KW): Oh Gott. Einmal im Jahr wurde gefegt [lacht].

　　Uwe Wieben (UW): Und dann kriegten die so ne goldene Hausnummer. Wenn mich U.S. aus Berlin, ein alter Boizenburger, wenn der am Telefon ist, ruft der mich an, und sagt, ja hier is S. vom berüchtigten „Aufgangweg der Jugend 26", da hat er doch gewohnt. Hab ich ihn immer so verscheißert, ihr seid doch die goldene Hausnummer. Ja, Warum haben sie die gekriegt? Weil die Unkraut vor ihrem Neubaublock gezupft haben und gepflegt haben.

　　KW: Vielleicht hatten sie noch die Grünfläche in Pflege genommen.

　　UW: Und weil die dann abgerechnet haben: unser Aufgang feiert noch zweimal im Jahr.

　　KW [belustigt]: 'Hausgemeinschaft'.

　　UW: „Wir treffen uns im Keller", hätten die auch sonst gemacht [lacht]. Aber so konnte das noch abgerechnet werden.

through the movement. To be sure, similar contests existed in West Germany too. Here, however, beautification initiatives were never linked to any party, and no pressure except local pride was exerted on individuals to participate. Major construction projects like building flats or laying sewage pipes were not part of the FRG's beautification movements, nor were these based on an ideology of personal transformation, betterment and patriotism. In marked contrast, in the GDR the participatory campaign connected the individual's sense of heimat and community to the exercise of citizenship. An engagement for the heimat thus became, according to the official transcript of state and party, an expression of socialist patriotism distinctive to the GDR.

In practice, 'Join in!' was an attempt by the SED to localize the economic and political shortcomings of socialism and encourage local solutions to shortages of labour, materials, tools and consumer goods. In a sense, 'Join in!' constituted a remarkable achievement. By inducing citizens to lay sewage pipes or clean up public spaces, the National Front effectively utilized local feelings of belonging and community to address some of the GDR's economic shortcomings. Consequently, individuals did not resign themselves to the deficiencies of the economy and state planning, but resolved to tackle them as best they could. By the same token, if villagers connected their houses to the water mains through voluntary work, or communities built a cultural centre, they did so because they did not expect the state to be able to provide these basic amenities in the foreseeable future. Far from reinforcing individual trust in the party and socialism, the competition reduced individual expectations that the state could be counted on to fulfil even the most minimal sanitary, cultural and infrastructural needs.

What was expected of the state was reduced further by the competition's shortcomings. Functionaries realized how soul-destroying it was if activists collected recyclable waste for which there were no containers;[117] if volunteers had agreed to pave a footpath but the paving stones were then not delivered;[118] or if gardens which they had planted were later destroyed by the construction of new housing.[119] More generally, the overemphasis on

---

[117] LHA Schwerin, Nationale Front Neubrandenburg 136: 'Informationsbericht Nr. 13/75. Bericht über Erfassung von Altrohstoffen und Initiativen in Wohngebieten im Kreise Prenzlau' (6 August 1975).
[118] LHA Schwerin, Nationale Front Neubrandenburg 135: 'Bericht über die Ergebnisse im „Mach Mit"-Wettbewerb des Jahres 1975' (Teterow, 9 January 1976).
[119] BArch-SAPMO, DY27 960, f. 176: 'Sitzung des Präsidialrates' (8 June 1977), introductory speech by Karl-Heinz Schulmeister.

construction during the Honecker years proved entirely misplaced, as this was never an activity that the majority of the population could engage in, for lack of skill, materials and tools. Moreover, participation was decidedly uneven across the country, as 'Join in!' was far more successful at rallying participants in the small towns and villages. In larger cities and new towns, by contrast, not only were overall participation rates much lower, the proportion of work for the 'Join in!' movement that was actually paid was much higher.[120]

Given that the campaign's economic returns were extremely uncertain, both in a statistical sense and in terms of economic added value, it is highly doubtful that the campaign's scale and ambition were commensurate with its economic achievements. If the state wanted to induce builders to do extra work at the weekends, or wanted villagers to build their own sewage system, there was no reason why more localized, targeted campaigns could not have fulfilled this aim at least as successfully. Given the economic and practical shortcomings of the campaign, why did state and party maintain and even expand it? Why did they develop a public transcript that linked local activism on behalf of the campaign inextricably to GDR citizenship and patriotism?

'Join in!' constituted a crucial strategy for the party to exercise its power in discreet ways. By subscribing, however formally and superficially, to local activities as acts of GDR citizenship, individual activists acknowledged the current political and economic conditions as 'given', and acknowledged the inescapability of state and party. In return, state and party could allow significantly greater freedom of individual local initiative. This also made acts of transgression, from expressing veiled criticism of the SED at the local church fair to illegally supplying building material, more palatable to state and party. For as long as such irregularities occurred under the guise of socialist citizenship, they did not threaten the authority of the state.

And yet this euphemization of power did not constitute a 'normalization' of everyday life. The ritualization of local activism through 'Join in!' did not induce citizens to accept this state of affairs as normal. Nor did the state and party's tolerance of instances of local cunning create some sort of pressure

---

[120] In 1981 in Neubrandenburg, a rural district with not a single town over 100,000 inhabitants and only one over 50,000, the amount of paid work was twice as high in larger towns as in villages and small towns; if participation in small towns and villages was three times that in larger towns, it follows that the amount of paid work in larger towns was six times that in villages and small towns! LHA Schwerin, Nationale Front Neubrandenburg 103: Lektion, 'Grundprobleme der Weiterführung des „Mach-Mit!"-Wettbewerbs [1978]', p. 30.

valve which made the experience of domination in other respects more tolerable. On the contrary, the citizens' acquiescence was bought at the cost of activists developing local meanings that were separate from, and even opposed to, those of state and party.

True to the ideal of the competition, in the cases of the Rennsteig Garden or the Neubrandenburg estate restored by Horst Meyer the citizens' initiatives had addressed the shortcomings of the local administration, to the benefit of all. However, such initiatives contributed not just to the strengthening of local community but also to a marked disrespect for authority. One such instance was described by Alfred Erck, as he commented on activists contributing to local preservation projects:

> A huge amount was messed up. Criteria were never applied to satisfy higher standards. And when professional conservationists or representatives from the Institute [of Conservation] in Weimar came and told them how to do it, [the locals] either stopped doing anything at all, or continued to do what they had planned to do anyway. There are many examples of this, but what is characteristic of all of them is this great problem, this local pig-headedness. We had no problems getting activists to participate, but the way they did it was pig-headed ... The professional conservationists worked themselves to exhaustion, and [when the work was completed] they stood there and didn't know whether to cry or not, but all they could do was praise the activists.[121]

This 'pig-headedness', which was far from untypical,[122] could pose some formidable challenges to the state, especially as activists saw that it could yield rewards. By encouraging individual initiative stemming from the local context, 'Join in!' reinforced the self-reliance of local actors and their relationships in dealing with the systemic deficiencies of socialism. Not least for this reason, 'Join in!' appears to have resonated particularly in

---

[121] 'Und da ist unheimlich viel verpfuscht worden. Da hat es nie Maßgaben gegeben die also höheren Ansprüchen genügten. Und wenn dann Denkmalpfleger kamen oder aus dem Institut aus Weimar kamen und haben gesagt, ihr müßt das so machen, dann haben die das entweder überhaupt nicht gemacht, oder trotzdem so gemacht, wie sie's für richtig gehalten haben ... Es gibt viele Beispiele dafür, aber eines ist sehr charakteristisch ... diese [lokale] Borniertheit ist das große Problem in allen solchen Dingen. Wir hatten keine Schwierigkeiten solche Sachen zu machen. Aber die Maßgaben waren borniert. Und wenn da von Oben her eingegriffen worden ist von denen, die es besser wußten, nichts worden gemacht oder es wurde einfach weiter gemacht ... [von den Denkmalpflegern] ist gearbeitet worden bis zum geht nicht mehr, und sie standen dann dort und wußten nicht richtig ob sie heulen sollten, aber sie konnten sie ja bloß loben!' Interview with Alfred Erck, 21 May 2003.

[122] Erck made a similar (though more indirect) point at a Cultural League Praesidium council meeting in 1977. BArch-SAPMO, DY27 960, ff. 203–4: 'Sitzung des Präsidialrates' (8 June 1977). Comments by Prof. Erck. See also *Natur und Umwelt im Bezirk Neubrandenburg. 2. Landschaftstag: „Mecklenburgisch-Brandenburgische Seenplatte" der Bezirke Schwerin, Potsdam, Neubrandenburg* (Neubrandenburg: Kulturbund der DDR, 1978), pp. 24–6; here p. 25.

communities in which it could reinforce already existing ties, whereas in areas where local ties and networks were less developed, such as in new towns, the competition appears to have made less of an impact.

Curiously for a movement that had originated in the desire to strengthen citizenship and the state, and which contributed to the maintenance of existing power relations, 'Join in!' reinforced meanings that were intensely individual and local. It did not reconcile citizens to the state, nor act as a safety valve for pent-up frustrations. Encouraging locals to deal with the shortcomings of socialism did not necessarily reduce frustration with these problems. Nonetheless 'Join in!' stabilized the GDR by euphemizing the party's domination and creating a public transcript which encouraged local initiatives to make do with socialism.

CHAPTER 6

Environmental destruction

INTRODUCTION

> Our heimat is not just the cities and villages,
> Our heimat is also all the trees in the forest.
> Our heimat is the grass in the meadow, the corn in the field
> And the birds in the sky and the animals on the ground
> And the fish in the river are the heimat.
> And we love the heimat, the beautiful heimat,
> And we protect it, because it belongs to the people,
> Because it belongs to our people.

One of the popular songs of the 'Young Pioneers', the party's children's organization, 'Our Heimat' emphasized the beauties of the socialist heimat. As the song made clear, the ideal of heimat was never just about its traditions, it was also essentially linked to the built and the natural environment. Both were beautiful, and both could only be protected in socialism where, as the song pointed out, the heimat belonged to the people. In socialism the environment was never held up as a good in itself, but as something that was continuously being transformed to fulfil the desires of all those who lived there. To the party, the changing built and natural environment was inextricably linked with the identity of the GDR citizen.

The significance of the environment for the public transcript of the heimat is illustrated by the TV show 'Heimat, We Greet You'. On 12 December 1987, the show featured the Schwarza valley in the Thuringian Forest.[1] To a series of heimat-related songs, the show introduced images of historic towns (Bad Blankenburg), monuments (a reconstructed historic windmill and Eberstein Castle), and scenic views of the valley.[2] There were

---

[1] DRA Schriftgutbestand Fernsehen: 'Landessender Sachsen-Anhalt. Sendekonzeption „Heimat, wir grüßen dich"' (23 September 1987).
[2] DRA Schriftgutbestand Fernsehen: 'Landessender Sachsen-Anhalt. Halle, 27. November 1987: Qualitätseinschätzung, Wirkungsabsicht'.

no references to factories, new towns or other socialist transformations of the environment. Instead, the show appealed to the viewers' senses. At Eberstein Castle, shots of beer tapped straight from a giant keg being tasted by the brewmaster himself visually reinforced the impression of a whole-some and individually crafted drink. While the Schenckensteiner Musikanten sang about what it was to be a Thuringian, close-ups featured sausages and meats. Subsequent shots of the lead singer shrouded in thick smoke arising from the grill visually transmitted the nourishing smell and smoky taste of this heimat feast. In addition to this scene, the show featured the lush green of the Schwarza valley, filmed alongside original sounds recorded on location. Quite intentionally, the producers sought to convey the 'moist, dark and misty' nature of the Schwarza's banks by capturing spider webs shimmering in the dew, and 'glistening, damp and colourful' leaves.[3] In the GDR the environment was something to be savoured, since socialism had made its beauty and its nourishment available to all.

Shows like these, or even the song quoted at the beginning of the chapter, refute David Blackbourn's claim that 'landscape as an expression of Heimat ... was rejected by the ruling party of the GDR'.[4] The problem, rather, was that the rustic ideal of the environment and its implications of abundance and purity were increasingly at odds with the individual experience of socialism in everyday life. Here, uncontrolled industrial pollution threatened the habitat of animals. Between 1970 and 1985, the number of endangered species increased from 203 to 296, and species of vascular plants on the verge of extinction rose from 103 to 166.[5] Moreover, as Honecker's construction programme continued apace the very existence of old towns was threatened, as old houses, some of them historic monuments, were often left to fall into disrepair. Paint was virtually unobtainable, so that grey came to prevail as the colour of buildings in towns and villages. Neither the countryside nor the built environment bore testament to the party's pro-fessed concern for the heimat.

There was a wide, and growing, gulf between the party's publicly articulated concern for the environment and a growing environmental crisis. This chapter examines the party's efforts to maintain the socialist transcript of heimat in the face of accelerating environmental degradation,

---

[3] DRA Schriftgutbestand Fernsehen: 'Landessender Sachsen-Anhalt. Sendekonzeption „Heimat, wir grüßen dich"' (23 September 1987).

[4] Blackbourn, *Conquest*, p. 326.

[5] Hardy Vogtmann, 'Vorwort zur 2. Auflage', in Regine Auster and Hermann Behrens (eds.), *Naturschutz in den Neuen Bundesländern – Ein Rückblick*, 2nd edn (Berlin: Verlag für Wissenschaft und Forschung, 2001), pp. 7–10; here pp. 8–9.

and the responses of those who were expected to subscribe to this transcript on the ground. How could the public transcript of the socialist heimat be maintained when heimat itself was exposed to such existential challenges?

The first part of the chapter explores these questions in relation to the built environment, as the party sought ways to reconcile the dilapidation of old towns with the provision of comfortable new flats in prefabricated units. The second part considers how the party attempted to channel environmental activism in ways that responded to the public transcript of the socialist heimat. By examining the two areas in which the ideal of the socialist heimat was most at odds with everyday experience, I shall explore further how successful the party was in encouraging activists to publicly acknowledge the socialist heimat ideal, and with it the power of the party.

'THIS IS MY HOME, HERE IS MY HEIMAT'

On 6 July 1978, Erich Honecker visited Hermann Großkopf and his family in the recently constructed new town of Berlin Marzahn to congratulate them as occupants of the one-millionth new flat constructed since the Eighth Party Congress. In his memoirs, Honecker described his emotions as he chatted with the family over coffee: one million flats, he wrote, equated to a million happy families. He felt proud as he looked out onto Marzahn, where just a few years ago he would have seen fields. Honecker noted the delight he felt not just at the quantity of new houses, but also at their quality. The architecture of new towns, he stated, should induce a feeling of comfort, allowing each and every resident to feel: 'This is my home, this is my heimat, where I can live in freedom and equality.'[6]

To Honecker, the new towns were the key to individual happiness within socialism. In 1975, he promised to solve the 'housing problem' by 1990, a promise which the party tried to fulfil by building prefabricated housing on a massive scale. By 1988, Marzahn, Hohenschönhausen and Hellersdorf, three Berlin districts that had not existed fifteen years previously, housed 164,318, 91,830 and 61,251 inhabitants respectively. This was clearly exceptional, but the building of new towns was impressive throughout the GDR. Half of Schwerin's population of 128,000 was living in its three adjoining new towns by 1988.[7] New towns became a desirable place of residence for many citizens looking for cheap and comfortable flats, and not just in the district capitals. Even in moderately sized towns like Eisenach, Altenburg or

[6] Erich Honecker, *Aus meinem Leben* (Berlin: Dietz, 1980), esp. pp. 303–4, 312–13.
[7] *Statistisches Jahrbuch 1988*, pp. 2, 6.

Mühlhausen, a substantial proportion of citizens were living by the 1980s in new neighbourhoods made up of prefabricated flats.[8] These new towns formed a fundamental part of the socialist transformation of heimat.

Prefabricated residential blocks offered new possibilities for the realization of the party's ideal of the 'developed socialist society'. Alongside the workplace, the party considered these residential areas to be the most important sphere in which individuals formed social relations and adjusted to the socialist way of life. The inhabitants of new towns had been uprooted from their previous neighbourhoods, and to the SED this presented a unique opportunity to instil new values, relationships and traditions.[9] The buildings were owned by the people, and all residents irrespective of social background lived in units that looked exactly the same. Such perfect conditions allowed residents to get to know each other, care for each other, and experience at first hand the fruits of socialism. New towns appeared as the microcosm of the 'developed socialist society', with their inhabitants turning into model socialist citizens.[10]

Given the scale of the new towns and their potential to make socialism a reality, the party might have been tempted to orientate the socialist heimat ideal solely towards the newly built environment, at the expense of the historic buildings in the town centres. However, at no time could the party be under any illusion that its ideal-type vision of a socialist community worked equally well in practice. As early as 1976, a large-scale survey of respondents in twelve new towns informed the party that only 8.1 per cent described their neighbourhood as a community that regularly met to socialize or to solve problems; 34.6 per cent stated that they only came together when absolutely necessary, 27 per cent that only a few tenants were interested in holding meetings as a community, and 33.5 per cent denied that they lived in a community of any kind.[11] The party found that new residents tended to neglect cultural activities in their new environment and were more concerned with domestic issues, such as following everyday

---

[8] Christine Hannemann, *Die Platte: Industrialisierter Wohnungsbau in der DDR* (Braunschweig: Vieweg, 1996), pp. 21–4. In Eisenach, for instance, 12,000 out of 50,000 inhabitants were living in the new town, Eisenach-Nord, by 1989.

[9] BArch-SAPMO, DY30 IV/B2 9.06 86: 'Material zum geistig-kulturellen Leben im Wohngebiet' (21 February 1977).

[10] 'Erste Mieter im Teil II des Dreeschs', *SVZ* (14 June 1976). Hannemann, *Die Platte*, pp. 97–102. 'Hier wohne ich – und so seh ich unser Haus'; 'Ein Haus und seine Menschen'; 'Ein Haus und unsere Politik', *SVZ* (14 May 1976). See also 'Wunder gibts nicht', *SVZ* (18 May 1976).

[11] BArch-SAPMO, DY30 IV/B2 9.06 86: 'Material zum geistig-kulturellen Leben im Wohngebiet' (21 February 1977), topic 1.2.4: 'Probleme und Hemmnisse bei der Entwicklung des geistig-kulturellen Lebens im Wohngebiet'.

routines within the family or buying new furniture. During the two years or so after moving in, a lack of communication with the outside world set in, which was difficult to overcome when residents became more interested in cultural activities.[12]

Even if residents wanted to immerse themselves in cultural life, this was difficult owing to the lack of meeting facilities.[13] For the 6,000 residents of the Leipziger Straße in Berlin only one central meeting space was planned, a club that could cater for 180 people. The inadequate meeting facilities in the centre of Berlin, where there were plenty of other cultural diversions in close proximity, were inconvenient enough. More serious was the lack of facilities in new towns all over the GDR, from Halle-Neustadt to Rostock. The poor provision of facilities there was compounded by inadequate transport facilities to the cultural centres of the nearby old towns.[14] Lack of cultural facilities was not only a problem in the large cities. As part of the 'Eichsfeld plan', the county town of Worbis in the Eichsfeld region (Erfurt district) had been expanded from 2,800 to 12,500 inhabitants (1960–78). Despite the heavy investment this entailed in industry and housing, no money had been spent on cultural facilities.[15] Occasionally, the Cultural League and the local authorities managed to secure individual apartments within residential blocks for use as cultural spaces, for instance as an art gallery, a meeting place, or a youth club. However, these had a strictly limited capacity, and had limited opening times.[16] The party was evidently unable or unwilling to divert funds from the construction of flats to the provision of cultural facilities.

The party invested much hope in promoting cultural life through the generation of 'new' heimat cultures for which large meeting spaces were not

---

[12] BArch-SAPMO, DY27 444, f. 98: 'Tagung des erweiterten Präsidiums des Kulturbunds der DDR am 17.10.1980 in Ahrenshoop', introductory lecture by Heinz Fox, Rostock.

[13] A relative majority of respondents asked by the Academy of Social Sciences (37.4 per cent) stated the lack of cultural centres close by as the most important reason why they did not attend cultural events. BArch-SAPMO, DY30 IV/B2 9.06 86: 'Material zum geistig-kulturellen Leben im Wohngebiet' (21 February 1977), topic 1.2.4: 'Probleme und Hemmnisse bei der Entwicklung des geistig-kulturellen Lebens im Wohngebiet'.

[14] BArch-SAPMO, DY27 444, passim. 'Tagung des erweiterten Präsidiums des Kulturbunds der DDR am 17.10.1980 in Ahrenshoop'. BArch-SAPMO, DY27 963: 'Stenografisches Protokoll, Präsidialratssitzung des Kulturbunds der DDR am 16.11.1979 in Berlin', comment by Dr Klaus Bursian, Rostock.

[15] KA Heiligenstadt, Rat des Kreises Worbis 4289: 'Gen. Dr. Ose, Mitglied des Rates für Kultur. Worbis, den 30.11.1978'.

[16] BArch-SAPMO, DY30 IV/B2 9.06 86: 'Material zum geistig-kulturellen Leben im Wohngebiet' (21 February 1977), topic 1.2.4: 'Probleme und Hemmnisse bei der Entwicklung des geistig-kulturellen Lebens im Wohngebiet'.

so necessary. The party was keen to encourage neighbourhood festivals,[17] but in practice functionaries found it difficult to organize residential festivals where few communal structures existed. In addition, the party and the Cultural League also encouraged the construction of heimat groups to foster new traditions. In the newly built environment, local historians and local chroniclers had a particular opportunity to 'record and locate' the transformation of the heimat, and to familiarize new residents with their environment. Residents would thus become rooted in the heimat, feel at home in it and engage with the socialist community.[18]

In practice, attempts to construct a distinct culture and 'heritage' for the new towns failed to take root to any significant degree.[19] The party and the Cultural League soon understood that the best hope for sustaining cultural life lay in relating traditions and activities in the new residential areas to the cultural traditions of the old towns. This was apparent in the party's decision to stop giving new towns functional names, as were given to earlier examples such as Leipzig-Nord or Halle-Neustadt. Names such as Großer Dreesch (Schwerin) and Lütten Klein (Rostock) were meant to express organic links to older parts of the town and its traditions,[20] while architectural features such as individual façades or monuments further underlined connections with the traditions of the wider region.[21] But such superficial linkages could not overcome the anonymity of the new towns, and only served to reinforce the importance of the old town for the local heritage. To provide the residents of the new towns with a sense of identity and community, the built environment of the old towns became more important than ever.[22]

In the GDR as in West Germany and other European countries, the cultural transformations of the late 1960s facilitated a renaissance of

---

[17] BArch-SAPMO, DY30 IV/B2 9.06 86. 'Material zum geistig-kulturellen Leben im Wohngebiet' (21 February 1977), topic 2.5: 'Wie vollzieht sich der Prozeß des immer stärkeren Zuwendens der Bürger zur sozialistischen Lebensweise im Wohngebiet?'

[18] BArch-SAPMO, DY27 962, ff. 76–7: 'Stenografisches Protokoll der Tagung des Präsidialrates des Kulturbundes der DDR am 19.1.1979', introductory lecture by Willibald Gutsche.

[19] BArch-SAPMO, DY30 IV/B2 9.06 86: 'Material zum geistig-kulturellen Leben im Wohngebiet' (21 February 1977), topic 3.4: 'Welche Kräfte müssen im Wohngebiet für die massenpolitische Arbeit besser genutzt werden?' BArch-SAPMO, DY27 960, f. 184: 'Protokoll der Sitzung des Präsidialrates am 8. Juni 1977', speech by Dr Preuß.

[20] 'Ein Haus und seine Menschen', *SVZ* (14 May 1976). BArch-SAPMO, DY27 444: *Sonntag* 44 (1980), 'Über Tage und Über Nacht', 7.

[21] In Rostock, for example, the façades of the prefabricated flats were decorated in traditional north German clinker brick. *Rostock*, 2nd edn (Leipzig: Brockhaus, 1982), p. 11. The first edition was printed in 1979.

[22] BArch-SAPMO, DY27 444, ff. 141–2: 'Tagung des erweiterten Präsidiums des Kulturbunds der DDR am 17.10.1980 in Ahrenshoop', comment by Dr Jürgen Karthaus.

preservationism. Rudy Koshar has linked these debates in both parts of Germany to a new sense of nationhood that legitimized itself through a connection with early modern and medieval narratives.[23] In the GDR, to be sure, the value of preservationism was reinforced not just by the anonymity of the new towns, but also by the party's emphasis, beginning in the 1970s, on the GDR's heritage. Historical, technical and scientific monuments such as castles or workshops could now be restored in the name of reinforcing local tradition,[24] while also yielding economic benefit as tourist attractions in themselves.[25]

The heritage ideal also affected the design of inner cities. Following the early examples of Rostock, Weimar and Wismar, central streets were restored as an architectural unit and turned into pedestrian zones,[26] inviting citizens to stroll along, window-shop, or perhaps stop for coffee or ice cream. Such streets were not just held up as meccas of consumerism, they were also sites displaying the skills of the master builders of past centuries. Here, one could admire different architectural styles, and take time to investigate the individuality of historic houses.[27] Although pedestrianized 'boulevards' had existed since the 1960s, from the 1970s their construction became a matter of local pride.[28]

The significance of historic buildings and monuments as part of the local (and the GDR's) heritage constituted a marked shift away from the utilitarianism of the Ulbricht era. This became clear to all concerned in 1974, when the Potsdam district authorities decided to pull down the historic royal stables of the Prussian dynasty in the centre of town. In that year also, the Dresden district authorities planned to relocate the golden statue of Albrecht the Strong away from its historic location in the city. The internal

---

[23] Rudy Koshar, *Germany's Transient Pasts*, ch. 7.

[24] BArch-SAPMO, DY27 2618: Dr Liesel Noack, 'Der Beitrag der Bezirksorganisation Leipzig des Deutschen Kulturbundes zur sinnvollen Freizeitgestaltung unserer Werktätigen unter besonderer Berücksichtigung der Arbeit in den Naherholungsgebieten [1967]'. BArch-SAPMO, DY27 423, ff. 64–6: 'Die weitere Entwicklung der Denkmalpflege in der DDR und die Aufgaben des Kulturbundes. Stenografische Niederschrift der Zentralen Kommission des Präsidiums des Kulturbundes am 29. und 30. Oktober 1976 in Magdeburg', speech by Prof. Nadler.

[25] BArch-SAPMO, DY27 2941: 'Neuordnung des Schutzes und der Pflege von Denkmalen der Geschichte und der Kultur in der Deutschen Demokratischen Republik' (6 August 1968). BArch-SAPMO, DY27 2618: 'Der Beitrag der Bezirksorganisation Leipzig des deutschen Kulturbunds zur sinnvollen Freizeitgestaltung unserer Werktätigen unter besonderer Berücksichtigung der Arbeit in den Naherholungsgebieten' (paper given by Lisel Noack, 2 March 1967).

[26] Ludwig Deiters, 'Zum neuen Denkmalpflegegesetz', *Denkmalpflege in der Deutschen Demokratischen Republik* 2 (1975), 1–4.

[27] *Rostock*, p. 14.

[28] Interview with Ludwig Deiters, 6 March 2003.

debates that surrounded these decisions ultimately came to Honecker's attention, and in both cases he decided in favour of the monuments' preservation. According to Ludwig Deiters, then head of the GDR's Institute for Preservationism, the following years marked a high point in his Institute's work, not least because the party's commitment to historic monuments was affirmed at the Ninth Party Congress in 1976.[29] This did not mean that preservationists acquired a significant status in the GDR's architectural debates. However, it did mean that in local architectural disputes, arguments pointing to the value of historic buildings and monuments as part of the nation's tradition carried more weight than before 1974, or during the 1980s.[30]

The new emphasis on preservationism was reflected in the Cultural League, where the number of preservationist hobby groups increased from forty-five (1968) to ninety (1976) and, following the creation of the Society for Preservationism, to 301 in 1981 and 382 by 1984.[31] By far the smallest of the three societies that succeeded the Friends of Nature and Heimat, it aimed to train and direct those members keen on preservationism, to enable them to pursue their hobby more effectively and under closer guidance. In practice, preservationists concentrated on three major tasks. First, they could catalogue monuments and buildings in their locality that were of particular value. This was an important strategy in alerting local authorities to the existence of historic buildings and 'shaming' officials into providing scarce resources for their preservation. Second, amateur preservationists helped in their spare time to take care of particular objects, cleaning and restoring them. Third, they acted as local experts when historic buildings were in danger of irreparable damage, either from neglect or from destruction to make way for new housing. In this capacity, they could also alert the Institute for Preservationism, which could reinforce their claims by

---

[29] The Ninth Party Congress emphasized not just the urgency of Honecker's construction programme, but also the importance of harmony between the old and the new, asserting the party's commitment to the renovation of old houses. *Protokoll der Verhandlungen des IX. Parteitages der Sozialistischen Einheitspartei Deutschlands* (Berlin: Dietz, 1976), vol. I, pp. 66, 178–83 (Erich Honecker and Kurt Knobloch, First Party Secretary of Leipzig).

[30] Interview with Ludwig Deiters, 6 March 2003.

[31] *Statistik zur Entwicklung des Kulturbundes der DDR: Bericht an den X. Bundeskongreß* (Berlin: Kulturbund der DDR, 1982), p. 9. The overall statistics were confirmed by reports on the ground. The contemporary significance of preservationism in the cities, and the constitution of new preservationist groups, are highlighted, for instance, in a 1976 report of the Cultural League in the Erfurt district. ThHStAWe Kulturbund der DDR Bezirksverwaltung Erfurt 19. Referat 17. Bezirksleitung (24 November 1977), pp. 4, 11–12. For the 1984 figures, see Lothar Kolditz, 'Bürgerinitiative zur Pflege von Denkmalen und ihrer Umgebung', in *Kulturbund in der entwickelten sozialistischen Gesellschaft 1982–1986*, ed. Sekretariat des Präsidiums des Kulturbundes der DDR (Berlin, 1987), pp. 189–91.

providing expert opinions, and by seeking support, if necessary, from the Cultural Ministry in Berlin. Legally, whenever preservationists raised objections before the local authorities that could not be resolved, the authorities were obliged to report to the Ministry of Culture.[32]

In the late 1970s, the party accepted the need for historic buildings and monuments, not least in the city centres, as being complementary to its construction programme for the new towns. Historic buildings and monuments stood as daily reminders of the locality's heritage, for citizens of both the city centres and the new towns.[33] For instance, the mayor of Magdeburg took great pride in the prefabricated tenement blocks that graced the town's centre and its outlying new towns, where a new flat was completed every eighty minutes. But he also emphasized the value of what little historic architecture remained, from the cathedral to the patricians' coats of arms that had survived the wartime destruction of the city centre. This combination of old and new allowed the citizens to appropriate Magdeburg's traditions, and contributed to their appreciation of history and their sense of heimat.[34]

The new towns were persistently linked to the heimat through traditional monuments and artefacts. From the late 1970s on, numerous articles in the travel and cultural sections of journals and magazines introduced the cultural traditions and sights of the GDR's cities. These articles regularly featured the amenities provided in prefabricated residential areas and the sheer number of flats that had been built. However, in contrast to the way factories had been represented as distinctive sights in their own right during the Ulbricht era, from the mid-1970s the tourist gaze was not directed towards the prefabricated towns. The cultural and journalistic focus remained firmly on each town's historic traditions, in travel reports and in touristic representations. New flats were presented not as the centre of attention, but as an added bonus (Figure 11).[35] New towns and the historic buildings and monuments of the old towns became perfect complements;

---

[32] Interview with Ludwig Deiters, 6 March 2003.

[33] BArch-SAPMO, DY27 423, ff. 165–70: 'Die weitere Entwicklung der Denkmalpflege in der DDR und die Aufgaben des Kulturbundes. Stenografische Niederschrift der Zentralen Kommission des Präsidiums des Kulturbundes am 29. und 30. Oktober 1976 in Magdeburg', comments by Dr Hanke on Berlin Marzahn.

[34] BArch-SAPMO, DY27 423, ff. 9–11: 'Die weitere Entwicklung der Denkmalpflege in der DDR und die Aufgaben des Kulturbundes. Stenografische Niederschrift der Zentralen Kommission des Präsidiums des Kulturbundes am 29. und 30. Oktober 1976 in Magdeburg'. Opening comments by Werner Herzig, lord mayor of Magdeburg. See also 'Goldene Leier, alter Stein', *Sonntag* (13 March 1977).

[35] See, for instance, 'Reisejournal: Eisenach', *Für Dich* 48 (1983), 23–6. 'Reisejournal: Gotha', *Für Dich* 49 (1978), 23–6. 'Burg, Bürger und Besucher', *NBI* 31 (1984), 36–7. 'Reisejournal: Mühlhausen', *Für Dich* 31 (1989), 23–6.

11. Plan of Mühlhausen. New flats are drawn in at the top, but they are not central to the imagery. At the centre-left of the image, the second church on the left is the Jacobikirche. The buildings around it are depicted as being built in the style of 'historical gap construction': these icons are almost indistinguishable from Mühlhausen's historic buildings. 'Reisejournal: Mühlhausen' (Travel Journal: Mühlhausen), *Für Dich* 31 (1989), 24–5.

citizens could live in the comfort of new apartment blocks, while enjoying the historic heritage.

In practice, there was a direct trade-off between the construction of new flats and the repair of old housing. Since export-intensive industries could pay far higher premiums than the work-intensive construction industry, the latter never employed sufficient numbers to realize the party's ambitious goals for the production of new flats, especially in the industrial districts of Karl-Marx-Stadt and Leipzig.[36] One roofer complained in 1974 that in his co-operative, roofers could earn a year-end premium of around 80 marks, a mere tenth of what they could obtain as industrial workers. Even worse, amongst those employed to fulfil Honecker's building programme, higher wages were paid to workers building the new towns than to craftsmen repairing traditional houses. In all of Halle, the GDR's sixth largest city with 230,000 inhabitants, only nine masons were employed in 1974 to carry out building repairs. At the same time, there were 700 chimneys in town whose state of repair presented a serious danger to the public. But the masons were needed for other repair work that was even more urgent, and even when they did have time to tackle a number of those chimneys, it was not at all clear that appropriate scaffolding was available. The general situation was compounded by a shortage of repair materials, especially clay, electrical switches, plugs and sanitary installations. A report for the GDR's People's Chamber noted that in all of Halle, not a single spare window frame or spare door could be obtained that could be fitted into an old house. Little wonder, then, that of 91,000 flats in Halle, 85 per cent needed repair.[37]

In 1976, preservationists estimated that over the next decade, more than 140 cities with 125 historic centres would have to be renovated or restored.[38] In the late 1970s the state of the inner cities became acute. In Grabow (Schwerin district), for instance, the town centre consisted of 710 flats, of which it was estimated in 1978 that between 30 and 40 per cent would have to be torn down.[39] This signalled a new, much more direct threat to historic

---

[36] Between 1970 and 1989 the number of workers employed in the construction industry increased by just 3 per cent. Hansjörg F. Buck, 'Wohnungsversorgung, Stadtgestaltung und Stadtverfall', in Eberhard Kuhrt (ed.), *Die wirtschaftliche und ökologische Situation der DDR in den achtziger Jahren* (Opladen: Leske & Budrich, 1996), pp. 67–109.

[37] BArch-SAPMO, DAI (Volkskammer der DDR) 11818: 'Stenografisches Protokoll. Sitzung des Ausschusses für Eingaben der Bürger in der Volkskammer der DDR am 24. Oktober 1974 in Berlin'.

[38] BArch-SAPMO, DY27 423, ff. 199–200: 'Die weitere Entwicklung der Denkmalpflege in der DDR und die Aufgaben des Kulturbundes. Stenografische Niederschrift der Zentralen Kommission des Präsidiums des Kulturbundes am 29. und 30. Oktober 1976 in Magdeburg', comments by Peter Schuster.

[39] 'Kleinstadt auf dem Moor', *Sonntag* (19 February 1978).

buildings and monuments. Whereas up to the mid-1970s, historic buildings had suffered largely from neglect owing to prefabricated construction outside the old towns, thereafter many houses in town centres became so derelict that they were under direct threat of being replaced by new buildings. By the end of the 1980s, 40 per cent of all buildings built before 1945 were considered by the GDR's own Academy of Construction to be severely damaged, with a further 11 per cent being uninhabitable.[40] The more resources the socialist plan devoted to the construction of prefabricated flats, the more historic flats deteriorated. By 1989 the net gains in housing stock had become minimal.[41]

Since damaged housing stock was particularly concentrated in the GDR's towns, whose centres had become depopulated, during the 1980s the tension between preservationism and new prefabricated construction turned into a dispute over the destruction of the GDR's historic city centres. A rift developed between the party's concentration on particular monuments and buildings and the preservationists' concern about the decay of older houses in general. The party clearly hoped that through better institutional guidance, preservationists would focus on particular objects. Moreover, in touristic representations of the country's historic towns, newspapers and magazines highlighted individual historical buildings, in this way also suggesting which buildings needed to be saved – and which did not (Figure 11).[42] Yet the vast majority of buildings in the centres of Mühlhausen and Quedlinburg, as well as towns like Eisenach and Meiningen, were of historical value. The policy of preserving houses on the main tourist routes while leaving houses in the back streets to decay could not be ignored by preservationists.[43]

The party hoped to reconcile this conflict through what it dubbed 'historical gap construction'. First developed in Halle, prefabricated building blocks were produced in a much smaller size, which could be used not just in large ensembles, but also on relatively small plots of land. Moreover, the façades could be adjusted to fit as much as possible into the local environment, by using prefabricated, stylized features such as gables and windows (Figure 12). To the party, this method was the saviour of the historic city centres, preserving their historic distinctiveness and individuality without

[40] Buck, 'Wohnungsversorgung', pp. 95–6.   [41] Kopstein, *Politics*, pp. 182–3.

[42] 'Reisejournal: Mühlhausen', *Für Dich* 31 (August 1989), 23–6; here 24–5.

[43] According to a West German study completed in 1990, around one third of Quedlinburg's centre was 'almost completely dilapidated' or 'badly damaged', and in a further 57 per cent of the buildings damage was 'medium' to 'serious'. 'Zaghafter Neubeginn am Ende des Schienenstrangs', *Junge Welt* (3–4 November 1990).

12. 'Historical gap construction', Merseburg. Using Merseburg as an example, the picture shows how the construction co-operative of Halle had managed to preserve the town's distinctive character: 'This new building, not really designed as a single block, is situated in the town square and stands in a visual relationship with neighbouring historic houses: through the vaulted roof, the colour (the windows in the grey buildings were painted dark brown and in the red buildings were painted white), through a loggia at the corner and the diversity of style of the shop windows.' 'Bauplatz nebenan' (construction site next door), *NBI* 8 (1983), 12.

compromising on the need for new and comfortable flats.[44] This was also the solution found for Mühlhausen, which faced a similar housing problem. The deplorable conditions of some of the buildings around the Jacobikirche led the authorities to demolish them in 1988, and 'rejuvenate' the area through the gap construction method (Figure 11). As the authorities argued, the new houses were built with painstaking attention to detail, leaving the

---

[44] 'Neuartige architektonische Lösung für das Zentrum von Quedlinburg', *Neues Deutschland* (5–6 January 1985); 'Neubau und Modernisierung paßt zur Schmalen Straße', *Freiheit* (Halle) (19 December 1984); 'Eigenheim – mitten in der Stadt: Wie die Naumbürger einen Rathausspruch verstehen', *National-Zeitung* (20/21 February 1988), weekend supplement, 1–2.

spirit and individuality of the Jacobikirche quarter intact. Here 'prefabricated blocks, tiled gables and historical reconstruction formed a trinity'.[45]

Despite the official transcript whereby prefabricated flats and historical tradition were reconciled, historic buildings were under greater threat than ever. Far from saving historic quarters, the new construction method endangered them by making prefabricated construction feasible in small spaces. Moreover, the erection of 'historic' prefabricated houses formed part of the rhetoric of 'restoration' rather than construction, enabling the party to claim this as part of its commitment to the upkeep of old housing stock.[46] Privately, the party left no doubt about what it was up to. In 1988, Karl Schmiechen, state secretary at the Ministry of Construction, noted that the repair of an old flat cost three times as much as the construction of a new, prefabricated flat. For as long as this imbalance continued, Schmiechen insisted that there was no economically viable alternative to replacing old houses with prefabricated flats.[47] During the 1980s, then, the GDR's historic city centres were seriously threatened by policies of neglect and destruction.

While the party continued to insist on the compatibility between its concerns for heimat and the construction of prefabricated housing in new towns and the city centres, the decay of historic buildings was clear for all to see. Against this background, the number of registered amateur preservationists grew. This raises the question how these activists responded to the decay of the inner cities, and what they hoped to achieve. To what extent was the party able to assert its meanings for the socialist heimat, and how willing were individuals to subscribe to the public transcript of the heimat whose physical decay they witnessed in their everyday lives?

In interviews with heimat activists across the former GDR, the new towns never featured unless I specifically asked about them (this applies even to heimat activists living in new towns). By contrast, the irretrievable destruction of historic houses to make way for new flats was often lamented. Interviewees constantly reminded me of the uphill struggle facing preservationists. Manfred Fiedler, who, as the Cultural League's deputy secretary responsible for the Friends of Nature and Heimat, had engineered the creation of the Society of Preservationists, left no doubt about this:

---

[45] 'Maßgeschneidertes Gewand für historische Stätten', *Neue Zeit* (3 December 1987). The quotation is in 'Reisejournal: Mühlhausen', *Für Dich* 31 (August 1989), 23–6; here 26.

[46] BArch-SAPMO, DY30 2845 (Büro Mittag), ff. 256–63. The interview was published in the women's magazine *Für Dich* on 18 September 1985 (no. 38).

[47] BArch-SAPMO, DAI 17301, ff. 45–7: 'Stenografisches Protokoll. Sitzung des Ausschusses für Eingaben der Bürger vom 25. bis 27. Oktober 1988 in Dessau'.

Given the sheer mass of country houses, preservationism was often overburdened. Materials were simply lacking and not available in the necessary quantities. I'm thinking of Stralsund for instance. I mean, what I saw there that was important and necessary from a preservationist's point of view, and not only there: the roofs of the historic buildings were collapsing, the walls were damaged, and we tried to urge as well as we could that something must be done, and if the building couldn't be restored they should at least try to secure it from further destruction. Especially a town like Stralsund with this medieval character that extended to entire streets, it was marvellous. But to walk through this, my goodness, [it was] unimaginable, and wherever else we went – Gotha, for instance [it was the same].[48]

Of the interviewees I spoke to, Fiedler was amongst the least critical of the party's care for the socialist heimat. Yet even he could not help oscillating between admiring the historic buildings of the inner cities, and lamenting their decay. The dilapidation of historic houses was clear for all to see, and no amount of party rhetoric could convince anyone that this was compatible with the party's care for the heimat. Instead, Fiedler and others spoke of preservationists in heroic language: how they had achieved so much despite adverse conditions. To be effective, preservationists needed to engage in time-consuming work, and be prepared to confront the local authorities where necessary. Indeed, finding a leader for the local preservationists was not always easy, because it was clear that this position meant trouble with the authorities.[49] By listing houses in need of preservation and reminding councils of their duty to the heimat, by carrying out minor repairs themselves, and by cleaning monuments and preventing them from falling into disrepair, preservationists did all they could in the face of adversity.[50]

Given the scale of the dilapidation of the inner cities, activists could not but feel a sense of powerlessness and frustration. One way of recording their concerns was through the monthly informative reports which every

---

[48] 'Aber was wees ich wer bei der Masse an Herrenhäusern war natürlich die Denkmalpflege och teilweise überfordert. Weil einfach Materialien fehlten, in dem Ausmaß gar nich da waren. Ich denke da zum Beispiel och an Stralsund. Also ich meen was ich da gesehen habe was denkmalpflegerisch wichtig und notwendig gewesen ist und nicht nur da. Die Dächer fielen ein von diesen historischen Gebäuden, de Mauern warn beschädigt, und also das, da ham wir eben och so gut es ging immer wieder darauf gedrungen das begonnen wird etwas zu machen, ne, man hat erstemal gesichert ohne das es schon wieder in Ordnung gebracht worden ist. Gerade so ne Stadt wie Stralsund mit dieser, mit dieser mittelalterlichen Bausubstanz. Ganze Straßenzüge, das is, das iss was wunderbares gewesen. Da durchzugehen und, ach nee, wenn man sich das so vorstellt oder in Gotha und wo wir überall gewesen sind.' Interview with Manfred Fiedler, 27 February 2003. (Fiedler came from Saxony.)

[49] Interview with Jürgen Thormann, 22 April 2005.

[50] Auster and Behrens, *Naturschutz in den neuen Bundesländern*, passim. Interview with Manfred Fiedler, 27 February 2003. On the preservationists' actions in Quedlinburg, see also Hans-Hartmut Schauer, *Quedlinburg: Fachwerkstadt, Weltkulturerbe* (Berlin: Verlag Bauwesen, 1999).

organization had to submit to the party.[51] According to Jürgen Thormann, Mühlhausen county secretary of the Cultural League and author of his organization's informative reports, it was crucial to use the right wording. In the 1970s, every report had to signal popular approval for the party's ideal, the 'unity of economic and social policy' postulated at the Eighth Party Congress.[52] In the 1980s, each report noted the members' concern for peace, their appreciation of Honecker's leadership, and their rejection of US policy.[53] Authors of the monthly reports did have the opportunity to voice criticism; in fact, they were required to do so. When I asked Thormann on what basis he decided which criticisms to include and which to leave out, he said he used to include those criticisms that were common knowledge, and those in which officials could be shown to have contradicted themselves and their own laws. In this way, no one could face retribution for anything they had said, while Thormann could affirm the organization's identity as speaking out for its members. Thormann, in short, ensured that his reports fitted the public transcript.

In the mid-1980s, three issues prevailed among Thormann's criticisms: problems in obtaining consumer goods, pollution mainly through litter and insufficient refuse collection, and the dilapidation of the old town. Taking reports filed in a six-month period in 1986 as an example, Thormann reported in February that his members had 'discussed plans for the recon-struction of the town to reflect preservationist concerns'. The following month, he was only marginally more concrete, stating that his members had discussed possible layouts for the Jacobikirche quarter. In May, Thormann noted that his members welcomed the party's initiative to solve the nation's housing problems, and appreciated its consideration for preservationist concerns. In the following month, members were reported to have queried why in Berlin the SED had lower electoral returns in recent elections than in Mühlhausen, even though Berlin was supported by the rest of the Republic through building material and food supplies. And in July, Thormann reported that members had wondered why the reconstruction of the central square in town was proceeding so much more slowly than construction in Berlin's Thälmann Park.[54]

---

[51] A number of historians have made extensive use of these reports as a gauge of public opinion. Mark Allinson, *Politics and Popular Opinion in East Germany, 1945–68* (Manchester University Press, 2000). Mark Allinson, 'Popular Opinion', in Major and Osmond (eds.), *The Workers' and Peasants' State*, pp. 96–111.

[52] Interview with Jürgen Thormann, 22 April 2005.

[53] See, for instance, StA Mühlhausen, Kulturbund Mühlhausen 4: Kulturbund der DDR Kreisleitung Mühlhausen, p. 5 (summer 1984).

[54] StA Mühlhausen, Kulturbund Mühlhausen 4: 'Politische Monatsberichte' (February–July 1986).

These statements hardly appear as trenchant criticisms of the party, but it is worth examining them in detail. Thormann's references from February to May 1986 relate to the Mühlhauseners' struggle to save the small quarter around the historic Jacobikirche from being torn down and replaced by 'historical gap construction'. Reminding the party of its rhetorical commitment to preservationism, or wondering what the Jacobikirche quarter would look like, was all that needed to be said in the GDR context to record frustration, upset and protest against the party's plans.

Thormann's other statements expressed the widespread frustration at the fact that the city had had to provide 250 building workers for the construction of the Thälmann Park in Berlin for that city's 750th anniversary in 1987, while locals had to watch their own historic buildings suffer continual decline.[55] Again, wondering at the 'low' vote in Berlin or the relatively fast progress of Mühlhausen's workers in Berlin represented a clear message to the party about the privileging of Berlin at the expense of the local heimat. This was, in fact, a common grievance: builders and materials from all over the GDR were used first and foremost for the reconstruction of Berlin, and district capitals also received a disproportionate share of the scarce resources. Provincial towns, in many of which the historical infrastructure had escaped the war relatively unscathed, were thus left to deteriorate not just owing to scarce resources, but also to the hierarchical system of allocation characteristic of 'democratic centralism'. Thormann's reports, in sum, demonstrate the depth of frustration about the dilapidation of the built environment, and not just among preservationists. They also show how this concern could be expressed in a nuanced manner, through the public transcript.

Registering dissent through information reports was one way of keeping to the public transcript; writing petitions was another. In 1984, planners proposed to demolish three gasometers in Berlin's Thälmann Park, to make way for a statue of the communist leader. The news of the impending demolition spread and caused a huge stir. Students and teachers of architecture at the Academy of Art protested against the decision, and citizens wrote passionate petitions on behalf of the gasometers. As E.B. wrote,

They are among the most striking landmarks of our city, especially Prenzlauer Berg. To me it seems perfectly possible to include the gasometers in the design of the park

---

[55] Interview with Jürgen Thormann, 22 April 2005. See also Peter Merseburger's report on Mühlhausen for the West German television show *Monitor*, in which he charted the frustrations of residents at the dilapidation of the old town. DRA Zeitschriftensammlung: 'Mühlhausen', in *Monitor* (25 May 1987), ARD, 9.10 p.m.

and thus create a synthesis of the old and the new. Technological monuments are also part of our heritage and must be protected.

Another resident, C.L.B., argued: 'after all we are dealing with a techno-logical monument, which is a landmark of our city, and ... forms part of the distinctive character of my local district'.[56] What is striking here is the way in which gasometers were declared, in the language of heimat, to be a landmark of Berlin. In fact, the park formed part of a redevelopment project that included a block of prefabricated flats for which old tenement blocks had to be demolished. The reason why the party responded with such nervousness to this incident (which was reported to Günter Mittag) was that the dispute did not concern the gasometers as such, or even the design of the park: it was an expression of protest against the clearance of old tenement blocks in an area of Berlin where a youth subculture was rapidly emerging.[57] By using the language of the socialist homeland and its heritage, protesters were able to challenge the meanings of heimat, and with it the party's hegemony. For this reason, the party was extremely concerned to keep the protest within the transcript and avoid open confrontation.

In the end, the Thälmann Park gasometers were destroyed. In Mühlhausen, the Jacobikirche quarter was demolished in 1988 and rebuilt by 1989. Preservationists could try and maintain historic sites as best they could. They could register their opposition to the destruction of buildings and monuments, appeal to the Institute of Preservationism, and write petitions. This could (and usually did) delay proceedings, but in the hous-ing arena, such activities rarely stopped the party in its endeavours.

In the early 1980s, rumours emerged in Mühlhausen that the local SED hierarchy wanted to build their headquarters on an old, historic cemetery. Preservationists and amateur historians in the Cultural League greatly valued the gravestones there; for dendrologists, the old bushes and trees in the cemetery were important. Thormann repeatedly went to the SED county leadership, where each time he was assured that this was groundless gossip. Thormann remembers how one day, whilst he was in a meeting, an activist stormed into the room; he had just come from the cemetery where he had witnessed tanks moving in to flatten the ground and make room for the building. Activists could never feel that they had any sort of entitlement on behalf of the heimat, because all power remained with the party. As

[56] BArch-SAPMO, DY30; Büro Mittag 2845, ff. 137–44: 'Eingaben' (June 1986), 'Brief der Parteileitung Kunsthochschule Berlin' (12 June 1984), 'Brief des Ministers für Bauwesen an Günter Mittag' (25 July 1984).
[57] Interview with Ludwig Deiters, 6 March 2003.

Thormann realized, ultimately 'the party did whatever it wanted, end of story!'[58]

If the party was so obviously dominant, why did more and more individuals become active on behalf of preservationism, and what did they hope to gain? In Meiningen (Suhl district), a local preservation society was formed under the aegis of the Cultural League in 1980. Among its twenty to thirty registered members, an inner core of nine or ten engaged in constant skirmishes with the town and county councils about the state of the town centre, the castle and the castle's historic English garden. Whenever the local authorities planned work on any building, the preservationists made clear that they expected to be consulted. This resulted in frequent angry written exchanges between the group's leader, Thomasius, and the local mayor, Wiebel, who, Thomasius felt, disregarded preservationists' concerns.[59] In 1981, the town proposed to tear down a historic building in the city centre. Alarmed by these plans, the preservationists wrote to the Institute for Preservationism in Erfurt, whose officers inspected the site. Eager for action, the mayor misrepresented the inspectors' opinions and tore down the building. This was a demonstration of the party's power, but it was not without consequences. To be sure, the demolition could not be undone, but the local preservationists and the Institute in Erfurt petitioned the district authorities until Wiebel was forced to admit that he had disregarded the law.[60]

When rumours began to circulate that the party planned to tear down parts of the city centre to make room for prefabricated houses, preservationists launched a campaign entitled 'Save Old Meiningen' in 1987. Protest was taken to these new levels by a young preservationist, Axel Wirth (b. 1962). From a Meiningen family, Wirth had abandoned his studies of urban planning in Weimar out of disillusionment, according to his own testimony, because the architectural ideals he was being taught could never be realized in practice. Wirth became active in one of the group's pet projects, the construction of a heimat museum in a derelict grotto in the English garden. His central involvement, however, related to the local authorities' plans, from the mid-1980s, to demolish part of the city centre to make way

[58] Thormann: 'und trotzdem: Die Partei machte, was sie wollte, aus die Maus!'
[59] StA Meiningen, IG Denkmalpflege 5: 'An den Rat des Kreises' (18 November 1982). IG Denkmalpflege 3: 'Stellungnahme zur Innenstadtbebauung' (14 January 1982).
[60] StA Meiningen, IG Denkmalpflege 6: Institut für Denkmalpflege Erfurt (26 March 1981); 'An den Bürgermeister' (26 March 1981); Bürgermeister Wiebel to Fenchel (13 May 1981); Fenchel to Bürgermeister Wiebel (14 May 1981); IG Denkmalpflege to Bürgermeister Wiebel (14 May 1981); Bürgermeister Wiebel to IG Denkmalpflege (22 October 1981).

for new construction. To prevent this, Wirth and his friends pursued a double strategy: to persuade local residents, desperate for better accommodation, of the value of historic buildings through talks, publications and other activities; and to use all possible legal means to stop, change or at least delay the plans.

The group was taken seriously because throughout the 1980s, local authorities had learned that preservationists could make life very uncomfortable for them. Activists were also encouraged by the feeling that, despite the enormous power of the party, victory might just be possible. Wirth described how the Cultural League's success at erecting a memorial to the town's Jewish residents in 1988, despite this subject having been taboo before, encouraged activists with a feeling that 'you can succeed with such topics'.[61]

The case of Meiningen does not merely reveal the importance of earlier experiences of recording protests and gauging how far one could go. It also demonstrates the significance of the particular local environment. In Meiningen, locals were proud of their theatre, which was linked to an attachment to the former ruling dynasty, and particularly Duke George II, whose patronage had made the town's theatre famous beyond the borders of Germany. Wirth surmised that most Meiningers had a picture of the Duke somewhere, either on open display or hidden away from public view.[62] Pride in Meiningen's cultural contribution was reinforced by rivalry with neighbouring Suhl, as locals could not forget that Meiningen had been demoted to a county town while 'plebeian' Suhl had become the district capital.[63] The strength of local identity often overrode party allegiance. Thomasius' membership of the SED did not prevent him from opposing his party's plans to deface the city centre, while Wirth's campaign benefited

---

[61] 'Die Aktivitäten um die Pflege des jüdischen Erbes der DDR, das ja eigentlich völlig Tabu war, was ja auch von Meiningen, und das hat uns auch damals in Sachen Innenstadt Mut gemacht, wo es auch von Meiningen aus 'ne große Initiative kam, das Erinnern an die Synagoge in Meiningen und die jüdischen Bürger in Meiningen, die hervorragende Verdienste hatten, hier zu pflegen, und nachdem das also 1988 auch zur Einweihung eines Denkmals gekommen war waren wir der Meinung, „OK, man kann bei solchen Themen durchaus Erfolg haben" und haben dann sofort das Thema Altstadt groß angesprochen.' Interview with Axel Wirth, 27 September 2007. This is not the only example among my interviewees where the experience of local activity to commemorate the Jews was named as an example of particular local progressiveness, even if, historically speaking, this was not necessarily the case.

[62] Axel Wirth explained how every Meininger possessed a picture of Duke George II, the patron of the theatre, and that, when the local heimat museum was opened in the English garden, it displayed the coat of arms not of the town, but of the Duke. Interview with Axel Wirth, 27 September 2007.

[63] Alfred Erck, president of the Cultural League in Suhl district, emphasized (and confirmed) the local hostility (and superiority) felt vis-à-vis Suhl. Interview with Alfred Erck, 21 May 2003.

crucially from his particular expertise and his standing in the city, which party functionaries, who were locals themselves, could not simply ignore.

Wirth could delay the council, but he could not stop it. In March 1989, Wirth sent out a final petition to the district, protesting against the authorities' plans.[64] This prolonged discussions with the district building commission well into May 1989, but Wirth failed to change the commission's mind. Having exhausted all legal means at his disposal, he persuaded the district leadership of his party, the NDPD, to take up the cause. Party leaders arranged yet another meeting between Wirth and the district building commission in late June 1989, which concluded with the customary outcome.[65] He had lost his battle, and on 19 October 1989 builders from the Suhl construction combine laid the foundations for the first prefabricated block of flats in the inner city.

Wirth's ambition to convince locals of the value of the city's historic centre shows how difficult it became for the party to sustain its argument that prefabricated buildings complemented the built environment. It is important to note that Meiningen is not the only example of the preservationists' growing frustrations. In the Mecklenburg town of Boizenburg, preservationists also developed activities that came close to challenging the public transcript of the socialist heimat. In 1988, Uwe Wieben, who served on the county council for the NDPD, refused to vote for the budget because it provided money for the reconstruction of Boizenburg's old town. As director of the heimat museum, Wieben then organized an exhibition, 'New Building in an Old Town', in which he invited locals to present their own plans for the redesigning of the city centre. Like Wirth's activities, Wieben's actions were far from illegal, but they do signify a growing unwillingness to accept the party's public transcript. By 1988, preservationists' open affirmation of the socialist heimat had become visibly strained.

HEIMAT AND THE ENVIRONMENT

The dramatic deterioration of the built environment was reinforced by the pollution of the natural environment. In 1987, West German scientists measuring pollution in the River Elbe reported that a total of 53,000 tons of ammonium, 16,000 tons of phosphate, 26 tons of mercury, and 126 tons of lead had got into this river alone. The Elbe fed from waters that crossed

---

[64] Axel Wirth Private Collection, 'Rat der Stadt Meiningen an Herrn Axel Wirth' (14 April 1989).
[65] Axel Wirth Private Collection, 'Brief Axel Wirth an Jürgen Hinrichs' (22 May 1989); 'Rat des Bezirks Suhl Bezirksbauamt an Axel Wirth' (June 1989).

territory inhabited by 80 per cent of the GDR's population, and its waters were used four to seven times over for personal consumption, industry and agriculture.[66] By 1989, the GDR's emissions of sulphur doxide were twenty-six times higher than those of West Germany, and had damaged 44 per cent of the GDR's forests.[67] If the drinking water in cities like Dresden had become a health hazard for small children by 1989,[68] what impact did this have on the public transcript of the socialist homeland? Granted, the socialist notion of heimat allowed for the transformation of the environment, but it precluded its wholesale destruction. Under these conditions, how could the ideal be sustained that only under socialism could heimat flourish?

Pollution had been a cause for concern for environmentalists throughout the history of the GDR.[69] However, from the late 1960s onwards, environmental concerns were aggravated by the plan. Large industrial complexes were created which oversaw all production processes. In addition, the 'industrialization of agriculture' resulted in the creation of large-scale farms specializing in livestock production. Mass production of animals, especially pigs, produced enormous quantities of dung which, unless disposed of carefully, contaminated the soil and the drinking water of the surrounding area with nitrates.

Unprecedented pollution through industry and agriculture was compounded by the lack of resources available for investment. During the 1970s and especially the 1980s, ageing industrial plants and agricultural machinery emitted more and more pollutants.[70] With the GDR's reliance on sulphuric brown coal increasing, resources for industrial investment, let alone investment in air filters and water treatment plants, declined.[71] Landolf Scherzer's impressions upon entering a wheel-spoke factory in Suhl district in 1987 were indicative of the problems this caused in everyday life. Working conditions resembled those of the early nineteenth century, with women dunking the spokes in molten chrome or nickel, their only protection from this 'sorcerer's brew' being a thin foil. The floor was covered in oil

---

[66] 'Zurück zur Natur', *Bild der Wissenschaft* (August 1991), 68–74. For 1988, Buck lists lower figures measured by the same institute: 4,300 tons of zinc, 970 tons of copper, 10 tons of cadmium, 16 tons of mercury and 180 tons of lead. Hansjörg Buck, 'Umweltpolitik und Umweltbelastung', in Kuhrt (ed.), *Die wirtschaftliche und ökologische Situation*, pp. 223–66; here pp. 244–5.

[67] Jörg Roesler, *Umweltprobleme und Umweltpolitik in der DDR* (Thüringen: Landeszentrale für Politische Bildung, 2006); here p. 59.

[68] 'Dresdens Trinkwasser für Kleinkinder ungeeignet', *Frankfurter Rundschau* (15 November 1990).

[69] Oberkrome, „*Deutsche* Heimat", pp. 347–556.   [70] Roesler, *Umweltprobleme*, pp. 37–59.

[71] Not only did reliance on brown coal increase, but continued underinvestment in technology led to increased pollution of water and soil in the mining area. Roesler, *Umweltprobleme*, p. 44.

and acid, and even the director was frightened of the poisonous conditions inside his factory, for the sake of his workers and of the environment – but there was simply no money to reduce the damage in what was the GDR's only wheelchair factory.[72] Environmental conditions deteriorated rapidly during the 1970s and 1980s, while environmental awareness, fuelled partly by the environmental debates broadcast on West German television, increased.

In the late 1960s, the growing demand for recreational sites not only reignited official encouragement for preservationism, it also put pressure on the party and the local authorities to consider the problems of environmental pollution in a new light.[73] In 1966, the Cultural League initiated a 'landscape conference' (*Landschaftstag*) for the district of Neubrandenburg, to discuss measures for improving the tourist infrastructure in the vacation areas around Lake Müritz. The meeting was attended by representatives from the Cultural League, the relevant counties and the district, the forestry and water management offices and the district departments of tourism and the environment. Although delegates were primarily concerned with promoting tourism, an important subtext of the debates was the understanding that, for nature to be enjoyed, it needed to be protected from agricultural and industrial pollution.[74]

The idea of bringing together representatives from different organizations to co-ordinate their work across administrative boundaries soon caught on. Beginning in 1968 the Cultural League of Suhl, Erfurt and Gera organized, in rotation, the biennial 'Thuringian Landscape Conference'. From 1970 on, a landscape conference for the Harz mountains was held every five or six years, with representatives from the relevant districts (Magdeburg, Halle and Erfurt). During the 1970s, these conferences became an important forum in which environmental problems were raised. At the second landscape conference in Neubrandenburg, held in 1976, officials from Schwerin, Potsdam and Neubrandenburg districts discussed how the lakes and forests in the north of the GDR could be kept free from pollution, as this was an area visited by 600,000 holidaymakers and 2.5 million day trippers every year. Participants were particularly

---

[72] Landolf Scherzer, *Der Erste*, 7th edn (Berlin: Aufbau Taschenbuch, 2002), pp. 162–71.

[73] BArch-SAPMO, DY27 946, ff. 121–2: 'Stenografisches Protokoll der Tagung des Präsidialrates des DKBs am 21. Februar 1969', comment by Alex Ständel.

[74] On the Cultural League's attempts to lobby for the 'Müritz-Seen-Park', see BArch-SAPMO, DY27 3696: 'Protokoll der Arbeitsausschusssitzung vom 15.3.1967.' On the landscape day, see Regine Auster, *Landschaftstage: Kooperative Planungsverfahren in der Landschaftsentwicklung; Erfahrungen aus der DDR*. Umweltgeschichte und Umweltzukunft (Marburg: Bund demokratischer Wissenschaftlerinnen und Wissenschaftler e.V., 1996), pp. 45–8.

concerned about deficient provision for the disposal of hazardous waste, the uncontrolled leakage of chemicals into the ground at many agro-chemical centres, and saturation with manure owing to faulty or overflowing containers.[75]

Landscape conferences were held in growing numbers for ever smaller areas, including places where tourism formed a much less important sector of the economy, including the Zittau hills (Dresden district, 1975), the central Ilm valley (Erfurt district, 1976) and the plains of Magdeburg ('Börde', Magdeburg district, 1981). During the 1980s, landscape conferences were held for even smaller areas, often for single counties, and even for urban areas. In 1986 the Cultural League noted with satisfaction that, between 1 January 1985 and 28 February 1986, there had been a total of 123 landscape conferences throughout the GDR covering 60 per cent of the country's counties, with 20,000 participants.[76] By 1989, the Cultural League claimed that 75 per cent of the GDR's counties were holding landscape and environmental conferences.[77]

A further forum for activity was the Society for Nature and the Environment (GNU), created in 1980 to combine those subdivisions of the Friends of Nature and Heimat which were particularly concerned with the environment, such as botanists, ornithologists and geologists. The GNU aimed to provide better networks among, and training opportunities for, its members. It also strongly encouraged mapping the environment. By charting the nature and location of plants, trees, animals and insects, members of the GNU could provide scientists with invaluable information. It was increasingly important for the GNU's mission that the organization record essential information to support environmental measures, for only what was known could be protected.[78]

The GNU became the Cultural League's fastest-growing organization. Encompassing some 1,300 local organizations upon its foundation, it grew to 2,974 by the end of 1986, which translated into 57,245 members, equivalent to 21.4 per cent of the Cultural League's membership. Much of this increase came from the creation of new types of groups that had not

[75] *Referate, Berichte, Ergebnisse, Aufgaben: 2. Landschaftstag „Mecklenburgisch-Brandenburgische Seenplatte".* Natur und Umwelt: Im Bezirk Neubrandenburg (Neubrandenburg: Kulturbund der Deutschen Demokratischen Republik, 1979).

[76] BArch-SAPMO, DY27 456: 'Einschätzung der Entwicklung der Gesellschaft für Natur und Umwelt im Kulturbund seit dem X. Bundeskongreß' (13 October 1986), p. 4.

[77] BArch-SAPMO, DY27 978, f. 235: 'Die Umweltpolitik der DDR und die Aufgaben des Kulturbundes. Präsidialratssitzung Kongreßhalle, 28.9.89', speech by Harald Thomasius.

[78] BArch-SAPMO, DY27 456: 'Der Kulturbund als Partner der Wissenschaft' (Büro Schulmeister, 10 June 1986).

existed in the 1970s, such as 'Urban Ecology' (2,917 members) and 'Environmental Protection', which within seven years had developed into the GNU's largest sub-organization, with 726 groups and 10,245 members.[79] As the GDR's official environmental organization, the GNU became a pre-eminent voice in the struggle to raise environmental awareness among citizens and authorities alike.

A final framework for environmental activity was provided by the nature protection law of 1970, which stipulated that each county was to be assigned environmental officers, who were to be led by a county environmental officer. Along with amateur preservationist officers acting at county level, their duty was to alert local authorities to particular environmental problems, advise them on the environmental impact of individual policies, and help find alternative solutions where possible. Environmental officers were usually in close contact with the Cultural League and the Institute for Environmental Protection in Halle, which provided training, professional expertise where necessary, and institutional support in case of local disputes. Environmental officers were allowed to veer from public paths in nature reserves, and had the right (and the duty) to inspect natural sites.[80] Most importantly, their position gave them the moral authority to engage in local environmental issues if they so chose.

The ways in which these different kinds of activists were meant to operate on behalf of the environment were explained in a programme on GDR television in 1982, entitled 'The People of the Cultural League'. Focusing on the environmentalists' activities in Güstrow county (Mecklenburg), the thirty-minute film observed ornithologists as they mapped the bird life of the area. Spearheaded by the county environmental officer, GNU members discovered that a local lake contained too many pesticides, and identified a local agricultural co-operative as the culprit. The film then showed a discussion between the environmental activists and representatives of the co-operative, and in the end it was agreed that the co-operative would build new containers for its manure. Lest viewers focus too much on the behaviour of this specific co-operative, the film ended with a shot of a landscape at the edge of the ornithologists' paradise which the viewers had just seen. Here was an illegal rubbish dump, which the local authorities were powerless to shut down in the face of the irresponsible actions of so many citizens.

[79] BArch-SAPMO, DY27 456: 'Statistik, Fakten, Relationen. Der Kulturbund der DDR 1987' (1 January 1987).
[80] Interview with Horst Baade, 19 April 2005.

'This is a concern', the film concluded, 'for all of us, not just the people of the Cultural League'.[81]

'The People of the Cultural League' was a rare example of environmental problems being openly articulated in the national media. Its central message, however, was conventional enough: environmental problems consisted of specific local or regional transgressions and could be dealt with at this level, by political, economic and individual co-operation, and through individual responsibility. This ideal underlined the public rhetoric of state and party on the subject of environmental activism throughout the 1970s and the 1980s. At the second landscape day held in Neubrandenburg, Walter Reichert, the Potsdam district councillor with responsibility for the environment, admitted the problems arising from the disposal of toxic waste. However, he implicitly denied that systemic shortcomings were responsible. Rather, the key to socialist environmental policy was ideological. The remedy lay in 'educating our people into a socialist relationship between the individual and the environment'.[82]

The final point made by 'The People of the Cultural League', about illegal waste disposal, was far from random. In most towns, waste disposal sites tended to be inadequate, and were often unsecured against toxic leakage into the subsoil; local refuse collection systems often collapsed entirely. As a result, illegal rubbish dumps had appeared throughout the countryside. Overflowing and decrepit litter bins, as well as irregular rubbish collection, defaced many towns in the eyes of their residents.[83] The problem of excessive litter fitted perfectly with the party's emphasis on individual responsibility and was thus publicized openly. Individuals carelessly throwing litter about were subject to frequent admonitions in the local pages of district newspapers. Articles 'shamed' citizens by contrasting the beauty of the historical heritage of a castle or a historic square with the 'crater-like landscape' of litter around it.[84] If, despite the commitment of the party and concerned activists, the environment did not improve, this was, according to the public transcript, down to the thoughtless disposal of waste that was so harmful to birds, plants and the

[81] *Die Leute vom Kulturbund*, broadcast 13 June 1982.
[82] Walter Reichert, 'Diskussionsbeitrag', in *2. Landschaftstag Neubrandenburg*, p. 19.
[83] StA Mühlhausen, Kulturbund 4: monthly informative reports for February, March, October and November 1986.
[84] 'Mit der kritischen Kamera unterwegs', *Das Volk* (Mühlhausen) (6 September 1968). ThHStAWe 18: Kulturbund der DDR Bezirksverwaltung Erfurt, 'Leider auch einige Wermutstropfen', *Das Volk* (Erfurt) (11 May 1978).

soil.[85] This was an act of lawlessness that directly contravened the party's ideal of an engagement with the heimat as an expression of socialist citizenship.

While the party could point the finger at citizens' irresponsible attitude towards the environment, this only carried so far. Under the conditions of central planning, it was difficult to address key environmental problems at local level. In a trade-off between economic and environmental investment, scarce resources were prioritized for economic production almost without fail.[86] In 1985, the Ernst Thälmann agricultural co-operative in Hollenbach (Mühlhausen county) was ordered to pay a penalty of 1,000 marks because its dung had infiltrated local waters. For a polluter to be fined was extremely rare, and in this case prompted the head of the co-operative to send a petition to the state council. He stated that in 1978–80 the co-operative had put into operation an intensive pig unit for 600 pigs, though it only had the facility to store their excretions for five days. To dispose of the dung properly in the nearby fields would require a storage capacity of ninety days, but the local council in Mühlhausen had been unable to meet the co-operative's request for the necessary construction materials. Faced with the choice of reaching its production targets or complying with environmental laws, the co-operative had chosen the former. The ministerial council intervened on the co-operative's behalf, rendering even this rare case of action against a polluter void.[87] Economic targets evidently trumped environmental concerns.[88]

Campaigning against pollution was difficult not just because of the primacy of the plan, but also because of the interdependence of actors in a system of scarce resources. Berthold Fritzlar was an environmental officer in the village of Langula, part of the Vogtei region in Mühlhausen county. Villagers either commuted to work in nearby Mühlhausen, or worked at the

---

[85] 'Eine Glühlampe im Nest: Aus dem Alltag der Fachgruppe Ornithologie Pirna', *Neue Deutsche Bauernzeitung* 14 (6 April 1984), 11. From the middle of the 1980s, there was a marked increase in reporting of negligent individual behaviour. On the Sächsische Schweiz region, for instance, see 'Pittoreske Felsenwelt soll auch die Enkel erfreuen', *Neue Zeit* (18 July 1987); 'Einmalig schöne Landschaft erhalten – Anliegen aller gesellschaftlichen Kräfte', *Sächsische Zeitung* (11 November 1987). This article on the third landscape day for the region contrasted the litter left by visitors with the success of industrial co-operatives in reducing emissions. See also 'Hauptwanderwege in der Sächsischen Schweiz gesäubert', *Neues Deutschland* (18 July 1988).

[86] According to Hugo Weinitschke, for instance, a planned treatment plant for the Buna chemical works in order to improve the quality of the River Saale had to be shelved owing to the need to construct a plant for the production of acetylene. Interview with Hugo Weinitschke, 7 February 2003.

[87] BArch-SAPMO, DY30, SED Zentralkomitee Abt. Landwirtschaft, ff. 8–11.

[88] Interview with Karl-Heinz Schulmeister, 11 November 2002.

local Thomas Müntzer agricultural co-operative. One of the more successful co-operatives in the district, it was often used as a showcase for foreign dignitaries, and for this reason lavished much of its cultural budget on Langula and its neighbouring villages. Consequently, the village boasted a thriving cultural life, enhancing its 'heritage' through a choir, a folklore group and an orchestra. When I interviewed him, Fritzlar spoke of his love for nature and heimat as the reason he became an environmental officer, and assured me that it was possible to make a difference on behalf of the environment.[89] I then asked him specifically whether there were problems with the storage and disposal of manure at the co-operative. Only at this point did he admit that these had been problems, as the co-operative spread its manure in an area whose groundwater fed into the local water supply. However, he and his colleagues had never complained, and there was no local debate about it. It was clearly something people learned to overlook.[90] This is not just an instance of individual impotence against the plan: Fritzlar and his wife both worked at the co-operative, whose economic success sustained its cultural budget, which the co-operative spent on heimat groups and the improvement of cultural facilities in the village. Challenging the co-operative without good reason might undermine the culture of heimat itself. The economic and cultural importance of many pollutants made it doubly hard for environmental activists to try to stop pollution, especially when the chances of success were remote to begin with.

Environmental activists, just like other citizens, required a good understanding of what kinds of action promised success and which would cause trouble. Activists learned this at times by transgressing the line and suffering the consequences. In 1973, for instance, the Mecklenburg Friends of Nature and Heimat discovered mercury in the livers of wild geese. They realized that this came from the seed coating used on winter grain, and published a couple of articles on the problem.[91] The association did achieve its objective, as the seed dressing was changed despite the higher costs this involved. But, by publishing articles on toxins, the Friends of Nature and Heimat had

---

[89] As an example, Fritzlar cited a depot of salt that had been left by the roadside to deal with icy roads in winter. On rainy days, the salt leaked into the ground, into a nature conservation area. Environmentalists managed to persuade the council to move the depot elsewhere. Interview with Berthold Fritzlar, 19 April 2005.

[90] Interview with Berthold Fritzlar, 19 April 2005.

[91] Interview with Huge Weinitschke, 7 February 2003. Gerhard Klafs, 'Die Arbeitsgruppe Greifswald des Institutes für Landschaftsforschung und Naturschutz', in Auster and Behrens (eds.), *Naturschutz*, pp. 325–48; here pp. 337–9.

gone too far, and the party responded by tightening central control over the magazine.[92]

Environmental activists learned that three boundaries could not be crossed: air pollution, water pollution, and any statistical information on pollution in any context were out of bounds. These 'red lines' were communicated less by law than by practice. In the early 1980s, Hartmut Baade, a teacher in Altenburg who was also an environmental officer for the county, helped his pupils organize a local environmental exhibition at their school. The exhibition documented how once a week when the local woollen factory changed its dye containers, the local river, the Pleisse, turned green, blue and red. This was common knowledge, but documenting it was another matter. The incident caused much discussion and suspicion among his superiors and the party, and subsequently Baade received an official warning.[93]

What these boundaries meant in practice can best be illustrated through the Windischleuba dam near Altenburg. Constructed to provide water for the heavy industry and brown coal mines of Leipzig district, the dam immediately became significant for recreational purposes. In the 1960s, an island made of sediment was declared a bird sanctuary, and a campsite was built at another part of the lakeside. Subsequently, environmental activists persistently tried to prevent encroachment on the sanctuary by boats. During summer, ornithologists acted as guards to send away trespassing boats, and they contacted the authorities if necessary. In this time-consuming manner, and by raising public awareness through publications and guided walks, ornithologists and environmental activists managed to keep the sanctuary going even though little was done by the authorities themselves to enforce the reserve's boundaries.

While successful in maintaining the sanctuary, nature activists were unable to prevent much greater overall environmental damage. The water behind the dam came from the River Pleisse, one of the GDR's most polluted waters. Water quality deteriorated further from the excrement of 15,000 ducks on a farm created in the mid-1960s, and from the pesticides used in surrounding woodlands. From the 1960s, locals no longer swam in the reservoir, and in 1980 it was officially closed for fishing.[94] These problems were clear to activists, who spent so much of their free time on the lake, and they did

---

[92] Interview with Hugo Weinitschke, 7 February 2003.   [93] Interview with Horst Baade, 19 April 2005.

[94] ThStA Altenburg Kulturbund: *Natur und Heimat* 31, 'Entwurf: Dokumentation zu ausgwählten Ergebnissen und Aufgaben der sozialistischen Landeskultur im Kreis Altenburg', ed. Kreisvorstand der Gesellschaft für Natur und Umwelt Altenburg (H. Baade, H. Etzold, H. Grosse) (April 1989).

discuss them – privately.[95] Publicly, the lake's levels of pollution could never be mentioned.[96]

Through persistence, hard work and commitment, environmental activists could nurture a bird sanctuary, but they could never address more fundamental pollution issues. This was not simply because the economic rationale of the plan always trumped environmental arguments. Activists also suffered from a lack of institutional support. The Cultural League in general, and the GNU in particular, were not strong enough to lobby effectively on behalf of their members' concerns, nor did they carry sufficient weight among the mass organizations to defend members who got into trouble. State and party functionaries were often uninterested in environmental matters and failed to consult with environmental officers.[97] Moreover, when local officials did commit themselves to environmental action, citizens were unable to hold them to account if action failed to follow words.[98] In the absence of administrative courts to which activists could appeal,[99] the GNU's authority as an organization was simply insufficient to instil the necessary respect among administrators and party officials. Many officials had insufficient knowledge of, and interest in, the GDR's environmental laws.[100]

The limitations on their influence caused such resentment among many activists that these issues began to occupy the GNU leadership. In a confidential letter to the first secretary of the Cultural League, Harald Thomasius, head of the GNU, reflected on the closure of the environmental library attached to the Zion Church in Berlin. Asking why so many people chose to get involved with ecological groups attached to the Church rather than the GNU, Thomasius wrote:

One reason, in my view, is the limited, often euphemistic and imprecise information about ecological facts and problems in our country. The result of this is that people get their information from the Western media … Another reason is our

95 Rare written evidence is in ThStA Altenburg, Kulturbund 1. 23: 'Stausee Windischleuba und NH-Freunde' (1964). See also 'Kreisleitungssitzung 2 August 1963'.
96 This had been different even in the early 1960s. Grosse, 'Der „Wartburg" und die Pleiße'.
97 See, for instance, a petition by H. N. (Waltershausen), in which he protested strongly against the felling of trees by local forestry officials against his explicit advice. BArch-SAPMO, DY30 SED Zentralkomitee Abt. Landwirtschaft, ff. 201, 206–7 (March/April 1977).
98 In 1974, for instance, the Zittau county Friends of the Heimat noted, in GDR parlance, that when the county had approved its environmental plan, it had not referred directly to the plans worked out by themselves. Moreover, the head of the local Friends had 'often lamented that agreed measures were not always adhered to consistently'. BArch-SAPMO, DY27 3509: 'Untersuchung der Aktivitäten des Kulturbundes zur Entwicklung der sozialistischen Heimatkunde und Landeskultur' (10 April 1974).
99 Caldwell, *Dictatorship*, ch. 2.
100 BArch-SAPMO, DY27 978, ff. 234–7: 'Die Umweltpolitik der DDR und die Aufgaben des Kulturbundes. Präsidialratssitzung Kongreßhalle, 28.9.89', speech by Harald Thomasius.

conciliatory attitude towards transgressions of environmental laws. In most cases, these are considered insignificant, and at best, they are punished with a nominal penalty.

In the light of the GDR's environmental problems, it was increasingly difficult for the party and even the GNU to convince its citizens that its concern for the environment was more than rhetoric. Indeed, often the GNU's activists were forced to obtain their information from the local pastor, who tended to be better informed through the Church-affiliated ecological groups.[101] Whereas the party succeeded in keeping GNU preservationists largely within the confines of the public transcript, in the 1980s the ideal of the socialist heimat was directly challenged by a small minority of individuals who refused to express their concerns for the environment through channels provided for by the party. The final part of this chapter explores how the transcript of heimat was openly challenged, and how the party responded.

In 1984, a number of young environmental activists in Eisenach formed an eco-group, the 'Eisenach Friends of Nature', attached to the Church.[102] Its members were concerned about the pollution emitted by the potash works in the area, the state of the local river, and more general topics discussed not least within the West German environmental movement, notably dying trees and the dangers of nuclear power. The motivations for engagement were different for each member, but it is instructive to consider one example. Ralf Päsler, the oldest member (b. 1955) was influenced by pacifist and environmental ideas coming over from the West, and refused military service. Conscripted to the alternative construction service (*Bausoldaten*) between 1981 and 1983, he heard upon his return to Eisenach that there was a group of environmental activists under the aegis of the Church, which he joined. By his own account, Päsler was driven by three motivations: an opposition to the political system as it was; a concern for the environment; and the social network within the eco-group.

According to Päsler (and this is borne out by the group's activities documented in the Stasi files), the group had two concrete aims. It wanted to inform the public and campaign on behalf of the environment, and to hold up a mirror to the state, to show that it was not keeping its own laws and was failing to live up to its own ideal of the 'socialist heimat'. To this

---

[101] BArch-SAPMO, DY456: Büro Prof. Schulmeister, 'Zusammenkunft mit Abgeordneten in Bad Saarow' (13 April 1988).

[102] BStU MfS and BV Erfurt, archivierter Operativer Vorgang (AOP) 1227/86: 'Beschluß über das Anlegen eines Operativen Vorgangs' (Eisenach, 11 May 1984).

end, the group organized walks in the nearby Hörsel hills, an area of particular natural beauty where the dying trees were evident for all to see. In 1986, it began organizing an annual environmental fair, the 'eco-forum', on church land, featuring information stalls and discussion evenings. The group sought the attention of activists throughout the district and beyond, and co-ordinated the writing of petitions to local authorities and the state council.[103] This was work on behalf of the heimat in direct opposition to the public transcript of the socialist heimat.[104]

The seriousness of this transgression was registered by the party's 'sword and shield', the Stasi. The eco-forum propelled the intelligence services into action, and the latter launched three successive operations from 1984, 'Maple Leaf', 'Garden' and 'Engagement'. Their primary purpose was *Kanalisierung* – directing the group's activities into channels that were more palatable to the official environmental transcript of the heimat. By influencing group members directly through informants and indirectly through the Church and other organizations, the group's leaders would become isolated and lose their influence over others.[105] The Stasi assigned to the case a number of 'unofficial informers' (IMs) who had links with the group and exerted pressure on local and regional Church officials. The organization was even able to recruit one member of the group directly, who filed reports as IM Riemann. One piece of the puzzle was still missing: the Stasi was quite clear that it needed an IM from the ranks of the GNU, who could communicate with the eco-group on matters of common interest. The Stasi did not have to look for very long: in September 1985 it contacted and recruited Heinrich Weigel as IM 'Fritz Braun'.

Resident in Erfurt since 1982, Weigel was a teacher at the local upper school and a member of the Liberal Democratic Party (LDPD). He soon involved himself in the GNU and became a tireless publicist of his new

[103] 'Umweltschutzwoche mit Trödelmarkt', *Thüringische Landeszeitung* (5 September 1986). According to the Stasi, the group had contacts in West Germany and the opposition movement around Rainer Eppelmann in Berlin. BStU, MfS, BV Erfurt, AOPK 785/88, 'Sachstandsbericht zur OPK „Garten"' (27 February 1987).

[104] 'Wir haben immer gesagt: zweigleisig – sowohl was tun, damit es nicht heißt, die reden nur, aber auch informieren, das war so Selbstverständnis der Gruppe. Das Zweite war natürlich ganz klar, dem Staat den Spiegel vorzuhalten, also ihm klar zu machen, die Ansprüche die Du hast (sozialistische Heimat: war ja Schutz der Umwelt, war ja durchaus ne gängige Floskel, die ja in keinster Weise irgendwo eingehalten werden konnte aus wirtschaftlichen Gründen) also dem Staat den Spiegel vorhalten und eigentlich auch ne Fortsetzung meines Engagements was ich ja auch schon als Bausoldat oder indem ich gesagt habe das sind keine demokratischen Wahlen, hier nehm' ich nicht teil, also dieses Engagement einfach auch in eine Richtung zu bringen.' Interview with Ralf Päsler, 29 September 2007.

[105] BStU, MfS, BV Erfurt, AOPK 785/88, f. 10. ('Einleitungsbericht zur OPK Garten', 2 May 1986).

'heimat of choice' (*Wahlheimat*), publishing within four years almost 180 articles and pamphlets on local walks, local geography and distinctive monuments. In June 1985, Weigel became the leader of the local GNU, which had been relatively inactive until then.[106] He focused the GNU's energies on two objects in particular: the rhododendron garden and the Hörsel hills. The former contained a number of rare species, which were particularly precious since rhododendrons did not normally grow on Thuringian soil.[107] The latter contained rich fauna, caves and bats, and the GNU prided itself on the fact that owing to its campaigning, parts of the area were declared a nature reserve in 1987.[108]

Weigel's activism undoubtedly expressed the interests of the GNU's members, but it was also directed at the eco-group. In his public and private contacts, Weigel consistently pushed for the group's practical participation in the GNU's projects, the rhododendron garden and the Hörsel hills. The gardens were particularly suitable for eco-group action, he and the Stasi found, because they were situated on church property. With the argument that, if the eco-group was so concerned about the environment, it should start in its own backyard, Weigel was able to instigate the creation of a rhododendron garden circle affiliated to the Church, which organized days of action along with GNU members. In this way, members of the eco-group began working together with the GNU and local authorities, directing their energies to environmental activities sanctioned by the party.[109]

In practice, 'channelling' the eco-groups' activities proved difficult. A number of members did engage with the rhododendron garden, but many young people objected to having to do 'gardening'.[110] In fact, the Stasi files confirm Päsler's recollections that he and his friends went there on occasion to tidy up, which was followed by a social event in the evening – but that this had no impact on the group's anti-systemic and social concerns, none of which could be reconciled with those of the Cultural League.

Weigel assisted the group in obtaining permits and meeting facilities for discussion forums, beginning with the 1986 environmental fair. In return for these favours, Weigel and a colleague would insist on being co-speakers

---

[106] BStU, MfS, BV Erfurt, KD Eisenach 363, vol. 1: 'Rat des Kreises Eisenach, Aktennotiz über Aussprache mit dem amtierenden Vorsitzenden der Gesellschaft Natur und Umwelt...', 10 June 1985. See also, in the same file: 'Herausforderung angenommen', *Thüringische Landeszeitung* (20 March 1986).

[107] 'Botanisches Kleinod im Mariental', *Thüringische Landeszeitung* (8 March 1986).

[108] StA Eisenach, Kulturbund 30: Heinrich Weigel, 'Eine Gesellschaft stellt sich vor' (1987).

[109] BStU, MfS, BV Erfurt, AOP 1227/86: 'Leiterinformation zum OV „Ahorn"'. Eisenach (4 March 1986).

[110] BStU, MfS, BV Erfurt, KD Eisenach 363, TII, vol. 1: 'Eindrücke über die Aussprache mit Sympathisanten des „Ökokreises" am 2.10.1985'.

at such events, with the goal of persuading the impressionable youngsters to accept the party's view of environmental activism.[111] The trouble was that as a speaker Weigel often encountered hostile opposition. The central tactic of eco-group members consisted in demanding that speakers cite concrete facts and figures about pollution levels – information neither Weigel nor any other speaker representing a mass organization were allowed to give.[112] At the 1986 eco-forum, Weigel spoke about his desire to see the Hörsel hills declared a nature reserve. Weigel's colleague from the GNU went on to talk about the bats of the Hörsel hills. But none of this was of much interest to the members of the eco-group, who pressed them to become more definite about the dying forests there.[113] When one activist forced Weigel to come clean by asking him whether or not acid rain existed in the GDR, Weigel was reduced to stating categorically, to general ridicule, that acid rain did not exist, and that if forests died, this was often because not enough new trees grew.[114] The Stasi files tend to confirm Päsler's estimation of Weigel: that he was an anal-retentive 'pedant before the Lord'. It is difficult indeed to see how this type of person could have made a positive impression on a group of rebellious youths.[115]

Perhaps most striking in this affair is how threatened the party felt by a handful of youngsters. Local Stasi officers were concerned that the group's activities might inspire others and spark a public demonstration against the state.[116] They were also concerned about their own careers, because it was important that no trouble in Eisenach caught the attention of the district command in Erfurt or, even worse, central command in Berlin. For instance, in February 1989, the Stasi ended 'Operation Engagement', noting with satisfaction its success at containing the group, but omitting the fact that the group had opened an eco-library on church premises a month earlier. Local Stasi officers needed to prevent open protests, but they also needed to be seen by the party to be doing so successfully.

In the light of the party's determination to contain the eco-group, and given the inequality of power relations, I asked Päsler why they carried on nevertheless. Päsler responded that they were held together by a common

---

[111] BStU, MfS, BV Erfurt, AOPK 345/89: 'Leiterinformation', Eisenach (26 September 1988).
[112] BStU, MfS, BV Erfurt, KD Eisenach 363, TII, vol. 1: 'Eindrücke über die Aussprache mit Sympathisanten des „Ökokreises" am 2.10.1985'.
[113] Ibid., 'Information zum Umweltforum' (2 October 1986).
[114] BStU, MfS, BV Erfurt, 433 NA, TII, vol. 1: 'Information zum Vortragsabend, IM Reimann', Erfurt (8 October 1986).
[115] Interview with Ralf Päsler, 29 September 2007.
[116] According to Päsler, this was also communicated to him by a local Stasi officer who tried to enlist him as an unofficial informer. Ibid.

joy in provocation, and by the successes they had, for instance when a barrage of petitions actually succeeded, or when they managed to propel the local environmental authorities into action. Given that they operated under the relatively safe umbrella of the local church, every concession by the authorities, however small, aroused the desire for further action.[117]

CONCLUSION

The state's disregard of its own laws was neither new[118] nor restricted to the environment;[119] nevertheless the destruction of the built and natural environment accelerated precisely as the socialist heimat was acquiring unprecedented importance in the articulation of socialist patriotism. Environmental pollution and the dilapidation of old towns were driven to critical levels by the state's own policies of underinvestment in modern industrial technology, the stubborn concentration on the construction of prefabricated housing developments, and the overall failure of the plan. The party's legitimacy, which from the 1970s could not be dissociated from its concern for the heimat, was critically undermined by the state's inability or unwillingness to prevent environmental destruction.

The importance of heimat to the party was also reflected in the creation of the preservation society and the GNU, which allowed the party to increase its own control over their activities and their discourse.[120] This does not mean that activists on the ground were instruments of the party or its ideology. Activists continued to act as they saw fit, identified areas in need of protection, and organized support as they considered necessary. But the growing attention of the party made it all the more crucial that activists were aware of the public transcript, and that they understood where the limits of their engagement lay.

Those activists portrayed here had all internalized how far they could go – they had to, in order to achieve success within the confines imposed by state

---

[117] Ibid.
[118] On violations of the environmental law of 1954, and the consequent frustrations of environmentalists in the late 1950s, see Oberkrome, „*Deutsche* Heimat", pp. 336–56.
[119] In fact, pointing to the authorities' own disregard of the state's laws and ordinances was a common way of articulating grievances in petitions. Merkel, *Meckerecke*, passim.
[120] Interview with Kurt Ludwig, 25 March 2003. As district secretary, Ludwig would have known that the break-up of the Society of Friends of the Heimat was ordered from the party only secondhand, from conversations with members of the Cultural League praesidium. Still, there are good reasons for believing that this decision was imposed upon the Cultural League. Hugo Weinitschke, who was on the central executive committee when the decision was made, argued strongly against the break-up but felt that the decision had already been made without consultation, from on high. Interview with Hugo Weinitschke, 7 February 2003.

and party. Jürgen Thormann used this knowledge to guide his members, and to phrase his reports to the party. Berthold Fritzlar, too, knew that there were too many other areas of concern for him to waste his energies on the pollution caused by his local co-operative. Meanwhile, Hartmut Baade had come to understand that certain information, even if it was widely known, must never be openly discussed. In these and other instances, the state was remarkably successful at channelling the activities of environmentalists in ways that corresponded to the official transcript of the socialist care for the heimat.

It would be too easy to dismiss the activists' actions as futile. There is an air of irrelevance about the Boizenburg GNU's attempt to preserve a plot of land on the local heath while the River Elbe next to it was in a state of ecological collapse.[121] Focusing on the Windischleuba bird sanctuary rather than on the quality of the water seems, in hindsight, beside the point. Yet, through persistence, ingenuity and commitment, activists did achieve significant successes. By alerting the authorities to the mercury in the seed coatings, environmentalists probably did save birds such as the sea eagle from extinction. Environmental activists were instrumental in the creation of a range of nature reserves and were sometimes even able to prevent the illegal construction of holiday homes in areas of particular beauty. Environmentalists clearly had a point when they argued that much could be achieved on behalf of the GDR's environment, and that without their activities, things would have been much worse.

Crucially, through each and every one of their actions, activists acknowledged the power of the party. The public transcript of the socialist heimat acted to euphemize the party's power, thinly veiling to preservationists and environmentalists the fact that they could only realize their interests if they subjected themselves to the rules the party imposed. Activism and citizenship on behalf of the heimat depended on the goodwill of the party.

The euphemism which the socialist heimat provided for the party's affirmation of power in everyday life was exposed by groups who refused to submit to the public transcript. The difference between the party's transcripts on preservationism and on the natural environment is that in the latter case, the SED declared particular aspects of environmentalism out of bounds. The decay of houses could be seen by all, and mentioned by all (albeit within clear boundaries). By banning any detailed information about the state of the environment from the public transcript, the party made itself vulnerable to those who used this language nonetheless. The fact that the

---

[121] Interview with Uwe Wieben and Karin Wulf, 16 June 2003.

Stasi mobilized such extensive resources against a handful of activists who chose to violate the transcript of the socialist heimat demonstrates just how vulnerable the party felt. The Eisenach eco-group directly challenged the SED's authority and exposed the public transcript on the environment for what it was: a tool for the instrumentalization of power.

The fact that the majority of environmental activists submitted to the public transcript cannot necessarily be taken as an expression of active support for the state. Individual engagement with nature and the heimat provided an important sense of individual agency and a sense of being able to make a difference, however small. But, it could also lead to frustration at not being heard, which was tantamount to one's commitment being discounted and unappreciated. Amongst ornithologists, activists on the ground felt increasingly powerless during the 1980s against the functionaries' arbitrary actions, and they increasingly expressed this frustration at meetings.[122] The Mühlhausen Cultural League's anger at the state of its town is palpable from the information reports submitted by Jürgen Thormann month after month. When I asked Horst Baade whether it was frustrating not to be able to address more fundamental issues about the environment, he replied:

Of course. This was frustrating, certainly. But today there is unemployment. It's part of the system, there are things that you just cannot change. And in GDR times everybody knew that, from, say, a technological point of view not everything could be realized. Everyone was sick and tired of the problem with the rubbish ... You had the problem every day, but you knew that you couldn't do anything about it. You just learned to live with it.[123]

For as long as activists believed that current power relations were there to stay, their frustrations did not endanger the party's power. Yet, beneath the veneer of the public transcript, frustration built up to such an extent that even the Cultural League warned of its dangers. Concern and anger at the state of the natural and built environment fundamentally undermined the identity with the GDR which the party so desired. Naturally, heimat enthusiasts did not act in a vacuum. Their concern for the environment alone did not cause the party to fall. But when the party's power was openly challenged in a variety of ways, in 1989, the citizens' frustrations at the conditions of the built and natural environment, which had long festered under the surface, burst out into the open, significantly reinforcing other open challenges to the power of the party.

---

[122] Erich Rutschke, 'Ornithologie in der DDR – ein Rückblick', in Auster and Behrens (eds.), *Naturschutz*, pp. 109–33; here pp. 127–8.
[123] Interview with Horst Baade, 19 April 2005.

PART 3

Power, practices and meanings

In Part 2 I showed that the socialist heimat ideal and its manifestations reinforced identifications with the locality and region, rather than the state. But if that was so, does that mean that forty years of socialism passed communities by completely? That was surely not the case. Precisely because through the public transcript socialism affected the experience of heimat at such a local and individual level, the party affected how individuals interacted with their community and their heimat. At the grass-roots level, socialism was linked even to the most trivial concerns. As Landolf Scherzer has shown for the small Thuringian town of Bad Salzungen, the party was held accountable for the cleanliness of the shop floor, the thickness of the slices of sausage served to army recruits in their canteen, and the availability of chocolate Father Christmases during Advent.[1] Given how closely the experience of socialism and the locality were intermeshed, it is hardly likely that socialism failed to impact the nature of heimat sensitivities. How, then, did socialism and the experience of power in the everyday affect local culture and communal relations?

Part 3 explores a crucial dimension of the everyday experience of power which we cannot grasp if we focus solely on the relationship between private and public transcripts. Scott's model assumes that people act rationally, always in their best interests. It presupposes that these interests are defined by the nature of domination, so that people and communities seek to maximize their freedom from domination. This approach, by definition, cannot account for the emotions and inconsistencies of actors. Individuals are rarely, if ever, consistent, rational actors; rather, in their practices they constantly 'meander' as they try to make sense of the shifting material and emotional conditions of their everyday life. Heimat practices became subject to individual meanings (*Eigen-Sinn*), which could subvert official constructions of the socialist heimat, but which, alternatively, could also

[1] Scherzer, *Der Erste*.

promote individual accommodation to existing power relations.[2] These issues can be explored in greater depth only at the micro-level, by exploring how people's sense of heimat changed over time, in relation to social relationships, cultural festivals and the experience of socialism.[3]

The following analysis explores practices and meanings in two locations which manifested near-extremes of the kinds of everyday behaviour possible in the name of the socialist heimat. I chose Holungen, because early on in my research, I came across a petition written on behalf of the Cultural League. This petition, against the proposed extension of the slag heap from the local mines, was submitted to the state council by the Cultural League as the village's largest mass organization, in the desire to protect the heimat. In the case of Holungen, it appeared that heimat was deployed to make a claim against the actions of state and party. By examining this village, it seemed possible to explore how local meanings of the heimat could be developed to undermine the meanings of socialism.

Dabel attracted my attention for the opposite reason. In a letter written to the secretary of the GDR-wide Cultural League, Karl-Heinz Schulmeister, Dabel's Cultural League secretary, pointed out with evident pride the exemplary activities of the villagers on behalf of their socialist heimat. Further research suggested that, unlike neighbouring Mestlin which was constructed in 1952 as a model socialist village, Dabel was not chosen by the party to be transformed into a model of the socialist heimat. Inasmuch as Dabel demonstrated what the socialist heimat might look like in a community setting, this was the achievement of the villagers themselves. Dabel, in other words, appeared to show that socialism did have the power to transform the practices, symbols and meanings of heimat.

The two localities chosen for an investigation of everyday practices of heimat are not typical in any way. No locality was 'representative' of the GDR in its totality, even if statistically some communities were more representative of the country's social composition than others. More to the point, the ideal of heimat itself was predicated on distinctiveness, not typicality. At least in the Honecker era, the most 'ideal' and 'typical' heimat community was that which was most distinctive in its traditions and practices. Moreover, the aim of this Part is to explore more carefully the complexity of the meanings which heimat practices could generate in their various local environments, contexts and situations. They demonstrate

[2] On this important ambivalence in the concept of *Eigen-Sinn*, see Lindenberger, 'Einleitung', in Lindenberger (ed.), *Herrschaft und Eigen-Sinn*, here pp. 24–5.
[3] On the relationship between 'micro-history' and 'macro-history', see Medick, 'Quo Vadis'.

precisely how the power of state and party acted in specific local contexts to give particular meanings to individuals and relationships. The ideal of the socialist heimat provided for different social dramas and relationships in each village, in each new town, and in each city.

This Part relies extensively on interviews with villagers, sometimes a whole series of interviews, between 2003 and 2007. I also had access to the private collections of Paul and Brigitte Hamelmann, which contained material about heimat festivals, and of Josef Kistner, who kept much material relating to the local struggle against the potash mines; the county archive also contains important documents. Although there is virtually no material relating to Dabel in the archives of Sternberg county or Schwerin district, I was fortunate to have access to the extensive collection of the Dabel heimat museum, which included rich records of the village's cultural life from the 1960s to the 1980s.

These sources were complemented by material from the state security services, the Stasi. This material, unearthed in a search lasting from 2004 to 2008, proved extremely difficult to assemble because Stasi files are archived by informant and by case, but not by theme. As a result, the overview I gained was based on excerpts taken from a number of different informants' files.[4] This allowed an insight into a range of practices by different actors on behalf of Stasi informants.[5] Whereas Stasi files in themselves are extremely problematic as sources, in conjunction with other texts they are highly valuable as accounts of particular incidents that are no less subjective than those we find in official reports and in oral testimonies.

[4] In line with the strict German laws on the privacy of individual actors in relation to Stasi files, only actors whose Stasi activity is beyond doubt can be named, and are named, in this book.
[5] By contrast, the fact that I was unable to see any files in their entirety makes it difficult to assess heimat-related Stasi activities in relation to other concerns of the informers.

CHAPTER 7

Social drama and the euphemization
of power

INTRODUCTION

With a fairly steady population of around 1,050 inhabitants in the decades before 1989, Holungen is a village in the Eichsfeld, equidistant from Bischofferode in the east and Duderstadt in the west.[1] For centuries the Eichsfeld had been part of the bishopric of Mainz, from which it was also governed until 1802. The Eichsfelders thus distinguished themselves from their predominantly Protestant surroundings through their Roman Catholicism, an enduring characteristic even during the nineteenth and twentieth centuries, when the Eichsfeld was divided administratively. In 1945, the border between the British and Soviet zones divided Eichsfeld again. 'Lower Eichsfeld' in the west, around Duderstadt, became part of West Germany. 'Upper Eichsfeld' in the east, by contrast, lay in what became the district of Erfurt (GDR), and comprised two counties, Worbis and Heiligenstadt.

The village of Holungen is around 320 metres above sea level, and is surrounded by hills (between 485 and 500 metres above sea level) in three directions: the Ohmgebirge in the south, the Wehnberg to the north, and two hills that separate Holungen from Duderstadt in the west: the Brunen Bühl and the Sonnenstein. Almost equidistant from Duderstadt, the Eichsfeld's historic capital, and the Sonnenstein ran the inner-German border. This meant that from 1952 Holungers could not venture to the largest town in the Eichsfeld. They even needed special permits to go to the neighbouring villages just beyond the Sonnenstein, since these lay within the five-kilometre restricted zone (*Sperrgebiet*) along the border.

---

[1] From the 1950s to the 1980s, the population remained remarkably steady, declining slightly from 1,097 in 1954 to 1,008 in 1986. Paul Hamelmann (ed.), 'Festschrift 725 Jahre Holungen' (Holungen, festival brochure, 1991), 14.

13. View of the slag heap at a relatively modest size, when most of the waste from the mining was being pumped back into the ground. The picture was taken from the Ihmberg, looking south, *c.* 1968.

Only to the east does the village not border on natural hills, so that the Bode stream, which originates from the Ohmgebirge before it enters the village, can make its way eastwards to Bischofferode, the next large town. About two kilometres to the the east of Holungen stood what developed into the village's and the area's largest employer: the 'Thomas Müntzer' potash mine. Founded in 1908, it expanded its production after 1945, and had a workforce of about 2,000 by 1979. Beside the entrance to the mine there was a reddish-brown slag heap of waste from the mining process. Up to the early 1960s, a substantial part of the residual salts was pumped back into the mines, so that the cone-shaped slag heap grew relatively slowly. From the 1960s this expensive procedure was discontinued and all residue was added to the slag heap (Figure 13). Coupled with growing production levels this transformed the slag heap into a hill similar in size to the Sonnenstein or the other surrounding hills, except, of course, that the noxious residue could never be integrated into the natural setting. By the late 1970s the slag heap had closed off almost the entire valley to the east (Figure 14).

14. View of the slag heap from Holungen cemetery in 1978, looking east. By the 1970s the slag heap had expanded to its natural limits.

The potash mines were the driving economic force of the village, but their poisonous fumes also added a sensuous dimension to village life. The slag heap dominated Holungen aesthetically, and cut off the village visually to the east, so that it was virtually hemmed in in all four directions. The slag heap produced a particular micro-climate, because in the autumn and winter months the new basin generated climatic inversions, whereby colder air was trapped in the valley beneath warmer air flowing over the surrounding hills.

Although the village became cut off visually, at a cultural level Holungers considered themselves the heart of their region. This was the birthplace of Hermann Iseke (1856–1907), a priest and author of many heimat poems. His most important lines became known as the Eichsfeld Song (*Eichsfelder Sang*, 1902), the definitive Eichsfeld hymn.[2] This ode to the beauty of the region and the longing for the Eichsfeld's soil did not name Holungen as such. But the song named the Sonnenstein, where,

[2] Daphne Berdahl has noted the emotional and symbolic importance of the Eichsfeld Song for Eichsfelders in the border village of Kahla. Daphne Berdahl, *Where the World Ended* (Berkeley: University of California Press, 1999).

when Iseke wrote the song, there was a large wooden cross that could be seen from afar. It symbolized the region's close connections with Catholicism, and transformed the Sonnenstein itself into *the* 'lieu de mémoire' for the Eichsfeld.

'WHERE THE CROSS TOWERS UPON THE HILL': SYMBOLS, PRACTICES AND SOCIAL DRAMA[3]

In late 1954, some Holungers formed a committee to plan a festival in honour of Iseke's one-hundredth anniversary in 1956. The idea of commemorating a priest who had ministered to the German imperial forces caught the county's cultural authorities in Worbis by surprise, as the county administrators, who were evidently not from the area, barely knew who this Iseke was.[4] Particularly problematic from their point of view was the Holungers' desire that this festival be open to all Eichsfelders, including those from the Federal Republic. However, officials had just heard a rumour that an all-Eichsfeld heimat festival was to be organized in Duderstadt in 1956. Holding such a festival in Holungen, they realized, would steal the West Germans' thunder, and would at least enable the local authorities to control the festival's proceedings.[5] The SED granted permission, but on the condition that the festival organizers joined the Cultural League.

Over the eighteen months during which the festival was prepared, two particular bones of contention emerged. Besides the erection of a memorial stone, quarried and cut by villagers in 1,300 hours of voluntary work, the committee focused its energies on the Sonnenstein. They planned to erect a 'cross of peace' ten metres high, with light bulbs attached, so that it could be seen day and night from Holungen to the east, and Duderstadt in the west. For Holungers, re-erecting the cross that Iseke had written about allowed them to reaffirm the unity of their heimat, whose essential unity across East and West could still be expressed as part of the official transcript in this particular period.

Unsurprisingly, the county and district authorities were extremely reluctant to grant permission for a giant cross serving as a symbol of unity, and

---

[3] Hermann Iseke. This line is taken from the fifth stanza of the Eichsfeld song.

[4] Brigitte and Paul Hamelmann Private Collection, 'Protokollbuch für die Vorbereitung des Heimatfestes anläßlich des 100. Geburtstages des Eichsfelder Heimatdichters Dr H. Iseke', entry for 23 February 1955.

[5] Hamelmann Private Collection, 'Protokollbuch', entry for 19 December 1954.

15. Wooden cross on the Sonnenstein, looking west towards Duderstadt. This view would only have been accessible to two Holungers who were allowed here once a year to undertake necessary repair works. This is a replica of the cross erected in 1956.

tried to persuade the villagers to change their plans. However, the longer the authorities hesitated, and the longer the festival preparations went on, the harder it became to refuse the villagers' demands. In the end, Holungers were allowed to erect their cross on the Sonnenstein, with a further 1,700 hours of voluntary work (Figure 15). [6]

The organizers' second concern related to publicity and fundraising, especially with regard to Eichsfelders from the Federal Republic. The county authorities demanded that all contact beyond family invitations be authorized. This did not stop the word from spreading across the demarcation line, nor did it stop the involvement of the Eichsfeld associations of the Ruhr district. Nevertheless, the authorities were able to restrict publicity. On the day of the festival, they also closed the nearby Teistungen border crossing and forced Western Eichsfelders to take a long detour via the Wartha checkpoint near Eisenach, thus limiting the number of West Germans who attended.

[6] Ibid., entry for 23 October 1955.

The Iseke celebrations began on Saturday, 7 July 1956, with a brass band playing in the village. Thereafter a procession of around 5,000 participants walked up to the Brunen Bühl hill, where the Iseke memorial was unveiled and blessed, to an enthusiastic rendition of the Eichsfeld Song. In a torchlight procession, participants moved on to the neighbouring Sonnenstein. There, the lights of the cross were switched on, and a bonfire next to it was lit. This 'fire of peace' was reflected by two bonfires on hills in the Western Eichsfeld, with the sound of church bells chiming in every village east and west of the demarcation line. The following morning started with mass, followed by drinks (*Frühschoppen*) and lunch. The festival's climax in the afternoon consisted of a pageant, with Eichsfelders from across the region wearing their traditional costumes. A crowd of between 8,000 and 20,000 spectators – between eight and twenty times the village population – lined up to see the pageant; between 800 and 1,500 spectators had come from the FRG. The festivities concluded with an address by Paul Schäfer, the head of the local school, and the director of Duderstadt county, Gleitze.[7]

The festival and its preparations reveal a striking diversity in the meanings of heimat. For the local authorities, this was an opportunity to reach a community which it had barely managed to access before. By providing crucial logistical and material assistance, the authorities could hope to be seen in a positive light by the local community. Moreover, the state had acquired lasting access to the village's cultural life, as those who had previously acted under the aegis of the local church had now become members of the Cultural League. Villagers were evidently happy to record their achievements in the public transcript of the National Reconstruction Effort (NAW), as they carefully listed the hours they had spent on behalf of their heimat in preparing the festival. Finally, while they were concerned to limit the number of West Germans attending, the festival represented, for local state and party officials, a demonstration of genuine regional traditions that proved the superiority of the heimat in the GDR.[8]

Villagers were under no illusions about the authorities' designs. Even at the very beginning of the festival organization, the local priest admonished villagers 'not to surrender our right to celebrate according to our will'.[9]

---

[7] The SED party paper for Erfurt District, *Das Volk*, listed the following attendance figures: 3,000 visitors at the Brunen Bühl and 8,000 at the main procession, while the CDU paper *Thüringer Tageblatt* noted that 800 Eichsfelders had come from the West. In 1981, the Stasi noted in an internal document that 20,000 had attended the festival (rather than 8,000).

[8] This is evident from a collection of cuttings from *Das Volk* and the *Thüringer Tageblatt* in the Hamelmanns' 'Protokollbuch'.

[9] Hamelmann Private Collection, 'Protokollbuch', entry for 19 December 1954.

Rather than oppose the authorities, however, villagers learned how to appropriate the authorities' designs to their own advantage. For them, membership in the Cultural League also had its benefits, as it could be used to establish allies and advocates at a higher level.[10] Moreover, frequent contact with the authorities enabled villagers to learn the public transcript of the party, which was not just in the party's interest but could also help the villagers. In early dealings, villagers tended to send Paul Schäfer to communicate with the local authorities, because as the local head teacher he was educated and was used to dealing with them. However, records of the preparatory meetings, at which outside officials were sometimes present, show how soon others in the committee learned to speak in the 'official' language of the socialist heimat. At their meeting in January 1956, for instance, Schäfer told the committee that throughout the GDR, the Cultural League now encouraged the writing of village chronicles and the mobilization of citizens to make their village more beautiful. At the following meeting, attended by functionaries from the county as well as from the Cultural League, the committee was well prepared. At the beginning of the proceedings, villagers took their guests by surprise by outlining how they were already working on the village chronicle.[11] To press home their point, the mayor then detailed the hours and the financial contributions donated by villagers towards the mainte- nance and care of the village.[12] Having proved their commitment to the socialist heimat in the public transcript, the committee was now in a much stronger position to discuss more sensitive issues, notably the proposed cross on the Sonnenstein. They had learned to 'play the rules' in responding to the language of heimat in socialism, especially when asking for favours in return.

Despite the villagers' concessions to the 'rules of the game', the meanings underlying both the symbols of heimat (the memorial stone and the cross) and the practices of preparing and running the festival could not present a starker contrast with the heimat ideals advanced by state and party. Villagers beautified their village not in response to the Cultural League's initiatives, but out of embarrassment over the 'disgraceful blots' (*Schandflecken*) in their village.[13] The cross erected was not just a symbol of peace and unity, though it was that too. It principally stood for the region's Catholicism. According to local legend, it was from the Sonnenstein that the Eichsfeld had been Christianized, and it was this cross that Iseke had immortalized in

---

[10] Ibid., entry for 8 January 1956.   [11] Ibid., entry for 8 February 1956.   [12] Ibid., 1956.
[13] Hamelmann Private Collection, 'Protokollbuch', entry for 29 January 1956.

the last verse of his Eichsfeld Song. The state subsequently forbade Eichsfelders to sing this verse owing to its Christian connotations:

> Eichsfelder wandering afar
> Happily and with song
> Home, at home stands all your heart and courage
> Your senses and your soul,
> Home where the cross towers above the hill
> And tells you of God's love!
> And when your final hour comes
> May it be on Eichsfeld soil![14]

The Roman Catholic meanings of the heimat were evident in other ways. The Iseke memorial stone was placed next to a wayside chapel. And in his speech at the end of the pageant, Paul Schäfer also emphasized that love of the Eichsfeld heimat could not but inspire everyone, just as it had inspired Iseke, to trust in goodness, mercy, kindness and charity.[15] For Holungers, this was not a festival to express their identification with socialism, but a festival to emphasize the Catholic bond between all Eichsfelders, east and west of the border.

Far from providing a context for village unity, the festival occasioned plenty of arguments among villagers. Some complained about the location of the memorial, others shirked doing their bit in the quarry, and less than a month before the festival many villagers had not fulfilled their commitment to help lay the sewage systems so that the work could be completed on schedule.[16] However, these problems receded into the background in dealings with the state and the mass organizations. When I asked Paul Schäfer about the problems they encountered in preparing the festival, he responded:

Well, the people from the Cultural League now wanted to take charge, and wanted to ensure that we did not bring in religion at any cost … but we remained steadfast to the end. We even started with a holy mass at the steps where we put up a statue of the Mother of God.[17]

---

[14] 'Eichsfelder mit Frohwanderblut / Und liederreicher Kehle, / Heim, heim steht all' dein Herz und Mut, / Dein Sinn und deine Seele, / Heim wo das Kreuz vom Hügel ragt / Und dir von Gottes Liebe sagt! / Schlägt deine letzte Stunde, / Es sei auf Eichsfelds Grunde!'

[15] *Festschrift zum Eichsfelder Heimattreffen in Holungen anläßlich des 100. Geburtstages des Heimatdichters Dr Hermann Iseke 1956*, ed. Heimatfreunde Holungen (Dingelstädt, 1956); here pp. 23–5. There is a short summary of Schäfer's speech in the *Thüringer Tageblatt* ('Iseke-Feier und Heimattreffen in Holungen'), which is in the 'Protokollbuch'.

[16] 'Protokollbuch', entries for 13 November 1955 and 8 January 1956. KA Heiligenstadt, Rat der Gemeinde (RdG) Holungen 65: 'Protokoll der Versammlung der Nationalen Front Ortsausschuß Holungen am 13. Juni 1956'.

[17] Interview with Paul Schäfer, 12 May 2005.

When I asked him why he thought the county had allowed the festival in the first place, Schäfer replied: 'We tricked the county into it, I would say. Later the head man of the county had to leave, because he had allowed this to happen.'[18]

What is evident from Schäfer's recollections includes, but also goes beyond, the notion of the 'villagers' cunning' described in Chapter 5. This was a feeling of distance, of opposition to how 'they' – a term encompassing all outside mass organizations and state authorities in county and district – wanted to impose 'their' secular conceptions of heimat upon 'us', the Holungers. This was not changed by the fact that the key figures in the organization committee, including Paul Schäfer and Josef Artmann (the chair), were members not just of the village Cultural League, but also of the local CDU and National Front committees.[19] Membership of these organizations may have served a practical purpose in achieving some of the villagers' goals, but this does not mean that members considered themselves as functionaries of these mass organizations, or even the state.

Holungen shows how even in a situation in which villagers consciously pitted their memory of the locality against that of the party, local interests and the mechanisms of state and party were nonetheless closely intertwined. Although villagers clearly distinguished between the public transcript of the socialist heimat and their own meanings of what it was to be an Eichsfelder (and Holunger), these private meanings did not just develop in contradistinction to the state. The meanings that developed also had to do with village relationships and one's place in them. The preparation and execution of the festival was thus also about leadership in the community, doing one's bit and asserting one's own meanings vis-à-vis the decisions of the organizing committee.

Although in practice its meanings were complex, the festival became enshrined in the collective memory of the villagers as a great spectacle, a time when the villagers had fought the authorities and the political system, and won. The subsequent dismissal of the leader of the Worbis county administration for allowing the festival to proceed in the way it did constituted, in the memory of the villagers, the ultimate triumph. In this way, a memory of the 'tricks' that Holungers had played on the party served to emphasize the limits of the party's reach into the community and into the Holungers' identifications with their community and locality.

[18] Ibid.
[19] KA Heiligenstadt, RdG Holungen 65: 'Protokoll der Versammlung der Nationalen Front Ortsausschuß Holungen am 13. Juni 1956'.

The state, meanwhile, offered its own response to the 1956 festival, to show just who had the final say. In 1961 the Ministry of the Interior extended the restricted zone of the border area westwards by a couple of hundred metres. Whereas before, the restricted area had just excluded the Sonnenstein with its cross, henceforth it just included both the Iseke memorial and the cross. Holungers could see their heimat symbols from the opposite side of the road, but they could never go there, nor were they allowed to stop on the road. Here was a permanent manifestation of state power, lest Holungers forget in whose gift the symbols of heimat ultimately resided.

Holungen continued to be a difficult terrain for state authorities. Between 1956 and 1968, the village saw the going and coming of four different mayors. At village meetings, citizens complained bitterly about the facilities they had to put up with: owing to the mines and the uncertain subsoil conditions in the village, no new residential flats could be built. The school building was in a deplorable condition, and there were no cultural facilities. The village priest complained that the few phone lines that had been laid were often out of order; the road to Worbis was in a terrible state; bus services to Worbis, not to mention Erfurt, were extremely poor. For many villagers, Holungen was effectively cut off from the outside world.[20]

Voluntary work on the part of the National Reconstruction Effort (NAW) did not subside after the Iseke festival, since the villagers recognized that nothing would happen in the village unless they did it themselves.[21] Moreover, the next big festival was looming on the horizon: in 1966, Holungen would celebrate its 700th anniversary. For this event, villagers continued to expand the sewage system; they created a pond for the amateur fire brigade, an open-air meeting space near the pond, and a building for the 'Konsum', the village shop.[22] Relative to other Eichsfeld communities Holungers shone for their contributions to the NAW.[23]

The most important endeavour in connection with the anniversary was the construction, as part of the NAW, of an open-air stage in the Wehnberg, to the north of the village. Plans began in 1962, and in 1968 the

---

[20] KA Heiligenstadt, RdG Holungen 65: 'Diskussion auf dem Einwohnerforum am 7.6.1963 in der Gemeinde Holungen'. Similar complaints were also raised in KA Heiligenstadt, RdG Holungen 49: 'Protokoll vom Einwohnerforum am 24. August 1961'. It appears from this that the frequency of the change in mayors was also criticized at the meeting.

[21] KA Heiligenstadt, RdG Holungen 65: 'Protokoll über die Einwohnerversammlung am 25. April 1968'.

[22] KA Heiligenstadt, RdG Holungen 65: 'Kommunalpolitischer und volkswirtschaftlicher Plan der Gemeinde Holungen für das Jahr 1965'.

[23] KA Heiligenstadt, RdG Holungen 59: 'An das Kreissekretariat der Nationalen Front Worbis, 19.8.65'.

stage was completed thanks to the involvement of one of the village's most active cultural groups, the amateur dramatic society directed by Josef Artmann. Under his passionate leadership, the group established a regional reputation for its performances, while the profits generated at the Wehnberg amounted to around 100,000 marks in 1966–69 alone. For this work, the Cultural League in Berlin officially recognized the Holungen organization as 'contributors to the creation of the socialist heimat'. Artmann himself received the Cultural League's highest awards, the Johannes R. Becher medal in silver (1963) and in gold (1967).[24] In 1969, the drama circle as a whole was awarded the 'Needle of Honour for Artistic Folklore' ('Ehrennadel für künstlerisches Volksschaffen'), with a cash prize in recognition of its efforts.[25]

As chair of the Iseke festival organization committee in 1956, Josef Artmann had been at the centre of local confrontations with the authorities. Yet the memory of these disputes, and the inclusion of the Iseke memorial and cross inside the restricted area in 1961, did not deter Artmann from seeking official recognition for his activities. In a letter to the local council Artmann asked that his group be honoured as an 'outstanding folklore collective', asserting that he and his collective had engaged in their labours out of commitment to the socialist fatherland, and out of love for the GDR.[26]

These practices related to the 'socialist heimat' reveal several layers of meaning. Most immediately, they show Artmann's energy and his passion for amateur theatre. Moreover, the ambitious construction of the theatre underlined Artmann's desire to shine locally and regionally. He had already displayed this energy to get things done in 1956. Constructing a stage was not like creating more essential provisions like the sewage system, for it attracted greater attention outside the village.[27] The open-air stage also shows how at the grass roots, individuals could use a succession of National Front initiatives to realize their own ambitions. Holungers benefited from the material provided by the county and the machinery of the local co-operative regardless of whether it was part of the NAW (up to

---

[24] Hamelmann Private Collection, 'Urkunde: Natur- und Heimatfreunde – Mitgestalter unserer sozialistischen Heimat'.

[25] Hamelmann Private Collection, Chronological Table: 'Dramatischer Zirkel – Kulturbund Ortsgruppe Holungen unter der Leitung von Josef Artmann'.

[26] KA Heiligenstadt, Rat des Kreises (RdK) Worbis 7515: 'Abrechnung der Stafette der Volkskunst zu Ehren des 20. Jahrestages der DDR'.

[27] KA Heiligenstadt, RdK Worbis 7515: 'Abschlußbericht über die Durchführung der Volkskunstinitiative und der „Stafette der Volkskunst" im Grenzkreis Worbis'. The report singles out the achievements of the Holungen dramatic circle on pp. 1–2, 5, 9.

1966), the Torgau Initiative (1967) or 'Join in!' (from 1968). Aside from these meanings, Artmann's initiative also shows how the language of social-ism had become part of everyday life. As villagers had come to understand by 1956, using the public transcript was important for justifying communal efforts and for obtaining official recognition. And this recognition not only enhanced feelings of local or personal pride: it could yield handsome cash rewards.

Artmann's motivations also derived from his occupational position. He had owned the village shop and bakery. The shop had been taken over by the 'Konsum' in 1955, during the busiest planning phase of the Iseke festival,[28] a fact which no doubt added greatly to Artmann's personal antipathy towards the state. Artmann still owned his bakery, which gave him a certain degree of political independence and an important role in the community, as his bakery was a daily meeting place for villagers. But Artmann's position was also precarious. Since his shop had been collectivized, he had every reason to fear that the bakery might one day be taken away, too. He might legitimately have hoped that his protestations of love for the GDR and his heimat would reduce the county's desire to take over his bakery, and persuade them to overlook his membership of the Iseke festival committee in 1956.

The drama circle's labours for their open-air stage did not end with its completion in 1968. On 14 June 1970, Josef Kistner heard rumours that the group was planning to construct, on the southern slope of the theatre, a wooden hut to serve as dressing rooms. In his capacity as head of the village council's building committee, Kistner went to see Artmann to explain that the hut could not be constructed within the next few years, as other work (such as the construction of the water mains, street lighting and a restaurant) had to take priority. Kistner's explanations notwithstanding, a low-loader with a caterpillar track appeared on the Wehnberg a few days later, with Artmann personally overseeing the work.

When Kistner heard of Artmann's clandestine operation, he was out-raged. Supported by the county building commission in Worbis, Kistner summoned Artmann and his drama group before the village building commission, with the mayor presiding. Artmann protested that his labour had all been for the public good. The minutes recorded that: 'he viewed his construction measures at the Wehnberg in relation to the "Beautiful village" initiative … He accused the community council of lacking initiative and failing to appreciate those who worked with the young people of the village.'

---

[28] Hamelmann (ed.), *Festschrift*, p. 11.

Artmann went on to complain that his group had not received from the village council the financial rewards that would be commensurate with their efforts on behalf of the socialist heimat. Returning to the matter at hand, Kistner said that if dressing rooms were erected, they should be built with sanitary facilities, for which a different location was more suitable. The local building commission threatened that if Artmann and his friends refused to co-operate, the construction site would be restored to its original state. Artmann retorted that he would carry out the restoration himself and resign from his position in the drama circle. His co-organizer of the drama circle, Pfafferodt, added ominously how difficult it would be in the future to get the young involved in communal and cultural projects.[29] After the meeting, Artmann and Pfafferodt wrote to the council, reiterating their threats. They announced their resignation, and with it the end of all cultural activities involving the young people of the village, since the council had so clearly derided all they had achieved in their work with the young.

In the end, Artmann and his friends did not resign, and a hut was eventually built. What the incident does show is how fickle this commitment to 'Join in!' and the NAW were, and how adaptable the language of the socialist heimat, the public transcript, was to the articulation of personal desires. Artmann's protestations of 'love for the GDR' did not stop him for one moment from transgressing the law when it suited him. It is worth noting the arguments Artmann brought forward. He emphasized not his cultural commitments *per se*, but his involvement in an area which he knew was vitally important to the state: the activities of the young. Artmann's protestations provide evidence of how easily concepts such as the sensible use of spare time, the edification of the young, the beautification of the heimat and the creation of values could be adapted to the pursuit of *Eigen-Sinn*.

After receiving so much recognition from authorities far beyond the village level, Artmann clearly felt entitled to carry out work on 'his' stage irrespective of what 'they', the authorities, said. This was a conflict articulated in terms of 'us' and 'them', but in contrast to the Iseke festival of 1956, the fault lines did not run neatly between the village and the state authorities. The functionaries were part of the village community themselves. The mayor opposed Artmann in this instance, even though he was also a

---

[29] KA Heiligenstadt, RdG Holungen 46, 'Protokoll über die Aussprache der Baukommission mit Vertretern des Kulturbundes und des dramatischen Zirkels am 23.8.1970, 20.30 Uhr, im Sitzungszimmer des Rates der Gemeinde' (2 September 1970).

personal friend. Kistner was a member of the village community, and an ally of Artmann's on other occasions, but in this dispute he used his official function to maximize his chances of winning and prevailing over Artmann. In fact, it is not at all clear that Artmann enjoyed the support of most villagers. He had already received quite a lot of recognition and favours; his drama circle may have been the most wily, but it was certainly not the only cultural group in the village, and the project did, after all, divert resources from other improvements which villagers badly needed.[30]

Heimat could provide a language and framework in which many conflicts were articulated, even if the underlying meanings remained very different. Josef Kistner and the village mayor may have been expressing their own visions of this local heimat, but they did so as local functionaries of the state, with all the advantages and disadvantages this entailed in Holungen. This example also provides further evidence for how 'Join in!' and notions of heimat provided a sense of agency to individuals, an agency which expressed personal desires within the parameters set by state and party. And, finally, it highlights the complex impact of the state and its economy, as well as the 'Join in!' movement, on village relations. Encounters with 'them', the state, and endeavours to overcome material shortages did not necessarily lead to greater communal solidarity. Instead, actors could use the language and institutions of state and party to further their own, deeply local and personal agendas. This phenomenon was far from unique to the GDR, or to socialism. However, in a system in which the state attempted to be present in so many spheres of everyday life, and in which alternative means of fulfilling one's desires were restricted, state institutions and state initiatives could be divisive, encouraging insecurities, jealousies and hostilities among individuals and groups. Personal relations had become entangled with individual experiences of the state and its functionaries.

THE VEILING AND UNVEILING OF DISSENT

Even the highest official recognition accorded to Artmann's drama circle, that of 'outstanding folklore collective of the GDR' (1972), failed to convince the county authorities that Holungen was now a shining example of socialist heimat culture. Yet, although no functioning village club existed in

---

[30] In addition to the written evidence quoted, jealousy among other village groups was also mentioned as a motive by Paul Hamelmann (interview, 12 May 2005).

the village,[31] cultural life continued to flourish. The significance of Artmann and his amateur drama circle declined from the middle of the 1970s, but other individuals assumed a prominent role. Paul Hamelmann, for instance, helped organize, under the aegis of the Cultural League where necessary, the village's Easter celebrations, seasonal dances and the annual church fair. The organization also looked after the local carnival, which Holungers prided themselves on as being the largest and most authentic in the area.[32]

Carnival presented a further basis for emphasizing the Cultural League's standing in the village. Along with theatre, carnival provided popular cultural activity for the young. The vast majority of those growing up in Holungen joined the Cultural League, not the Free German Youth.[33] So popular was the carnival that on the day of the procession none of the local children went to school. When in 1981 the head teacher summoned all the parents to give them a dressing down about this practice, only one family appeared.[34] Clearly, carnival was big in Holungen, and had acquired the status of a major religious holiday. It allowed Holungers to vent some of their frustrations in the pageant, at the beer table or in speeches. Here, after all, was an annual 'ritual of reversal' which, even more strongly than other cultural practices, created moments of anti-structure that reversed habitual roles and relations to allow participants to reflect on the structures guiding everyday life.[35]

Carnival was also a source of local pride. In the Holunger's own estimation, nobody could celebrate the festival like they did. Indeed, carnival provided a sole point of contact between the cultural centre of the hated potash mines and the Cultural League. Every year, the Holungen Cultural League organized the carnival celebrations of the workers. Although in every other respect Cultural League leaders wanted nothing to do with the potash works, here they made an exception, for two reasons. First, the fact that they were asked ahead of everyone else in the area proved that Holungers really were best at celebrating the carnival, and that even the directorate of the

[31] KA Heiligenstadt, RdK Worbis 4332: 'Einschätzung der Entwicklung des geistig-kulturellen Lebens in der Gemeinde Holungen' (24 February 1976). KA Heiligenstadt, RdK Worbis 6517: 'Jugendförderungsplan der Gemeinde Holungen für das Jahr 1961' (12 January 1961). On the authorities' attempts to set up a village club, see BStU, MfS, BV Erfurt, AOPK 2664/ 84, ff. 28–30: 'Information über die Durchführung des Erfahrungsaustausches zur Vorbereitung der Bildung eines Dorfklubs in Holungen' (Worbis, 4 August 1981).
[32] Interview with Paul Hamelmann, 12 May 2005.
[33] BStU, MfS, BV Erfurt, AOPK 2664/ 84, ff. 314–15: 'Information zu Jugendarbeit in Holungen' (19 April 1985).
[34] Ibid., f. 120: report by GMS 'Jugend' (Worbis, 8 September 1981).
[35] Turner, *The Ritual Process*, ch. 5.

potash works had to acknowledge this. Second, organizing carnival for the potash works provided an important source of income that saw the Cultural League through the rest of the year, and made them independent of sponsorship by the authorities.[36]

While the authorities continued to be concerned about the regular cultural activities of Holungers, local anniversaries continued to provide the main points of friction in the cultural sphere. In 1981 the village planned to celebrate the 125th anniversary of Hermann Iseke's birth. With the borders closed, this could never be a repetition of the festival of twenty-five years ago, but, according to Paul Hamelmann, 'we wanted to demonstrate that we could still celebrate as before'.[37] The high point of the festival was to be a torchlight march to Iseke's birthplace. The Cultural League kept quiet about its plans, but six weeks before the festival was due to start on 29 July, the local village mayor, an SED member and an unofficial informer for the Stasi, heard rumours about the festival.[38] Enough time remained for the authorities to exert pressure on the Holungers about how the festival could be celebrated.

By now, officials had learnt that they had to tread carefully. When they tried to prevent the 700th village anniversary festival in 1966 from becoming a celebration of Catholicism, officials had received a protest from the Bishop who had been invited to the village. At that time, Artmann and Schäfer had left the Worbis authorities in no doubt that Holungers 'would do what they want, anyway', and that they would only accept the authority of the Church.[39] Fifteen years later Hamelmann was asked to report to the Worbis cultural authorities to explain what they were up to, and to be reminded that any plans for the festival required the county's permission. When Hamelmann retorted that the Holungers would go ahead with their Iseke festival with or without the authorities' consent,[40] officials could be in no doubt that the Holungers meant business.

---

[36] Interview with Paul Hamelmann, 12 May 2005. See also the vague, brief and non-committal 'Jahreskulturplan der Gemeinde Holungen' (1985 and 1984), which shows clearly the lack of interest in co-operating with the cultural authorities. KA Heiligenstadt, RdK Worbis 4332.

[37] 'wir wollten demonstrieren, wollten zeigen, wir haben früher gefeiert und können auch heute feiern'. Interview with Paul Hamelmann, 12 May 2005.

[38] BStU, MfS, BV Erfurt, AOPK 2664/ 84, ff. 10–12: 'Einleitungsbericht – OPK „Iseke"'.

[39] BStU, MfS, BV Erfurt, AIM 1154/ 87, TII, vol. 4: 'Mündlicher Bericht des GHI „Jürgen Gerlach"' (Worbis, 23 June 1966).

[40] 'Da bin ich zu dem Chef [vom Rat des Kreises, Abt. Kultur] gegangen, der hat mir das Buch genommen [und] hat es zugeklappt: „Das machen wir nicht so wie Sie das denken mit dem Festprogramm." „So pass mal auf", hab ich zu ihm gesagt, „ob Sie das wollen oder nicht, ich sage wir ziehen unser Fest durch wie wir das für richtig halten, da frag ich aber keinen in Worbis drum." Ich sag: „das haben Sie doch damals '56 gesehen wie die das in Holungen durchgezogen haben", ich sag: „ich zeige Ihnen das wir das heute auch noch können."' Interview with Paul Hamelmann, 12 May 2005.

A few days later, Hamelmann was invited to a village council meeting. After trying in vain to change Hamelmann's mind, the mayor asked him in private to meet him and a colleague from the county's department of culture at the priest's house the following day. Hamelmann agreed, and so the next morning he approached the priest's house. Just before reaching the house, he saw the mayor and his colleague sitting inside the mayor's car:

I look inside, but nobody from the department of culture is inside the car. There sits our mayor and Department of Interior. Big Sunglasses, I knew him, he wore dark glasses like a mafioso, I thought: I know this guy from somewhere. Ah yes, he had me lying down once before to ask me about carnival. Now we've arrived at the Priest's house, and he opens the door – an old Silesian, I can still see him before me as he opens the door – 'hey, Paul, what pals have you brought here?' I say 'they're no pals of mine, they invited *me* – I'm sure they want to have a natter over coffee and cake', I say, joking. And then goes this appearance from Berlin, Department of the Interior, Mr T: 'we must have a talk.' 'Ok.' Then the priest opened the door a little, let me and Berlin inside, and our mayor – I don't remember whether he had just left the Church or his sons – anyway, when he tried to enter, he says: 'you stay outside, I didn't ask for you', and shut the door. Now this Department of the Interior stood alone with us both in the hallway. He was like a deer in the headlights, he just stood there. And then the priest said, 'so what do you want?' He started to stumble, he just couldn't get going.[41]

Mr T., the official from the county office for internal affairs, for whom Hamelmann used the interesting shorthands of 'Department of Interior' and 'Berlin', had a proposition to make: if Holungers cancelled their torchlight procession and refrained from singing the Eichsfeld Song, the district concert agency in charge of organizing professional concerts

---

[41] 'Aber guck ich darein, ist der von der Abteilung Kultur gar nicht drinne in dem Wagen. Da sitzt unser Bürgermeister drin und Abteilung Inneres. Große Sonnenbrille, ich kannte den, so ne dunkle Brille wie so ein Mafioso, ich dachte den … hab ich den irgendwo schon mal gesehen. Ach so durch Karneval hat der mich schon mal liegen gehabt … Jetzt steh ich beim Pfarrer … da macht der Pfarrer die Türe auf, so richtig so ein alter Schlesier, seh ich noch wie heute, macht die Tür auf, „na Paul, was hasten da für Kumpels?" Ich sag sind nicht meine Kumpels, ich sag die ham mich auch eingeladen hier. Da wollten die doch sicherlich nen Kaffeekränzchen machen, hab ich noch gelästert." Und dann hat sich der Berlin Vogel Abt. Inneres, der Herr T.: „Wir müssten mal diskutieren." „Könn mer machen." Da hat der Pfarrer die Tür nen bisschen aufgemacht, hat mich reingelassen und den Berlin und unser Bürgermeister – ich weiß nicht ob er aus der Kirche getreten war oder kurz vorher oder seine Söhne – jedenfalls, wie der reinwollte, sagt er [der Pfarrer]: „Sie bleiben draußen, Sie hab ich nicht bestellt", hat er die Tür zugemacht. Jetzt stand dieser Abteilung Inneres allein mit uns beiden im Flur. Der war wie so ein aufgeschrecktes Reh, stand der da. Und da hat der Pfarrer nun erzählt, ja was issen? Da kam er richtig ins Stocken, der war wie vor dem Kopp geschlagen, der kam gar nicht richtig zum Zuge.' Ibid.

throughout the district would fund a cultural programme to the tune of 3,600 marks.[42] Hamelmann accepted, since this brought a cultural programme to the village which would normally have only been affordable by large co-operatives or towns.

Despite these attempts, Holungers still found a way to express 'their' meanings of the Iseke celebration. When the dancers and musicians from the district concert agency arrived, they asked Hamelmann where they could change. Hamelmann responded that he was not responsible for their coming, and that they should go across the festival lawn, to where the mayor lived. While the mayor was busy dealing with his unexpected guests, Hamelmann and his mates set up the box office, demanding an entrance fee of everyone who came in (their friends excepted).[43] When the mayor appeared, it was too late for him to intervene. He was left to complain bitterly to the Stasi, in his capacity as IM 'J. Gerlach'. The Cultural League had, he reported, taken an entrance fee even though they had not incurred any cost for the evening. Moreover, on this and all other evenings, he noted, the Cultural League had reported attendance figures that were far too low (hence pocketing the fees of those unaccounted for), while for two events they had not reported any attendance figures (or revenues generated) at all. IM 'J. Gerlach' was outraged, and demanded that the party look into the funds that were unaccounted for immediately – though in fact, there was little the party could do.[44]

On the surface, the mayor's frustration appears to be surprising, since the authorities had managed to transform the festival, not least through the presence of outside performers. More importantly, the council's department for internal affairs successfully prevented Paul Schäfer, the festival's orator in 1956, from speaking publicly at any point during the festival. Moreover, the priest, who had been asked to give the opening speech, was replaced by the village mayor. Sample postcards that showed two Holungers in Eichsfeld costume with the text of the Eichsfeld Song were confiscated,[45] no torchlit procession was held, and the Eichsfeld Song was not sung at the official celebrations.

---

[42] Hamelmann remembered a figure of 7,000–8,000 marks. Despite this exaggeration, the essence of the state's desire to influence the festivities by funding them generously remains. For the lower figure, see BStU, MfS, BV Erfurt, AOPK 2664/ 84: Worbis, 1 August 1981 (information on the concert).

[43] Interview with Brigitte and Paul Hamelmann, 17 June 2003. Interview with Paul Hamelmann, 12 May 2005.

[44] BStU, MfS, BV Erfurt, AOPK 2664/ 84, f. 32: 'Tonbandabschrift FIM „J. Gerlach"' (19 August 1981).

[45] BStU, MfS, BV Erfurt, AOPK 2664/ 84, ff. 24–5. 'Information über die eingeleiteten Maßnahmen in Holungen' (Worbis, 22 July 1981).

Yet the authorities' victory had been one of form, not substance. On the Sunday of the festival, the priest held mass in remembrance of Iseke and spoke of him as an example to all. As the congregation came out from the church into the churchyard, one of Iseke's descendants started singing the Eichsfeld Song – and the congregation joined in, singing also its final, forbidden verses.[46] Here, on Church territory, the state had no means to prevent this. Moreover, at the festival itself, a heimat-themed evening with slides opened with the first two – permitted – verses of the Eichsfeld Song. Many of the slides featured the Sonnenstein and the Brunen Bühl, and to another slide featuring a Holunger in folklore dress, the speaker quoted parts of the third – forbidden – verse. If the state had won the battle over the heimat festival's meanings, it had done so merely on a technicality.

The Iseke festival of 1981 represents in part a further variant to the theme of 'us', the villagers, versus 'them': the functionary from the county had lost his personal identity and simply stood for 'them', the centralized state. As in 1956, this was an affirmation of the Catholic meanings of heimat, meanings that had to be upheld in opposition to the state. Indeed, for the villagers, as well as for the state, the repertoire of engagement in subsequent cultural practices and social dramas since 1954 loomed large. Once again, this was not simply an instance of village unity against 'the' state. The Cultural League planned the 1981 festival, but the meanings they ascribed to it did not correspond to those of all villagers, many of whom principally wished to have a good time. Moreover, other cultural groups did not have a voice in the proceedings, not least the village choir, whose sponsorship by the potash works provided plenty of tensions with the Cultural League. In the end, the elaborate festival generously sponsored by the district concert agency may have been welcomed by the villagers, but it was Hamelmann who stuck his neck out – by charging entrance fees while letting in his friends for free he showed the party, and the villagers, who called the shots.

The festival also shows how personal meanings, in this case rivalries and animosities, were deeply intertwined with the development of public and private transcripts. The mayor's clandestine reports to the Stasi make palpable his sense of frustration against the Catholic/Cultural League 'network' in the village against whose social and cultural power he, the

---

[46] Interview with Paul Schäfer, 12 May 2005. Interview with Paul Hamelmann, 12 May 2005. Hamelmann Private Collection, 'Holunger Erinnern: Festschrift zum Fest des Heimatvereins am 23. Mai 1998', 20.

representative of state and party, appeared to be so powerless. Even so, the severity and the nature of reactions is surprising: why would the county pay for a day of high-class entertainment, in a small village tucked away in the outer corner of the district (and of the GDR), which few of the districts' citizens even knew about, let alone cared about? The actions of villagers and officials, and the significance of the festival, can only be understood fully against the background of a wider confrontation that had begun three years earlier, in 1978.

In summer 1978, word spread that the potash works planned to extend its slag heap further northwards, a measure that would close off the valley completely.[47] The heap had grown to a point where a further extension northwards was prevented solely by the natural flow of the River Bode. The slag heap could not be extended to the south-west because here stood the village sports grounds and open-air swimming pool. Immediately to the east of the heap a plant had been installed to regulate the water supply to the mines. Since the slag heap could be extended in no other direction, there-fore, the potash works had decided to construct a tunnel beneath the existing slag heap in order to divert the river and make the extension possible. Moreover, they planned to extend the heap westwards by 150 metres. This would bring the 150-metre high slag heap within fifty metres of the house of Theo Iseke, a great-nephew of Hermann Iseke (Figure 16).

Upon hearing of the plans Theo Iseke demanded a meeting with the mine's director, only to find that the plans were final. In response, Iseke wrote a petition to Erich Honecker,[48] and this was flanked by a second petition sent in by Josef Artmann on behalf of the Cultural League, which, as the village's largest mass organization, claimed to speak for the entire village. While Iseke based his complaint on the abuse of socialist democracy, arguing that he had not been properly informed, Artmann pointed to the potential environmental damage of the extension. The main problem consisted of the danger of flooding, once the valley was closed off and the Bode could only flow through the tunnel. In extreme weather conditions after unusually heavy rainfall, the tunnel would be insufficient for all the water that needed to go through it, causing flooding in the village (Figure 17). Moreover, Artmann complained at the sulphur and chloride emissions from the mines, which already settled in the valley under current

---

[47] KA Heiligenstadt, RdK Worbis 6572: 'VEB Kombinat Kali Sondershausen. Erweiterung – Neue Schlammabsatzanlage im Bodetal' (15 June 1978).

[48] Josef Kistner Private Collection, 'Abschrift: Eingabe Theo Iseke an den Vorsitzenden des Staatsrates…' (24 October 1978).

16. House of Theo Iseke. The picture shows the extension of the slag heap by around August 1989, before it was extended (temporarily) still further northwards.

conditions and damaged local trees and the local harvest. Like Iseke, Artmann insisted that the decision to extend the slag heap was in breach of socialist law, because local representatives had not been consulted.[49] In response to the petitions, the deputy head of environmental affairs in the district council, Zänker, came to Holungen to explain the decision to extend the slag heap. As far as the state was concerned, that was the end of the matter.[50]

The matter was far from over. The village council demanded further information from the potash works, asserting its right to be consulted.[51] Moreover, the Cultural League sent a second petition to Erich Honecker. Once again invoking the constitutional guarantee that the beauty of

[49] ThHStAWe Kulturbund der DDR, Bezirksverwaltung Erfurt 19: 'Drohende Gefährdung der Landeskultur und des Umweltschutzes der Gemeinde Holungen, Kreis Worbis, Bezirk Erfurt' (4 November 1978).
[50] KA Heiligenstadt, RdK Worbis 6572: 'Stellvertreter des Vorsitzenden für Umweltschutz und Wasserwirtschaft' (21 December 1978).
[51] KA Heiligenstadt, RdK Worbis 6572: 'Ergebnis der Beratung'.

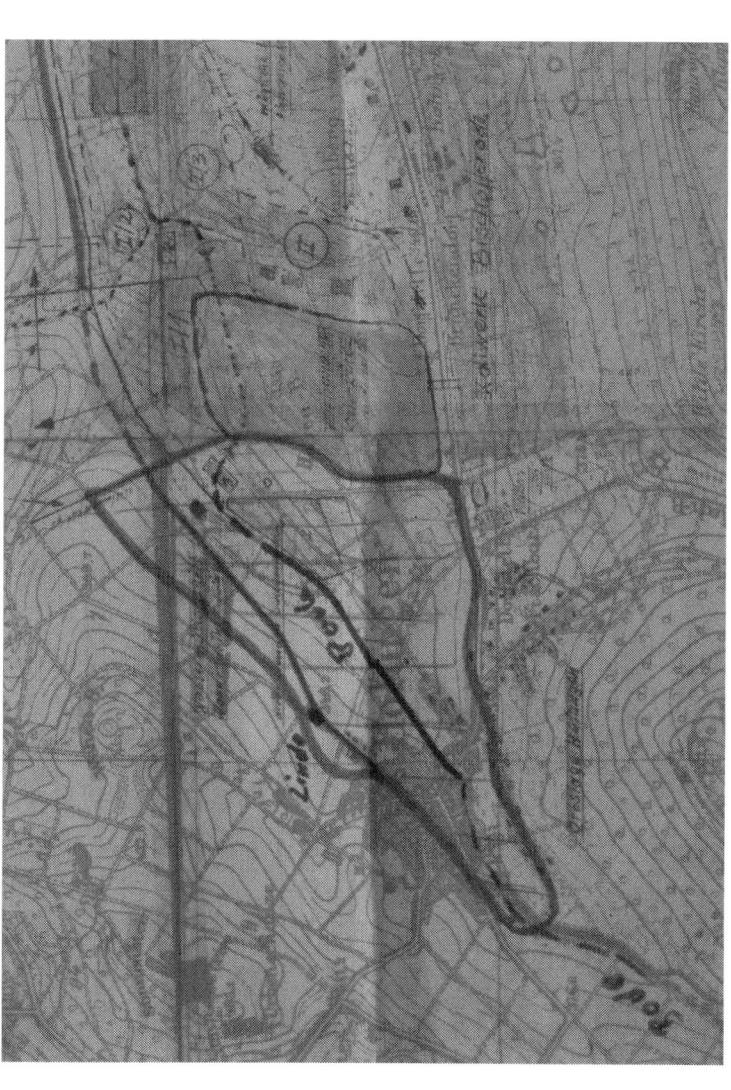

17. Map annotated by Holungers indicating the proposed northward extension of the slag heap and its consequences. The Bode river would be diverted into a tunnel going beneath the existing slag heap, while the ground covered by the slag heap would increase by 50 per cent. The map also indicates the total area which villagers expected to be flooded if the tunnel got clogged up at a time of heavy rainfall, with half of the village being affected. The shaded area beyond the rectangular line shows the northbound extension of the slag heap planned in 1980. The arrow pointing up from the slag heap shows the direction of envisaged future extensions to it. The dark line denotes the Bode river, with its diversion via a tunnel through the extended slag heap shown by dotted lines. The shaded area within the line of the river shows the area of possible flooding following the tunnelling of the Bode river at a time of heavy rains. Kistner private collection, c. 1980.

the heimat would be protected, the villagers asserted that the mines and the district had not taken sufficient account of alternative proposals drafted by the villagers, and the opinions of other experts. The petitioners listed seventeen offices to which they had addressed a plea for help, including the ministries of environmental protection, agriculture, culture, sciences and mines, the district Cultural League and the Institute for Environmental Protection. Holungers demanded to be heard and to receive responses from these offices.[52] In addition, in early 1979 both the village council and the village assembly issued an order to the potash mines to stop all building activities and reverse all planning decisions made at higher levels. The order was overturned by the county council two weeks later. The village assembly refused to accept this, and lodged a formal complaint against the county council's decisions.[53]

This extraordinary challenge to the higher authorities led to much commotion in the district. On 27 March 1979, Zänker returned to the village, flanked by representatives from the mining ministry in Berlin, the head of Worbis council, industrial and environmental functionaries from district and party, and representatives of the local potash mine and its parent combine. Against these heavyweights, the six members of the village council stood little chance. In the course of the discussions it transpired that the village mayor had indeed been informed as the law required, but had not passed on any information to other villagers.[54] Immediately after taking on the village council, the delegation of experts addressed the larger village assembly in a second meeting, pointing out that other villages in the GDR, notably those close to dams, faced far greater risks of flooding. The state simply could not make provisions for an eventuality that was only likely to happen once every two hundred years.

The villagers knew they had lost this particular battle,[55] but that did not end their hostility, far from it. Theo Iseke, for one, set out to prove that the tunnel would not work, and he did not have to wait for two hundred years. On 19 April 1983, heavy rainfall and the blocking of the tunnel's entrance with rubbish and bits of wood caused rising water levels; flooding was

[52] Josef Kistner Private Collection, 'An den Vorsitzenden des Staatsrates' (26 December 1978).
[53] KA Heiligenstadt, RdK Worbis 6572: 'Vorsitzender Rat des Kreises Worbis an den Bürgermeister Rat der Gemeinde: Worbis, den 8. Februar 1979'. See also KA Heiligenstadt, Rat der Gemeinde Holungen, Beschluß Nr. xxix–9/79.
[54] KA Heiligenstadt, RdK Worbis 6572: 'Protokoll der 5. Sitzung des Rates vom 27.3.1979 der Gemeinde Holungen'.
[55] KA Heiligenstadt, RdK Worbis 6572: 'Protokoll über die xxx. Sitzung der Volksvertretung am 27.3.1979'.

averted only because the Bode's old river bed had not yet been filled by the slag heap, so that the water could escape along it. Carefully documented by Theo Iseke,[56] the tunnel's failure was further proof that the villagers had nobody to rely on apart from themselves – and the Church.

The Holungers did not wait until 1983 to continue their resistance against the mines. Under the leadership of Josef Kistner, they presented an 'innovation proposal' (*Neuerervorschlag*) to the potash mines in which they evaluated and provided quotations for an alternative proposition for expanding the slag heap. This forced the potash mines into another round of discussions. Perhaps not altogether surprisingly, the proposal was rejected at a meeting on 21 April 1979, and – equally unsurprisingly – the signatories to the proposal issued a complaint against the rejection.[57] Ultimately, however, all legal means had been exhausted, and there was nothing more the villagers could do.

Since this row had technically been about the construction of the tunnel, villagers were still determined to fight futher extensions to the slag heap northwards.[58] The ensuing debates in 1979 largely mirrored those of the previous year. The mayor sent a representative to the potash works who gave his verbal consent to the planned measures there and then, without ever informing the village council. On 28 December 1979 the village assembly issued a decree forbidding a further extension to the slag heap, noting that its representative had not been authorized to give his consent. The decree was not signed by the mayor, who wrote to the county separately stating that he disagreed with the decree, and that he had not been informed by the villagers of their actions.[59]

Once again, the mine prevailed, but not before its directors, the county officials and the district authorities were reminded that some villagers would fight to the bitter end. In fact, although the mine managers had won the right to close off the valley they shied away from doing so. For as

---

[56] Josef Kistner Private Collection, photographs taken by Theo Iseke, 19 April 1983 at 8.15 p.m., 8.45 p.m., and 9 p.m.

[57] KA Heiligenstadt, RdK Worbis 6572: 'Neuererkollektiv des Kulturbundes der DDR: Neuerervorschlag zur Veränderung der geplanten Rückständekalihaldenerweiterung und zur Anlegung einer Schlammabsatzanlage' (11 December 1979). See also 'Bürgermeister Hesse an den Rat des Kreises Worbis, Beschluß Nr. 17 – III/ 79 (15.1.1980)'.

[58] KA Heiligenstadt, RdK Worbis 6572: 'Einladung zur Standortvorberatung zum Investitionsvorhaben Stabilisierung der Produktion 350kt im Kaliwerk Bischofferode' (26 April 1979).

[59] KA Heiligenstadt, RdK Worbis 6572: 'Volksvertretung der Gemeinde Holungen Beschluß Nr. 17-III/79 vom 28.12.1979'. 'Antrag zur Standortbestätigung der Halden- und Schlammabsetzungsanlagenerweiterung des Kaliwerkes vom 8.8.1979 und 02.11.1979 gemäß Standortberatung vom 09.05.1979'; 'Bürgermeister Hesse an den Rat des Kreises Worbis, Beschluß Nr. 17–III/79 (15.1.1980)'.

18. Devotional monument by Iseke's house, consecrated by the Church to the Virgin Mary.

long as possible, they extended the heap in other ways, as villagers were clearly not going to take this lying down.

Extending the slag heap without filling in the old river bed essentially meant extending its base westward. This took the toxic hill to within fifty metres of Theo Iseke's house; further expansion westwards could proceed only if his house, and the devotional monument to the Virgin Mary standing next to it, could be destroyed (Figures 16, 18). Iseke refused to move, and since the monument had been consecrated, he could (and did) count on the support of the Church. After years of fighting over this issue, by August 1989 the authorities had no choice: since 80 per cent of the potash mined at Holungen was exported for hard currency, the state could no longer afford to respond to the Holungers' concerns. Sparing Iseke's house, the mines began to close off the Bode valley. Ultimately, the villages had managed to delay the closing of the valley by some ten years. But they were never able to change the authorities' mind. Power ultimately continued to reside with the state, until 1989.[60]

---

[60] Interview with Josef Kistner, 14 October 2007. Interview with Paul Hamelmann, 12 May 2005. Interview with Paul and Brigitte Hamelmann, 17 June 2003.

The continuing disputes surrounding the potash mines constitute a backdrop to the cultural events in the village, not least the Iseke Festival of 1981. The ongoing confrontation explains the party's willingness to lavish so much money on the local community and thereby prevent the *Eigen-Sinn* expressed through the festival from becoming an open expression of distance or even opposition. Moreover, the controversy illustrates the joy that the Cultural League campaigners must have felt at outsmarting the village mayor at the box office. Clearly, sympathy for the man who, in their eyes, had sold out the village to the mines was non-existent. In turn, such events were doubly significant for the local community. Amidst all the frustrations which the setbacks in the tussle against the slag heap provoked, an event like this, and the victory – however small or imagined – it represented against 'Berlin' and all the representatives of state and party provided important moments of self-affirmation, self-respect and local pride. The significance of these moments was reinforced by their essentially public nature. They were not challenges to the public transcript as such, but open assertions of alternative meanings, of the private transcript: rare moments in which the power of individuals and symbols against authority could be demonstrated for all to see, while the mayor felt his humiliation all the more strongly because it had been public.[61]

The cultural performances and the political disputes between villagers, the mines directorate, local officials and outside experts 'varnished' the power of the party to impose a solution, and the hostility of many villagers to the status quo. At the same time, these skirmishes were flanked by unvarnished reminders of state power, notably the border, institutions like the Department of the Interior, and the state security services. Villagers had frequent contact with these, for instance when Hamelmann was called to explain himself to the county's interior department in Worbis, or when Kistner was forbidden to visit his mother, who lived in the restricted zone near the border. Indeed, in the early 1980s Artmann faced the real threat of losing his bakery if he continued with his struggle against the mines, whereafter he took more of a back seat in subsequent developments. So how did villagers respond to such open manifestations of power, and how did this impact on the effectiveness of the public transcript?

---

[61] This provides a further reason why it is more helpful to speak of 'private' rather than 'hidden' transcripts. In Scott's work, open assertions of the 'hidden' transcript automatically challenge the public transcript. This was clearly not the case here, though his general observation about the significance of public expressions of distance holds true. Scott, *Domination*, pp. 213–16.

Despite these frequent intrusions, and perhaps even because of them, there appears to have been a core belief amongst Holungers that the village community was a sphere free from state interference. Indeed, even Josef Kistner, whose activities were bound to make him a target for Stasi surveillance, insists that he did not think it possible at the time that unofficial informants would report on him; in reality, ten unofficial informants at his workplace and in the village were spying on him. But, in Holungen the power of the state was limited in its impact in two ways. First, it appears that the Stasi never made it into the inner circle of the Cultural League. As unofficial informers, the mayor or the head of the Cultural League in Worbis county could provide some information, for instance that Cultural League leaders in Holungen met in secret. But they were not privy to what was said at the meetings. Stasi influence extended widely, but it did not extend everywhere. Second, irrespective of what state officials and the Stasi knew, it appears that some of the main actors spent little time thinking about whether the Stasi was or was not present in the village, even if they had come into contact with Stasi officials on other occasions.[62] This was not the same for everyone, as individuals like Artmann, who had much to lose, could scarcely afford to overlook the state's coercive power. Nonetheless, collecting money at the box office against the mayor's protest, or singing the Eichsfeld Song, confirmed many of the Cultural League's leaders in their view that the essence of local culture and local relationships lay outside the meanings intended by the party. At the local level, the state did not belong.

Holungen was far from being the only village affected by potash mines along the border, nor was it the only village directly affected by increasing environmental pollution. At the same time, the intensely local and personal nature of the conflict is striking. Although the confrontation was headed by the Cultural League leader, Artmann, and supported by others like Hamelmann, the person who stands out in this conflict is Josef Kistner. With two engineering degrees, he had worked at the potash mine (1961–8) until the director forced him out owing to his refusal to join the party. Underlying the conflict between Kistner and the director was thus a long history of personal antipathy and rivalry, nurtured by the former's Catholicism and the latter's party allegiance. In 1968, Kistner took over the electrical operations at the GDR's largest cement works in Deuna. Kistner had the necessary skills and connections to take on the management

---

[62] Josef Kistner, like Päsler, was asked at one point whether he wanted to co-operate with the Stasi. Interview with Josef Kistner, 14 October 2007.

of the mines; he was perfectly capable of finding viable alternative solutions for the slag-heap extension. Moreover, the Stasi noted with horror that he had obtained access to confidential planning documents from the mines, while he used his connections at the district and GDR levels to maximize pressure on local officials.[63]

Even more important was Kistner's local influence, which can be measured by the fact that he managed to persuade the majority of the village council, including SED members, to vote against the district authorities. Kistner and his Cultural League friends achieved this through more than the force of their arguments. Thanks to his qualifications he served as the head of the village's building commission, and every local building and building extension needed his approval. Those who owned a house or wished to build one in the future could not risk voting against him.[64] Kistner eventually lost his job at the building commission, but his informal influence remained considerable. Moreover, his comrades-in-arms from the Cultural League were in a similarly strong position to take on the authorities. Hamelmann and his closest League friends were a group of bachelors, with no children that could be discriminated against at school. Moreover, Hamelmann worked in construction in Nordhausen, far away from local employers. Like Kistner, Hamelmann was thus relatively free from local pressure, while his access to supplies of building material made him and his friends less dependent on patronage from the authorities for official allocations for their endeavours.[65] Finally, the leadership of Kistner (and Hamelmann at the cultural level) would not have been possible in this way without the Church. The fact that the church council almost duplicated the Cultural League leadership provided the village's informal leadership structure with an alternative institutional endorsement, one that was clearly linked to the villagers' sense of heimat.

CONCLUSION

The example of Holungen raises the important question of how *Eigen-Sinn* related to the private transcripts of the community, and to the public

---

[63] BStU, MfS, BV Erfurt, AIM 677/ 85, f. 74: 'Abschrift mündlicher Bericht des IM „Lore"' (Worbis, 21 July 1981).

[64] BStU, MfS, BV Erfurt, AIM 677/ 85: 'Mündlicher Bericht GMS „Friedrich"' (received on 27 June 1980).

[65] Hamelmann and his friends often organized building supplies for their neighbours, including material for the region's largest beer stall inside the festival tent for the 1980 village festival. Interview with Paul Hamelmann, 12 May 2005. Interview with Paul and Brigitte Hamelmann, 17 June 2003.

transcript of the socialist heimat. Kistner, Artmann, Hamelmann and Schäfer are just some of the more notable examples of how individuals developed their own meanings in relation to the community and the state. Indeed, as this account has shown, the state could impact upon individuals and the community in contradictory ways. Yet village life was rich with cultural practices and social drama, and it is these which related the *Eigen-Sinn* of individuals to the transcripts of the community.

Victor Turner has suggested that through cultural performances, communities reflect on day-to-day social practices. Cultural performances constitute 'magic mirrors, each interpreting as well as reflecting the images beamed to it, and flashed from one to the others'.[66] Cultural practices in Holungen, from the weekly celebrations of mass to amateur theatre, offered individuals the opportunity to reflect on, and assert, where they stood in relation to the community, and to express their identification with it. Moreover, village festivals, from carnival to Iseke celebrations, created – at the point of celebration – genuine, creative liminal spaces in which individuals and the community could express desires ('a mood of feeling') and meanings normally deeply embedded in the cultural fabric.[67] In the cultural setting of carnival, for instance, villagers were able to articulate publicly their controversy with the potash mines (Figure 19), a ritual of reversal in which victory could be imagined (albeit temporarily). This not only provided encouragement for further political action, it also helped integrate the dispute into the self-identifications of Holungers.

Local culture, a sense of homeland, and the local experience of state and party were thus closely interwoven, with each reinforcing the other. In this sense, Holungen contradicts Turner's assumption that rituals of reversal (such as carnival) restore and reaffirm relations by presenting those of 'low' status with a 'pressure valve' to let off steam.[68] Rather than helping to reduce tensions with state and party, carnival and other cultural practices provided occasions for villagers to euphemize their distance to state and party.[69]

Cultural practices necessarily stand in close relation to 'social dramas', i.e. crises caused by breaches of regular norm-governed social relations, which force people to take sides. In such dramas, meaning is engendered by

---

[66] Victor Turner, *The Anthropology of Performance* (Baltimore: PAJ Publications, 1987), pp. 23–4.
[67] Turner, *Anthropology of Performance*, pp. 22–7, 123.   [68] Turner, *The Ritual Process*, p. 177.
[69] Scott, *Domination*, pp. 172–87.

19. 'Holungen in Seenot' (Holungen at risk of drowning): a carnival float created by Holungers, which illustrates the villagers' concerns that the village was at risk of severe flooding through the proposed extension of the slag heap.

relating current problems to a rich communal past.[70] As these conflicts are resolved, they offer a more acute and conscious reflexivity than cultural practices; hence the latter draw meaning and force from social dramas.[71] Cultural performances and social dramas offer moments of communal reflexivity which inform, adjust and in this way strengthen the group's self-knowledge.

Incessant disputes among individuals at village level did not, therefore, hinder the development of common transcripts at community level. On the contrary, social drama followed by reconciliation furthered the development of common transcripts. Each drama, whether it related to Artmann's hut or to Hamelmann's involvement in the 1981 Iseke festival, allowed communal relations to be slightly readjusted depending on the individuals involved and the dispute at hand. As the example of Holungen shows, state

[70] Victor Turner, 'Dewey, Dilthey and Drama: an essay in the anthropology of experience', in Victor W. Turner and Edward M. Bruner (eds.), *The Anthropology of Experience* (Urbana: University of Illinois Press, 1986), pp. 33–44; here p. 40.
[71] Turner, *Anthropology of Performance*, p. 94.

and party impacted on how the drama was enacted and resolved through its economic, political and cultural resources. Yet the state did not determine the outcome of the social drama among Holungers. Through the reflexive phase that followed each encounter, meanings were constructed that may not have been shared by all, but which were mutually understood and accepted, and persistently reaffirmed in cultural practices, until they were challenged in further social drama. Local, private transcripts thus evolved that related to state and party, but maintained their distinctiveness throughout.

The focus of this chapter has remained on a few individuals who, over the decades, led the Cultural League and were in very close contact with one another. Even if this group represented only a few of the Holungers, their significance in the village can be best understood as that of a 'star group'. Victor Turner asserts that in most communities in which multiple memberships exist, a 'star group' forms which most wish to join, and which is distinguished by a particularly high intensity of social contact and 'psychic energy'. Such a group could have a particular influence on cultural performances and on the outcome of social dramas.[72] In this sense, the actors presented in this chapter, notably Schäfer, Artmann, Hamelmann and Kistner, as well as their friends (including the Iseke nephews), had a disproportionate influence on the identifications of Holungers and the meanings of heimat.

The Holungers' manifestations of *Eigen-Sinn* raise a further crucial question: why did individuals take the trouble to keep the authorities at arm's length in this way? Their acts bordered on opposition, and they were not without danger. The state's prioritization of economic profit was evident not just in Holungen, but also in environmental problems throughout the land. Certainly after the initial meetings with the political and economic representatives of the district, as well as encounters with 'Berlin', it seems difficult to understand why villagers persisted in making a fuss over an apparently futile issue at every opportunity.

The possibility cannot be excluded that Holungers hoped that their arguments might convince, however unlikely this must have appeared. At least as important, perhaps, was that protesting constituted an act of local belonging. This does not imply that everybody approved of the obstinacy of the Cultural League members led by Artmann and Kistner. After all, many villagers worked in the mines, and many from the

---

[72] Ibid., pp. 44–6.

surrounding villages also depended on the mines for their livelihood.[73] For such villagers, disagreeing with Kistner and Iseke did not imply a lack of local allegiance. But for the Holungen Friends of Nature and Heimat, the extension of the mine fundamentally threatened their locality. It transformed their sensuous experience of the heimat because of the slag heap's appearance and the heavy smoke lingering in the village on calm sunny days. The slag heap threatened the very existence of the heimat through the possibility of flooding. Such an encroachment on the local heimat could not be taken lying down, even if any action was likely to be futile. Concern for Holungen and roots in this community could not be better expressed than by doing whatever was possible to protest against the decisions of the 'outsiders', the mine directorate and the state authorities.

These 'social dramas' of the late 1970s and early 1980s not only reaffirmed relations and identifications among Holungers, they also reinforced the unofficial authority of the Cultural League leaders. Hamelmann's recollections of meeting 'Berlin' at the priest's house not only reversed normal power relations, putting him and the priest in the driving seat; when told to the other villagers the story manifested clearly who the leaders of the community were who alone could teach 'Berlin' a lesson. With every conflict against the authorities, and with the social dramas these provoked inside the village, it appears that the Cultural League emerged strengthened and emboldened. In these skirmishes, 'winning' against the authorities was secondary. Above all, these activities were to be understood as the assertion of one's self-understanding as a Holunger and of one's standing within the community.

This raises one final, related question: why did the state care so much about the villagers' disquiet? Even in the unlikely event that the villagers had chosen to protest openly, the state could easily have used force to overcome this. Instead, representatives of state and party engaged in endless meetings long after the mines had secured the legal right to expand. More puzzling still, why did the state make so much fuss (and incur such heavy expenses) just to prevent two verses of the Eichsfeld Song from being sung?

The Holungen controversies bring to light the euphemization of power evident in the socialist heimat. The power of state and party rested, in James C. Scott's terms, on its being seen as unavoidable. And for hegemony to appear as inevitable, open challenges must be avoided at

---

[73] Hamelmann remembered how he had been subject to criticism precisely because he was unmarried, and thus presumably did not have to think about his employment in the same way as the married men from the mines. Interview with Paul Hamelmann, 12 May 2005.

all costs. Hence state and party were careful to exert as much power as possible without open confrontation. The threat of the law or the use of force was always there, symbolized not least by the border and the villagers' inability to access 'their' cross on the Sonnenstein. Yet, precisely because the extension of the slag heap might have brought latent confrontation out into the open, it was held off for as long as possible. Meanwhile, the authorities tried to encode their power in many aspects of everyday life, including the festivals discussed here. In their own everyday lives, meanwhile, Holungers used heimat as a euphemism to see just how far they could take their foot-dragging, their skirmishes against authority and their struggle over symbols of heimat. Holungen represents a particularly dramatic instance of a contestation over the symbols and practices of the heimat: heimat contributed to both a euphemization of power and a 'varnishing' of dissent – through encounters that did much to reinforce, over time, a belief that power could be shifted at the margins while, at its core, the rule of the party was there to stay.[74]

---

[74] On the practices of domination and subordination, which rest on hegemony being accepted as unavoidable, and the role of euphemization in this process, see Scott, *Domination*, chs. 4 and 6.

CHAPTER 8

Cultural practices, Eigen-Sinn and hidden meanings

INTRODUCTION

Geographically, economically and culturally, Dabel appears to be a complete contrast to Holungen. Located in the north of the GDR, far from the border, it lies six kilometres away from its former county town, Sternberg, and forty kilometres from Schwerin, the former district capital. In contrast to Holungen, most Christians in Dabel are Protestants, though by the 1970s and the 1980s these formed a minority among villagers. Dabel's population grew considerably, from 1,052 in 1960[1] to between 1,400 and 1,500 by the end of the decade. From the 1970s, Dabel's population effectively doubled through the construction of an army barracks at the edge of the village. Situated in the flat Mecklenburg Lake district, lying in the shadow of the windmill that served as the village's emblem, Dabel was much more spread out than the enclosed Holungen (Figure 20; Map 2, p. 282), bordering the small Lake Dabel in the east, and Holzendorf Lake in the west. It took over two kilometres to get from one end of the village to the other, with the western and northern parts of the village over 1.5 kilometres away from the village centre.

Dabel was an uncommonly large village for its area, and it was distinctive in socio-economic terms. It provided a range of essential shops and services, including a butcher's and two grocery stores as well as a barber's and a painter. More unusually, the village had never been dominated by a single landowner, and had a diverse economic base. In the late 1960s only around 12 per cent of the adults in the village worked at the two local agricultural co-operatives. Around 14 per cent worked at the Fritz Reuter metal and wood processing plant, 12 per cent worked in trade, and a further 12 per cent

---

[1] BStU, MfS, BV Schwerin, AIM 413/63 vol. 2: 'Strukturplan der Gemeinde Dabel' (Dabel, 8 August 1960).

20. View of Dabel, north to south from the centre of the village (2008). The first building on the left is the old school, the building on the far left is the church.

in education and other social occupations.[2] Even though an unusually small proportion of the inhabitants were farmers, collectivization was keenly felt in Dabel, both by contemporaries and in village memory. Every villager had personal or family connections with farmers whose land had been collectivized, or who had chosen to flee to the West leaving all their worldly goods behind.[3]

Heimat is intertwined with community. Practices and ideals relating to the homeland are affirmed, qualified or rejected by other members of the community, while personal identifications are communicated and developed in social dramas and common rituals. This chapter investigates how a community very different from Holungen developed notions of heimat, and what practices and dramas characterized the individuals within it.

[2] HStD: 'Material für Dorfchronik, Ergebnisse der Dorfbefragung in Banzkow und Dabel', p. 20. See also the preface. The two largest groups among the adult population consisted of retired people (16 per cent) and housewives (18 per cent).
[3] Interview with Uwe Schliehe, 30 August 2005. Interview with Helga Böhnke, Rosemarie Bartelt, Wolfgang Cords and Karl-Heinz Schwabe, 5 July 2003.

In considering the impact of state and party on notions of community and heimat, few tasks are more challenging than to assess the impact of the state security services as one of a range of factors that impacted on everyday life. I have already shown that the state security services (Stasi) directly affected people who openly challenged the public transcript of the socialist heimat. However, it is also the case that the majority of citizens – and Dabel is a perfect example of this – did not openly challenge the public transcript of socialism. The example of the socialist heimat in everyday practices shows that most citizens managed to express their individual desires and concerns within the framework of the socialist order. The difficulty for the historian arises from the latency of Stasi power. Even if a majority of villagers were never directly confronted by officers of the state security services, this does not necessarily mean that the Stasi had no impact. How can we assess contemporaries' awareness that the Stasi could intervene if it wished to, and how did this awareness affect cultural practices, and individual identifications with heimat, the community and the GDR?

The question of Stasi impact is particularly poignant in a village setting. In such an intimate social context, it was very likely that if the Stasi confronted one villager, others would know. At the same time, the example of Holungen suggests that the possibility of villagers becoming involved with the Stasi themselves was something that could be imagined only with great difficulty, if at all. How, then, did the possibility of overt and covert Stasi activity in a village affect relationships? This question about how, if at all, the quiet presence of the Stasi was communicated breaks down the notion of transcripts, which depend on communication and mutual intelligibility. How can we evaluate communications about village life made to the Stasi which were foreclosed to other villagers, and what do these communications tell us about individual and communal identifications? How can we include the silence veiling the Stasi, amongst covert informers and those apprehensive about Stasi interference, in our assessments about the meanings of community and identity in the GDR?

In this chapter I shall address these questions more directly, while trying not to exaggerate the impact of the state security services. I shall show how, in one of the most exemplary communities of the socialist heimat, local identifications and notions of community were shaped by individual leadership, common traditions, social drama, rituals of reversal and a remarkable responsiveness to shifts in the ideological priorities of the party. At the same time, it emerges that the state security services affected each of these factors, though never exclusively. I shall attempt to make a start at integrating the Stasi into our understanding of how state and party affected everyday life in the GDR, as one of a number of diverse factors that affected the cultural life of one very distinctive community.

A BEACON OF SOCIALIST CULTURE

In 1969, Horst Roggenbau invited the first secretary of the Cultural League, Karl-Heinz Schulmeister, to visit Dabel. Roggenbau took enormous pride in the village's transformation, and wanted Schulmeister to see how the village had been turned into a model for the socialist heimat. 'When you come to Dabel', he wrote, 'you will not recognize it. I simply cannot list all the improvements here – such as pavements, street lighting, a bowling alley, green spaces, the creation of a leisure site … It is almost incredible what has been created in such a short period of time.' Roggenbau knew his addressee would be appreciative. Three years earlier, the Cultural League praesidium of the GDR had recognized Dabel as a model of the socialist heimat, commending the village to the rest of the country as 'a beacon of culture'.[4]

If Dabel could be represented as a model of the socialist heimat, this is particularly remarkable because up to the early 1960s, Dabel was notable, if anything, for its lack of cultural enterprise. As elsewhere in Mecklenburg, the substantial number of expellees (from Germany's former eastern territories now under Polish or Soviet sovereignty) that settled in the village represented a new beginning for the community.[5] This was scarcely evident in the public appearance of village culture, whose origins lay predominantly in the pre-war era. The voluntary fire brigade continued to provide a focus for cultural activity, as did the sports teams now organized under the purview of the local machinery-lending station.[6] Dabel's Cultural League was founded in 1955 with thirty-seven members under the leadership of Hans-Georg Merten, a local teacher. The League's membership and activities remained limited, however. In 1956, a major event of pre-war popular culture was revived with the celebration of carnival, but the fun to be had at this event was short-lived. In the 1961 carnival pageant, the village mayor

---

[4] HStD Kulturbund Protokolle, entry for 2 November 1966. *725 Jahre Dabel: Eine Chronik*, ed. Fritz Ahrens *et al.* (Dabel: Interessengemeinschaft Heimatgeschichte/Chronik der Ortsgruppe des Kulturbunds Dabel, 1977), p. 32.

[5] I was unable to obtain exact figures for population movements in the village, though interviewees certainly remembered the expellees as a significant presence in the village. Hardly any archival material (even newspapers) appears to have been preserved outside the village. The rich collections of the Dabel Heimatstube begin in the early 1960s with the revival of the local Cultural League.

[6] *725 Jahre Dabel*, pp. 31–2. The continuation of pre-1945 traditions into the socialist era was also emphasized by Karl-Heinz Schwabe, former head of the village club in the 1960s. Interview with Helga Böhnke, Rosemarie Bartelt, Wolfgang Cords and Karl-Heinz Schwabe, 5 July 2003.

was paraded through the village inside a cage atop one of the floats. This led to much amusement in the village – but less among the state authorities. In subsequent years the pageant was prohibited, and only one carnival evening per year was organized.

Crucial to the transformation of local village culture was the local school. A host of new teachers who arrived in the second half of the 1950s were not only uniformly socialist, they also transformed local cultural life. The new physical education teacher, Heinrich Garling, founded a popular gymnastics group; the new arts teacher helped produce posters, invitations and flyers for the Cultural League;[7] meanwhile, Horst Roggenbau himself, a biology teacher, set up the young philatelists' association. Constituting just under 20 per cent of the Cultural League's membership during the 1960s, teachers formed a disproportionately large occupational group in the League, and they were also exceptionally active.[8]

It is not clear whether the founding members of the Cultural League felt some initial unease about these energetic young teachers who had come in from the outside, or were frustrated at the authorities' criticism of their carnival celebrations, or both. In any case, between 1955 and early 1963 the Cultural League membership declined despite the addition of the teachers, from thirty-seven to thirty-one members. In the early 1960s, meetings consisted of events organized for pupils, and of slide shows and discussion evenings attended by a dozen or so villagers.[9] By the early 1960s Roggenbau had taken over the running of the Cultural League, but up to 1963 its activities made but a minimal contribution to Dabel's culture.

In 1962 the village celebrated its 700th anniversary with a festival. The village festival, held annually thereafter, transformed the Cultural League's standing in the village. As part of the 1963 festival, Roggenbau organized a Mecklenburg heimat-themed evening. When the performers hired from the county town pulled out at the last minute, Roggenbau was forced to put together a programme of his own, involving the local agitprop group (led by a fellow teacher), the gymnasts and the postman, Uwe Schliehe, with whom Roggenbau performed Low German sketches. The evening proved a tremendous success. Roggenbau had shown that he could not only enlist his

---

[7] HStD Material für Dorfchronik, 'Begründung zur Auszeichnung des Freundes Werner Schade mit der Ehrennadel der Nationalen Front in Bronze' (no date, *c.* 1969).

[8] HStD Kulturbund: 'Übersicht über die berufliche Zusammensetzung. Dabel, den 7.4.1964'; 'Deutscher Kulturbund Tätigkeitsbericht. November 1966–März 1967'.

[9] HStD Material für Dorfchronik: 'Tätigkeitsbericht der Ortsgruppenleitung für den Monat Februar 1963'; 'Tätigkeitsbericht der Ortsgruppenleitung für den Monat April – Juni 1963'.

own students as his audience, but also speak to the villagers, in their own language and through their own culture.[10]

The Dabel Cultural League was keen to capitalize on its success, creating a photography circle and organizing further Low German evenings throughout the winter months. In the 1964 festival, twenty-five Cultural League members were involved in the organization of eight (out of twenty-two) events which included book readings, slide shows, the Mecklenburg folk evening, and a folk culture (*Volkskunst*) exhibition which alone drew 910 visitors. By 1967, the Cultural League was organizing seventeen out of thirty-five events, which included a hobby exhibition, a cultural conference and a festival evening in honour of the Great Socialist October Revolution. Thanks to the Cultural League's involvement in the village festival, its membership grew to 42 in December 1963, 98 in December 1965, and 117 in March 1967.[11] With 138 members in 1974, the Dabel Cultural League now represented almost a third of all Cultural League members in Sternberg county.[12] The significance of the League in Dabel increased through its expanding involvement in the village festival, and in turn the festival was invigorated through the contributions of the Cultural League.

With a plethora of events related to socialism in name and in content, the Dabel village festival represented precisely the kind of socialist festival which the SED and the National Front sought to encourage. Yet, as the first part of this book has shown, the creation of a socialist culture was particularly difficult to realize where the collectivization of agriculture was having severe effects. In Dabel, too, the Cultural League found it extremely difficult throughout the 1960s to enlist farmers as active members.[13] Yet, given the relatively small size of the farming population there, the festival could thrive whether farmers attended or not.[14]

---

[10] HStD Material für Dorfchronik: 'Kurzbericht über die Veranstaltungen der Ortsgruppe zu den II. Dabeler Dorffestspielen vom 31. August – 8. Sept. 1963' (Dabel, 15 September 1963).

[11] HStD Material für Dorfchronik: 'Tätigkeits-Bericht der Ortsgruppenleitung für den Monat März 1964'; 'Tätigkeits-Bericht der Ortsgruppenleitung für den Monat April 1965'; 'Tätigkeits-Bericht der Ortsgruppenleitung für den Monat November 1966 bis März 1967'; 'Tätigkeits-Bericht der Ortsgruppenleitung für den Monat Oktober und November 1965'.

[12] HStD Material für Dorfchronik: 'Prüfungsbericht der zentralen Kommission Natur- und Heimat über die Ergebnisse der Untersuchung der Aktivitäten des Kulturbundes zur Entwicklung der sozialistischen Heimatkunde und Landeskultur im Kreis Sternberg (1974)', p. 3.

[13] In February 1964, for instance, the Cultural League admitted its first members from the agricultural co-operatives. However, these were the cadres of the two co-operatives, and they were responding to pressure from the village council and from Roggenbau who had publicly lamented their absence in village culture. HStD Kulturbund: Tätigkeitsbericht der Ortsgruppenleitung für Februar 1964.

[14] Interview with Uwe Schliehe, 30 August 2005. Schliehe could not recollect a significant presence of farmers during the 1960s.

Whether or not the festival was branded as being 'socialist' in nature, villagers could endow it with an intensely local meaning that had little to do with socialism. Indeed, while socialist cultural authorities encouraged the concept of a 'village festival', for Dabelers this was not a completely new idea. During the Weimar Republic and into the Third Reich, Dabelers had celebrated the 'Mecklenburg Village Day'. It had been organized by the shooting association, and its centrepiece consisted of a pageant.[15] The celebration of local culture through the pageant was continued in carnivals up to 1961, and in 1962 the pageant was resurrected as part of the village festival. The festival, then, allowed the continued expression of local folk traditions that villagers held dear.

As the village festival developed, cultural life expanded. Reviewing the Cultural League's activities over the past three years, Roggenbau noted in 1970 that, quite apart from its pivotal contributions to the village festivals, the League had organized 151 events which had attracted 8,390 people.[16] The Cultural League organized day trips to various parts of the heimat,[17] while also developing cultural programmes for the Young Pioneers and the election of the SED village leadership.[18]

The cultural achievements of Dabelers in the 1960s were recognized far beyond the Cultural League in Berlin. The gymnasts won the bronze medal at the Fifth German Sports and Gymnastics Festival in Leipzig in 1969, and in 1972 they won gold at the workers' festival in Schwerin.[19] The philatelists won medals throughout the district and even around the GDR, and participated in exhibitions in Poland and Czechoslovakia. Even the National Front considered Dabel to be a model, as in 1969 the village recorded contributions to 'Join in!' totalling one million marks.[20]

Socialism affected almost every cultural event organized by the Cultural League in those years, and this was not imposed from above, nor was it mere window-dressing. In 1970, the Cultural League committed itself to a comprehensive celebration of the hundredth anniversary of Lenin's birth.

[15] HstD Bildersammlung (photo album): '10. Mecklenburgischer Dorftag Dabel 1934'.
[16] HStD Material für Dorfchronik: 'Wie hat sich in Dabel die sozialistische Lebensweise entwickelt und wie ist die Ortsgruppe des Deutschen Kulturbundes Dabel ihren geistig-kulturellen Aufgaben gerecht worden? [1970]'.
[17] HStD Kulturbund, Protokolle: entries for 10 December 1966 (Potsdam and Hiddensee), 8 April 1967 (Berlin), 15 May 1969 (Spreewald).
[18] HStD Material für Dorfchronik: 'Tätigkeitsbericht der Ortsgruppenleitung für den Monat November/Dezember 1966 und Januar, Februar, März 1967'.
[19] HStD Material für Dorfchronik: 'Begründung zur Auszeichnung der Freundin Jutta Bülow mit der Ehrennadel für das künstlerische Volksschaffen' (Sternberg, 30 June 1969). See also *725 Jahre Dabel*, p. 36.
[20] HStD Kulturbund, Protokolle: entry for 2 November 1966. *725 Jahre Dabel*, p. 32.

The indefatigable Roggenbau organized a programme that included slide shows on Leningrad, talks on 'Lenin and Gorki' and 'Lenin – Model and Leader', a quiz evening on Lenin, and a discussion forum entitled 'Learning from Lenin Means Learning to Win'. Other events dedicated to Lenin included debates held at election time, discussions with the young people of the village about military service, and readings of Soviet literature.[21] Not all of these plans materialized. Of seventeen events envisaged for the youth club, only ten were actually held. Yet, even if the most ideological events were cancelled, occasions such as Erwin Bekier's book reading entitled 'Tracing Lenin' ('Auf Lenins Spuren') were still overtly political, reminding villagers of the times and the society in which they were living.[22] For Horst Roggenbau, as for the Cultural League in Berlin, Dabel was a 'beacon' of culture not (just) because Dabelers enjoyed more culture than other villages, but because he had managed to initiate a village culture that reflected the socialist currents of the 1960s far better than anywhere else in the region.[23]

There were several reasons why village culture became politicized in this way. Roggenbau himself was highly energetic. His wife also participated in some of the Cultural League's activities, but a marriage that was by all accounts unhappy encouraged Roggenbau to pour all his energies into his cultural interests. Roggenbau's first love, in the memory of villagers, was philately. In reality he was as committed to politics as to his stamps. As an amateur correspondent for the Sternberg county page of the *Schweriner Volkszeitung*, he contributed 253 articles and notices between 1961 and 1963 alone. Such articles were an excellent way not just to publicize his activities, but also to mention – and in this way honour – others for their commitment. In these columns, Roggenbau also registered his impatience, for instance with the local agricultural co-operative's apparent lack of commitment to the plan and to socialism. Roggenbau inspired, encouraged and cajoled, but never at the cost of his political commitment.[24]

Thanks to his charisma Roggenbau built up a network of like-minded individuals. In addition to his colleagues at school, this included the

[21] HStD Material für Dorfchronik: '„Zehn Aufgaben im Jahre des großen Lenins": Arbeitsprogramm der Ortsgruppe des Deutschen Kulturbundes Dabel für das Jahr 1970'; 'Vereinbarung zwischen dem Jugendklub Dabel und der Ortsgruppe des Deutschen Kulturbundes … für das Lenin-Jahr 1970'. BArch-SAPMO, DY27 3423: 'Arbeitsprogramm des Dorfklubs Dabel vom 1. September bis 1. Mai 1971'.
[22] HStD Material für Dorfchronik: 'Vereinbarung zwischen dem Jugendklub Dabel und der Ortsgruppe des Deutschen Kulturbundes … für das Lenin-Jahr 1970'.
[23] BArch-SAPMO, DY27 3423: letter from Roggenbau to Schulmeister, 'Werter Genosse Schulmeister (Dabel, den 3.1.1970)'.
[24] HStD Volkskorrespondent Roggenbau, Zeitungssammlung.

successive heads of the local village club, and the village librarian. He could also count on the help of some of his former pupils. One of these was Wolfgang Cords, who became head of the local youth club in 1966 before eventually becoming a full-time cultural functionary at the county cultural club.[25]

However, when measured not by the number of political events but by their popularity, it is less evident that socialism really had become part of village culture. At the Fourth Village Festival in 1965, the Mecklenburg folklore evening attracted an audience of 200, and a popular art exhibition received 400 visitors. By contrast, a talk on 'socialist leadership' was attended by just twenty-two people. Five years later, the opening night to the Ninth Dabel Village Festival dedicated to Lenin, which featured a village dance, attracted a crowd of 150 people, while the 'Day of Socialist Combat Sport' ('Tag des sozialistischen Wehrsports') drew 190 people. Only seven people, on the other hand, were present at the festival's most political event, a discussion group with veteran soldiers,[26] and literary discussions were not particularly popular either.[27] Political discussions were not always unpopular. In 1967, the Cultural League organized a youth forum with an army officer. It was attended by 120 people, but the event also included a performance by the gymnasts, which was followed up by a dance.[28] Three years later, Roggenbau organized a talk by the same officer. This time, no entertainments were linked to the event and the talk had to be cancelled owing to poor attendance. Overtly advertised political debates could draw a significant audience, but apparently only if they included other attractions besides.[29]

Roggenbau could claim high audience figures for socialist events because they were often specifically aimed at school children, and, given the teachers' involvement with the Cultural League, it was difficult for the children

---

[25] Interview with Helga Böhnke, Rosemarie Bartelt, Wolfgang Cords and Karl-Heinz Schwabe, 5 July 2003.

[26] HStD Plakate: 'IV Dabeler Dorffestspiele 1965'; 'IX Dabeler Dorffestspiele 1970'. Many posters are available on which the number of attendees is marked. The fact that such low numbers are also presented internally and informally suggests that the figures given are reliable.

[27] As part of the Fifth Dabel Village Festival, for instance, a literary evening broadcast by Schwerin the district's radio station attracted an audience of six, while even a humorous literary evening in Low German attracted a mere nineteen people. HStD Material für Dorfchronik: 'Tätigkeitsbericht der Ortsgruppenleitung für den Monat August/September/Oktober 1966'.

[28] 'Gymnasts' is an imperfect translation of *Sportwerbegruppe*: the group delighted its audiences not just with pure gymnastics, but also with gymnastic formations and dances.

[29] HStD Material für Dorfchronik: 'Tätigkeitsbericht der Ortsgruppenleitung für den Monat April, Mai, Juni, Juli, August 1967. Vereinbarung zwischen dem Jugendklub Dabel und der Ortsgruppe des Deutschen Kulturbundes … für das Lenin-Jahr 1970'.

not to attend. Moreover, in 1964 Roggenbau created a recitation group made up of a few pupils from each year-group. The group's performance of poems and texts became a staple of every official occasion, be it a celebration of the local SED, election-day events or the 'baptism of youth'. Such occasions were attended by numerous villagers. In 1971, the recitation group performed at four events in celebration of the twenty-fifth anniversary of the SED's foundation in the village, allowing Roggenbau to claim these as Cultural League events with a total audience of almost 1,000 people.[30] Roggenbau could (and did) claim for his Cultural League a mass appeal in the village which in reality it never had.

In 1970, a survey of local culture was conducted, based on interviews with 212 individuals representing 81 per cent of Dabel's households. The results made sobering reading for Roggenbau. When Dabelers were asked which of the village's cultural groups they were aware of, a clear majority identified the gymnasts (60 per cent), followed by the philatelists (32 per cent) and the bowling group (32 per cent), with the Cultural League a poor fourth (19 per cent). Those who had named at least one group were asked if they were particularly interested in any one of these groups' activities. Again, the gymnasts came first (17 per cent), followed by philately (4 per cent) and a category that comprised other Cultural League activities (recitation group, literature circle, village chronicle, etc., 4 per cent in total). Almost half (46 per cent) were not interested in any of the cultural activities offered in Dabel at present.[31]

The survey shows that Roggenbau's activities through his recitation group and his political campaigns were not considered to be integral to village culture. What was accepted as constituting part of local culture was Roggenbau's specific hobby group, the philatelists. Clearly, the village population delighted in attending philately exhibitions, or dance shows or Low German performances. Those events, by contrast, that were ideological not just in name but in nature relied for their existence on a core of activists (and pupils) who could be relied on to organize and attend.[32] The Cultural League in Berlin and Roggenbau himself may have considered Dabel a 'beacon' of socialist culture. However, after seven years of socialist activism

[30] HStD Material für Dorfchronik: 'Veranstaltungstätigkeit der Ortsgruppe des Deutschen Kulturbundes zum 25. Jahrestag der Gründung der SED im Monat April 1971'.

[31] HStD Material für Dorfchronik: 'Ergebnisse aus der Dorfbefragung in Banzkow und Dabel', tables 3 and 4.

[32] An unofficial informant for the Stasi reported one villager as saying that, if the school did not participate in political events, these would be totally lamentable ('wäre es ganz jämmerlich'). The great majority of Dabelers were apathetic. BStU, MfS, BV Schwerin, HAXX 10187, f. 448: '14.7.1966. Gespräch mit Herrn XXX aus Dabel am 12.7.1966'.

culminating in comprehensive celebrations of Lenin's anniversary, the vast majority of Dabelers did not accept socialism as part of their heimat culture.

PRIVATE MEANINGS

The ambiguous relationship between socialism and the practices and meanings of heimat persisted in Dabel through the 1970s and the 1980s, when individuals became much more free to follow their own desires in the pursuit of the heimat's 'heritage'. Dabel continued to be recognized as a model community of the socialist heimat throughout the 1970s and 1980s. Over thirteen years, Dabel was recognized five times (1969, 1974, 1979, 1980 and 1982) as one of the top contributors to the 'Join in!' competition in the district.[33] Every year, Dabelers drew up a plan which clearly outlined the responsibility of individuals and groups for cleaning particular areas or streets. This was not simply a matter of organization: it also allowed villagers to put pressure on those who neglected their participatory duties.[34] Dabel's cultural life continued to thrive in other respects, so that Dabelers expressed, in the eyes of the Sternberg county National Front, 'the citizens' pride and joy in what they had achieved'.[35] The National Front organization in Schwerin district expected that Dabel's example would inspire a deeper love of heimat and pride in the country everywhere, especially amongst the district's more 'backward' communities.[36]

There are good grounds for doubting that Dabelers engaged in 'Join in!' out of motives of socialist citizenship. They were in a virtuous circle. Since it had been recognized as a model participant in 1969, the village had become one of three locations in the district which received privileged supplies of materials and logistical help.[37] Moreover, since the SED had already recognized Dabel as a beacon of socialist culture, it was in the party's interest to sustain this state of affairs. Dabelers never had to cope with the materials shortages and supply problems that increasingly frustrated other

---

[33] LHA Schwerin, Nationale Front Schwerin 114: 'Zur Auszeichnung für vorbildliche Leistungen im Wettbewerb Schöner unsere Städte und Gemeinden – Mach Mit! (Koll. Thide) [1982]'.

[34] HStD Dorfklub: 'Arbeitsplan des Ortsausschusses der Nationalen Front Dabel [1968–1969]'.

[35] LHA Schwerin, Nationale Front Schwerin 158: 'Nationale Front, Kreisausschuß Sternberg: Sternberg, den 4.1.80. betr: Bericht über alle durchgeführten Wohngebiets- und Hausfeste im Jahr 1979'.

[36] LHA Schwerin, Nationale Front Schwerin 158, 'Kurzvortrag durch Genossin Ellie Massel' (28 November 1987).

[37] LHA Schwerin, Nationale Front Schwerin 150: 'Streng Vertraulich! Auswahl von Gemeinden, die zum Teil durchgängig verschönert und architektonisch weiter im Wettbewerb „Schöner unsere Städte und Gemeinden – Mach mit!" gestaltet werden sollten [1975]'.

communities in the participatory campaign, especially during the 1980s.[38] Celebrating the Dabel Village Festival and participating in 'Join in!' brought tangible material benefits to the community.

More importantly, what has been shown in previous chapters was true for Dabel also: 'Join in!' worked because it reinforced existing traditions and mentalities. Dabel was a village with a relatively high degree of home ownership, with private gardens located in front of the houses bordering on the street (Figure 20). Given this relatively fluid transition from private to communal spaces, villagers had a personal interest in ensuring that their gardens did not look onto untidy streets. The concern of villagers to help each other keep their gardens in order is a common theme in the villagers' memories of the period before 1989.[39] This significance of the garden was further confirmed by the 1970 village survey, in which 33 per cent of the respondents identified working in the home and garden as their favourite pastime, a remarkable result given that this was not listed as one of the categories in the questionnaire.[40]

This importance of the garden for the village community was one of the first impressions gained by the village pastor upon arriving in the village in 1983:

Many people gave us presents, like fruit and similar things, but always adding the sentence: 'Well, next year you'll have these things yourself.' ... So I understood that the garden had to be done, and when the first hedge had grown at the front [of the garden], people got the impression that the pastor also had some notions about gardening ... You have to come to terms with the fact that in the countryside, you could buy hardly any fruit or vegetables.[41]

---

[38] The supply problems throughout the district are discussed in LHA Schwerin, Nationale Front Schwerin 114: 'Zur Führung des Mach-mit-Wettbewerbs im I. Quartal 1982. Ergebnisse, Zielstellungen, Probleme, Erfahrungen und Schlußfolgerungen' (12 April 1982).

[39] Wolfgang Cords remembered the common sight, in his childhood, of people sitting on their doorstep playing the *Trekfidel*, the local version of the accordion. Interview with Helga Böhnke, Rosemarie Bartelt, Wolfgang Cords and Karl-Heinz Schwabe, 5 July 2003. According to Schliehe, one of the central ruptures to village life after 1989 was that public life moved from the street into the private backyard: 'Früher haben wir alle 'ne Bank vorm Haus gehabt und haben abends im Sommer draußen vorm Haus gesessen ... heut sitzen'se alle hinten im Garten, heute hat keiner mehr 'ne Bank vorm Haus.' Interview with Uwe Schliehe, 30 August 2005.

[40] HStD Material für Dorfchronik: 'Ergebnisse aus der Dorfbefragung in Banzkow und Dabel', esp. table 2.

[41] 'Nun war damals, im Grunde ja auch, nun der Garten mußte neu angelegt werden ... so daß uns dann sehr viele Leute was geschenkt haben, was weiß ich, Obst und ähnliche Dinge, aber immer so'n bisschen mit dem Satz: „also im nächsten Jahr, dann haben Sie's ja selbst." Da war mir also klar, man muß also auch im Garten was tun, obwohl ich nun mit Garten sonst nicht so wahnsinnig viel im Sinn hatte, denn ich bin Stadtmensch, ich habe 30 Jahre praktisch in Rostock gewohnt. Und mir war denn klar auch der Garten mußte gemacht werden. Und als dann hier vorne diese Hecke ... angewachsen

What the pastor, Lange, was describing here was precisely the mentality that Knut Kreuch and Alfred Erck identified as the reason why 'Join in!' had worked in Thuringia.[42] People cared about their gardens and their streets, a concern reinforced by the scarcity of fruit and vegetables in the shops. 'Join in!' succeeded where it did through a particular combination of scarcity, mutual reliance and local tradition.

Even though Dabel continued to be considered a model village of the socialist heimat during the 1970s and the 1980s, it would be misleading to characterize this period as a mere continuation of what had been developed before. In the 1970s, village life (and with it, village culture) changed significantly owing to the creation of barracks for the National People's Army (NVA) in 1972. Built on the edge of the village, these barracks and the new flats for officers became known as 'Dabel 2', and housed a population the size of Dabel again, of whom only a minority came from Mecklenburg.

The arrival of the soldiers proved a mixed blessing for Dabel. Villagers benefited from a brand new school building as well as a meeting hall. Moreover, some Dabelers found employment at the base, sparing them a commute to Sternberg or even further afield. Nonetheless the effective doubling of the town's population created huge cultural, economic and social tensions. These became manifest, for instance, through the military convoys that chose to roar through the main street every second day or so (instead of taking the bypass round the village), adding to pollution and damaging the road surface and roadside pavements constructed through 'Join in!' In 1988, a leak from Dabel 2 spilled oil into the local lake, making the leisure area around it (also constructed through 'Join in!') unusable for the villagers.[43]

The military convoys' passage through the village was only the most glaring reminder of the power differential between the original Dabelers and the people of Dabel 2, which villagers just referred to as 'up there'. When I asked about Dabel 2 in 2005, the subject still evoked strong emotions. According to Uwe Schliehe:

These were two separate worlds, we did not want anything to do with them, or they with us. They were a step above us, they looked down on us. This starts with the

---

war, hatten die Leute den Eindruck, also der Pastor versteht auch was vom Garten ... Auf dem Lande, muß man eben sehen, weil man eben selbst kaum was kaufen konnte, Obst und Gemüse selbst war auf dem Lande im Grunde nichts da.' Interview with Hansherbert Lange, 23 August 2005.

[42] See Chapter 5.

[43] Interview with Hansherbert Lange, 23 August 2005. LHA Schwerin, Nationale Front Schwerin 342: 'Ergebnisse, Erfahrungen und Probleme bei der Führung der Gemeinschaftsaktion „Gepflegte Landschaft – gepflegte Umwelt" (Sternberg, den 26.2.1988)'; 'Nationale Front Kreis Sternberg: Protokoll über die Sekretariatssitzung am 16.3.88'.

workers' bus that went to Sternberg [and beyond to Schwerin], THEY all had seats whereas OUR WOMEN had to stand.

Rosemarie Bartelt, the village librarian who also attended this interview, concurred, as she had been reliant on this bus:

They had to pay 70 Pfennigs, whereas we who boarded the bus in the village, had to pay 80. And they had the seats – do you think that we ever got a seat? Whether you were pregnant or whatever, the LADIES and GENTLEMEN, they just sat there.[44]

In relation to the soldiers, Dabelers found themselves relegated to second-class status. Coveted new flats were being built 'up there', but these were out of reach for any Dabeler who was not a member of the party. The school building, too, may have been brand new, but the fact that it had been constructed 'up there', forcing all the children to move from the centre of the village to the vicinity of the barracks, was a further affront felt by Dabelers and their children at an everyday level.[45]

From the beginning, Horst Roggenbau was keen to include the army in the Cultural League's activities. He created a Cultural League branch in the barracks which was joined by some thirty to forty officers and their wives, and invited a representative of the army group to attend meetings of the Cultural League's planning committee.[46] In return, the army group allowed the Cultural League to use the army's facilities for cultural events.[47] Thereafter the more formal and political of these events, such as award ceremonies and discussion evenings, often took place 'up there'.

The army's involvement in village culture was not particularly popular. Its band was welcome to play at village events, but if officers participated in the celebrations, they were not welcome. 'As soon as the officers got among

[44] U.S.: Das waren zwei getrennte Welten, wir wollten mit denen nichts zu tun haben, und die nicht mit uns. Die waren eine Stufe höher, die guckten auf uns herunter. Das geht [los] schon wenn morgens der Arbeiterbus nach Sternberg fuhr ... DIE hatten allen ihren Sitzplatz während UNSERE FRAUEN stehen mußten.
    R.B.: Die mußten 70 Pfennig bezahlen, wir die im Dorf zugestiegen sind mußten 80 bezahlen ... und da ging's schon los. So, DIE hatten Sitzplätze, glauben Sie, daß wir mal EINEN Sitzplatz bekamen? Ob man schwanger war oder was, die DAMEN und HERREN die saßen da.
    The emphases reflect a particular intonation of the interviewees which made palpable their emotional agitation. Interview with Uwe Schliehe and Rosemarie Bartelt, 30 August 2005.
[45] Rosemarie Bartelt: 'auch wenn bei uns die Wohnungsknappheit war, wir durften ja da oben auch keine Wohnung in Anspruch nehmen. Nur Genossen oder [Offiziere] – aber n'einfacher Arbeiter [der nicht]. Und die Schule nachher sollte ja eigentlich hier ... gebaut werden, aber dann mußten ja die Kinder von den Offizieren ins Dorf fahren, wie sollte DAS wohl gehen? UNSERE mußten entweder zu Fuß oder mit dem Fahrrad ... aber DIE, nein blos nicht.' Ibid.
[46] HStD Kulturbund, Protokollbuch: 'Leitungssitzung 5 November 1974'.
[47] HStD Material für Dorfchronik: letter from Roggenbau to Karl-Heinz Schulmeister: 'Lieber Bundesfreund Schulmeister (Dabel, den 11.1.1975)'.

us, it was over for us', Uwe Schliehe explained. 'This was true of carnival, it was true of everything. They thought up there that they were a better class of people.'[48] Interestingly, this rejection did not arise (at least primarily) from disapproval of the political commitment these officers had made. Rather they were rejected as outsiders who had no real interest in integrating into local culture and customs. The local, private transcript never included those who had moved into Dabel 2.

With the army, Roggenbau now had a good partner (and a reliable audience) for the Cultural League's most overtly political events.[49] The army's co-operation in this respect became particularly important because Roggenbau's own group of pupils, the recitation group, was disbanded in 1976. This meant that the role of politics in village culture declined, something that is also evident in the programmes of the Dabel Village Festival. In 1976, Cultural League members added to the programme an evening of *Snacks*, or storytelling in Low German. The following year, another tradition was invented after Wolfgang Cords and his contemporary, Fritz Döscher, teamed up with another friend to form the 'Miller's Lads' ('Die Müllerburschen'). This folklore group became the central feature of the 'Dance on the Storage Floor' ('Tanz auf dem Sackboden'), an event thought up by Döscher and Cords. Döscher was the son of the local miller who had managed to retain his economic independence; for these dances, the Lads cleared the windmill's storage floor of sacks of flour to make space for the folklore evening.

The 'Dance on the Storage Floor' became the highlight of the village festival, with additional evenings attracting visitors from the entire region throughout the year. So popular did this event become that it attracted the attention of the district radio station, Radio Schwerin. From January 1983, the station broadcast a fortnightly programme of Low German storytelling and folk music from the windmill in a show entitled the 'Plappermoel' (the 'chatting mill').[50] The show remained extremely popular and presented a successful alternative to the West German radio show 'Talk in Low German' (*Talk op Platt*) on the regional North German Broadcasting Station (NDR). Once again, Dabel had become a showcase for the socialist

---

[48] 'Ja, da kam ja das nachher auch schon so, wenn die Offiziere dazwischen waren, denn war ja für uns schon Schluß. Da haben sich viele zurückgezogen. Das war beim Karneval so, das war bei allem so. Die haben sich da oben gerechnet als Menschen 1. Klasse.' Interview with Uwe Schliehe, 30 August 2005.

[49] Nevertheless, a small number of political events continued to be held in the village. HStD Plakate: 'Der Kulturbund Ortsgruppe Dabel lädt ein anläßlich des 40. Jahrestages der Befreiung durch die Sowjetarmee … in die Dorfgaststätte „Blauer Bock"' (3 May 1985).

[50] *725 Jahre Dabel*, pp. 33–4.

21. 'Snacks ut de Plappermoel' (Stories from the chatting windmill). A two-page spread in the GDR's most widely distributed illustrated journal, the television and radio guide *FF-Dabei*. Talking to officials from Radio Schwerin are Horst Roggenbau (second from left) and Fritz Döscher (third from left) outside Dabel's windmill. *FF Dabei* 26 (1983), 4.

heimat in Mecklenburg, the GDR and beyond (Figures 21, 22).[51] Whereas in the 1960s the village appeared to be an ideal-type reflection of the socialist heimat ideal of the Ulbricht era, by the mid-1970s it had come to represent the regional heritage and folkloristic customs so prized under Honecker's leadership.

Even if the transformation of village culture appeared to be a perfect reflection of the ideological transformations of the party at the GDR level, this does not mean that this process occurred seamlessly, without friction. In 1977, Roggenbau resigned the leadership of the Cultural League for health reasons, and was succeeded by Döscher. Roggenbau also exerted

[51] Anita Karau, 'Snacks ut de Plappermoel', *FF Dabei* 26 (1983), 4–5. Evidently the 'Plappermoel' continued to be associated with Dabel and its windmill even after the first fifty programmes, when the show moved to larger and more convenient broadcasting facilities in Schwerin: *FF Dabei* 6, 'Rund um die „Plappermoel"' (1986), 46. (This article introduced a TV show about the 'Plappermoel' in Dabel, broadcast on 4 February 1986, at 8 p.m. on DDR I.)

22. 'Snacks ut de Plappermoel'. Playing next to the musical editor of Radio Schwerin are the Miller's Lads (Dieter Krüger, Heinz-Georg Selke and Wolfgang Cords), with Dabel's windmill in the background. *FF Dabei* 26 (1983), 5.

less cultural influence through the school, which he left in 1980 in order to take up a position as full-time functionary for the Cultural League in Sternberg county. Roggenbau did not take his declining influence lightly. He was appalled by the prominence of the Miller's Lads' activities, and he felt that Döscher failed to give sufficient encouragement to the traditional activities of the Cultural League. This was reinforced by a personal dislike of Döscher. According to one villager, both men wanted to be 'number one' in the village.[52] In 1983 Döscher was ousted by a group inside the Cultural League, with Roggenbau re-assuming the leadership of the local organization.[53]

Behind the façade of energy and ideological conformity, the 1970s in Dabel were characterized by substantial conflict. The arrival of the army and the creation of Dabel 2 transformed most aspects of the villagers' life, as outsiders to their community had suddenly settled in their midst. Moreover, the cultural transformations in particular were underwritten by

[52] Interview with Elsa Schmidt, 15 November 2007.
[53] BStU, MfS, BV Schwerin, AIM 143/90, ff. 45–7: AIM 'Kämpfer', 15 November 1983.

generation change, as a younger generation with less interest in constructing socialism through culture assumed responsibility in the Cultural League. The cultural innovations of this period, however, were there to stay. Even after Roggenbau had regained leadership, he could not turn back the clock, as the 'Miller's Lads' and new traditions such as the 'Beach Festival' show. For what emerged in the 1970s was the reinvention of a folk culture that had in fact always existed. The activities of Döscher and Cords may not have found the approval of the Cultural League's 'old guard', but they clearly spoke to many villagers far beyond the confines of the Cultural League.

Dabel shows how, at the local level, individuals appropriated ideological shifts in the GDR in order to increase their own freedom of manoeuvre. The Miller's Lads could point to the 'heritage' debate to underline the political value of their passions, and use the new political currents of the Honecker era to serve their own interests. This also underlines why the 'heritage' concept became so popular: it allowed villages and towns to return to traditions that were still rooted deep within the community.

In 1983, Hansherbert Lange arrived in the village as the new young Protestant pastor. His predecessor had lived in an outlying village and had been relatively absent from village life. The Church had remained relatively significant, however, to one section of the village's population, the new citizens. Five of the Dabelers I spoke to agreed that the tensions between 'Mecklenburgers' and new citizens had been significant after the war, but diminished over time. Compared to the divisive impact of the army as the new, privileged 'outsiders', the division between expellees and Mecklenburgers receded into the background, at least for Mecklenburgers. And yet tension between expellees and natives remained to some degree.[54] The church became an important marker of difference, because a disproportionate number of active churchgoers were Protestant expellees from Eastern Prussia and Silesia. For these groups, the Church was part of their heimat in a way that it never was for 'Mecklenburgers'. Indeed, Hansherbert Lange remembered how in many pastoral conversations with new citizens a sense of being 'different' had persisted into the 1980s:

Considerably more of these people went to church than the Mecklenburgers, because actually for them this was still a link to the heimat ... so I had a number who came from East Prussia, Silesia etc., disproportionately more than

---

[54] The major division was not between Dabelers and expellees, but between Mecklenburgers and expellees: Mecklenburgers like Roggenbau were integrated quickly, not least through the language. They also came to Dabel under conditions that were very different from those of the expellees: either through marriage, or because a relative lived there, or because they were given a job there.

Mecklenburgers. That could not be got over. You didn't notice this in their clothing or that sort of thing … I noticed this once when I started [my new job], I organized a service in Low German, just to do something different. And it dawned on me that I would only do this once, and never again, because many of them simply did not know what to do with it.[55]

Because of the significance of new citizens to the Dabel church as late as the 1980s, Low German never became its language. Moreover, whereas new citizens rarely held leading positions inside the Cultural League, they occupied key positions in the church. While overt tensions between villagers undoubtedly receded over time, differences between new citizens and 'Mecklenburgers' remained.

Lange brought a new dimension to village culture by initiating new traditions related to the church. Following a donation of handbells from the United States, Lange was able to create a handbell-ringers' society in 1987. In 1988, the group performed throughout the region and was even filmed for television. The bell-ringers' society was one example of the international dimension Lange brought to the village. It relied mostly on American and English musical arrangements, and kept in close contact with its American sponsors. Lange encouraged children to become penfriends of children in the US, the Netherlands or other countries. In fact, the church developed a cultural programme of its own, which included, apart from bible classes, guitar, flute and operetta groups, while a cellar was converted for the village's young people to 'hang out' in. Lange also instituted new village traditions, including a St Martin's procession on 11 November (St Martin's Day), when, after the service, around 100–150 parents and their children would take part in a procession from the church down to the lake, with the children holding lanterns.

Four years after Lange's arrival, one villager, 'Elvira', noted that

one somehow has the impression that in Dabel a lot, if not everything, is somehow geared towards the church. You don't hear anything about culture, the Free German Youth or the Cultural League. Only the well-known individuals … who are in the 'Miller's Lads' are active. If something is happening in the village, then [it's] always in the church.

---

[55] 'wesentlich mehr sind von diesen Leuten in die Kirche gekommen als die Mecklenburger, denn das war für sie im Grunde ja noch ein Stück Verbindung zur Heimat … da habe ich eben eine ganze Reihe gehabt die aus Ostpreußen, Schlesien usw. kamen, prozentual wesentlich mehr als Mecklenburger … Das war auch nicht rauszukriegen. Man hat's nicht gesehen an der Kleidung oder so … Ich habe das einmal gemerkt als ich anfing, mach ich einen plattdeutschen Gottesdienst, mal um was anderes zu machen. Und dann hab ich gemerkt: das machst du bloß einmal, und nie wieder, weil eben sehr viele damit gar nichts anfangen konnten.' Interview with Hansherbert Lange, 23 August 2005.

This confirms that during the 1980s, after Roggenbau had reasserted his leadership, the Cultural League's traditional activities received relatively little attention outside its own membership. Culturally, the 'Miller's Lads' continued to be in great popular demand, with the church also rising to cultural prominence. Elvira's remarks also point to a further significant dimension in Dabel village life, the state security services (Stasi): 'Elvira' was a Stasi informant from the village.[56]

The involvement of the Stasi was no secret to Lange. He had frequent encounters with Stasi officers, not least in relation to the St Martin's procession. Lange remembers how they came into the church to witness the opening service; he also knew that his procession outside Church land was closely watched. One year, the authorities threatened him with imprisonment if he persisted with it. Lange responded by staying on Church ground where, in accordance with the 1978 Church–State Agreement, the state could not actively intervene. The service was accompanied by frequent ringing of the handbells. For the ensuing procession, the congregation walked three times around the church and the cemetery, to the incessant ringing of the church bells. 'This', concluded Lange, 'was surely the loudest and most striking St. Martin's service that I ever conducted.' Never again did the state try to stop the procession to the lake.[57]

The Stasi exerted pressure in other ways. When Lange was visited by two pastors from the USA, figures in long, dark coats stood on the other side of the street and constantly watched the house. Such types of surveillance would, of course, be noticed not just by Lange; word would spread around the village, too. Direct surveillance by the state security services was not confined to Lange. Rosemarie Bartelt [R.B.], the village librarian, remembers being asked to get into a car that had pulled up beside her while she was walking through the village:

'They collected me with the pram, with the baby, Roland, and Frank and Peter [her other children], they picked me up from the street.' I [J.P.] asked: 'Why?'
R.B.: Well, why, why, what a stupid question! So that I could be interrogated.

---

[56] BStU, MfS, BV Schwerin, AOP 397/90: 'IM-Kand. „Elvira"', 30 September 1987.
[57] 'Ich mußte ja dann irgendwann immer wieder zum Rapport antreten, und dann hat man mir gedroht und mich belehrt … bis dahin, daß sie mir einmal irgendwann so mordmäßig gedroht haben, so ungefähr wenn ich das [den Umzug] jetzt mach, so ungefähr, dann werde ich gleich verhaftet. Und dann hab ich gesagt, na gut, dann bleib ich auf kirchlichem Gelände … [Während des Gottesdienstes] haben immer die Handglocken geläutet … Wir sind [anschließend] im Kreis mindestens dreimal nicht nur um die Kirche sondern um den Friedhof so herum, und das war sicher der lauteste auffälligste Laternengottesdienst den ich je gemacht hab.' Interview with Hansherbert Lange, 23 August 2005.

Uwe Schliehe (U.S.): Imagine, I was the postman. So the Stasi thought that I would know everything. How often they picked ME up for an interrogation I cannot even tell you. My wife can confirm this. How often, how often. 'YOU MUST KNOW SOMETHING, YOU GO INTO EVERY HOUSE.' ... Yes, that's how they started. That I can tell you.

[R.B.]: And yet these were good times.

U.S.: Yes, because we didn't know about it. I mean, we certainly did know [i.e. about the Stasi interrogations], but that one person was induced to spy on another, THAT we did not know.[58]

The state security services were a fact of everyday life, and in their recollections Dabelers acknowledged that they knew this at the time. Schliehe and Bartelt remembered the Stasi as something from 'outside', something that had to be faced from time to time, but that was imposed on the village community from elsewhere. Since the Stasi was seen as alien to village life and community, it was inconceivable that the saboteurs should have been in their midst, that one of them could bring this outside intervention and this level of insecurity upon his or her own community.

In a village where there were fluid boundaries between the public and private spheres, it was not a problem if someone was a member of the SED. Horst Roggenbau was a frequent dinner guest in the Schliehe household, even though Schliehe's daughter was discriminated against in Roggenbau's school because she had been confirmed in church (Schliehe himself was a member of the NDPD). But at village level such political differences could recede into the background. Individuals learned to live together, and so it was possible for the two passionate Low German speakers, postman Schliehe and Roggenbau the philatelist, to be friends despite Roggenbau's political commitment. In other words, for as long as Roggenbau subscribed to the private transcript of the local community, he could still be part of the village community. By contrast, the Stasi was obfuscated and could not be dealt with within the community. By definition, there could be no

---

[58] R.B.: Die haben mit dem Kinderwagen, und mit dem Kleinkind, mit Roland, und Frank und Peter [waren auch noch da], da haben die mich von der Straße geholt.

J.P.: Warum?

R.B.: Ja, warum, warum? Die Schule ist abgebrannt! Na, zum Verhör.

U.S.: Was glauben Sie wohl, ich war Briefträger! Da hat man von Seiten der Stasi gedacht, der weiß alles. Wie oft ICH weggeholt wurde zum Verhör, das kann ich ihnen gar nicht sagen. Meine Frau kann das bestätigen. Wie oft, wie oft. „SIE MÜSSEN DAS WISSEN, SIE KOMMEN IN JEDES HAUS". Die Leute erzählen Ihnen alles. Ja, so ging das los. Ja, das kann ich Ihnen sagen.

R.B.: Und trotzdem war die Zeit schön.

U.S.: Ja, weil wir dass nicht gewußt haben. Ich meine das haben wir wohl gewußt, aber das einer auf den anderen angesetzt war, DAS haben wir nicht gewußt.

Interview with Rosemarie Bartelt und Uwe Schliehe, 30 August 2005.

transcript relating to the Stasi. It was imposed from the outside and remained impenetrable, partially hidden from the view of those who were spied on. Like the army in Dabel 2, the Stasi was seen as an outside force that was irreconcilable with the village community.

Yet, is it really believable that Schliehe could have been unaware that unofficial informers might have existed inside the village? Other villagers recollected their response very differently. When I asked Mr and Mrs Teschner if they suspected that unofficial informants were spying on them, they said:

We suspected that some of them did, and in the end some of our best friends did spy on us. That's your 'village community' for you. For this reason we never went to village events. We closed in upon ourselves and our closest family, and when we celebrated we sat down out there in the garden where nobody could hear us, since here in the house they could plant listening devices.[59]

The Teschners were not the only ones keeping their guard. Elsa Schmidt remembers that a West German relative in Frankfurt (am Main) once informed her that all the letters she had received from her had been opened. Schmidt did not take an overly active part in village life, though she said this was because she lived too far away from the centre, and she did not attribute the interference directly to the Stasi.[60] Still, both examples indicate a range of responses to the possibility of Stasi surveillance. What they share is a tacit acknowledgement that if one embraced the possibility of Stasi surveillance (without being part of it oneself), it was difficult to be involved in local culture. Covert Stasi activity was clearly incompatible with the working of a village community that relied on shared understandings of trust, honour and openness.

OBFUSCATED AND HIDDEN TRANSCRIPTS

The change of attitude by Rosemarie Bartelt and Uwe Schliehe from allowing me an insight into their feelings about the Stasi to assuring me that life was good all the same suggests that I was touching upon private, hidden meanings that were not necessarily meant for an outsider. Indeed, the Stasi is etched deep onto village memory, though it was only after years of research and interviewing, once I could show that I knew about the Stasi's history in the village and could ask direct questions, that villagers spoke

---

[59] Interview with Mr and Mrs Teschner, 15 November 2007.
[60] Interview with Elsa Schmidt (name has been changed), 15 November 2007.

about this issue at all.[61] The meanings of the Stasi are still hidden today, and what follows represents a highly imperfect attempt by an outsider to uncover them as well as possible.

The files of the State Security Services reveal that during the 1960s, Dabel was not only a model of cultural activity; it was also a place of deep concern to the party and its 'sword and shield', the Stasi. Between 1953 and 1968, twenty-eight acts of sabotage and anti-state propaganda had been committed within and around the village. At the 1954 elections an election poster had been written over with the slogan 'We want free elections.' On 31 March 1957, Dabelers could see four new slogans painted on boards in the middle of the village (Map 2), including the phrase 'Any donkey can govern with bayonets' (Bebel). In the night of 29/30 November 1957 four slogans were painted across propaganda boards, including phrases like 'Freedom is always just the freedom of those who think differently' (Rosa Luxemburg), 'The GDR is a political prison', and 'Unity through free and secret elections: fight for it!'[62] The slogans had not been painted just anywhere – they were found, once again, on boards put up in the village centre, a few metres away from the mayor's office and the school (Figure 23; Map 2).[63] Here they would be seen by most villagers, and no spot could be more provocative to functionaries – until the culprits came up with an even better idea. In the night of 24/25 April 1958, a long slogan to protest against the stationing of Soviet nuclear missiles on Rügen Island was written, in tar, right across the wall of the local policeman's house (Figure 24; Map 2). Further slogans were painted on each of the other walls, and the phone line was disconnected. The daubs on the policeman's house near the village centre were a sensation for villagers as well as the Stasi, albeit in different ways.

All the slogans were in the same handwriting. They were written by someone of good education who knew how to cover his tracks. Since all the slogans were written in such prominent locations, at least one person must have stood guard.[64] Even so, witnesses must have seen the culprits. As the

---

[61] To put it another way, the Stasi was not mentioned, or was mentioned only in very superficial ways, in the interviews I conducted in the first years of my research. Only through a throwaway line by one of the interviewees, about a villager committing suicide after being imprisoned for arson on false charges, and through references in my first sightings of relevant Stasi files, did I become aware of this issue. Further enquiries to the Federal Stasi Archives in Schwerin revealed a range of documents which then allowed me to raise specific questions with the villagers I interviewed towards the very end of my research.

[62] BStU, MfS, BV Schwerin, AOP 654/70, ff. 11–17: 'Eröffnungsbericht zum Operativ-Vorgang „Todfeinde"', 20 November 1967.

[63] Ibid., f. 13.   [64] Ibid., ff. 16–17.

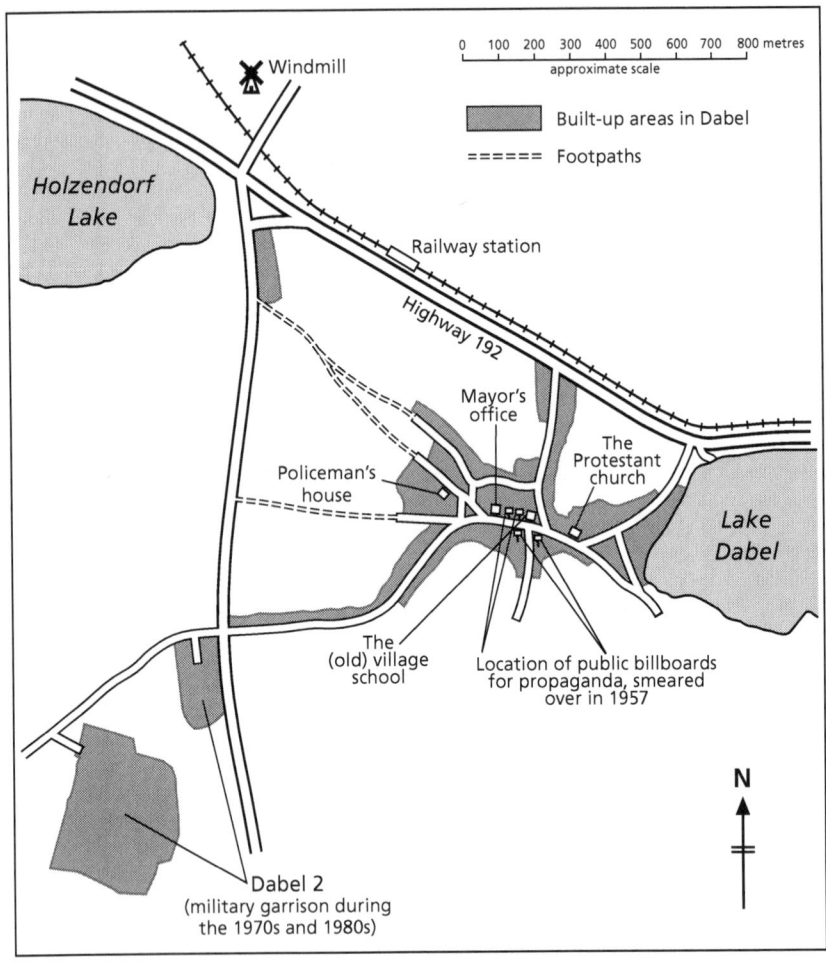

0   100 200 300 400 500 600 700 800 metres
approximate scale

Built-up areas in Dabel

====== Footpaths

Windmill

Holzendorf
Lake

Railway station

Highway 192

Mayor's
office

The
Protestant
church

Policeman's
house

Lake
Dabel

The
(old) village
school

Location of public billboards
for propaganda, smeared
over in 1957

N

Dabel 2
(military garrison during
the 1970s and 1980s)

2. Dabel

village painter noted, it would have been impossible for an ordinary person to paint the slogans at night without a light, and painting four slogans together would have taken at least two hours, not counting interruptions when passers-by approached.[65] In consequence, the Stasi was never concerned about finding the culprits through the evidence alone: it was convinced that more than one villager knew about these deeds and who the

[65] BStU, MfS, BV Schwerin, AIM 1856/63, vol. 2: GI „Paul Racker", Sternberg, den 4.4.1957. 'Bericht'.

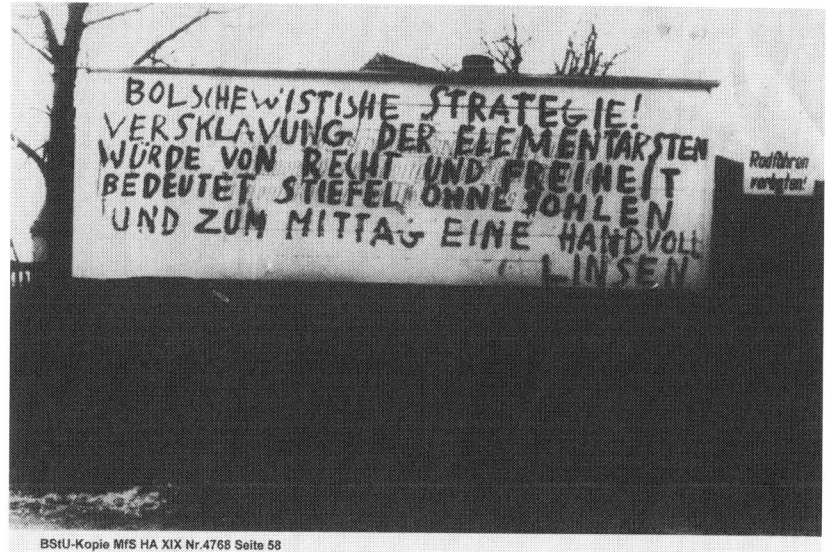

BStU-Kopie MfS HA XIX Nr.4768 Seite 58

23. 'Bolschewistische Strategie. Versklavung der elementarsten Würde von Recht und Freiheit bedeutet Stiefel ohne Sohlen und zum Mittag eine Handvoll Linsen.' (Bolshevist strategy: enslavement of the most fundamental dignity of justice and freedom means boots without soles and a handful of lentils for lunch.) Slogan painted on a billboard opposite the school, in the village centre. The original slogan was painted over with white paint, and once that had dried the new slogan was painted on in black. 28–29 November 1957. MfS HA XIX No. 4768, p. 58.

culprit was, and so finding out about village rumours, the 'hidden' transcripts of villagers, was critical.

On top of these acts of propaganda, sabotage caused substantial damage to the local economy. In 1958 a goods train was derailed by sabotaging the local rails. A number of collectivized companies were damaged by arson attacks. Most significant in village memory were two attacks committed on 2 and 16 November 1967 respectively, when first a giant haystack and then the wooden barracks housing parts of the school burnt down.[66]

The Stasi left no stone unturned to get to the bottom of these attacks, even setting up, at one time, a permanent covert office in Dabel – a strategy normally reserved for operations abroad, at the GDR's embassies.[67] Every

[66] BStU, MfS, BV Schwerin, AOP 080/77: 'Operativer Maßnahmeplan zur Aufklärung der Staatsverbrechen im Kreisgebiet Sternberg', 20 November 1967.
[67] I am grateful to Jens Gieseke for this information.

24. 'Unsere Mailosung: Wir Dabeler Arbeiter kämpfen gegen die geheimen Atomraketen-Abschusszentren der russ. DDR auf [*sic*] Insel Rügen' (Our May resolution: we workers of Dabel fight against the secret nuclear launch centres of the Russian GDR on Rügen Island). One of a number of slogans daubed in tar on the house of Dabel's policeman in the night of 24/25 April 1958. MfS HA xix No. 4768, p. 49.

clue to a possible culprit, however tentative, was followed up. When a villager reported to the Stasi that he had heard the teacher, Marten, say with an ironic grin that nobody in the village would dare to commit such acts, and that the culprit had to be an outsider, this was sufficient for the Stasi to take very seriously the suspicion that Marten himself could be responsible. He was educated, a handwriting sample had been taken which did not rule out the possibility that he had written the slogan, and shortly after he had taught about Schiller's *Wilhelm Tell*, villagers woke up to find Tell's words written on a board: 'Be united, united, united!' Another person under constant suspicion was the village painter, who by the early 1960s could no longer stand the pressure and moved out of the village. This did not put him out of the Stasi's reach. The organization continued to collect evidence against him, and enlisted a friend and former prisoner to call round and elicit indiscretions that might incriminate him. The two villagers serve as good examples of how the Stasi responded to every rumour, every lead and every person who fitted its broad profile of the culprits.

No conclusive evidence was found against the two suspects or anybody else. In the course of the investigations, however, a number of villagers were imprisoned for acts that came to light in the course of the investigation. In 1958, seven of them were sentenced to an average of three years in prison for remarks made against the socialist order, the possession of Western literature and the singing of two 'militarist' songs in the village pub. The Stasi was fully aware that it had not found the culprits; this only made it all the more important to demonstrate openly that power remained within the party. Given the party's frustrations, 'varnishing' its power was no longer enough in a village like Dabel.

In the 1950s and 1960s the village was under special observation by the Stasi, and no villager was exempt from the suspicion that they might be hostile to the socialist order. Villagers still have a remarkably clear memory of the attacks, and the response of the Stasi. Elsa Schmidt recalled:

Yes, it was terrible, it was awful. So, a large haystack burned down; then a wooden hut used by the school burned down. Imagine how active the Stasi was here! Really, whenever we saw these black limousines, which you could not see into, drive past we were fed up. And you know, they got hold of people and interrogated them, cross-examined them. They got all the men, also many women.[68]

Mr (H.T.) and Mrs (I.T.) Teschner had left Dabel for the West in 1953, but returned when they were offered the chance to inherit their aunt's farm in 1954. Since they had left the GDR before, they were regarded with great suspicion by the Stasi. When I mentioned the arson attacks (without even getting to the question), the Teschners interjected:

H.T.: Do you know about the fire in the Reichstag [in 1933]? That's how it was here. The real culprits were not the ones they caught, they did it all themselves. We were interrogated by the Stasi, hundreds of times … The railway lines had been cut through. This was in 1953 or 1955. Nobody even had a saw that could cut through iron in those days … Our brother-in-law, he worked on the railways, he was imprisoned for three and a half years for this.

I.T.: A hundred metres away from us was a large haystack, which was burned down. Someone was locked up for this. People were just locked up indiscriminately.

---

[68] Interview with Elsa Schmidt, 15 November 2007.

H.T.: The school burned down, we were really lucky then [we had an alibi] …
we were celebrating [nearby], and that was the night it was burned down.
I.T.: Yes, so it was our turn again.
H.T.: Just interrogations, again and again.[69]

What is remarkable is not just the accuracy with which acts of sabotage
were remembered.[70] The recollections are also consistent in the impression
they give of the brute power of the state: individuals remembered black
limousines which one could not see into, endless indiscriminate interrogations which affected almost everyone in the village, and arbitrary arrests. It
did not take much for the villagers to believe that the state was responsible
for these acts, that it was out to penalize them individually and collectively
for reasons they could not quite fathom. For instance, the tar daubs on the
policeman's house were a particularly daring act of sabotage, well remembered by contemporaries. Elsa Schmidt described how the Stasi inspected
every ladder in the village for traces of tar, which it duly found on a number
of them since people worked with tar for all sorts of reasons.[71] What was
considered by the Stasi to be a vital piece of evidence was, in the minds of
villagers, a mere excuse for the Stasi to violate the community and terrorize
its individuals.

There is no evidence that the Stasi was behind the attacks, or that it
fabricated evidence in order to punish villagers indiscriminately. However,
the interrogations did lead to the imprisonment of villagers who had
nothing to do with the attacks, while persistent interrogations of individuals
in a small village were unlikely to have been hidden from others. Since the
culprits were never found, villagers could never look back on these years
with a sense of closure. Moreover, the attacks present a crucial dimension to
village life in the 1950s and 1960s, and make the village's cultural 'renaissance' in the 1960s all the more remarkable.

The arrival of new teachers in the school, for instance, reflected the Stasi's
suspicion in the 1950s that most of the teachers were politically unreliable, a
suspicion that had been confirmed by an official inspection months before
the first attacks were committed, in 1953.[72] The report provided the official
basis for replacing the headmaster and some teachers, and for increasing the

---

[69] Interview with Mr and Mrs Teschner, 15 November 2007.
[70] The Teschners also recollected the daubs on the policeman's wall. Interview with Mr and Mrs
Teschner, 14 November 2007.
[71] Interview with Elsa Schmidt, 14 November 2007.
[72] HStD, Rat des Kreises Sternberg Abt. Volksbildung: 'Schulinspektor. Sternberg, den 15.1.1953:
Überprüfung der Zentralschule Dabel. Protokoll über die Auswertungskonferenz der Überprüfung
am 10.2.1953 (Dabel, den 12. Februar 1953)'.

number of teachers.[73] Thereafter there was no doubt about the teachers' political commitment. All teachers participated in ideological training events, while at election times or at harvest time, the school and its pupils campaigned publicly on behalf of state and party.[74] Since the teachers were obviously committed to raising a new socialist generation, it is no accident that they were behind the 'renaissance' of village culture in the 1960s.

More generally, if cultural life in the 1950s appeared to be relatively dormant in relation to socialist cultural institutions, this reflected a refusal to have anything to do with an organization that represented socialism. The acts of sabotage also provided a crucial context for understanding the appearance of the float in the 1961 carnival. Representing the mayor in a cage was no random choice of themes in which villagers jested about what they would like to do to their mayor; it constituted a direct protest against the random imprisonment of villagers, and aired the villagers' suspicion that the real culprits were the authorities. The functionaries' response shows that these meanings were not at all hidden from the state.

There was another consequence of Stasi activity in the 1950s and the 1960s. As Dabelers who consulted their Stasi files after 1990 found out, the Stasi tried hard to uncover the culprit(s) of the attacks by extending its network of unofficial informers. This was not always straightforward. The Stasi was often frustrated by villagers who agreed to spy on their neighbours, but either failed to do so in practice or delivered only reports that never included any incriminating material. Nonetheless, many informers did spy on their neighbours. They formed part of the socialist heimat, and were an integral part of village life. Twenty-six informants spied on Mr and Mrs Teschner. No fewer than forty-six informants, and at least ten from Dabel, spied on Hansherbert Lange in the 1980s. One of these spies was Horst Roggenbau.

Horst Roggenbau was enlisted as an unofficial informer ('Geheimer Informator', GI) in 1958, the year before he arrived at Dabel, with a special mission to influence, and inform on, his fellow teachers and provide information on individuals who had aroused the suspicion of the Stasi.[75] As he became more prominent in the village, agitating more forcefully on

---

[73] In 1951, there were seven teachers for 340 pupils, while in 1967 there were twenty-six teachers for 407 pupils. *725 Jahre Dabel*, p. 31.

[74] HStD Volkskorrespondent Roggenbau Zeitungssammlung. See the newspaper notices for 1961: 'Zur Weiterbildung', 'Schüler helfen LPG', 'Pioniere helfen der LPG', 'Dabel am Vortage der Wahlen'.

[75] BStU, MfS, BV Schwerin, AIM 479/71, vol. 1, ff. 21–2: 'Einschätzung des GI „Kämpfer"' (6 January 1960).

behalf of the party, his duties changed as he became less useful as an informant about suspicious individuals. Instead, he was charged with evaluating individuals in the village (and in this way recommending possible co-informants), assessing the mood prevalent in the village, and alerting the Stasi to cases they might take up.[76] Through his prospering local activities and his growing international philatelic contacts Roggenbau became more important for the Stasi as the 1960s went on, but towards the end of the decade he became more reluctant to co-operate. He began to avoid meetings and failed to pass on proceedings from the village that were of interest to the Stasi, so that in 1971 co-operation ceased.[77]

Roggenbau's co-operation with the Stasi was reactivated in 1983. He served again as an unofficial informant, and also provided the Stasi with rooms for conspiratorial activities: those of the Cultural League in Dabel, which Roggenbau now controlled again. They were situated in the middle of the village and could be used not just for undercover meetings, but also for observing the village centre.[78]

Horst Roggenbau's activities invite us to explore a particular, but clearly not uncommon, 'dialectic of surveillance' (Scott) that affected relations between the party and the citizens in the GDR. Roggenbau's basic motivations, in his dealings with the Stasi as in his 'open' activities within the village, appear to have been remarkably consistent: he wanted to be at the centre of things. To be sure, he believed in socialism and was passionately interested in philately, but he clearly needed to be the man in charge, a central figure in village life. This desire for influence determined the dialectical relationship between his secret and his public activities: as his importance in village life increased, his Stasi activities waned; after his cultural influence had declined considerably, he resumed his undercover activities.

In his dealings with the state and with the villagers, Roggenbau developed a multiplicity of actions and meanings which appear to be highly inconsistent unless his basic motivations are taken into account. He tried hard to use his reports to the Stasi not just to underline his own significance in village life, but also to slight those with whom he disagreed. Continuing a number of 'social dramas' by subversive means, Roggenbau complained, in 1965, that the Cultural League's representation on the village council was

---

[76] BStU, MfS, BV Schwerin, AIM 479/71, vol. 1, ff. 69–70: 'Einschätzung des GI „Kämpfer"' (20 March 1967).

[77] Ibid., ff. 111–12: 'Abschlußbericht zum IMS-Vorgang „Kämpfer"' (28 May 1971).

[78] Ibid., ff. 49–52: 'Vorschlag zur Verpflichtung einer IMK/KW' (3 January 1984).

not commensurate with its membership.[79] In 1969, he complained that villagers were too unresponsive to (his) cultural work.[80]

Roggenbau was not the only Dabeler reporting social conflict to the Stasi. In 1968, another informant wrote to the Stasi to vent her frustration about Roggenbau. She had called a meeting to finally create a village branch of the Free German Youth, but at the meeting Roggenbau had successfully torpedoed her endeavour. Roggenbau already led a youth group in the village, and rather than set up the Free German Youth there too, he demanded that his current group be promoted first. To the villagers' approval, Roggenbau asserted that the Free German Youth was interested merely in politics, whereas he was concerned not to alienate the youngsters.[81]

Roggenbau is a striking example of how we need to consider the private, social and cultural contexts of individual actors if we are to fully understand what motivated their actions. Here is a person who sought agency not against the party and state control, but through it. He informed on villagers *for* the party. But he also opposed the establishment of the Free German Youth (FDJ), *against* the party. In 1970, he dedicated cultural events to Lenin, *for* the party. But at this time he was also trying to put a stop to his personal Stasi activities, *against* the party. Roggenbau's apparently contradictory behaviour does not fit into frameworks established by social historians: it can be explained neither through a dichotomy between state and society, nor by showing how closely enmeshed they were. Rather, his behaviour must be explained by the way he related local culture, his social relationships, state and party to his own personal desires, specifically his goal to be at the centre of village life.

Roggenbau's position in the village was never uncontested. He, too, had to submit to most of the political decisions that affected the community. And, just as he informed on members of the community, others in turn spied on him. Roggenbau shows particularly clearly how individuals 'tacked' between different meanings, in a way that cannot be captured by Scott's binary opposition between the 'dominant' and the 'subordinate'. Roggenbau was both the object and the subject of power, often at the same time.

Cultural and social life was thus determined by a series of skirmishes among the villagers themselves. Arguments about who ran the Cultural

---

[79] BStU, MfS, BV Schwerin, AIM 479/71, vol. 2, f. 248 (Dabel, 29 August 1965).
[80] Ibid., vol. 3, ff. 1–3. 'Bericht über die Situation in der Gemeinde Dabel' (17 July 1969).
[81] Ibid., vol. 1, ff. 84–6. 'KP „Anneliese Klohse"' (14 February 1968).

League, the formation of the village club, or the role of the army in village culture were matters affecting many local groups, involving reflections on what kind of culture villagers wanted. In social dramas of this kind, the state was always present, even if villagers chose not to take this fact into account. In Dabel as elsewhere, the Stasi clearly offered a way to take local disputes to new, clandestine levels. If social dramas and cultural practices act as a hall of 'magic mirrors' (Turner) vis-à-vis the community, some of them reflected the state, whose influence was distorted by all other mirrors to the point that the influence of state and party could no longer be determined clearly. Whatever the crisis, someone was likely to think of the party (through the Stasi) as a 'silent' contributor to this drama and so report to it, or at least consider the possibility of being reported on.

To assert the significance of the state is not to assume that state and party were all-knowing, or in total control. Far from it. But the state did set the framework through which the heimat could be lived and celebrated. And it constituted some element in the reflexivity that informed individual and collective identifications through the locality. Even if villagers rejected the 'socialist heimat' ideal and an 'identity' with the GDR, state and party were nevertheless consistently present in the cultural practices and the social dramas of the heimat, overtly and covertly.

CONCLUSION

If ever there was a model of the socialist heimat, Dabel appears to have been it. Through village festivals, heimat-themed evenings, and participation in 'Join in!', the community reflected the changing public transcripts of the socialist heimat. While Dabel culture seemed to manifest the socialist community of people in the 1960s, in the Honecker era Dabelers spearheaded the revival of the region's Low German heritage. The Miller's Lads became regional celebrities, and were even celebrated in the national press. In fact, the emblem of the Miller's Lads and of the village, the windmill, became known throughout the GDR during the 1980s, as the image on the ten-pfennig stamp (Figure 25). When millions of letter-writers and philatelists looked at this stamp, they did not just see a windmill, they also paid, in most cases unwittingly, tribute to an ideal type of the socialist heimat.

Socialism affected cultural and social practices and meanings in significant ways. At the most obvious level, many cultural events became highly political, while Dabelers also related some of their activities to political events, such as elections, party celebrations and army days. Socialism also

25. GDR ten-pfennig stamp displaying Dabel's windmill, 1981.

had an impact on the meanings of cultural practices. Becoming a handbell-ringer or going to the St Martin's pageant was not just a cultural activity like any other. Joining in these activities exposed a person to the suspicions of the party (and the Stasi), and they signalled a wish for distance from the offerings of the Cultural League and the Free German Youth. Finally, socialism affected personal relationships and communal identifications. Roggenbau sought to reassert his cultural predominance in the village with the help of the Stasi, while the organization of the village festival and its political flavour raised acute questions about who really called the shots in this village community.

Given the prevalence of the Stasi in the 1950s and 1960s and its open (and covert) activities, how can we believe villagers who assert that they had no idea that covert Stasi informers could be in their midst? Clearly, some villagers, like the Teschners, were convinced that clandestine Stasi operations were afoot in the village, and as a result they withdrew from actively influencing village culture. Yet, given the physical and especially the emotional violence caused by the Stasi's activities in the 1950s and the 1960s, whose scars ran deep in the memories of the villagers forty years on, it is remarkable that village culture experienced such an upswing during the 1960s. Those who participated in this cultural renaissance, like Uwe Schliehe, could apparently do so only on the premise that whatever the Stasi did, it remained an outside force, one that could not impact on the essence of the village and its community. The actual and potential reach of state and party into the community made it even more significant to distinguish the villagers from outsiders, reinforcing a sense of community and localness.

The incompatibility of village community and the Stasi illustrates that communities are not just shaped through private transcripts – they are also shaped through a tacit agreement on what should remain unsaid. Just like identifications at the national level, local communities were forged through the act of forgetting, by agreeing on what should not be spoken of.[82] The act of forgetting, made manifest through silence, is closely linked to common suffering, a collective grief that unites the memory of the community.[83] Silence and forgetting were necessitated not merely by grief. The Stasi had been intimately connected with social drama deep within the village community. In Turner's typology, social drama consists of (1) a breach of regular norm-governed social relations, (2) a crisis that forces people to take sides, (3) a redressive phase, a period of stock-taking and critique of events, and (4) the reconciliation of the social groups previously at odds with each other.[84] This causality ensures the dynamism of community, as the redressive phase, in particular, provides for a period of reflexivity and liminality which allows the group to develop. For the conflicts sparked in Dabel by the attacks of the 1950s and the 1960s, there was no redressive phase, so there could be no reconciliation. Cultural events allowed one outlet for reflection and redress, but – as the 1961 carnival procession showed – this could never include one of the main parties to the drama, the party. There was no closure, even after the attacks stopped in 1968. Silence and forgetting constituted the best way for the community to go on and rebuild relationships. What Dabelers experienced at the hands of the Stasi, collectively and individually, could never be mentioned openly, but it was no less powerful for that in shaping collective experiences. In Dabel, silence became a crucial basis for the community and its memory.

Dabelers may have put the conflicts of the 1950s and the 1960s behind them; but the latency of the power of state and party was something they were never allowed to forget. The military camp, the privileges of Dabel 2 and the military convoys roaring through the village centre all served as daily reminders of the precariousness of socialist citizenship. Dabelers again tried to deal with this 'aggression' by excluding these influences from the private transcripts of the village community. Ultimately, however, they could be under no illusion that their ability to express their culture and develop their identifications relied on the goodwill of state and party.

[82] Ernest Renan, 'What is a nation?', in Geoff Eley and Ronald Grigor Suny (eds.), *Becoming National: A Reader* (New York and Oxford: Oxford University Press, 1996), pp. 42–55.
[83] Helmut Walser Smith, *The Continuities of German History. Nation, Religion, and Race across the Long Nineteenth Century* (Cambridge University Press, 2008), pp. 74–6.
[84] Turner, *Anthropology of Performance*, p. 34.

Although there was little villagers could do about the party's covert and overt assertions of power, it is clearly unhelpful to consider Dabelers as passive objects. Far from it; the renaissance of local culture from the 1960s, and the improvements achieved through the 'Join in!' competition, testify to the Dabelers' ability to shape their everyday lives and tack between different situations in order to make this possible.[85] Because it offered unusual scope for individual agency, the socialist heimat created particularly significant spaces for 'tacking' between different positions, depending on the context. Individuals could move across a range of opinions somewhere between approval and dissent, and develop a multiplicity of meanings.

By 'tacking' from one position to the next depending on the circumstances, individuals sought to make the most of their situation by exploiting 'the rules of the game', playing the system 'to their least disadvantage' (Hobsbawm).[86] What made this so difficult was that these rules were never 'normalized' or standardized.[87] Rather they changed constantly, necessitating individual flexibility and adaptability. For the rules of the game in everyday life did not relate solely to state and party, though these were never far away. As this part of the present book has shown, such rules also included individual relations with the community, and personal preferences as to how to pursue one's free time. These spheres developed in close relation to each other, but also remained clearly demarcated from each other. It was thus wise for citizens to pursue multiple strategies simultaneously. This is what made it possible for Uwe Schliehe to remember the fate of his brother and sister-in law, who had had to flee to the West because they were about to be imprisoned for hoarding some seed corn for the coming season, while engaging with the Cultural League and the National Democratic Party at the same time.[88] And it was possible for Roggenbau to be indefatigable in his pursuit of socialism, while doing everything in his power to prevent the Free German Youth from taking root in Dabel.[89] Tacking between such positions, maintaining different stances almost simultaneously depending on the context, maximized one's own

[85] On individual options for 'meandering', see Alf Lüdtke, '„Fehlgreifen in der Wahl der Mittel": Optionen im Alltag militärischen Handelns', *Mittelweg* 36 (2003), 61–75.

[86] Quoted in Scott, *Weapons*, p. xv.

[87] Fulbrook (ed.), *Power and Society in the GDR*, Introduction. Fulbrook, *The People's State*, esp. pp. 4, 236–41.

[88] Interview with Uwe Schliehe, 30 August 2005.

[89] Such 'tacking' was more common than not, even outside the two villages. Thus W.K. was able to celebrate the heimat and enjoy GDR-wide recognition with his folklore group while never forgetting that his father had died while interned at Buchenwald by the Soviets after 1945. Interview with W.K., Thuringia, 21 April 2005.

opportunities in the increasingly distinct spheres of everyday life. These spheres were distinct, but never separate.[90] Individuals learned to employ multiple registers in relation to state, party, personal desires and communal relationships. In so doing, actors found it increasingly difficult to develop any wholesale acceptance of local culture, state, party and socialism, and establish an identity between them.

Through the manifold influences which state and party exerted on cultural practices and social conflicts, the heimat served as an important forum in which current practices of domination were, in their essence, accepted as a given. Not until 1989 was the party's hegemony openly challenged, and in that situation its power, and that of the state, quickly collapsed. By that time an arsenal of alternative meanings and practices had evolved. The SED's fall from power made possible the articulation of meanings of heimat that had developed beneath the public transcript. For a brief period, between autumn 1989 and the local elections of May 1990, the power that had been exerted by the Stasi moved towards the centre of village politics to a degree that was unusual even by the standards of the day. Even at this time, however, the subject of the village's past was not directly mentioned; rather, debates revolved around a covert telecommunications station which had been discovered in the village, while the SPD and the CDU urged villagers not to elect former Stasi elites. On the surface, this was not a debate about the impact of the Stasi on individual lives, nor were the scars of the 1950s and the 1960s openly displayed. And even today, whereas villagers can talk about the arbitrariness of state power as experienced by Dabel 2, many still cannot bear to consult their own Stasi files for fear of what they might find. Two decades after the collapse of socialism, the memory of the Stasi is difficult to reconcile with notions of community. To this day, the community of Dabel and its memory are built on silence and the act of forgetting.

---

[90] On the differentiation of spheres in everyday life, see Lindenberger, 'Diktatur der Grenzen', pp. 31–6. The interrelationship between these spheres raises the question of whether the term *Grenzen* is appropriate to describe the distinction between them.

CONCLUSION

From citizens to revolutionaries

> To be living here, today, is incredible! I hardly have time to sleep. Many have a feeling of solidarity that our generation has never known. Everything is moving, taboos are being broken, energies freed which we never knew existed, and which are yet so limited ... nothing will be as it was ... Never have I seen so much boundless energy, but also so many tears shed by grown men. The people on the street, the masses, these are the experiences of my lifetime – of a whole generation.[1]

In mid-November 1989, Uwe Wieben read out these words at a citizens' gathering ('New Forum') in Boizenburg; they had originally been written to friends who had just left for West Germany. As Wieben explained, the period following Erich Honecker's resignation on 19 October, when the party's power was no longer unassailable, was unlike anything citizens had ever known, and would be unlike anything they would ever experience again. This period did not end with the fall of the Berlin Wall on 9 November 1989. It continued until the establishment of new structures, a process, launched with parliamentary elections on 18 March 1990, which ended on 3 October with German unification. The months between autumn 1989 and late spring 1990 presented a remarkable liminal moment for East Germans. Politically, socially and culturally this was a time when everything could be challenged, and anything seemed possible. In this moment of 'anti-structure' East Germans could reflect on what they were, and what they ought to be. Examining this liminal period more closely provides us with important insight into the identities East Germans had developed up to 1989, and how this affected the nature of the East German revolution.

It was not at all self-evident that an actor like Wieben, a long-time member of the NDPD, would emerge as one of the leaders of the local revolution. Following his frustration with the SED's plans to reconstruct the inner city, which culminated in his refusal to be re-elected to the

---

[1] Uwe Wieben Private Collection, open letter: 'Liebe Uta, Lieber Wolfgang!', 7 November 1989.

county council in the local elections of May 1989, Wieben focused on his own academic interests as a historian. He also directed his energies towards the organization of talks and discussion evenings hosted by the Boizenburg heimat museum, which he directed. From the late summer onwards Boizenburgers used these discussion evenings to voice their criticisms of the party with increasing openness. Wieben had provided a valued forum for the articulation of local discontent, and when in November 1989 the opposition and the local council needed a neutral meeting ground, the museum was the natural choice. Wieben first became the obvious candidate to mediate talks between the local opposition and the party, and then, from January 1990, served as Boizenburg's first post-Communist mayor.[2] As a leading heimat activist, Wieben had reinforced the public transcript of the socialist heimat for years. In 1989, he became a key figure in the local revolution.

Wieben's case was far from unusual. In Meiningen, Axel Wirth continued his opposition to the destruction of the city centre until September 1989. Through a series of last-minute petitions he was able to postpone the execution of the SED's plans by over six months, but on 19 October 1989 the first part of the old town was destroyed. Coincidentally, on that day Erich Honecker resigned, whereupon the revolution gathered momentum throughout the GDR. In Meiningen, as in towns throughout the GDR, local demands became increasingly prominent as the demonstrations continued into October. Two issues came to the fore in the citizens' protests: the environment and the condition of the old town. On 14 November, the first Monday demonstration after the fall of the Berlin Wall, Wirth spoke to thousands of Meiningers in the church and on the market square, to remind them about the old town's historical importance in German history.[3] In the following days public pressure became so strong that on 16 November Meiningen's building commissioner reluctantly agreed to suspend the planned further demolition of the old town;[4] Wirth led the campaign to make this decision permanent, and by early 1990 the Meiningen friends of the heimat had won the argument. By using the momentum of the revolution, the friends succeeded as revolutionaries where they had failed as citizens.

[2] Uwe Wieben, *Veränderung. Wende. Verantwortung* (Rostock: Neuer Hochschulschriftenverlag Ingo Koch, 1998), pp. 25–40.

[3] Horst Strohbusch, *Das Licht kam aus der Kirche: Wende in Meiningen 1989–90* (Meiningen: Verlag Börner PR, 1999), pp. 81–100. Axel Wirth Private Collection: 'Notizen Friedensgebet 14.11.1989'.

[4] Axel Wirth Private Collection: 'Forderungen der Kreisorganisation Meiningen des Kulturbundes der DDR zur Verbesserung des denkmalpflegerischen Zustandes unserer Kreisstadt' (15 November 1989). See also the local page of the 17 November 1989 issue of the *Freies Wort* (Meiningen edition).

Wieben and Wirth are just two examples of local actors whose frustrations, having previously developed within the socialist transcript of the heimat, emerged into the open once the unavoidability of existing power relations was challenged. Neither Wieben nor Wirth developed their dealings with the authorities before and during 1989 in a vacuum. The two were deeply embedded in their respective localities, were involved in the local branches of the GDR's mass organizations, and were both native to the town in which they acted. They benefited, in other words, from a local repertoire of engagement which had developed and extended tactics of stubbornness and foot-dragging within a distinctive local context. Even within their respective small communities, these two citizens were far from the only ones to act. At a time when the party's structures of authority were increasingly being contested without being replaced with new ones, other individuals took on prominent roles, propelled by the concerns they had nurtured for years. The debates and decisions that accompanied the revolution in the capital thus acquired a deeply local character, informed not only by the particular problems of the locality, but also by the experiences and frustrations which actors had encountered before 1989.

At the local level, policies could be changed immediately and perceptibly. In addition, many local issues symbolized wider frustrations. One of the first demands which even local SED leaders embraced was the return of builders and craftsmen who had been seconded to the construction of East Berlin. Evidently, after forty years the SED had still not succeeded in integrating the capital into popular notions of heimat, nor in making the privileging of Berlin palatable to the rest of the population. Moreover, in the winter of 1989–90 the main advocates of continuing with the construction of new flats were the local residents' administrations, which had previously been responsible for allocating flats to the people. For locals who had depended on these administrations for the allocation of living space,[5] they epitomized at local level the SED's power and the failures of socialist planning. This was not only a fight for the city centres, it was also a struggle against the party's arrogance of power.

If the actors and the themes of the revolution were deeply rooted in the locality, so too were some of the solutions. Between October 1989 and April 1990, communities were faced with the rapid erosion of the party's power and that of the central state. Moreover, citizens refused to accept the authority of the districts, whose administrations continued to be staffed largely by SED functionaries, even after the first free elections to the GDR

---

[5] Kopstein, *Politics*, p. 185.

parliament on 18 March 1990. Local communities relied on their own initiatives to respond to the plethora of demands and problems voiced by the citizens. In a period of flux and uncertainty, East German towns and villages began looking towards West Germany.

Through pre-existing or spontaneous twinning arrangements, East German localities looked for, and received, vital technical, practical and administrative assistance. The West German city of Marburg, for instance, supplied its twin city, Eisenach, with buses, equipment for paving streets and equipment for treating sewage. The Marburg city council also opened an advice bureau in Eisenach to provide help in practical ways: how to issue local licences, for example.[6] Individual organizations, associations and newly formed parties also quickly looked to West Germany for help.[7] Certainly the newspaper reports of the time, as well as oral and written reflections on this period, do not suggest that this was seen as West German 'imperialism': since East Germans had to 'learn' democracy at break-neck speed, West German material, technical and political support was gratefully received.[8]

Contacts between cultural groups proliferated, in part helped by official twinning arrangements, but mostly in response to individual dispositions and local circumstances. Walter Kamrodt, from the Vogtei region near Mühlhausen, described how he had been active for decades in a folklore group sponsored by the Thomas Müntzer agricultural co-operative. On 27 December 1989 his group was invited to perform at the European Youth Week in Ludwigstein Castle, in Hesse:

I agreed, but I didn't know what the European Youth Week was, I didn't know what happened at Ludwigstein, and if you now think I'm ignorant, we had forty years of the GDR, we never knew what Ludwigstein was ... This was a tremendous experience. There was a group from Belarus, one from Czechoslovakia, from the USA, from Italy. And one was from Kassel [in northern Hesse], they had a director, a dance teacher, and they performed like we did ... And we lived there for a week

---

[6] On the significance of Neu-Ulm for how Meiningers 'learned' democracy (and received important financial assistance), see Strohbusch, *Das Licht*, pp. 179–181.

[7] 'Weil so viele darauf warten: Als nächstes Gewerbegenehmigungen'; 'Noch mehr als 1000 Mal von Eisenach nach Marburg', *Oberhessische Presse* (25 January 1990), no. 2.

[8] For Meiningen see Strohbusch, *Das Licht*, pp. 179–81. Jürgen Kuhlmann, who headed the SPD in Dabel in 1990, has very bitter memories of the unification and post-unification period, but spoke in enthusiastic terms about the help he received from the SPD in Probsteierhagen. No connections had existed prior to 1989, but Probsteierhagen SPD offered their help, and Dabelers accepted – the beginning of an association that has lasted to the present day. Interview with Jürgen Kuhlmann, 14 November 2007. For the case of Eisenach, it was of more than symbolic significance that the first 'Round Table' meeting between local authorities and opposition leaders was chaired jointly by the mayors of Eisenach and Marburg.

and we bonded so tightly, and when we returned from that week the GDR was dead for us. That's perhaps a bit exaggerated, but we saw that there was life outside the GDR.[9]

Upon his return, Kamrodt was asked if his group would perform at a folklore festival in Röllshausen in northern Hesse, in the summer of 1990. This was the start of what would become an official partnership between the two communities. It is unlikely that no individual members of the folklore group had ventured into West Germany in the weeks after 9 November, so Kamrodt's suggestion that seeing other places transformed them forever should perhaps be considered as being coloured by hindsight, as he himself suggests. Nevertheless the feeling of possibility, of community with other international groups, and especially with the West Germans from neighbouring northern Hesse, should not be discounted. In that week at the festival, the two German groups recognized just how much they had in common.

The Germans' encounter through heimat did not always proceed without tensions. In Meiningen, many heimat enthusiasts left the Cultural League to join the Rhön Club, founded in 1876 but which during the German division could only exist in the West German part of the mountain range. One of those joining the Rhön Club was Alfred Erck, the long-time president of the district Cultural League. However, he encountered haughty attitudes from some club members who appeared to dismiss the Easterners' long-standing commitment to, and identification with, their heimat. Erck was so hurt by this that he left the club and redirected his energies on behalf of the heimat towards the East, towards the Thuringian Forest, despite his emotional attachment to the Rhön as his heimat.[10]

Notwithstanding such instances, it appears that at local level East–West encounters were less laden with the tensions that developed at the national level, where unification was negotiated, or in the economic sphere, where the imbalance of power between East and West Germans manifested itself equally quickly. At local level, Germany's reunification suggested itself long before the formal details of unification were agreed between the two states. For East Germans, it was natural to look to West German communities and to the federal states for practical help, and for West Germans it was natural to give it. The period 1989–90 is remarkable for the spontaneity and flexibility with which local communities supported each other. At the

[9] Interview with Walter Kamrodt, 21 April 2005. [10] Interview with Alfred Erck, 21 May 2003.

level of local culture and in the strength of local identifications, Germans in both countries still understood one another, even after forty years of division.

As this book has shown, private notions of belonging and community were reinforced by conditions of scarcity, continued distrust of the 'centre' and of Berlin, and the party's emphasis on the cultural diversity of local tradition. This provided localities with considerable strength and resourcefulness in 1989–90, while the political structures around them collapsed. In August, Holungen's potash mine had started to fill up the old river bed of the Bode and close off the valley. On 17 October 1989, the Holungen Cultural League wrote a new petition signed by 600 people; significantly, it was no longer addressed to the Head of the Council of State, but to the People's Chamber. From October to November, Holungers took to the street in regular, weekly demonstrations, but the potash mines continued to seal off the valley. On 30 November, Josef Kistner contacted the West German television channels, ARD and ZDF. Stating that they had too much material already, they referred Kistner to contacts in the GDR media.[11] The authorities caught wind of this, and to avoid potential public embarrassment, the Ministry for Mining announced the following day that the slag heap extension would be temporarily suspended while alternative solutions were being considered.

Over Christmas, a heated debate unfolded, as the directors of the mines warned that alternative solutions would threaten two hundred Holungers' jobs.[12] In search of new allies, Kistner contacted the Ministry of Environment in Lower Saxony (West Germany) in early January 1990. The Minister for the Environment, Werner Remmers, and his chief of staff, Hermann Kues, thus became involved in the mediation of the conflict.[13] This culminated in a meeting in Hanover on 13 February, attended by representatives of the mines and of the village. The management agreed to change the direction of the slag heap extension and remove the spoil that had begun to close off the valley, with the Ministry providing the expertise needed to do this. The opening to the valley was saved.[14]

---

[11] Josef Kistner Private Collection: notes from telephone conversation, 30 November 1989. Interview with Josef Kistner, 14 October 2007.

[12] Josef Kistner Private Collection: 'VEB Kalibetrieb „Südharz" Werk „Thomas Müntzer" an Arbeitskreis der Pfarrgemeinde sowie Ortsgruppe des Kulturbundes' (9 January 1990). 'Dichteprüfung', *Das Volk* (21 December 1989). 'Existenz des Dorfes bedroht?', *Eichsfelder Tageblatt* (16 December 1989).

[13] Josef Kistner Private Collection: newspaper cutting dated 11 January 1990 (*Lingener Tagespost*): 'DDR-Dorf hofft auf Remmers'. The name of the (West German) newspaper is not preserved.

[14] Josef Kistner Private Collection: 'Remmers ringt DDR-Managern Zugeständnisse ab', *Lingener Tagespost* (3 February 1990). 'Talverschluß in Holungen vom Tisch', *Harz-Kurier* (15 February 1990).

That Holungers should have turned to the Lower Saxon Ministry of Environment for help is hardly surprising. West German authorities had a certain credibility which GDR officials lacked, and since the West German part of the Eichsfeld lay in Lower Saxony, turning to the Ministry there was the obvious thing to do. Yet there was more to this than meets the eye. Both Remmers and Kues came from Lingen in the Emsland, a small region which constituted one of three Catholic enclaves in Lower Saxony, and which had in the nineteenth century formed part of the constituency of Ludwig Windthorst (1812–91), the creator of the Roman Catholic Centre Party. In Lingen, Catholicism still affected public life, not least in terms of election results, with Remmers and Kues both heavily involved in local Catholic organizations.

Remmers and Kues were able to communicate with villagers in ways that the SED never could. When Remmers came to Holungen on 1 February, the whole village was decorated with (West) German flags. Following a custom Holungers normally reserved for heimat rituals like Church festivals and carnival, children stayed home from school that morning. Remmers' visit officially began at the church, where he was welcomed to the village. He then proceeded to hold a number of meetings with miners, the management and villagers, first at the mines and then in the church hall. In the evening, Remmers was the guest of honour at a special mass in the church. As deputy chair of the committee of German Catholics, Remmers himself gave the sermon on the political responsibility of Christians. Mass was followed by a get-together with villagers in the church hall. To Holungers Remmers was not simply a politician from West Germany. He was one of them.[15] After forty years of separation, Germans still understood each other through the language of heimat.

In this book I have examined how the GDR's socialist party, the SED, attempted to gain popular appeal and consolidate power by constructing a distinctive sense of nationhood. The socialist state was founded on an ideology which most citizens did not share; its security was guaranteed by Soviet troops, which most citizens did not want. To make matters worse, its legitimacy was persistently challenged by its larger, and increasingly wealthier, neighbour, the Federal Republic of Germany. Precisely because of the

---

[15] In turn, the importance of Catholicism to the Holungers' identity was picked up by Remmers' local newspaper, the *Lingener Tagespost*, which strongly emphasized the Catholic dimensions of the visit. Josef Kistner Private Collection: 'Remmers ringt DDR-Managern Zugeständnisse ab', *Lingener Tagespost* (3 February 1990).

precariousness of the GDR's existence, the party recognized from the beginning that it could not appeal to its population on the basis of socialism alone. Constructing a distinctive 'national' identity, through which citizens could develop a sense of patriotism specifically for the GDR, was essential for the viability of the party and of its creation, the GDR.

The party defined nationhood through heimat, and in this way related socialism to popular culture. Heimat also offered a language and imagery of nationhood which the population understood. In linking heimat to socialism from the late 1940s onwards, the party could emphasize the cultural specificity of the GDR's regions even at a time when Germany's division did not yet appear to be final in the eyes of the people. Heimat endowed the GDR with an authenticity and a cultural rootedness which socialism alone could never provide.

The construction of the socialist heimat was remarkably successful in a number of ways. It provided a consistent ideological rationale for socialist transformation from the late 1950s onwards, while also offering individuals a framework within which they could pursue their cultural desires. The party's encouragement of the socialist heimat enriched the lives of millions participating in heimat festivals, going on walks signposted by heimat activists, and enjoying heimat shows on television. Through the socialist heimat the party fulfilled desires for the production and consumption of culture and recreation.

Because heimat was linked not just to nationhood, but also to socialist citizenship, especially during the Honecker era, heimat enabled citizens to realize some of their ambitions, including the creation of local museums and projects like the Rennsteig Garden in Oberhof. On a more mundane but no less important level, communities were able to improve their standard of living by taking the initiative to construct basic amenities like drainage systems and pavements. Affirming the socialist ideal of heimat allowed citizens to improve the material and cultural conditions of everyday life. In practice, this link between heimat and citizenship was often strained to the point of incredibility. Villagers eating sausages on village festivals hardly did so out of feelings of citizenship and GDR nationhood. Still, the relationship between socialism and popular culture formed a marked contrast to the early 1960s, when the party was largely at odds with popular cultural desires. Through the construct of socialist citizenship developed from the late 1960s, the party was able to relate in positive ways to the popular practices which it had encouraged.

The socialist heimat ideal helped the party secure its power, but never achieved the identity between the citizens and the state which the party so desired. For the construction of identity, the socialist heimat ideal was at once too expansive and too restricted. The socialist heimat ideal was too ambitious in that it was used in an attempt not just to construct identities, but also to overcome a vast range of shortcomings. The party attempted to legitimize the inner-German border by claiming it protected the socialist heimat, but this could scarcely reduce popular frustrations generated by that border. The party emphasized the value of each locality to the GDR, but this sharpened rather than overcame consternation at the unequal distribution of scarce resources, especially the privileging of Berlin. The SED insisted on the beauty and the cultural wealth of the socialist heimat, but this never overcame the citizens' desire for foreign travel. The heimat beautification campaigns enabled communities to alleviate some of the most glaring shortcomings of the socialist plan, but this was hardly conducive to establishing positive identifications with socialism. Finally, functionaries praised the perfect harmony between citizens and their environment, but this was belied by dying forests, polluted waters and sulphurous air. In linking heimat to some of the major strains experienced in everyday life, the party in fact rendered the ideal of the socialist heimat more alienating, and reminded citizens of socialism's shortcomings.

By providing possibly the clearest definition of heimat in German history, the party denied the socialist heimat ideal the quintessential ambiguity through which identifications could be generated. Identifications develop through liminal moments which act as a 'hall of mirrors – magic mirrors, each interpreting as well as reflecting the images beamed to it'.[16] Each of these moments prefigures the return to the structuredness of the community, but they never entail a return to the *status quo ante*. In this way, moments of liminality are essential for the dynamic construction of identifications, but they are predicated on a degree of unpredictability, of 'anti-structure' (Turner). Such unpredictability was possible at local level, but only there. At local level, cultural practices from carnival to the state-sponsored Mayday festivities provided much room for local specificities and communal bonds to be expressed, reframed in moments of liminality, and strengthened in turn. Of course, there was no shortage of GDR-wide festivals that related to socialism and the GDR. However, here no unpredictability was allowed, no liminality became possible, and no evolution could occur. Local and regional identifications evolved, whereas

---

[16] Turner, *Anthropology of Performance*, pp. 21–6; here p. 24.

the party's construction of a 'national', GDR-wide identity remained static and devoid of vibrancy.[17]

Heimat was never just about the construction of identity; ultimately, it was central to the construction of power, through the party's attempt to root itself and the GDR in popular culture, and the citizens' responses. The socialist heimat ideal is thus best understood as part of the public transcript, the open interaction between the party and its citizens, which was governed by particular norms, expectations and language. Within the public transcript of the socialist heimat, individuals and communities were able to develop their own, separate meanings of heimat. The public transcript was at once remarkably effective and singularly vulnerable. It was effective precisely because in acknowledging the existence of socialism in their everyday practices, citizens recognized that the party was there to stay, and that open contestation was pointless. Right up to the end of the GDR, most of those who were frustrated by environmental destruction in town and countryside continued to express their practices and ideas within the transcript of the socialist heimat. At the same time, the elasticity of the concept of socialist heimat enabled those willing to defy the state to push against the boundaries, challenging the party's transcript from within. How seriously the party took this challenge is attested by the vehemence with which it responded to such open contestations of its power. The actions of a few Catholic villagers, or of a tiny eco-group in Eisenach, were much more than local skirmishes. They were in fact critical, because they endangered the foundations of the public transcript – the assumption that existing power relations were there to stay, and that open challenges would be futile.

As in other socialist states in the Soviet bloc, the weakness of socialism forced the party to refer to the idea of nationhood as the central basis of its symbolic appeals during the 1970s and 1980s.[18] Although the economic circumstances of the GDR, to say the least, varied considerably from those in other socialist states, during the 1960s the SED, too, was forced to

---

[17] In the second half of the 1980s, the Zentralinstitut für Jugendforschung (ZfJ) was concerned to find a growing gap between a consistently high identification among young adults with their home town and the region, and declining levels of identification with the state. By 1988, 68 per cent identified with their home town, while 50 per cent identified unequivocally with the GDR. While these (and other ZfJ figures) support the argument presented in this book, they are not included as evidence because the figures have to be treated with extreme caution. This is not simply because 'identity' means all things to all people, but because the ZfJ asked only young people in and around Leipzig. For the ZfJ, 'representativeness' related to class and party affiliation, not to regional origin or the respondents' origin from either town or countryside. ZfJ, 'Aspekte des staatsbürgerlichen Bewußtseins älterer Schüler' (Leipzig, May 1989), ff. 16–23; here tables 15 and 16; 'Politisch-historische Einstellungen der Jugendlichen 1988' (Leipzig, December 1988), f. 16.

[18] Verdery, *National Ideology*, pp. 101–33.

recognize the failure of successive attempts to create a socialist society. The party had come to appreciate the need to construct identifications that were emotionally more effective than socialism. Heimat complemented the rational arguments of socialism with a rich arsenal of emotions, enabling the party to present its achievements and its vision in the emotive language of community and belonging.

The construction of nationhood was important not solely because of the failure of the socialist utopia. As Verdery has argued, 'contestation, not mere repetition, is the vehicle of ideology'.[19] By connecting their ideology with popular ideas of the nation, the socialist parties of Eastern Europe reached their citizens in new ways, even if they could not necessarily control the nature of that discourse. Through appeals to nationhood, the party engaged with sections of the population that socialism alone could not reach. Recognizing the insufficiency of class struggle to maintain their legitimacy, socialist parties in the GDR, as elsewhere in Eastern Europe, attempted to generate instead a distinctive, socialist sense of nationhood.

What distinguished the GDR from its Eastern neighbours was not *that* nationhood became central to the construction of identity from the 1960s, but *how* this process occurred. In a sense, the GDR was a constructivist's dream: whereas in Poland, Romania or Czechoslovakia the communist leadership had to contend with symbols and ideas of nationhood that predated communism and existed outside it, this was not inevitably the case in the GDR. Since the GDR was not related to a distinct and exclusive nation, in theory identities could be constructed from scratch. In the GDR (as in West Germany), writers reflecting on contemporary political conditions and on Germany's recent past had few reasons to embrace the nation. In addition, marred by the increasingly radical nationalism that had characterized much of Protestantism before 1945, the Church was in no position to formulate rival ideas of the nation. Institutionally and intellectually, little stood in the way of the party's invention of a new nation.

The existence of a second German state west of the Iron Curtain made it all the more necessary for the GDR leadership to construct an identity that was unique, and one which reflected its ambitions for moral and cultural renewal. Yet as early as the late 1940s the party recognized that it could not just wish popular traditions away. The SED tried, especially in the late 1950s and early 1960s, to construct a new, socialist popular culture. However,

---

[19] Ibid., p. 126.

popular culture cannot be imposed; it is only effective for as long as individuals reflect it in their practices. As the party found to its chagrin, individuals refused to participate in 'new' socialist festivals, either actively (as organizers or participants) or passively (as consumers). Even though the conditions for the construction of nationhood were unique to the GDR, socialist leaders found that, just as in other countries, the construction of nationhood could proceed only by relying on pre-existing traditions and ideas. The party came to appreciate that its most realistic option was to acknowledge the popularity of the idea of heimat, and mould the national images and connotations which heimat had already transported for at least a century into expressions of nationhood in socialist Germany. As East German leaders found, there were clear limits to the extent to which national identity could be constructed without reference to pre-existing popular concepts of community and belonging.

The elasticity that allowed heimat to become so central to definitions of German identity amidst all the economic, political and territorial transformations of the nineteenth and twentieth centuries also allowed it to be adjusted to the conditions of socialism. Indeed, the idea of heimat was arguably more central to the invention of popular 'national' traditions than in any other state in German history. Whereas previous German states had recourse to other effective symbols of unity – the monarchy, culture, the Führer, for instance – in the GDR, few alternative myths and identifications that were rooted in popular culture were available to the party. Ironically, then, in constructing a national identity, the most centralized state in German history turned out to be the most reliant on local identity and regional diversity.

The attempt to tie socialism to popular traditions and culture came at a price. As this book has shown, the elasticity of heimat allowed the development of alternative meanings, which could be communicated even within the public transcript itself. In contrast to other socialist states, rival concepts of the nation never developed in public discourse, and not simply because there were no institutions encouraging this. The notion of heimat proved sufficiently elastic to allow the development of private transcripts that were very different from the party's heimat ideals, but which could still be communicated in the language and imagery of the socialist heimat.

In the GDR, just as in other periods of German history, heimat provided a mediating framework that reconciled tradition and change. In the GDR, heimat reconciled the familiarity of village life with bustling urban conditions, untouched landscapes with new towns, as well as peaceful idyll and the martial desire to defend it. Heimat offered a frame-work for the party to accommodate the tensions of the 'socialist modern' in everyday life.[20] In turn, the idea of heimat allowed local communities to make sense of socialism, to reflect on it in social drama cultural practices and visual representations (for example, on carnival floats or in festival magazines). The politics of heimat consisted in the tension that resulted from the different, and often conflicting, ways in which individuals, communities and the state made sense of the ideological, social, economic and cultural changes around them.

This book has sought to tackle the 'ogre that awaits every cultural historian': the issues of the reception, transmission, diffusion and meanings of representation.[21] From this perspective, it can make some contributions to the scholarly debate on how heimat enabled locality and nationhood to be imagined. Local and regional identities are no less invented than national ones,[22] and in the GDR, regional identifications proved to be complex and highly individual. Whereas through language, theatre and music, citizens in Dabel and Boizenburg – to name just two places covered in this book – probably considered themselves Mecklenburgers (with the notable exception of expellees), those in Thuringia had much less of a shared Thuringian identification. For instance, Eichsfelders identified with Catholicism first and foremost, Meiningers professed their identification with the former dynasty, and many from that region felt a sense of belonging to Franconia, whose dialect they still spoke. If in 1990, the federal states that had existed between 1945 and 1952 replaced the GDR's administrative districts, this was not really because these federal identifications had persisted as such. Rather, states like Thuringia could be most easily reconciled with the local and regional identifications which citizens had developed before 1989; more easily, in any case, than the SED's districts, which cut across many of those regional identifications.

The socialist heimat defined each location's specific position in relation to the whole.[23] From Rostock's international harbour in the north to the winter sports resort at Oberhof, the less spectacular Altenburg (famous for its playing cards) and Mühlhausen (home of Thomas Müntzer), icons on 'identity maps', magazine features and television shows all reinforced the particularity of individual locations. Given the difficulty of foreign travel,

---

[20] Katherine Pence and Paul Betts, 'Introduction', in Katherine Pence and Paul Betts (eds.), *Socialist Modern. East German Everyday Culture and Politics* (Ann Arbor: University of Michigan Press, 2008), pp. 1–34.
[21] Confino, *Germany*, p. 178. [22] Kühne, 'Imagined regions'.
[23] For a contrasting view, see Confino, *Germany*, ch. 1; here p. 48.

it was politically essential to insist that the GDR heimat boasted unsurpassed regional and cultural diversity. This could not be left to the political imagination. Heimat was constructed through the specificity of place.

The precision with which the GDR heimat was constructed as the sum of its parts does not mean, however, that the officially redefined spaces of heimat translate well into individual imaginations of heimat. The popularity of the journals *Neue Berliner Illustrierte* and *FF Dabei*, in which these specific representations and iconographies were illustrated, suggests that there was a receptive audience for such images. The popularity of heimat representations on television further suggests that the party's representations of Rostock or Oberhof resonated among the population. Based on this evidence, I have argued that such 'specific' representations of heimat did create a high degree of popular awareness of individual locations, and of how these helped define the GDR. At the same time, this 'flooding' of images provided ample space for individual interpretations, since the failure to present heimat as a 'generic' national metaphor made it harder to link specific representations of heimat to the individual imagination. This reinforces Alon Confino's central observation about the representation of heimat in German history: that it has been most effective when it could act as a metaphor that allowed space for individual meanings.[24]

Creating viable sites of memory that related specifically to the GDR, like Rostock's international harbour or the skiers' paradise of Oberhof, rendered the public transcript of socialist nationhood and heimat viable. However, there is no evidence that the socialist heimat, and the nationhood it defined, ever came to define private meanings of community and belonging. Even for a Stasi informer and SED loyalist like Horst Roggenbau, it appears that his standing as part of the local community was the central factor in guiding his actions. More generally, this explains why the revolutionary period from 1989 to 1990 is striking for the absence of popular demands that related to the idea of an East German nation. Although a diverse range of motivations clearly fuelled the citizens' desire for unification, the emphatic way that individuals turned to the locality and contemplated the surrender of a distinctive GDR statehood is truly remarkable. In the forty years of the GDR's existence, the party had failed to construct a popular 'national' identity through the 'socialist heimat', the GDR.

---

[24] Confino, *Germany*, passim, esp. ch. 3.

My argument in this book about the construction of identity through heimat has provided a new perspective through which we can better understand the nature of power in the GDR. By looking at the construction of power in everyday practices, I have sought to overcome the chasm between political and cultural history that still marks much of the historiography of the GDR. This analysis has shown how cultural and political history can (and must) be considered in close relation to each other. This is particularly (though not exclusively) evident in relation to the state security services, whose role in GDR history (and memory) is still fiercely contested.[25] A fundamental argument continues to divide political historians who insist that we cannot comprehend the GDR without understanding the repressive mechanisms of the party, and those who emphasize that other categories, such as generational change or consumer experiences, were much more meaningful to citizens in their everyday lives than the presence of the Stasi. Much of this debate has been guided by historians' use of different kinds of sources, as cultural historians have rarely looked at Stasi files, while historians of state and party have been relatively uninterested in everyday life.[26]

If we seek to understand everyday life, we can neither ignore the workings of the Stasi nor privilege it above other forms of power. This book has underlined how the party's 'hard' instruments of power, such as the Stasi, were closely and inseparably linked to its 'soft' power, notably its ability to elicit compliance without recourse to formal instruments of power. Even if we allow for the possibility that individuals were untroubled by the existence of secret informers, each of the villagers I spoke to, in Holungen and in Dabel, could refer to dealings they had had with the state security services. They had been questioned, had witnessed Stasi actions in their midst, or had been asked to be unofficial informants. The party's 'hard' power provided a rigid framework within which citizens could develop their own meanings of everyday life. Villagers may have found it impossible to reconcile 'hard' instruments of power such as the Stasi with the private transcripts of village relations, and they may have done their best to ignore

---

[25] For an example of the passions aroused by this question, see the discussion following the Gary Bruce's review of Andrew I. Port's book *Conflict and Stability*, on h-german, October 2007. www.h-net.org/logsearch/?phrase=port&type=keyword&list=h-german&hitlimit=25&field=&nojg=on&smonth=00&syear=2007&emonth=11&eyear=2008&order=relevance.

[26] See Dolores L. Augustine's contribution to the debate on Port's book on 23 October 2007: h-net.msu.edu/cgi-bin/logbrowse.pl?trx=vx&list=h-german&month=0710&week=d&msg=ric35JS88 CzrSyQG83Y3nA&user=&pw= (accessed on 14 October 2008).

the Stasi's existence in their midst. But the strategy of ignoring the possibility of Stasi surveillance in their everyday lives itself represented a decision on how to deal with the latency of the Stasi's power.

The party could not convince the citizens of the unavoidability of its domination without its 'hard' instruments of power. However, as the events of 1989 showed, these instruments became ineffective once the party had lost its 'soft' power, that is, the citizens' acceptance of everyday power relations. What this book has shown for the party's construction of national identity would, by extension, also hold for other policy arenas in which the party attempted to construct identity, notably its policies of social welfare, housing, and responding to consumer desires. None of these policies succeeded in establishing a firm bond between citizens and party. Their significance did not derive from their ability to create identifications with the GDR; none of them could convince the majority of citizens of the overall superiority of socialism. They did allow citizens, by contrast, to subscribe to the public transcript of socialism. For as long as these policies were sufficiently successful to allow the vast majority of citizens to publicly acknowledge the party's proclamations of social justice, identity and moral superiority over the FRG, current power relations – and hence the domination of the party – remained unchallenged.

For all their dynamism and vibrancy, individual and local identifications were predicated on the act of forgetting, and on silence. This is not to suggest that citizens were pained by the existence of the Wall and the party's security apparatus every waking hour. Yet the importance of silence extends far beyond the case of Dabel discussed in this book. It affected V. L., from the Vogtei, whose brother died in mysterious circumstances in Buchenwald after the war, and whose death could never be mentioned before 1989. It affected expellees who participated fully in their socialist environment without ever forgetting that their 'real' heimat lay in Pomerania or Eastern Prussia. It marked almost all border communities which had been 'purged' of villagers deemed politically unreliable in 1952, a loss which villagers could never speak about until 1989. Silence also shaped every village community whose members had been expropriated by the collectivization drives of the late 1950s. None of this meant that citizens stopped engaging fully with their socialist environment; but the sheer power imbalance between the party and the citizens was a fact of life which citizens had to internalize if they wanted to play the system 'to their least disadvantage' (Hobsbawm). The violence with which the state could, and did, interfere in individual and communal lives could not be openly admitted to the community, and this applied also to the possibility of betrayal by Stasi informers. Individuals and communities could not exist without mutual understanding of what could not be said, and what needed to be forgotten.

This conclusion has important repercussions on how we can reconcile historical scholarship on the GDR with the memories of historical witnesses. As Mary Fulbrook has pointed out, many citizens do not remember the GDR in terms of repression, hardship or the peculiarity of their state; rather, they simply remember the 'normality' of the lives they lived back then.[27] In this book I have suggested that, in exploring the workings of the public transcript, we can begin to examine 'the perceptions, actions and practices of the vast majority of the population' and relate them to the conditions of dictatorship, the domination of the party.[28] In aiming to help overcome the state–society dichotomy, I share an important concern with Mary Fulbrook and others who approach the GDR through the concept of 'normalization'. Yet most attempts to recognize the memories of former GDR citizens fail to acknowledge that their memories of the 'normal' lives they experienced were predicated on the latency of power, the power of the party that was felt, that was (or could be) known, but which was not spoken about. This silence presents one of the most difficult methodological challenges for the study of the GDR, as historians need to find ways to take account of that which was felt, avoided or suppressed, but remained unarticulated.

The difficulty inherent in understanding the latency of the party's power extends to an assessment of East Germans' memories. So many years after the end of the GDR, many villagers I met still refused to access their Stasi files for fear of what they might find, and of how this knowledge might relate to their local community. If Renan is correct in asserting that identity is forged through common forgetting, this may explain why the Stasi is so difficult to reconcile with the nostalgic longing for everyday life in the GDR often described as *Ostalgie* ('Eastalgia'). East German memories of 'normality' are predicated on the practice of forgetting.

A term like 'normalization' obstructs, rather than creates, a more sophisticated understanding of how different spheres of power related to everyday life. The normalization paradigm asserts that the majority of GDR citizens were able to lead perfectly 'ordinary' lives. From the mid-1960s to the early 1980s, the 'rules of the game' of how to behave in the GDR were

---

[27] Mary Fulbrook, 'Putting the people back in: the contentious state of GDR history', *German History* 24, no. 4 (2006), 608–20; here, 610–11. Fulbrook, *People's State*, pp. 15–16.
[28] On the importance of doing this, see Fulbrook, 'Putting the people back in'; here p. 610.

internalized by the population, and 'began to appear more ordinary, more "normal".[29] Millions of citizens became involved in public activities, whereby citizens reinforced, wittingly or unwittingly, the state whose normality they accepted.[30] Unfortunately, 'normalization' takes as a given that which should be analysed. If it is the case that every 'established order tends to produce ... the naturalization of its own arbitrariness',[31] then asserting that most citizens experienced life as 'normality' accords the party an extraordinary success in establishing its authority.[32] Yet, if the vast majority of citizens accepted life as 'normal', why did the state not only maintain its security apparatus, but expand it significantly throughout the supposed period of normalization?[33] Asserting 'normality' hides, rather than does justice to, the complexity of everyday experience. To be sure, millions of citizens engaged in activities sanctioned by the party and the National Front, and mass participation in 'Join in!' and the socialist heimat more generally is a perfect case in point. But simply noting this activism as indicating a sense of 'normalcy' hardly does justice to the complex inter-action of personal desires, communal relationships, and the parameters of socialism which affected individual actions. As this book has shown, indi-vidual activities affirmed existing power relations, but they also created distance, and alienation, from the party's desire for an identity between the GDR and its citizens as one socialist community.

The party managed to sustain its power because most citizens came to accept the unavoidability of current power relations. The concept of the public transcript avoids the pitfalls of the term 'normality'. Instead, it simply asserts that in accepting the public transcript of socialism, most citizens accepted the party's power as unavoidable. There is no value judge-ment inherent in this; individuals may have welcomed this unavoidability, or they may have resented it – but by and large, they acknowledged that, for the foreseeable future, the SED's domination was there to stay.

The unavoidability of existing power relations before 1989 makes it particularly important to explore the meanings that developed beneath the veneer of socialist citizenship. This perspective makes it much easier to reconcile the apparent stability of the GDR before 1989 (especially relative to its Eastern neighbours) with the suddenness and the totality of

---

[29] Fulbrook, *People's State*, pp. 258–9, 293.   [30] Ibid., pp. 8–10.
[31] Pierre Bourdieu, *Outline of a Theory of Practice* (Cambridge University Press, 1977), p. 164.
[32] Bourdieu's description is reminiscent of the ways in which Eastern European dissidents and scholars have understood the term 'normalization'. Yurchak, *Everything*, esp. ch.2.
[33] For instance, between 1965 and 1983, the number of full-time employees of the state security services almost trebled, from 29,137 to 82,684. Gieseke, *Die hauptamtlichen Mitarbeiter*, pp. 552–7.

its collapse in 1989–90. For as long as the party appeared to be unshakeable, and existing power relations seemed unavoidable, citizens had little reason to challenge them. Yet the relative absence of open challenges does not mean that citizens were content with the conditions of socialism, that they identified with them, or that they considered them as 'normal'. Heimat represented just one sphere in which individuals developed repertoires of meanings, identifications and engagement which were very distinct from those aspired to by state and party.

Once existing power relations were challenged, and the party's power was no longer unassailable, citizens no longer had to express their meanings and desires through the socialist transcript. At the Meiningen Monday prayer meeting on 24 October 1989, a local ophthalmologist, Horst Strohbusch, spoke of the power of the party which had caused each individual to lead a 'dual existence':

Thus, there was always a great rift between our word and our being … Even in school every young person realized that they had to lead a private and a public life at one and the same time … This double existence continued at university, in apprenticeships and at work … So we took part in all the social rituals of everyday life … This dual existence has damaged our identity and undermined our loyalty as citizens of this GDR.[34]

The 'socialist heimat' formed an important, though by no means the only, aspect of the dual existence of citizens, the public transcript of identity to which they had to conform. As Strohbusch asserted, the 'dual existence' which socialism had constructed was effective for the maintenance of power, but not for the construction of identity. Once socialism collapsed, the GDR identity which the socialist heimat had defined collapsed with it. What remained were the meanings of community and locality which had evolved despite democratic centralism, and which constituted a common platform of understanding between East and West Germans.

---

[34] Strohbusch, *Das Licht*, pp. 66–7.

Bibliography

ARCHIVE SOURCES

BUNDESARCHIV-STIFTUNG DER PARTEIEN UND MASSENORGANISATIONEN DER EHEMALIGEN DDR (BARCH-SAPMO)

DA1 (Volkskammer der DDR)
DR2 (Ministerium für Volksbildung)
DR6 (Staatliches Rundfunkkomittee)
DY6 (Nationalrat der Nationalen Front der DDR)
DY27 (Kulturbund der DDR)
DY30 (Sozialistische Einheitspartei Deutschlands)
Zentralinstitut für Jugendforschung

LANDESHAUPTARCHIV SCHWERIN (LHA SCHWERIN)

Deutsche Volksbühne
Kulturbund Neubrandenburg
Ministerium für Volksbildung
Ministerium für Volkskultur
Nationale Front Bezirk Neubrandenburg
Nationale Front Bezirk Schwerin
Rat des Bezirks Neubrandenburg
Rat des Bezirks Schwerin

KREISARCHIV (KA) HEILIGENSTADT

Rat der Gemeinde (RdG) Holungen
Rat des Kreises (RdK) Worbis

BUNDESBEAUFTRAGTE FÜR DIE UNTERLAGEN DES STAATSSICHERHEITSDIENSTES DER EHEMALIGEN DEUTSCHEN DEMOKRATISCHEN REPUBLIK (BSTU)

Ministerium für Staatssicherheit (MfS), Bezirksverwaltung Erfurt
Ministerium für Staatssicherheit (MfS), Bezirksverwaltung Schwerin

HEIMATSTUBE DABEL (HSTD)

Bildersammlung
Deutscher Kulturbund Protokolle
Deutscher Kulturbund Tätigkeitsberichte
Dorfklub
Material für Dorfchronik
Plakate
Rat des Kreises Sternberg, Abteilung Volksbildung
Übersicht über die berufliche Zusammensetzung
Volkskorrespondent Roggenbau, Zeitungssammlung

THÜRINGISCHES HAUPTSTAATSARCHIV WEIMAR (THSTAWE)

Kulturbund der DDR Bezirksverwaltung Erfurt
Nationale Front

STADTARCHIV (STA) MEININGEN

Interessengemeinschaft (IG) Denkmalpflege
Sammlung Wende

STADTARCHIV (STA) MÜHLHAUSEN

Kulturbund Mühlhausen
Sammlung Wende

STADTARCHIV (STA) EISENACH

Feste
Kulturbund Ortsgruppe Eisenach
Sammlung Wende

THÜRINGISCHES STAATSARCHIV (THSTA) ALTENBURG

Deutscher Kulturbund
Deutsche Volksbühne
Nachlaß Kuno Apel
Nachlaß Günther Hauthal

DEUTSCHES RUNDFUNKARCHIV BABELSBERG (DRA)

Schriftgutbestand Fernsehen
Television programmes:
    Schlager einer kleinen Stadt. Runde 6: Waren-Müritz (22 October 1966)
    Dolles Familienalbum (1969)
    Klock 8, achtern Strom (25 October 1969)

Schlager einer großen Stadt, Karl-Marx-Stadt (17 April 1971)
Mein Thüringen, mein Heimatland (14 August 1977)
Die lange Straße (1979)
Im Strom der Zeit (24 March 1981)
Märkische Chronik (1983)
Heimat, wir grüßen Dich (12 December 1987)
Oberhofer Bauernmarkt (26 March 1989)
Zeitschriftensammlung

ONLINE SOURCES

Discussion forum on Andrew I. Port, *Conflict and Stability*: h-german http://www.
h-net.org/logsearch/?phrase=port&type=keyword&list=h-german&hitlimit=
25&field=&nojg=on&smonth=00&syear=2007&emonth=11&eyear=2008&
order=relevance

PRIVATE COLLECTIONS

Brigitte and Paul Hamelmann (Holungen)
Günther Hauthal (Altenburg)
Josef Kistner (Holungen)
Uwe Wieben (Boizenburg)
Axel Wirth (Meiningen)

INTERVIEWS

I have listed only those interviewees whose conversations I have used directly for
this book. Interviews conducted on the same day but listed separately were
conducted separately.

Peter Apel (Eisenach): Born in 1945, he became an electrician. As a 'Stiegker' he
became one of the central organizers of the *Sommergewinn* in Eisenach during
the 1970s and 1980s, advancing to become head of the organizational team
(*Zunftmeister*) during the 1990s (12 June 2003).

Hartmut Baade: Born in 1941, he moved to Altenburg in 1961, where he taught
biology and chemistry, and was involved as county officer for environmental
protection (*Kreisnaturschutzbeauftragter*) (19 April 2005).

Horst Benneckenstein: Born in Neudietendorf near Erfurt in 1927, he lived in Erfurt
and was active in the Cultural League there. He moved to Neudietendorf in the
1980s, and 'invented' the annual woad festival to commemorate the medieval
dye produced in the village (28 April 2003).

Reinhold Brunner: Head archivist at Eisenach (20 May 2003).

Ludwig Deiters: Head of the Institute for Preservationism (Generalkonservator des
Instituts für Denkmalpflege der DDR), 1961–86 (6 March 2003).

Alfred Erck: Born in Meiningen, he became professor of aesthetics and cultural
theory at the Technical University at Ilmenau. He continued to live in

Meiningen, and in 1969 became district president of the Cultural League in Suhl (23 May 2003).

Manfred Fiedler: District secretary of the Cultural League in Karl-Marx-Stadt from 1966, secretary of the Cultural League of the GDR with special responsibility for the Friends of Nature and the Heimat (and its successor organizations) from 1974 (27 February 2003).

Inge and Berthold Fritzlar, with Armin Walter: Residents of Langula in the Vogtei region (Thuringia). Walter worked in Mühlhausen and was the long-serving chronicler of the village. Inge joined Berthold in 1948, and both worked at the Thomas Müntzer agricultural co-operative, with Berthold serving as environmental protection county officer (*Kreisnaturschutzbeauftragter*) (18 April 2005).

Heinrich Gemkow: Member of the Institute of Marxism and Leninism, member of the presidium of the Cultural League, vice-president of the Cultural League from 1968 (4 February 2003).

Gertrud Glandt: Born in the Rhineland, she moved to Rudolstadt during the Second World War. She married a local and joined the SED, becoming secretary of the Cultural League (20 April 2003).

Günther Hauthal: Born near Gera, he moved to Altenburg, where he joined the teacher training college at Altenburg in 1952. He continued at the institute until 1990, and became a keen publisher of heimat history (19 May 2003).

Erik Hühns: Director of the Märkisches Museum (the heimat museum in Berlin) and deputy general director of the National Museums on the 'Museums Island', and member of the praesidium of the Cultural League from the 1960s (3 December 2003).

Walter Kamrodt: Born in 1927, he became a baker and lived in Oberdorla (Vogtei region) near Mühlhausen. Kamrodt led the local folklore ensemble between 1978 and 1992, and served as county environmental protection officer 21 April 2005.

Manfred Kastner: He moved to Neuhaus am Rennsteig in the Thuringian Forest in 1963. As head of the local organization of the Cultural League in the 1980s he helped instigate a cultural revival in the village that culminated in the 500th anniversary celebrations in 1989 (29 March 2003).

Jürgen Klapczynski: He moved to Eisenach in 1951, and from 1974 to 1990 served as Lord Mayor of Eisenach, doing much to support the *Sommergewinn* festival.

Knut Kreuch: Born in 1966, he founded Wechmar's group of heimat historians in 1982, and was the guiding spirit of the revival of local history celebrations during the 1980s. After 1989 he became mayor of his village, and in 2006 was elected Lord Mayor of Gotha.

Dieter Kuhla: Manager of Eisenach's handball team, involved in the organization of the *Sommergewinn* festival despite not being born in Eisenach (23 June 2003).

Horst Meyer (name changed): Creator of a heimat museum through 'Join in!' in Mecklenburg (5 February 2003).

Ralf Päsler: From Eisenach. He refused to do military service, instead serving as a *Bausoldat* (1981 –3). Upon his return he joined the Eisenach eco-group and became active on its behalf (29 September 2007).

Karl Heinz Schulmeister: First Secretary of the Cultural League of the GDR, 1957–90 (11 November 2002).

Jürgen Thormann, secretary of the Cultural League for Mühlhausen county during the 1970s and 1980s (29 April 2003; 22 April 2005).

Hugo Weinitschke: Head of the Friends of Nature and the Heimat (Halle district), member of the praesidium of the Cultural League of the GDR and member of the Institute for Regionalism and Environmental Protection (Institut für Landesforschung und Naturschutz) in Halle (7 February 2003).

Uwe Wieben and Karin Wulf: Wieben served as director of the heimat museum in Boizenburg (Mecklenburg) and secretary of Boizenburg's Cultural League since 1978. Wulf succeeded Wieben as head of the heimat museum in the 1990s (26 June 2003).

Axel Wirth: Born in Meiningen, he became active in preservationism in his home town in the 1980s, campaigning against the destruction of historic buildings from 1987 (27 September 2007).

Günter Würfel: Served as Lord Mayor of the Mühlhausen Church Fair for thirty years, from the mid-1970s onwards (21 April 2005).

INTERVIEWS IN DABEL

Rosemarie Bartelt (village librarian), Wolfgang Cords (one of the Miller's Lads and pupil of Horst Roggenbau), Helga Böhnke (formerly active in the Women's League) and Karl-Heinz Schwabe (former head of the village club) (5 July 2003).

Rosemarie Bartels and Uwe Schliehe: Schliehe had been Dabel's postmaster. A friend of Horst Roggenbau, he was a member of the Church (20 August 2005).

Hansherbert Lange: Originally from Rostock, Lange was the village pastor from 1983 onwards (23 August 2005).

Jürgen Kuhlmann: Moved to Dabel from Schwerin in the early 1980s, and in 1989–90 headed the local social democrats group (15 November 2007).

Elsa Schmidt (name changed) (15 November 2007).

Mr and Mrs Teschner: They moved to Dabel during the War, but left in 1953, only to return in 1954 to inherit a farm there. Their brother-in-law had been one of the victims imprisoned by the Stasi in 1958, in connection with the arson attacks, of which he was not found guilty (15 November 2007).

INTERVIEWS IN HOLUNGEN

Brigitte and Paul Hamelmann: Paul was born in Holungen, and took up a job in construction. He took a lead in organizing Cultural League activities from the 1970s, and was a member of the Church council (17 June 2003).

Paul Hamelmann (12 May 2005).

Paul Schäfer: Originally from Erfurt, he moved to Holungen after the War when he married into the village. He became headmaster of the local primary school (12 May 2005).

Josef Kistner: Kistner worked at the potash works as an engineer until 1968, when
he took up a position in the GDR's largest cement works, Deuna, in charge of
its electrical operations (14 October 2007).

CONTEMPORARY NEWSPAPERS AND ILLUSTRATED JOURNALS

Altenburger Kulturspiegel (1955–7)
Aquarien- und Terrarien-Jahrbuch (1953–5)
Aus der Arbeit der Natur- und Heimatfreunde im Deutschen Kulturbund (1956–60)
Bauern-Echo (1952)
Berliner Zeitung
Bild der Wissenschaft (1991)
B.Z. am Abend
Das Volk (Mühlhausen and Erfurt editions)
Der Bote aus Thüringen
Der Morgen
Die Aussprache 4 (1949) – 9 (1954)
FF Dabei
Frankfurter Rundschau (1990)
Freie Presse (Karl-Marx-Stadt)
Freies Wort (Suhl)
Freiheit (Halle)
Für Dich
Gothäer Heimatzeitung
Heimatgeschichte
Heimatkalender der Kreise Altenburg und Schmölln (1959–61)
Junge Welt
Kulturspiegel der Kreise Altenburg und Schmölln (1958–70)
Mach Mit: Zeitschrift für die Ausschüsse der Nationalen Front der DDR
Mitteldeutsche Neueste Nachrichten (1976)
Mitteldeutsches Land (1957)
National-Zeitung
Natur und Heimat
Neue Berliner Illustrierte
Neue Deutsche Bauernzeitung (1984)
Neue Deutsche Presse
Neue Zeit
Neuer Tag (Frankfurt an der Oder)
Neues Deutschland
Norddeutsche Neueste Nachrichten (Rostock) (1969)
Oberhessische Presse (1990)
Ostseezeitung (Rostock)
Sächsische Neueste Nachrichten (1989)
Sächsische Zeitung (1987)
Schweriner Volkszeitung (Schwerin)

Sonntag
Strausberger Kreis-Echo
Volkswacht (Gera-Stadt)
Tagesspiegel (1970)
Tägliche Rundschau (1952)
Thüringische Landeszeitung
Vorwärts (1957)
Wochenpost
Zeit im Bild

SECONDARY LITERATURE

500 Jahre Neustadt am Rennsteig 1489–1989: Eine Ortschronik in den Bildern des historischen Festumzugs (Neustadt am Rennsteig: Rat der Gemeinde, 1989).

725 Jahre Dabel: Eine Chronik, ed. Fritz Ahrens *et al.* (Dabel: Interessengemeinschaft Heimatgeschichte/Chronik der Ortsgruppe des Kulturbunds Dabel, 1977).

Adorno, Theodor W., 'How to look at television', *Hollywood Quarterly* 6, no. 3 (1952), 222–40.

Allinson, Mark, *Politics and Popular Opinion in East Germany, 1945–68* (Manchester University Press, 2000).

'Popular opinion', in Major and Osmond (eds.), *The Workers' and Peasants' State*, pp. 96–111.

Anderson, Benedict, *Imagined Communities: Reflections on the Origin and Spread of Nationalism*, revised edn (London: Verso, 1991).

Applegate, Celia, *A Nation of Provincials: The German Idea of Heimat* (Berkeley: University of California Press, 1990).

Auster, Regine, *Landschaftstage: Kooperative Planungsverfahren in der Landschaftsentwicklung; Erfahrungen aus der DDR.* Umweltgeschichte und Umweltzukunft (Marburg: Bund demokratischer Wissenschaftlerinnen und Wissenschaftler e.V., 1996).

Auster, Regine and Behrens, Hermann (eds.), *Naturschutz in den Neuen Bundesländern – Ein Rückblick*, 2nd edn (Berlin: Verlag für Wissenschaft und Forschung, 2001).

Barker, Peter, *Slavs in Germany: The Sorbian Minority and the German State since 1945* (Lampeter: Edward Mellon Press, 2000).

(ed.), *The GDR and its History: Rückblick und Revision. Die DDR im Spiegel der Enquete-Kommissionen* (Amsterdam: Rodopi, 2000).

Bartel, Horst, 'Aufgaben und Probleme der regionalgeschichtlichen Forschung und Propaganda in der DDR', in *Aufgaben und Probleme der regionalgeschichtlichen Forschung und Propaganda in der DDR* (Berlin: Gesellschaft für Heimatgeschichte im Kulturbund der DDR, 1978), pp. 27–39.

Bastine, Werner, 'Zur Beziehung zwischen Heimatkunde und Geschichtsunterricht', in *Die Heimat im Geschichtsunterricht: Materialien zur Verwirklichung des heimatkundlichen Prinzips im Geschichtsunterricht* (Berlin: Volk und Wissen, 1957), pp. 24–30.

Bauer, Herbert, 'Heimat – Vaterland – Sozialismus', in *Zur Unterstützung des heimatkundlichen Unterrichtes* (Suhl: Deutscher Kulturbund, 1962), pp. 10–35.

Bauer, Theresia, *Blockpartei und Agrarrevolution von oben: Die Demokratische Bauernpartei Deutschlands, 1948–1963* (Munich: Oldenbourg, 2003).

Bauerkämper, Arnd, 'Von der Bodenreform zur Kollektivierung: Zum Wandel der ländlichen Gesellschaft in der Sowjetischen Besatzungszone Deutschlands und DDR 1945–52', in Kaelble *et al.* (eds.), *Sozialgeschichte der DDR*, pp. 119–43.

Ländliche Gesellschaft in der kommunistischen Diktatur: Zwangsmodernisierung und Tradition in Brandenburg 1945–1963 (Cologne: Böhlau, 2002).

Becher, Johannes R., 'Frieden und nationale Einheit', in *Natur- und Heimat Jahrbuch* (Dresden: Vereinigung Volkseigener Verlage, 1951), pp. 31–4.

Schöne deutsche Heimat (Berlin: Aufbau-Verlag, 1952).

Bentzien, Ulrich, 'Probleme regionaler Volkskultur: Einleitendes Referat zum Thema des Symposiums', *JbVkKg* 29, Deutsche Akademie der Wissenschaften (Berlin: Akademie-Verlag, 1986), pp. 17–36.

Berdahl, Daphne, *Where the World Ended* (Berkeley: University of California Press, 1999).

Berger, Stefan, 'National paradigm and legitimacy: Uses of academic history writing in the 1960s', in Major and Osmond (eds.), *The Workers' and Peasants' State*, pp. 244–61.

Bessel, Richard and Jessen, Ralph, 'Einleitung: Die Grenzen der Diktatur', in Richard Bessel and Ralph Jessen (eds.), *Die Grenzen der Diktatur: Staat und Gesellschaft in der DDR* (Göttingen: Vandenhoek und Ruprecht, 1996), pp. 7–24.

Blackbourn, David, *The Conquest of Nature: Water, Landscape and the Making of Modern Germany* (London: Jonathan Cape, 2006).

Blackbourn, David and Retallack, Jim (eds.), *Localism, Landscape, and the Ambiguities of Place: German-Speaking Central Europe, 1860–1930* (Toronto University Press, 2007).

Blaschke, Karlheinz, 'Die marxistische Regionalgeschichte: Ideologischer Zwang und Wirklichkeitsferne', in Georg G. Iggers *et al.* (eds.), *Die DDR-Geschichtswissenschaft als Forschungsproblem*, Internationale Tagung über Geschichtswissenschaft in der DDR (Munich: Oldenbourg, 1998), pp. 341–68.

Blessing, Benita, *The Antifascist Classroom: Denazification in Soviet-occupied Germany, 1945–9* (New York: Palgrave Macmillan, 2006).

Boa, Elizabeth and Palfreyman, Rachel, *Heimat: A German Dream. Regional Loyalties and National Identity in German Culture, 1890–1990* (Oxford University Press, 2000).

Bock, Helmut, 'Es gibt kein historisches „Niemandsland": Zu aktuellen Problemen des Erbes und der Tradition im Sozialismus von heute', in Helmut Meier and Walter Schmidt (eds.), *Erbe und Tradition in der DDR: Die Diskussion der Historiker* (Cologne: Pahl-Rugenstein, 1989), pp. 218–39.

Bondzin, Erwin, 'Wohnverhältnisse verbessern: Was kann die Nationale Front der DDR dazu tun?', *Mach mit: Zeitschrift für die Ausschüsse der Nationalen Front der DDR* 10 (1976), 4–9.

Bourdieu, Pierre, *Outline of a Theory of Practice* (Cambridge University Press, 1977).

Boym, Svetlana, 'Paradoxes of unified culture: From Stalin's fairy tale to Molotov's lacquer box', in Lahusen and Dobrenko (eds.), *Socialist Realism without Shores*, pp. 120–34.

Breitkopf, Jerzy, 'Masseninitiative der VR Polen', in *Verbesserung der Wohnbedingungen – wichtigste Aufgabe im 'Mach Mit!' Wettbewerb*, Gemeinsame Tagung des Sekretariats des Nationalrats der Nationalen Front der DDR und des Ministeriums für Bauwesen am 24. Okt. 1973 in Eberswalde-Finow (Berlin, 1973), pp. 35–6.

Breuer, Reiner, Donath, Friedrich, Jacobeit, Wolfgang and Moeller, Karl-Heinz (eds.), *Unsere Ortschronik: Hinweise und Anregungen zu ihrer Führung*, Arbeitsmaterial für die Fachgruppen Heimatgeschichte, Ortschroniken des Kulturbundes der DDR 4 (Berlin, 1978).

Breuilly, John, 'Conclusion: Nationalism and German Reunification', in John Breuilly (ed.), *The State of Germany: The National Idea in the Making, Unmaking and Remaking of a Modern Nation-State* (Harlow: Longman, 1992), pp. 224–38.

Bruner, Jerome, 'The narrative construction of reality', *Critical Inquiry* 18 (1991), 1–20.

Buck, Hansjörg F., 'Wohnungsversorgung, Stadtgestaltung und Stadtverfall', in Eberhard Kuhrt (ed.), *Die wirtschaftliche und ökologische Situation der DDR in den achtziger Jahren* (Opladen: Leske & Budrich, 1996), pp. 67–109.

'Umweltpolitik und Umweltbelastung', in Eberhard Kuhrt (ed.), *Die wirtschaftliche und ökologische Situation der DDR in den achtziger Jahren* (Opladen: Leske & Budrich, 1996), pp. 223–66.

Bundesvorstand des FDGB (ed.), *Geschichte des Freien Deutschen Gewerkschaftsbundes* (Berlin: Tribüne, 1982).

Caldwell, Peter C., *Dictatorship, State Planning and Social Theory in the German Democratic Republic* (Cambridge University Press, 2003).

Castillo, Greg, 'Peoples at an exhibition: Soviet architecture and the national question', in Thomas Lahusen and Evgeny Dobrenko (eds.), *Socialist Realism without Shores* (Durham, NC / London: Duke University Press, 1997), pp. 91–119.

de Certeau, Michel, *The Practice of Everyday Life* (Berkeley: University of California Press, 1984).

Confino, Alon, *The Nation as a Local Metaphor: Württemberg, Imperial Germany, and National Memory, 1871–1918* (Chapel Hill: University of North Carolina Press, 1997).

Germany as a Culture of Remembrance: Promises and Limits of Writing History (Chapel Hill: University of North Carolina Press, 2006).

Connelly, John, *Captive University: The Sovietization of East German, Czech and Polish Higher Education* (Chapel Hill: University of North Carolina Press, 2000).

Connor, Ian, *Refugees and Expellees in Post-War Germany* (Manchester University Press, 2007).

Crew, David (ed.), *Consuming Germany in the Cold War* (Oxford: Berg, 2003).

Davies, Charlotte Aull, 'A oes heddwch? Contested meanings and identities in the Welsh National Eisteddfod', in Felicia Hughes-Freeland (ed.), *Ritual, Performance, Media* (London: Routledge, 1998), pp. 141–59.

Deiters, Ludwig, 'Zum neuen Denkmalpflegegesetz', *Denkmalpflege in der Deutschen Demokratischen Republik* 2 (1975), 1–4.

Deutsche Verwaltung des Innern, *Verordnung zur Überführung von Volkskunstgruppen und volksbildenden Vereinen in die bestehenden demokratischen Massenorganisationen* (12 January 1949).

Dix, Andreas, *„Freies Land": Siedlungsplanung im ländlichen Raum der SBZ und der frühen DDR* (Cologne: Böhlau, 2002).

Donath, Friedrich, 'Bemerkungen zur Diskussion um die Begriffe Heimat – Vaterland – Nation', *Aus der Arbeit der Natur- und Heimatfreunde* 9 (1959), 226–8.

'Bürgerliche oder sozialistische Heimat?', *Sächsische Heimatblätter* 6 (1960), 258–60.

Ehlert, Hans and Rogg, Mathias (eds.), *Militär, Staat und Gesellschaft in der DDR* (Berlin: Links, 2004).

'Entschließung des VIII. Parteitages der Sozialistischen Einheitspartei Deutschlands', in *Protokoll der Verhandlungen des VIII. Parteitages der Sozialistischen Einheitspartei Deutschlands, 15.-19. Juni 1971 in der Werner-Sellenbinder-Halle zu Berlin*, vol. II (Berlin, 1971).

Epstein, Catherine, *The Last Revolutionaries: German Communists and their Century* (Cambridge, MA: Harvard University Press, 2003).

Eschenbach, Insa, 'Zur Umcodierung der eigenen Vergangenheit: Antifaschismuskonstruktionen in Rehabilitationsgesuchen ehemaliger Mitglieder der NSDAP, Berlin 1945/46', in Alf Lüdtke and Peter Becker (eds.), *Akten, Eingaben, Schaufenster: Die DDR und ihre Texte* (Berlin: Akademie-Verlag, 1997), pp. 79–90.

Fahrmeir, Andreas, 'National colours and national identity in early nineteenth-century Germany', in David Laven and Lucy Riall (eds.), *Napoleon's Legacy: Problems of Government in Restoration Europe* (Oxford: Berg, 2000), pp. 199–216.

'Discussion', *German History* 23 (2005), 405–11.

Farmer, Kenneth C., *Ukrainian Nationalism in the Post-Stalin Era: Myth, Symbols and Ideology in Soviet Nationalities Policy* (The Hague: Martin Nijhoff Publishers, 1980).

Feinstein, Joshua, '*Spur der Steine*: Zum Verhältnis von Gegenwart und Geschichte im DEFA-Spielfilm der sechziger Jahre', in Martin Sabrow (ed.), *Verwaltete Vergangenheit: Geschichtskultur und Herrschaftslegitimation in der DDR* (Leipzig: Akademische Verlagsanstalt, 1997), pp. 217–36.

Fenemore, Mark, *Sex, Thugs and Rock'n'Roll. Teenage Rebels in Cold-War East Germany* (New York/Oxford: Berghahn, 2008).

'The limits of repression and reform: youth policy in the early 1960s', in Patrick Major and Jonathan Osmond (eds.), *The Workers' and Peasants' State: Communism and Society in East Germany under Ulbricht, 1945–1971* (Manchester University Press, 2002), pp. 171–89.

Festschrift zum Eichsfelder Heimattreffen in Holungen anläßlich des 100. Geburtstages des Heimatdichters Dr Hermann Iseke 1956, ed. Heimatfreunde Holungen (Dingelstädt, 1956).

Fingerle, Stephan, *Waffen in Arbeiterhand? Die Rekrutierung des Offizierkorps der NVA und ihrer Vorläufer* (Berlin: Links, 2001).

Fischer, Walter R., *Human Communication as Narration: Toward a Philosophy of Reason, Value and Action* (Columbia: University of South Carolina Press, 1987).

Fiske, John and Hartley, John, *Reading Television*, 2nd edn with a new foreword by John Hartley (London: Routledge, 2003).

Fitzpatrick, Sheila, *Stalin's Peasants: Resistance and Survival in the Russian Village after Collectivization* (New York and Oxford: Oxford University Press, 1994).

François, Etienne and Schulze, Hagen (eds.), *Deutsche Erinnerungsorte I–III*. Vol. 1, 4th edn (2003); vols. 2, 3, 2nd edn (2002) (Munich: C. H. Beck).

Fulbrook, Mary, 'Nation, state and political culture in divided Germany, 1945–90', in John Breuilly (ed.), *The State of Germany: The National Idea in the Making, Unmaking and Remaking of a Modern Nation-State* (Harlow: Longman, 1992), pp. 177–200.

'Nationalism in the Second German Unification', in John Breuilly and Ron Speirs (eds.), *Germany's Two Unifications: Anticipations, Experiences, Responses* (Basingstoke: Palgrave, 2005), pp. 241–60.

The People's State: East German Society from Hitler to Honecker (New Haven: Yale University Press, 2005).

'Putting the people back in: the contentious state of GDR history', *German History* 24, no. 4 (2006), 608–20.

(ed.), *Power and Society in the GDR, 1961–1979. The 'Normalisation of Rule'?* (New York: Berghahn, 2009).

Gemkow, Heinrich, 'Über Wert und Mißbrauch der Heimatliebe: Gedanken zu Inhalt und Funktion des Heimatbegriffs', *Beiträge zur Geschichte der deutschen Arbeiterbewegung* (1962), no. 3/4, 657–70.

Gerrig, Richard J., *Experiencing Narrative Worlds: On the Psychological Activities of Reading* (New Haven/London: Yale University Press, 1993).

Gieseke, Jens, *Die hauptamtlichen Mitarbeiter der Staatssicherheit: Personalstruktur und Lebenswelt 1950–1989/90* (Berlin: Links, 2000).

Der Mielke-Konzern: Die Geschichte der Stasi 1945–90, 2nd edn (Munich: Deutsche Verlags-Anstalt, 2006).

Gilsenbach, Reimar, 'Liebhaberei oder Wissenschaft? Zum Geleit', *Aquarien- und Terrarien-Jahrbuch* (1954), 7–8.

Glaessner, Gert-Joachim (ed.), *Die DDR in der Ära Honecker: Politik, Kultur, Gesellschaft* (Opladen: Westdeutscher Verlag, 1988).

Gramann, Werner, *Nationale Front und Bürgerinitiative: Die Rolle der Nationalen Front der DDR – das Zusammenwirken der Ausschüsse mit den Volksvertretungen bei der Organisierung des „Mach Mit!"-Wettbewerbes in den Städten und Gemeinden* (Berlin: Staatsverlag der Deutschen Demokratischen Republik, 1973).

Green, Abigail, *Fatherlands: State-Building and Nationhood in Nineteenth-Century Germany* (Cambridge University Press, 2001).

Grieder, Peter, *The East German Leadership, 1946–1973* (Manchester University Press, 1999).

Grosse, Horst, 'Der „Wartburg" und die Pleiße', *Kulturspiegel Altenburg Schmölln* (May 1962), 134–5.

Gutsche, Willibald, 'Aufgaben und Probleme der marxistisch-leninistischen Regionalgeschichtsforschung und -propaganda in der DDR', in *Aufgaben und Probleme der regionalgeschichtlichen Forschung und Propaganda in der DDR* (Berlin: Gesellschaft für Heimatgeschichte im Kulturbund der DDR, 1978), pp. 9–25.

'Platz und Aufgaben der Ortschronik in der geschichtswissenschaftlichen und geschichtspropagandistischen Arbeit in der DDR', in *Heimatgeschichte* 11 (1981), pp. 35–54.

Haase, Horst, *Erben für unsere Zeit: Tagung des Präsidialrates des Kulturbundes der DDR am 21. Januar 1988* (Berlin: Kulturbund der DDR, 1988).

Haase, Horst *et al.* (eds.), *Die SED und das kulturelle Erbe: Orientierungen, Errungenschaften, Probleme*, Akademie für Gesellschaft wissenschaften (Berlin: Dietz, 1986).

Hager, Kurt, *Ergebnisse und Aufgaben unserer sozialistischen Kulturpolitik* (Berlin: Dietz, 1975).

Haider, Magdalena, *Politik – Kultur – Kulturbund: Zur Gründungs- und Frühgeschichte des Kulturbunds zur demokratischen Erneuerung Deutschlands 1945–54 in der SBZ/DDR* (Cologne: Verlag Wissenschaft und Politik, 1993).

Hall, Stuart, 'Encoding/decoding', in Stuart Hall *et al.* (eds.), *Culture, Media, Language: Working Papers in Cultural Studies, 1972–79* (London: Hutchinson/ The Centre for Contemporary Cultural Studies, University of Birmingham, 1980), pp. 128–38.

Halsall, Robert, 'GDR Architecture and town planning in post-unification Germany: "Geschichtsaufarbeitung" or aesthetic autonomy?', in Peter Barker (ed.), *The GDR and its History*, pp. 185–214.

Hamelmann, Paul (ed.), 'Festschrift 725 Jahre Holungen' (Holungen, festival brochure, 1991).

Hanisch, Ernst, 'Die linguistische Wende: Geschichtswissenschaft und Literatur', in Wolfgang Hardtwig and Hans-Ulrich Wehler (eds.), *Kulturgeschichte heute* (Göttingen: Vandenhoeck & Ruprecht, 1996), pp. 212–31.

Hanke, Irma, 'Heimat DDR', in Hans-Georg Wehling (ed.), *Politische Kultur in der DDR* (Stuttgart: Kohlhammer, 1989), pp. 180–93.

Hannemann, Christine, *Die Platte: Industrialisierter Wohnungsbau in der DDR* (Braunschweig: Vieweg, 1996).

Harbers, Dorothee, *Die Bezirkspresse der DDR (unter besonderer Berücksichtigung der SED-Bezirkszeitungen): Lokalzeitungen im Spannungsfeld zwischen Parteiauftrag und Leserinteresse* (Marburg: Tectum, 2003).

Hartewig, Karin and Lüdtke, Alf (eds.), *Die DDR im Bild: Zum Gebrauch der Fotografie im anderen deutschen Staat* (Göttingen: Wellstein, 2004).

Häussler, Helmut, *Kulturbund und Wohngebiet* (Leipzig: Bezirksleitung des Kulturbundes, 1963).

Heimatgeschichte und Geschichtsunterricht: 3. Gemeinsames Kolloquium der Ernst-Moritz-Arnd-Universität Greifswald, des Rates des Bezirkes Neubrandenburg und der Gesellschaft für Heimatgeschichte im Kulturbund der DDR am 22. Oktober 1987 in Neubrandenburg (Greifswald: Universität Greifswald/ Neubrandenburg Bezirk/Gesellschaft für Heimatgeschichte, 1989).

Heimatgeschichte und Jugend, Heimatgeschichte 13 (Berlin: Kulturbund der DDR, 1982).

Heitzer, H. *et al.*, *DDR: Werden und Wachsen. Zur Geschichte der Deutschen Demokratischen Republik*, Akademie der Wissenschaften der DDR/ Zentralinstitut für Geschichte (Berlin: Dietz, 1974).

Herbert, Ulrich, '*Liberalisierung als Lernprozeß: Die Bundesrepublik in der deutschen Geschichte*', in Ulrich Herbert (ed.), *Wandlungsprozesse in Westdeutschland: Belastung, Integration, Liberalisierung 1945–1980* (Göttingen: Wallstein-Verlag, 2002), pp. 1–52.

Herman, David, 'Stories as a tool for thinking', in David Herman (ed.), *Narrative Theory and the Cognitive Sciences* (Stanford: CSLI, 2003), pp. 163–92.

Heunemann, Kurt, 'Gründliche Vorbereitung, exakte Planung, rechtzeitige Information', in *Verbesserung der Wohnbedingungen*, pp. 57–9.

Heydemann, Günther and Schmiechen-Ackermann, Detlef (eds.), *Diktaturen in Deutschland – Vergleichsaspekte* (Bonn: Bundeszentrale für Politische Bildung, 2003).

Hinterthür, Bettina, *Noten nach Plan: Die Musikverlage in der SBZ/DDR – Zensursystem, zentrale Planwirtschaft und deutsch–deutsche Beziehungen bis Anfang der 1960er Jahre* (Stuttgart: Franz Steiner, 2006).

Hirsch, Francine, 'The Soviet Union as work-in-progress: ethnographers and the category of nationality in the 1926, 1937 and 1939 census', *Slavic Review* 56 (1997), 251–78.

Hobsbawm, Eric, 'Mass-producing traditions: Europe, 1890–1914', in Eric Hobsbawm and Terence Ranger (eds.), *The Invention of Tradition* (Cambridge University Press, 1983) pp. 263–308.

Hoff, Peter, 'Von "Da lacht der Bär" über "Ein Kessel Buntes" – ins "Aus". Politische Geschichte der DDR in Unterhaltungssendungen des DDR-Fernsehens', in Heide Riedel (ed.), *Mit uns zieht die neue Zeit … 40 Jahre DDR-Medien. Eine Ausstellung des Deutschen Rundfunk-Museums* (Berlin: VISTAS, 1993).

Hoffmann, Dierk, *Aufbau und Krise der Planwirtschaft: Die Arbeitskräftelenkung in der SBZ/DDR 1945–63* (Munich: Oldenbourg, 2002).

Honecker, Erich, *Aus meinem Leben* (Berlin: Dietz, 1980).

Hühns, Erik, 'Nation – Vaterland – Heimat', *Aus der Arbeit der Natur- und Heimatfreunde* 8 (1959), 169–79.

'Noch einmal: Nation – Vaterland – Heimat. Antwort an Dr Donath, Leipzig', *Aus der Arbeit der Natur- und Heimatfreunde* 9 (1959), 228–9.

'Das Volk gestaltet seine Heimat', *Aus der Arbeit der Natur- und Heimatfreunde* 4 (1960), 67–9.

'Zum Stand der Diskussion um den sozialistischen Heimatbegriff', *Aus der Arbeit der Natur- und Heimatfreunde* 10 (1960), 229–33.

Heimat, Vaterland, Nation (Berlin: Tribüne/Deutscher Kulturbund, 1969).

Humm, Antonia Maria, *Auf dem Weg zum sozialistischen Dorf? Zum Wandel der dörflichen Lebenswelt in der DDR und der Bundesrepublik Deutschland 1952–69* (Göttingen: Vandenhoek & Ruprecht, 1999).

Hürtgen, Renate, *Zwischen Disziplinierung und Partizipation: Vertrauensleute des FDGB im DDR-Betrieb* (Cologne: Böhlau, 2005).

Hürtgen, Renate and Reichel, Thomas (eds.), *Der Schein der Stabilität: DDR-Betriebsalltag in der Ära Honecker* (Berlin: Metropol, 2001).

Jarausch, Konrad (ed.), *Dictatorship as Experience: Towards a Socio-Cultural History of the GDR*, translated by Eve Duffy (New York / Oxford: Berghahn, 1999).

Jenkins, Jennifer, *Provincial Modernity: Local Culture and Liberal Politics in Fin-de-Siècle Hamburg* (Ithaca, NY / London: Cornell University Press, 2003).

Judt, Matthias, '„Nur für den Dienstgebrauch" – Arbeiten mit Texten einer deutschen Diktatur', in Lüdtke and Becker (eds.), *Akten*, pp. 29–38.

Käbisch, Edmund, 'Die letzten Jahre der DDR: Mein Alltag als evangelischer Pfarrer in Zwickau', in Clemens Vollnhals and Jürgen Weber (eds.), *Der Schein der Normalität: Alltag und Herrschaft in der SED-Diktatur* (Munich: Olzog, 2002), pp. 373–416.

Kaelble, Hartmut, Kocka, Jürgen and Zwahr, Hartmut (eds.), *Sozialgeschichte der DDR* (Stuttgart: Klett-Cotta, 1994).

Kahle, Werner, 'Zur Einheit von Historischem und Aktuellem beim Aneignen des Erbes', in *Sozialistische Lebensweise und kulturelles Erbe: Auszüge aus einer Diskussion* (Berlin: Kulturbund der DDR, 1976), pp. 57–63.

Kalous, Vaclav, 'Politische Aktivität des Bürgerkomitees – wichtige Vorbedingung für die „Aktion Z"', in *Verbesserung der Wohnbedingungen*, pp. 33–4.

Keil, Heinz, 'Deutscher Schwarzwald', *Natur und Heimat* (1952), no. 6, 14–16.

'Braunschweig – Notizen einer Westdeutschlandreise', *Natur und Heimat* 8 (1952), 10–12.

Klafs, Gerhard, 'Die Arbeitsgruppe Greifswald des Institutes für Landschaftsforschung und Naturschutz', in Auster and Behrens (eds.), *Naturschutz in den Neuen Bundesländern*, pp. 325–48.

Klessmann, Christoph, *Die doppelte Staatsgründung: Deutsche Geschichte 1945–55* (Bonn: Bundeszentrale für Politische Bildung, 1991).

Zwei Staaten – Eine Nation. Deutsche Geschichte 1955–1970 (Göttingen: Vandenhoeck und Ruprecht, 1988).

Kligman, Gail, *The Wedding of the Dead: Ritual, Poetics and Popular Culture in Transylvania* (Berkeley: University of California Press, 1988).

Căluş: Symbolic Transformation in Romanian Ritual, 2nd edn (Bucharest: The Romanian Cultural Foundation Publishing House, 1999).

Kneschke, Karl, 'Volksbildende Vereine und Gruppen', *Die Aussprache* 4, 6/7 (1949), 9–10.

'Vom Werden und Wachsen', *Natur und Heimat* 1 (1952), 2–3.

'Deutschland – unsere Heimat', *Natur und Heimat* 3 (1952), 1–2.

'Von der Wissenschaft zur Tat', *Natur und Heimat* 6 (1952), 1–3.

Koch, Hans, 'Kulturbund und kulturelles Erbe', *Mitteilungsblatt des Kulturbundes der DDR* 2 (1975), 2–20.

Kolditz, Lothar, 'Bürgerinitiative zur Pflege von Denkmalen und ihrer Umgebung', Sekretariat des Präsidiums des Kulturbunds der DDR (ed.), in *Kulturbund in der entwickelten sozialistischen Gesellschaft 1982–1986* (Berlin, 1987), pp. 189–91.

Komitee für Touristik und Wandern des Bezirkes Gera / Deutscher Kulturbund, Bezirkskommission Gera der Natur- und Heimatfreunde, *Wanderungen im Bezirk Gera* (Leipzig: Brockhaus, 1963).

Kopstein, Jeffrey, *The Politics of Economic Decline in East Germany, 1945–1989* (Chapel Hill: University of North Carolina Press, 1997).

Körner-Schrader, Paul, 'Wir blättern in einer Dorfchronik', *Natur und Heimat* 6 (1952), 10–13.

Koshar, Rudy, *Germany's Transient Pasts: Preservation and National Memory in the Twentieth Century* (Chapel Hill: University of North Carolina Press, 1998).

'"What ought to be seen": tourists' guidebooks and national identities in Germany and modern Europe', *Journal of Contemporary History* 33 (1998), 323–40.

German Travel Cultures (Oxford: Berg, 2000).

Kott, Sandrine, 'Zur Geschichte des kulturellen Lebens in DDR-Betrieben: Konzepte und Praxis der betrieblichen Kulturarbeit', *Archiv für Sozialgeschichte* 39 (1999), 167–95.

Kühne, Thomas, 'Imagined regions: The construction of traditional, democratic and other identities', in James Retallack (ed.), *Saxony in German History: Culture, Society and Politics, 1830–1933* (Ann Arbor: University of Michigan Press, 2000), pp. 51–62.

Kulturkonferenz 1960: Protokoll der vom Zentralkommittee der SED, dem Ministerium für Kultur und dem Deutschen Kulturbund vom 27. bis 29. April 1960 im VEB Elektrokohle, Berlin, abgehaltenen Konferenz (Berlin: Dietz, 1960).

Kulturpolitisches Wörterbuch, 1st edn (Berlin: Dietz, 1970).

Kulturpolitisches Wörterbuch, 5th edn (Berlin: Dietz, 1989).

Lahusen, Thomas, 'Socialist Realism in search of its shores: Some historical remarks on the historically open aesthetic system of the truthful representation of life', in Lahusen and Dobrenko (eds.), *Socialist Realism*, pp. 5–26.

Lahusen, Thomas and Dobrenko, Evgeny (eds.), *Socialist Realism without Shores* (Durham, NC / London: Duke University Press, 1997).

Land zwischen Saale und Elster, introduced by Armin Müller (Leipzig: Brockhaus, 1963).

Landsman, Mark, *Dictatorship and Demand: The Politics of Consumerism in East Germany* (Cambridge, MA/London: Harvard University Press, 2005).

Lange, Günter, *Heimat – Realität und Aufgabe: Zur marxistischen Auffassung des Heimatbegriffs*, 2nd edn (Berlin: Akademie-Verlag, 1975).

Lauerwald, Paul, 'Notwendigkeit und Möglichkeiten der propagandistischen Nutzung der Ortschroniken', in *Platz und Aufgaben der Ortschronik bei der geschichtswissenschaftlichen und geschichtspropagandistischen Arbeit in der Deutschen Demokratischen Republik*, Heimatgeschichte 11 (Berlin: Zentrale Ortschronistenkonferenz der DDR, 1981), pp. 68–76.

Leo, Annette and Reif-Spirek, Peter (eds.), *Vielstimmiges Schweigen: Neue Studien zum DDR-Antifaschismus* (Berlin: Metropol, 2001).

Lindenberger, Thomas, 'Diktatur der Grenzen: Zur Einleitung', in Thomas Lindenberger (ed.), *Herrschaft und Eigen-Sinn in der Diktatur: Studien zur Gesellschaftsgeschichte der DDR* (Cologne: Böhlau, 1999), pp. 22–3.

Volkspolizei: Herrschaftspraxis und öffentliche Ordnung im SED-Staat 1952–68 (Cologne: Böhlau, 2003).

'Einleitung', in Thomas Lindenberger (ed.), *Massenmedien im kalten Krieg: Akteure, Bilder, Resonanzen* (Cologne: Böhlau, 2006).

'Home, sweet home: desperately seeking heimat in early DEFA films', *Film History* 18 (2006), 46–58.

Lotz, Christian, *Die Deutung des Verlusts: Erinnerungspolitische Kontroversen im geteilten Deutschland um Flucht, Vertreibung und die Ostgebiete* (Cologne: Böhlau, 2007).

Lüdtke, Alf, 'Herrschaft als soziale Praxis', in Alf Lüdtke, *Herrschaft als soziale Praxis: Historische und sozial-anthropologische Studien* (Göttingen: Vandenhoek und Ruprecht, 1991), pp. 9–63.

'Introduction: What is the history of everyday life and who are its practitioners?', in Alf Lüdtke (ed.), *The History of Everyday Life: Reconstructing Historical Experiences and Ways of Life* (Princeton University Press, 1995), pp. 3–40.

'What happened to the "fiery red glow"? Workers' experiences and German fascism', in Alf Lüdtke (ed.), *The History of Everyday Life: Reconstructing Historical Experiences and Ways of Life* (Princeton University Press, 1995), pp. 198–251.

'Alltagsgeschichte – ein Bericht von Unterwegs', *Historische Anthropologie* 11 (2003), 278–95.

'„Fehlgreifen in der Wahl der Mittel": Optionen im Alltag militärischen Handelns', *Mittelweg* 36 (2003), 61–75.

Lüdtke, Alf and Becker, Peter (eds.), *Akten, Eingaben, Schaufenster: Die DDR und ihre Texte* (Berlin: Akademie-Verlag, 1997).

McDougall, Alan, *Youth Politics in East Germany: The Free German Youth Movement, 1946–1968* (Oxford: Clarendon Press, 2004).

McLellan, Josie, *Antifascism and Memory in East Germany: Remembering the International Brigades, 1945–1989* (Oxford: Clarendon Press, 2004).

Madarász, Jeanette, *Working in East Germany: Normality in a Socialist Dictatorship, 1961–79* (Basingstoke: Palgrave Macmillan, 2006).

Major, Patrick, 'Vor und nach dem 13. August 1961: Reaktionen der DDR-Bevölkerung auf den Bau der Berliner Mauer', *Archiv für Sozialgeschichte* 39 (1999), 325–54.

Major, Patrick and Osmond, Jonathan (eds.), *The Workers' and Peasants' State: Communism and Society in East Germany under Ulbricht, 1945–1971* (Manchester University Press, 2002).

Marssolek, Inge and von Saldern, Adelheid (eds.), *Zuhören und Gehörtwerden. Radio im Nationalsozialismus und Radio in der DDR der fünfziger Jahre*, 2 vols. (Tübingen: edition diskord, 1998).

Martin, Terry, *The Affirmative Action Empire: Nations and Nationalism in the Soviet Union, 1923–1939* (Ithaca, NY/London: Cornell University Press, 2001).

Mayer, Franz C. and Palmowski, Jan, 'European identities and the EU – the ties that bind the peoples of Europe', *Journal of Common Market Studies* 42 (2004), 573–98.

Medick, Hans, 'Quo Vadis, historische Anthropologie? Geschichtsforschung zwischen historischer Kulturwissenschaft und Mikro-Historie', *Historische Anthropologie* 9, no. 1 (2001), 78–92.

Meier, Helmut, *Der Kulturbund im politischen System der DDR in den siebziger Jahren*, Hefte zur DDR Geschichte 62 (Berlin: Helle Panke/Gesellschaftswiss. Forum, 2000).

Meier, Helmut and Schmidt, Walter (eds.), *Erbe und Tradition in der DDR: Die Diskussion der Historiker* (Cologne: Pahl-Rugenstein, 1989).

Meinecke, Friedrich, *Die deutsche Katastrophe: Betrachtungen und Erinnerungen* (Wiesbaden: Eberhard Brockhaus, 1946).

Merkel, Ina, *Wir sind doch nicht die Meckerecke der Nation! Briefe an das Fernsehen der DDR* (Berlin: Schwarzkopf, 1997).

Meuschel, Sigrid, *Legitimation und Parteiherrschaft: Zum Paradox von Stabilität und Revolution in der DDR 1945–89* (Frankfurt: Suhrkamp, 1992).

Mohr, Hubert and Hühns, Erik (eds.), *Einführung in die Heimatgeschichte* (Berlin: Deutscher Verlag der Wissenschaften, 1959).

Mohrmann, Ute, 'Ergebnisse und Grenzen praxisbezogener Volkskunstforschung der DDR in den fünfziger Jahren', *Volkskunst als Kulturgeschichte: Kultur und Lebensweise* 1 (1981), 53–65.

'Sitten und Bräuche im Lebenszyklus der DDR-Bürger – eine volkskundliche Forschungsaufgabe', in *Zur Formierung der sozialistischen Nation: Forschungsbeiträge* (Berlin: Akadamie für Gesellschaftswissenschaften beim ZK der SED, 1984), pp. 110–17.

von Moltke, Johannes, *No Place like Home: Locations of Heimat in German Cinema* (Berkeley: University of California Press, 2005).

Müller, Heiner, *Krieg ohne Schlacht: Leben in zwei Diktaturen*, 2nd edn (Cologne: Kiepenheuer & Witsch, 1994).

Müller, Karl, *Erinnerungen an meinen Freund Herbert Roth* (Suhl: WOG-Verlag, 1996).

Murdock, Caitlin, 'Constructing a modern German landscape: tourism, nature and industry in Saxony', in Blackbourn and Retallack (eds.), *Localism*, pp. 195–213.

Museumsdorf Cloppenburg, Kulturamt der Stadt Oldenburg, Stadtmuseum Oldenburg (eds.), *Regionaler Fundamentalismus? Geschichte der Heimatbewegung in Stadt und Land Oldenburg* (Oldenburg: Isensee, 1999).

Natur und Umwelt im Bezirk Neubrandenburg. 2. Landschaftstag: „Mecklenburgisch-Brandenburgische Seenplatte" der Bezirke Schwerin, Potsdam, Neubrandenburg (Neubrandenburg: Kulturbund der DDR, 1978).

Neutsch, Erik, *Spur der Steine*, new edn (Munich: DTV, 1995).

Newcomb, Horace (ed.), *Television: The Critical View*, 7th edn (Oxford University Press, 2007).

Nothnagle, Alan L., *Building the East German Myth: Historical Mythology and Youth Propaganda in the German Democratic Republic, 1945–89* (Ann Arbor: Michigan University Press, 1999).

Oberkrome, Willi, *„Deutsche Heimat": Nationale Konzeption und regionale Praxis von Naturschutz, Landschaftsgestaltung und Kulturpolitik in Westfalen-Lippe und Thüringen (1900–1960)* (Paderborn: Schöningh, 2004).

Olsen, Jon Berndt, 'Tailoring the truth: Memory culture and state legitimacy in East Germany, 1945–1989', PhD Dissertation, University of North Carolina (2004).

Ortschroniken in Vergangenheit und Gegenwart, Heimatgeschichte 14, Arbeitsmaterial für die Fachgruppen Heimatgeschichte, Ortschroniken des Kulturbundes der DDR (Berlin, 1982).

Palmowski, Jan, *Urban Liberalism in Imperial Germany: Frankfurt am Main, 1866–1914* (Oxford University Press, 1999).

'Travels with Baedeker: The guidebook and the middle classes in Victorian and Edwardian England', in Rudy Koshar (ed.), *Histories of Leisure* (Oxford: Berg, 2002), pp. 105–31.

'Building an East German nation: the construction of a socialist heimat, 1945–61', *Central European History* 37 (2004), 365–99.

'Regional identities and the limits of democratic centralism in the GDR', *Journal of Contemporary History* 41, no. 3 (2006), 503–26.

'Staatssicherheit und soziale Praxis', in Jens Giesecke (ed.), *Staatssicherheit und Gesellschaft: Studien zum Herrschaftsalltag in der DDR* (Göttingen: Vandenhoek und Ruprecht, 2007), pp. 253–72.

'Citizenship, identity and community in the GDR', in Geoff Eley and Jan Palmowski (eds.), *Citizenship and National Identity in the GDR* (Stanford University Press, 2008), pp. 73–91.

'Local activists and renegotiations of heimat in the GDR, 1949–90', in Fulbrook (ed.), *Power and Society in the GDR*.

Pence, Katherine, 'Schaufenster des sozialistischen Konsums: Texte der ostdeutschen „consumer culture"', in Alf Lüdtke and Peter Becker, *Akten, Eingaben, Schaufenster: Die DDR und ihre Texte* (Berlin: Akademie-Verlag, 1997), pp. 91–118.

Pence, Katherine and Betts, Paul (eds.), *Socialist Modern. East German Everyday Culture and Politics* (Ann Arbor: University of Michigan Press, 2008).

Pike, David, *The Politics of Culture in Soviet-Occupied Germany, 1945–1949* (Stanford University Press, 1992).

von Plato, Alice, '„Gartenkunst und Blütenzauber": Die Internationale Gartenbauausstellung als Erfurter Angelegenheit', in Adelheid von Saldern (ed.), *Inszenierte Einigkeit: Herrschaftsrepräsentationen in DDR-Städten* (Stuttgart: Steiner, 2003), pp. 183–234.

Poiger, Uta G., *Jazz, Rock and Rebels: Cold War Politics and American Culture in a Divided Germany* (Berkeley: University of California Press, 2000).

Port, Andrew I., *Conflict and Stability in the German Democratic Republic* (Cambridge University Press, 2007).

Prase, Tilo and Kretzschmar, Judith, *Propagandist und Heimatfilmer: Die Dokumentarfilme des Karl-Eduard von Schnitzler* (Leipziger Universitätsverlag, 2003).

Protokoll der Verhandlungen des IX. Parteitages der Sozialistischen Einheitspartei Deutschlands, 2 vols. (Berlin: Dietz, 1976).

van Rahden, Till, *Juden und andere Breslauer: Die Beziehungen zwischen Juden, Protestanten und Katholiken in einer deutschen Großstadt von 1860 bis 1925* (Göttingen: Vandenhoeck & Ruprecht, 2000).

Referate, Berichte, Ergebnisse, Aufgaben: 2. Landschaftstag „Mecklenburgisch-Brandenburgische Seenplatte". Natur und Umwelt: Im Bezirk Neubrandenburg (Neubrandenburg: Kulturbund der Deutschen Demokratischen Republik, 1979).

Reichel, Thomas, 'Die durchherrschte Arbeitsgesellschaft: Zu den Herrschaftsstrukturen und Machtverhältnissen in DDR-Betrieben', in Renate Hürtgen and Thomas Reichel (eds.), *Der Schein der Stabilität: DDR-Betriebsalltag in der Ära Honecker* (Berlin: Metropol, 2001), pp. 85–110.

Reiseführer Deutsche Demokratische Republik (Leipzig: VEB, 1961).

Renan, Ernest, 'What is a nation?', in Geoff Eley and Ronald Grigor Suny (eds.), *Becoming National: A Reader* (New York and Oxford: Oxford University Press, 1996), pp. 42–55.

Retallack, Jim, '"Why can't a Saxon be more like a Prussian?" Regional identities and the birth of modern political culture in Germany, 1866–67,' *Canadian Journal of History* 32 (1997), 26–55.

von Richthofen, Esther Eugénie, 'Bridging culture to the masses: Control, compromise and participation in the GDR. A case study of the *Bezirk* Potsdam', PhD thesis, University of London (2006).

Roesler, Jörg, *Umweltprobleme und Umweltpolitik in der DDR* (Thüringen: Landeszentrale für Politische Bildung, 2006).

Ross, Corey, *Constructing Socialism at the Grass-Roots: The Transformation of East Germany, 1945–65* (Basingstoke: Macmillan, 2000).

Rossman, Gerhard, *et al.*, *Geschichte der Sozialistischen Einheitspartei Deutschlands: Abriß*, Institut für Marxismus-Leninismus (Berlin: Dietz, 1978).

Rostas, Susanna, 'From ritualization to performativity. The concheros of Mexico', in Felicia Hughes-Freeland (ed.), *Ritual, Performance, Media* (London: Routledge, 1998), pp. 85–103.

Rostock, 2nd edn (Leipzig: Brockhaus, 1982).

Rowell, Jay, 'Wohnungspolitik' in Dierk Hoffmann and Michael Schwartz (eds.), *Geschichte der Sozialpolitik in Deutschland seit 1945* (Baden-Baden: Nomos, 2004), vol. VIII, *1949–61: Deutsche Demokratische Republik*, pp. 699–726.

Rutschke, Erich, 'Ornithologie in der DDR – ein Rückblick', in Auster and Behrens (eds.), *Naturschutz*, pp. 109–33.

'Entertainment, gender image, and cultivating an audience: Radio in the GDR in the 1950s', in Adelheid von Saldern, *The Challenge of Modernity* (Ann Arbor: University of Michigan Press, 2002), pp. 348–78.

Saldern, Adelheid von (ed.), *Inszenierte Einigkeit: Herrschaftsrepräsentationen in DDR-Städten* (Stuttgart: Steiner, 2003).

Schaarschmidt, Thomas, 'Regionalbewusstsein und Regionalkultur in Demokratie und Diktatur 1918–61: Sächsische Heimatbewegung und Heimat-Propaganda in der Weimarer Republik, im Dritten Reich und in der SBZ/DDR', *Westfälische Forschungen* 52 (2002), 203–28.

Regionalkultur und Diktatur: Sächsische Heimatbewegung und Heimat-Propaganda im Dritten Reich und in der SBZ/DDR (Weimar/Cologne/Vienna: Böhlau, 2004).

Schauer, Hans-Hartmut, *Quedlinburg: Fachwerkstadt, Weltkulturerbe* (Berlin: Verlag Bauwesen, 1999).

Scherzer, Landolf, *Der Erste*, 7th edn (Berlin: Aufbau Taschenbuch, 2002).

Schlenker, Wolfram, *Das „kulturelle Erbe" in der DDR: Gesellschaftliche Entwicklung und Kulturpolitik 1945–1965* (Stuttgart: Metzler, 1977).

Schmidt, E., 'Sprachforschung auf dem Thüringer Wald', *Kulturbund zur demokratischen Erneuerung Deutschlands Kreisleitung Ilmenau: Monatsprogramm Oktober 1955*, 12–13.

Schöner unsere Städte und Gemeinden – Mach Mit! Zum 20. Jahrestag der DDR, ed. Nationalrat der Nationalen Front (Berlin: Staatsverlag der Deutschen Demokratischen Republik, 1968).

Schramm, Rudolf, *Das Liebschwitzer Ranzenmärchen: Volkssagen und sagenhafte Erzählungen des mittleren Elstertals vorwiegend aus den Kreisen Gera-Stadt und Gera-Land* (Greiz: Kulturbund der DDR Kreissekretariat Greiz, 1980), vol. II.

Die Wunderblumen vom Röschnitzgrund: Sagen und sagenhafte Erzählungen des mittleren Elstertals aus den Kreisen Greiz und Zeulenroda, 2nd edn (Greiz: Kulturbund der DDR Kreissekretariat Greiz, 1981), vol. I.

Schroeder, Klaus, *Der SED-Staat: Partei, Staat und Gesellschaft, 1949–1990* (Munich: Hanser, 1999).

Schwär, Oskar and Czok, Karl, *Oberlausitz* (Dresden: Sachsenverlag, 1961).

Schwartz, Michael, *Vertriebene und „Umsiedlerpolitik": Integrationskonflikte in den deutschen Nachkriegs-Gesellschaften und die Assimilationsstrategien in der SBZ/DDR 1945 bis 1961* (Munich: Oldenbourg, 2004).

Schwarz, Sigrid, 'Die Liebe zur Heimat, ein wesentliches Ziel unserer patriotischen Erziehung', PhD thesis, Humboldt University Berlin (1956), 2 vols.

Scott, James C., *Weapons of the Weak: Everyday Forms of Peasant Resistance* (New Haven: Yale University Press, 1985).

Domination and the Arts of Resistance: Hidden Transcripts (New Haven: Yale University Press, 1990).

Seegers, Lu, '„Die Zukunft unserer Stadt ist bereits projektiert." Die 750-Jahrfeier Rostocks im Rahmen der Ostseewoche 1968', in von Saldern (ed.), *Inszenierte Einigkeit*, pp. 61–106.

'„Schaufenster zum Westen": Das Elbefest und die Magdeburger Kulturfesttage in den 1950er und 1960er Jahren', in von Saldern (ed.), *Inszenierte Einigkeit*, pp. 107–44.

Seidel, Werner, 'Verbesserung der Wohnbedingungen – gemeinsames Anliegen der KWV und Nationaler Front', pp. 55–6.

Shanahan, James and Morgan, Michael, *Television and its Viewers: Cultivation Theory and Research* (Cambridge University Press, 1999).

Siebeneicker, Arnulf, 'Kulturarbeit in der Industrieprovinz: Entstehung und Rezeption bildender Kunst im VEB Petrolchemisches Kombinat 1960–1990', *Historische Anthropologie* 5 (1997), 435–53.

Slezkine, Yuri, 'The USSR as a communal apartment, or how a socialist state promoted ethnic particularism', in Sheila Fitzpatrick (ed.), *Stalinism: New Directions* (London: Routledge, 2000), pp. 313–47.

Smith, Anthony D., *Chosen Peoples: Sacred Sources of National Identity* (Oxford University Press, 2003).

Smith, Helmut Walser, *The Continuities of German History. Nation, Religion, and Race across the Long Nineteenth Century* (Cambridge University Press, 2008).

Sommer, Ulf, *Die Liberal-Demokratische Partei Deutschlands: Eine Blockpartei unter Führung Deutschlands* (Münster: Agenda, 1996).

Sommergewinn: Heimatliches Volksfest in der Wartburgstadt Eisenach, ed. Fachgruppe Sommergewinn der Arbeitsgemeinschaft der Natur- und Heimatfreunde im Deutschen Kulturbund (1973).

Sommergewinn: Heimatliches Volksfest in der Wartburgstadt Eisenach, ed. Fachgruppe Sommergewinn der Arbeitsgemeinschaft der Natur- und Heimatfreunde im Deutschen Kulturbund (1974).

Sozialistische Lebensweise und kulturelles Erbe: Auszüge aus einer Diskussion (Berlin: Kulturbund der DDR, 1976).

Spilker, Dirk, *The East German Leadership and the Division of Germany: Patriotism and Propaganda*, 1945–1953 (Oxford University Press, 2006).

Staritz, Dietrich, *Geschichte der DDR* (Frankfurt: Suhrkamp, 1996).

Staritz, Dietrich, 'Die SED und die Opposition', in Dietrich Staritz, *Was war: Historische Studien zu Geschichte und Politik der DDR* (Berlin: Metropol, 1994), pp. 137–68.

Statistik zur Entwicklung des Kulturbundes der DDR: Bericht an den X. Bundeskongreß (Berlin: Kulturbund der DDR, 1982).

Statistisches Jahrbuch der Deutschen Demokratischen Republik 1956, Staatliche Zentralverwaltung für Statistik (Berlin: Staatsverlag der DDR, 1957).

Statistisches Jahrbuch der Deutschen Demokratischen Republik 1968, Staatliche Zentralverwaltung für Statistik (Berlin: Staatsverlag der DDR, 1968).

Statistisches Jahrbuch der Deutschen Demokratischen Republik 1978, Staatliche Zentralverwaltung für Statistik (Berlin: Staatsverlag der DDR, 1978).

Statistisches Jahrbuch der Deutschen Demokratischen Republik 1988, Staatliche Zentralverwaltung für Statistik (Berlin: Staatsverlag der DDR, 1988).

Steeger, Bernhard, *Menschenwege* (Halle: Mitteldeutscher Verlag, 1974).

Steiner, André, *Von Plan zu Plan* (Munich: Deutsche Verlags-Anstalt, 2004).

Steinmetz, Max, 'Die Aufgaben der Regionalgeschichtsforschung in der DDR bei der Ausarbeitung eines nationalen Geschichtsbildes', *Zeitschrift für Geschichtswissenschaft* 9 (1961), 1735–73.

Strittmater, Karl, *Ole Bienkopp* (Berlin: Aufbau Verlag, new edn, 2005).

Strobach, Hermann, 'Methodologische Probleme bei der historischen Erforschung und Darstellung der Volksdichtung', *Beiträge zur historischen Erforschung der Volksdichtung: Kultur und Lebensweise* 2 (1980), 71–85.

Strohbusch, Horst, *Das Licht kam aus der Kirche: Wende in Meiningen 1989–90* (Meiningen: Verlag Börner PR, 1999).

Suny, Ronald Grigor, *The Making of the Georgian Nation*, 2nd edn (Bloomington: Indiana University Press, 1994).

Thacker, Toby, *Music after Hitler, 1945–1955* (Aldershot: Ashgate, 2007).

Thomas, Rüdiger, 'Kulturpolitik und Künstlerbewußtsein seit dem VIII. Parteitag der SED', in Glaessner (ed.), *Die DDR in der Ära Honecker*, pp. 589–608.

Turner, Victor, *The Ritual Process: Structure and Anti-Structure* (London: Routledge & Kegan Paul, 1969).

Dramas, Fields, and Metaphors: Symbolic Action in Human Society (Ithaca, NY: Cornell University Press, 1974).

From Ritual to Theatre. The Human Seriousness of Play (New York: PAJ Publications, 1982).

'Dewey, Dilthey and Drama: an essay in the anthropology of experience', in Victor W. Turner and Edward M. Bruner (eds.), *The Anthropology of Experience* (Urbana: University of Illinois Press, 1986), pp. 33–44.

The Anthropology of Performance (New York: PAJ Publications, 1987).

Ulbricht, Walter, 'Durch schöpferische Initiative wird unsere Heimat schöner und reicher als je zuvor', in Nationalrat der Nationalen Front, ed., *Schöner unsere Städte und Gemeinden – Mach Mit! Zum 20. Jahrestag der DDR* (Berlin: Staatsverlag der Deutschen Demokratischen Republik, 1968), pp. 18–19.

Um unsere sozialistische Heimat: Referat und Diskussionsbeiträge einer Tagung am 20. Juni 1958 in Berlin (Berlin: DKB, Zentrale Kommission Natur- und Heimatfreunde, 1958).

Unterlauf, Max, 'Die Nutzung der Ortschronik Leuenberg in der Geschichtspropaganda', in *Heimatgeschichtliche Arbeit – Positionen, Probleme, Erfahrungen*, Arbeitsmaterial für die Fachgruppen Heimatgeschichte/Ortschroniken des Kulturbundes der DDR (Berlin: Kulturbund der DDR, 1985), pp. 49–53.

Verbesserung der Wohnbedingungen – wichtigste Aufgabe im „Mach Mit!" *Wettbewerb*, Gemeinsame Tagung des Sekretariats des Nationalrats der

Nationalen Front der DDR und des Ministeriums für Bauwesen am 24. Okt. 1973 in Eberswalde-Finow (Berlin, 1973).

Verdery, Katherine, *National Ideology under Socialism: Identity and Cultural Politics in Ceauşescu's Romania*, 2nd edn (Berkeley: University of California Press, 1995).

Vogler, Günther, 'Staatsgedanke und Staatsrealität im absolutistischen Preußen', in *Preußen in der Geschichte des deutschen Volkes: Beiträge aus der Veranstaltung der Zentralen Kommission Wissenschaft des Präsidialrates und der Bezirksleitung Potsdam des Kulturbundes der DDR am 5. und 6. Juni 1980 in Potsdam* (Berlin: Kulturbund der DDR, 1981), pp. 31–8.

Vogtmann, Hardy, 'Vorwort zur 2. Auflage', in Auster and Behrens (eds.), *Naturschutz in den Neuen Bundesländern*, pp. 7–10.

Volks- und Heimatfeste, gestern, heute, morgen: Referat und Diskussionsbeiträge einer Beratung, die der Deutsche Kulturbund – Zentrale Kommission Natur- und Heimatfreunde – am 25. und 26. Oktober 1958 in Magdeburg veranstaltete (Berlin: Deutscher Kulturbund Zentrale Kommission Natur- und Heimatfreunde, 1959).

Vorsatz, Mareike, 'Unsere Heimat, die schöne – Agitation und Propaganda der "ABZ-Zeitung"', in Christoph Lüth and Klaus Pecher (eds.), *Kinderzeitschriften in der DDR* (Bad Heilbrunn: Klinkhardt, 2007), pp. 90–120

Weber, Hermann, *Geschichte der DDR*, 2nd edn (Munich: DTV, 1999).

Weichlein, Siegfried, *Nation und Region: Integrationsprozesse im Kaiserreich* (Düsseldorf: Droste, 2004).

Weimann, Robert, 'Diskussion um Plenzdorf: Goethe in der Figurenperspektive', *Sinn und Form* 25 (1973), vol. I, 222–38.

Weisbrod, Bernd, 'Medien als symbolische Form der Massengesellschaft: Die medialen Bedingungen von Öffentlichkeit im 20. Jahrhundert', *Historische Anthropologie* 9 (2001), 270–83.

Wentker, Hermann, *Justiz in der SBZ/DDR 1945–53: Transformation und Rolle ihrer zentralen Institutionen* (Munich: Oldenbourg, 2001).

Wieben, Uwe, *Veränderung. Wende. Verantwortung* (Rostock: Neuer Hochschulschriftenverlag Ingo Koch, 1998).

Wierling, Dorothee, *Geboren im Jahr Eins. Der Jahrgang 1949 in der DDR: Versuch einer Kollektivbiographie* (Berlin: Links, 2002).

Wiesener, Albrecht, 'Halle an der Saale – Chemiemetropole oder "Diva in Grau"?', in Karin Hartewig and Alf Lüdtke (eds.), *Die DDR im Bild*, pp. 51–68.

Wietstruk, Siegfried, 'Von den Ländern zu den Bezirken: Die DDR 1949 bis 1952', *Staat und Recht* 38, no. 9 (1989), 753–60.

Woeller, Waltraud, *Berliner Sagen* (Berlin: Interessengemeinschaft für Denkmalpflege, Kultur und Geschichte der Hauptstadt Berlin im Kulturbund der DDR, 1980).

Wolfrum, Edgar, 'Die Preußen-Renaissance: Geschichtspolitik im deutsch–deutschen Konflikt', in Martin Sabrow (ed.), *Verwaltete Vergangenheit: Geschichtskultur und Herrschaftslegitimation in der DDR* (Leipzig: Akademische Verlagsanstalt, 1997), pp. 145–66.

Yurchak, Alexei, *Everything was Forever, until It Was No More* (Princeton University Press, 2006).

Zatlin, Jonathan R., *The Currency of Socialism: Money and Political Culture in East Germany* (Cambridge University Press, 2007).

Zentraler Ausschuß für Jugendweihe in der Deutschen Demokratischen Republik, *Vom Sinn unseres Lebens*, 4th edn (Berlin: Verlag Neues Leben, 1986).

Zirkler, Albert, 'Von der Mundartdichtung', *Natur und Heimat* 8 (1952), 20.

Zwischen Rennsteig und Rhön, introduced by Walter Werner and Rolf Tröstrum (Suhl: Deutscher Kulturbund, Bezirksleitung Suhl, 1966).

Index

Certain topics (e.g. heimat, identities, socialism, SED) occur throughout the book. References in the index are to particularly revealing or specific passages.

NEW STUDIES IN EUROPEAN HISTORY

Books in the series

Royalty and Diplomacy in Europe, 1890–1914
RODERICK R. MCLEAN

Catholic Revival in the Age of the Baroque
Religious Identity in Southwest Germany, 1550–1750
MARC R. FORSTER

Helmuth von Moltke and the Origins of the First World War
ANNIKA MOMBAUER

Peter the Great
The Struggle for Power, 1671–1725
PAUL BUSHKOVITCH

Fatherlands
State-Building and Nationhood in Nineteenth-Century Germany
ABIGAIL GREEN

The French Second Empire
An Anatomy of Political Power
ROGER PRICE

Origins of the French Welfare State
The Struggle for Social Reform in France, 1914–1947
PAUL V. DUTTON

Ordinary Prussians
Brandenburg Junkers and Villagers, 1500–1840
WILLIAM W. HAGEN

Liberty and Locality in Revolutionary France
Six Villages Compared, 1760–1820
PETER JONES

Vienna and Versailles
The Courts of Europe's Dynastic Rivals, 1550–1780
JEROEN DUINDAM

From Reich to State
The Rhineland in the Revolutionary Age, 1780–1830
MICHAEL ROWE

Re-Writing the French Revolutionary Tradition
Liberal Opposition and the Fall of the Bourbon Monarchy
ROBERT ALEXANDER

Provincial Power and Absolute Monarchy
The Estates General of Burgundy, 1661–1790
JULIAN SWANN

Printed in Great Britain
by Amazon

53107797R00206